D1446898

# Main Street to Mainframes

Best Wishes,

SUNY SERIES, AN AMERICAN REGION:
STUDIES IN THE HUDSON VALLEY

THOMAS S. WERMUTH, EDITOR

# *main street*
## *to*
# MAINFRAMES

## LANDSCAPE AND SOCIAL CHANGE IN
# POUGHKEEPSIE

## HARVEY K. FLAD and CLYDE GRIFFEN

**e** excelsior editions

AN IMPRINT OF STATE UNIVERSITY OF NEW YORK PRESS

The Lucy Maynard Salmon Research Fund of
Vassar College provided support for this publication.


Published by
STATE UNIVERSITY OF NEW YORK PRESS, ALBANY

© 2009  State University of New York

For information, contact State University of New York Press, Albany, NY
www.sunypress.edu

Production and book design, Laurie Searl
Marketing, Susan M. Petrie


**Library of Congress Cataloging-in-Publication Data**

Flad, Harvey K., 1938–
   Main street to mainframes : landscape and social change in Poughkeepsie / Harvey K. Flad
and Clyde Griffen.
       p.  cm. — (An American region : studies in the Hudson Valley)
   Includes bibliographical references and index.
   ISBN 978-1-4384-2613-6 (hardcover : alk. paper)
   1. Poughkeepsie (N.Y.)—History. 2. Poughkeepsie (N.Y.)—Economic conditions.
   3. Poughkeepsie (N.Y.)—Social conditions. I. Griffen, Clyde, 1929– II. Title.
   F129.P9F53 2009
   974.7'33—dc22
                                                                                                2008042638


10   9   8   7   6   5   4   3   2   1

For
Mary Flad
and
Sally Griffen

# Contents

# Illustrations

# Acknowledgments

═══════════════════════════════

The authors' interest and knowledge of Poughkeepsie and the mid-Hudson valley region have been gained over the past four decades by living and working in the area. Both of us came to teach at Vassar College. Our families have grown and prospered here, working in the community in numerous nonprofit organizations and raising children who graduated from local public schools. Our teaching and scholarship often focused on the history and landscape of the urban realm; many of our students also examined local social and material culture, and their research found its way into this work as well. As noted in the Introduction, our jointly-led field trips through Poughkeepsie's neighborhoods offered many of the stories that frame themes in this work; a visual representation of the urban field trip has been produced as *A Digital Tour of Poughkeepsie* by Vassar College in 2007. References in the annotated bibliography constitute much of our own research relevant to this study.

Over the years, a number of individuals—neighbors, friends, scholars—have helped us understand the city and its region. We wish to especially acknowledge those whose knowledge and personal stories have been instrumental in the research for this work. The authors held formal and informal interviews and conversations with the following individuals; their contributions have been most welcome: Doris and Ralph Adams, Roger Akeley, Rudolph and Katherine Albanese, Frank Bauer, Anna and Werner Buchholz, Fred and Alice Bunnell, Sam Busselle, Ray Boedecker, John Clarke, Steve Cole, Anne Conroy, T. J. Cunningham, Elizabeth Daniels, Frances Dunwell, Julia Dunwell, Jesse and Leah Effron, Jack Economou, Bernice and Edwin Fitchett, Mary Flad, Lou Glasse, Brian Godfrey, Burt Gold, Fredrica Goodman, Sally Griffen, James Hall, Sam Im, Armine Isbirian, Jeh and Norma Johnson, Sipra Johnson, Robert Kaminski, Ben LaFarge, Agnes Langdon, Charles Lawson, Peter Leonard, Eric Lindbloom, David Lumb, Stephen Lumb, Maisry MacCracken, May and Lawrence Mamiya, Greg McCurty, Marque Miringoff, Victor Morris, Ronald Mullahey, John Mylod, Fred

Nagel, Leonard Nevarez, Peter O'Keefe, Sandra Opdycke, Lucille Pattison, Sandra Ponti, Richard Reitano, William Rhoads, Brian Riddell, Francis Ritz, Klara Sauer, George Schnell, Pete Seeger, Joan and Jonah Sherman, Bernard Slade, Gerald Sorin, Sam Speers, Kenneth Toole, Norma Torney, William Van Loo, Richard Varbero, Louis Voerman, Jr., Richard Wager, Arthur Weintraub, Craig Wolf, and Louis Zuccarello.

We appreciate the assistance of many who have shared documents or helped us find them: John Ansley, Special Collections Librarian, Marist College; Stephen Cole, Director, External Relations, IBM materials; Sheila Appel, IBM Community Relations, and Dawn Stanford and Paul Lasewicz, IBM archives; Christine Crawford-Oppenheimer, Reference Librarian, CIA; Ann Davis, Director of Marist Bureau of Economic Research; Lynn Lucas, Curator, Local History Room, and other research librarians, Adriance Library; Stephanie Mauri and Eileen Hayden, Dutchess County Historical Society; reference librarians at Franklin D. Roosevelt Library, National Park Service; Jonah Sherman; Vassar College Library, Special Collections; and Thomas Wermuth, Director, Hudson River Valley Institute, Marist College. Rick Jones in the Earth Science and Geography department, Bayard Bailey and Jessica Chong in Media Cloisters, and Carol Jones and her crew in computer services at Vassar College furnished welcome technical assistance.

A special thanks to Tim Allred for access to his personal photo collection; Spencer Ainsley at the *Poughkeepsie Journal* and John Clarke at Dutchess County Department of Planning and Development for use of selected photographs; Meg Stewart for maps; Chip Porter and Mary Ann Cunningham for assistance with illustrations; Walter Brueggeman and Fortress Press, and Anne Whiston Spirn for quotation permission; Bernard Weisberger for his extended reminiscing about boyhood time in Hudson; James Merrell for his helpful criticism, reading the entire manuscript in an earlier version; reviewers for SUNY Press for their informative comments, and James Peltz and Laurie Searl for their advice and encouragement.

The cover painting "Main Street Façades" by Margaret Crenson was painted in April 2004 of Main Street, Poughkeepsie, between Academy and Hamilton Streets, and is used by permission of the artist.

Lastly, the authors recall, in memorium, Dr. Edna Cers Macmahon (1901–1983), professor of economics at Vassar College, for her dedication to the social welfare of the city of Poughkeepsie, her collection of reports and documents related to the city's social and economic development, and her mentoring of her students and ourselves.

# Introduction

———————————

Place is space which has historical meanings, where some things have happened which are now remembered and which provide continuity and identity across generations.
—Walter Brueggeman, 1977

*Main Street to Mainframes* tells a story of changes and continuities in society and landscape during the twentieth century in Poughkeepsie, New York, and, to a lesser extent, in the mid-Hudson River valley. Introductory chapters provide historical background for developments since 1900 and, more broadly, for the evolution from a city with diversified manufacturing and commerce focused by trolley transportation on downtown—Main Street—to an urban region transformed by IBM's success with mainframe computers. Continuity in diversification from the early nineteenth century gave way after IBM's arrival in World War II to a giant, benevolent employer that recruited or trained a more highly skilled labor force than the region had previously. That changed local society, especially in the townships surrounding IBM's three major valley sites.

During the twentieth century, small urban centers in the northeastern United States, such as Poughkeepsie, have been buffeted by global change in the economy, by national shifts in civic engagement, and by the problems posed by suburban sprawl. Hudson River valley cities have seen their prospects surge and ebb, then begin to revive again, as they head into the twenty-first century. Those leaders most concerned with the future talk about and plan for more focused economic and residential development, including the revival of Main Street without its previous commercial dominance, and clusters of high-tech employers without the previous overwhelming dominance of IBM. They look to the revitalization of urban riverfronts as part of the increased importance of tourism in the valley's

1

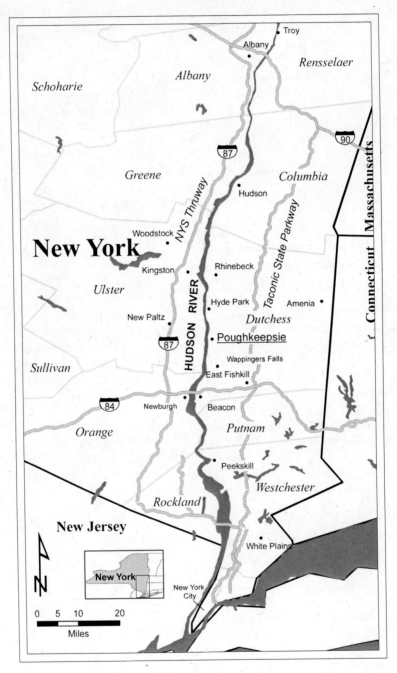

FIGURE I.1. Location map

economy. Tourism had flourished in the valley and the Catskill Mountains early in the nineteenth century, continued on a lesser and less publicized scale since then, but from the 1990s onward has loomed large in local planning for future economic growth.

Poughkeepsie is located 75 miles north of New York City on the eastern bank of the Hudson River. Its urban landscape has changed dramatically, from a relatively compact cityscape centered on downtown, to an urban realm with a multiplicity of centers. A car-centered society has led to a social network and landscape without boundaries, largely divorced from, yet still related to, its place-centered history. "Main Street" serves as a metaphor for an American community's identity. That identity depends on a visible streetscape of social relations, a cityscape where a community can recall its past, orient itself to the present, and imagine its future. Since World War II, however, suburbanization has spread everywhere in urban regions. In Poughkeepsie, as in many older communities, it hurt the city. IBM, by locating outside the city, hastened suburbanization in the adjacent townships. For nearly half a century, the area's largest employer brought prosperity to the new suburbs, but not to the city.

"Main Street" also can serve as metaphor for the social and economic turmoil that has been the story of so many American communities in the last hundred years. Poughkeepsie shares the experience of similar small cities in the United States, especially the constant need to adapt to change. In the twentieth century, when most of the commerce and manufacturing that had fueled its prosperity diminished or moved elsewhere and annexing the suburbs failed, the community faced the task of redefining itself and confronting major social challenges without the resources to pay for them. Business leaders, at least since the 1830s, have been boosters, sometimes caught up for a time in expansive visions of what their city might become and always anxious to be "up-to-date" in the facilities and goods they offered to investors and customers. But their constant aim has been to attract new firms, with a variety of incentives, to offset those failing or leaving. In that respect, the more things change, the more they stay the same. The reception of successive waves of immigrants and migrants also has strong continuities, notably in the recurrent movement from initial alarm among residents to gradual accommodation, despite striking differences in the national origin, race, and ethnicity of the newcomers.

With the exception of exuberant times like the 1830s and late 1860s when Poughkeepsie launched a variety of risky enterprises or made major investments in improving municipal utilities, the city has favored modest measures like Progressive era cleanups. Transportation improvements, like bridges and paved highways, although expensive, seemed necessary, if only to keep even with regional competitors. Community leaders sometimes moved more boldly, as in securing more grants for urban renewal than most cities in the 1960s and 1970s, but the resulting demolition of so much of the old downtown pockmarked Poughkeepsie for years to come, discouraging new investment. Yet, during the same years, the leaders of educational institutions in the valley made changes that not only strengthened them individually but also, inadvertently, made them more important as local employers in the wake of IBM's radical downsizing in the 1990s. The consolidation and cooperative ventures of regional hospitals had a similar result in expanding the importance of the non-profit sector of the local economy. By the twenty-first century, cultural and heritage tourism offered new economic opportunities even as the gravitational pull of New York City and the metropolitan area more firmly exerted its power. The mid-Hudson region's population continued to expand as residential and commercial sprawl covered much of the former rural landscape.

## A FRAMEWORK

This book began as a story of how the village of Poughkeepsie grew over two centuries: first, into a thriving central place that by 1900 had been given the booster title "Queen City of the Hudson," and then, by the beginning of the twenty-first century, into an urban region. It has become an attempt to show how time and space, as reflected in landscape and society, have come together in one small city and its region. The story tells how the area's population changed in composition as it increased in size, what natives and newcomers did to earn their livelihoods, where they chose to live, and how they related to each other and to their localities. In the early nineteenth century, Poughkeepsie was one of the four biggest river towns in the four counties (Columbia, Dutchess, Orange, and Ulster) of the mid-Hudson valley, so our story early on considers how these towns differed then and what experiences they shared during that century. We will return from time to time in telling our story to the larger regional context of economic and social connections between the valley's people and and its landscapes.

Our story pays special attention to three subjects. It emphasizes the diversification in Poughkeepsie's manufacturing up until World War II, when the arrival of a single new corporation, IBM, transformed the region. In the early twentieth century, Pougkeepsie had, for workers, the bad reputation of being a low-wage city, unfriendly to unions outside the building trades. IBM also shunned unionization, but brought a higher level of prosperity to the Poughkeepsie urban region for nearly half a century, increasing the size and the educational and skill level of its workforce as it shifted its focus to computers. With better wages, salaries, and perquisites than other local industries, it aroused both resentment and gratitude. IBMers' consumption supported an increase in the number and prosperity of local businesses. With two of its major facilities in Dutchess County and one in Kingston across the river, and workers often shuttling between them, IBM also inadvertently fostered a greater sense of connectedness in the mid-Hudson region.

Our second emphasis is on a recurrent process that has reshaped so many urban populations in the United States: successive waves of immigrant newcomers from Europe, the American South, the Caribbean, South and East Asia, and most recently Latin America, especially Mexico. These waves had many similarities, like chain migration in which firstcomers paved the way for migration to Poughkeepsie for others from their families and old neighborhoods. But these waves also differed not only in race or ethnicity, religion, and often language, but also in their reception by local residents and in the ease and success of their adaptation to their new world, including their occupations and residential locations.

Our third emphasis is on the changing physical landscape of this developing urban region. We locate the initial settlement overlooking its landings on the Hudson River waterfront. We note the city's changed relation to the river with the coming of the railroad in the mid-nineteenth century and the settling of industry. We discuss the profound impact on opportunities for both urban and rural populations with the development of the highway network in the mid-twentieth century.

We map the form and shape of the city itself as it changes from the irregular layout of the early village to the radial spatial pattern with downtown Poughkeepsie as its center that accompanied the coming of electrified trolleys in the 1890s. That pattern, common to so many cities at the turn of the century, centered social and economic forces on Main Street, but it, in turn, gave way with the triumph of the automobile to a progressive suburbanization, which by the beginning of the twenty-first century has become "spread city." Our story of the changing landscape in Poughkeepsie and environs includes the withering of downtown through urban renewal, white flight, and dispersion of retailing. It also tells of shifting tastes in public, commercial, and domestic architecture, from the work of pioneer landscape designers such as Andrew Jackson Downing and Calvert Vaux in the nineteenth century to the role of local resident President Franklin Roosevelt in the design of federal post offices.

This interdisciplinary work in urban studies by a social historian and a cultural geographer draws upon both disciplinary perspectives as well as the sociological insights of urban community studies. In describing where people lived, we examine the extent to which members of different social groups clustered together or dispersed and how their residential patterns changed over time. We will be looking at social mixing or segregation in voluntary associations, from churches to civic organizations. We will consider events and places that brought Poughkeepsians of all sorts together, like the Poughkeepsie Regatta, Fourth of July parades, Arbor Day celebrations, and public parks.

For the last half of the twentieth century, oral history contributes much to this study. Our interviews have constantly reminded us of the differences in interests, perceptions, and perspectives we all bring to viewing our past. For example, the city's business leaders have long been preoccupied with encouraging growth in the economy and population. Their interests often overlapped with, but sometimes have differed from, the visions of a smaller number of citizens concerned with improving local government and cultural opportunities with various kinds of reform. Women, for example, led the way in some of these reform efforts, championing "municipal housekeeping" and "good government" as they did in other American cities during the first half of the twentieth century.

The goals of wage earners and their perspective on employee-employer relations in Poughkeepsie are harder to discover in a city without strong labor unions. We find more direct evidence among foreign immigrants in our city of a dual preoccupation with preserving their ethnic identity while assimilating to meet everyday expectations of the marketplace. At the other extreme in documentation, we found abundant evidence for the fissures in the urban system that developed during the Depression, the period of urban renewal and Model Cities, and the efforts to promote civil rights in local schools.

What this historical-geographic study will not include is a narrative of politics and government at the municipal and county levels. That dimension will appear only when it is relevant to our primary concern with social, economic, and cultural change and their effect upon the physical landscape, social interaction, and civic participation. As we bring our project to a close, we, like others who have delved into the pasts of particular communities, think regretfully of the many voices we have not heard and the stories we have missed or not included. We hope our selection of voices and stories helps in understanding the history we share, but we know that it, like all written history, is incomplete.

The organization of this book is broadly chronological, beginning with the nineteenth century and moving to the end of the twentieth. But the treatments of some topics within chapters overlap in time, as in the comparison of how the Hudson valley's major river towns met their challenges during the nineteenth century. So, too, does the story of the spread of IBM and IBMers as that corporation moved toward its triumph with the 360 computer. That story overlaps in time with the early days of urban renewal in Poughkeepsie, when the city proved remarkably successful in winning federal funds but failed in its aim of urban revitalization. IBM's mainframes brought prosperity to the towns surrounding Poughkeepsie, but in so doing contributed to Main Street's decline. The history of the city, like the history of any place, continues to unfold as residents and newcomers adapt to changed circumstances and opportunities.

We hope to make our study a usable past for residents of the Poughkeepsie urban region by highlighting both continuities and major changes in the city's past to help us think about our present prospects. As we try to shape our future, we can learn a lot from the adaptability of both natives and newcomers over two centuries. At the opposite historical extreme, we need to learn whatever we can about the persistence into our time of habits of mind and patterns of behavior that have hampered civic cooperation in the valley's past. The authors hope that the examples included here may help us become more imaginative in discovering possibilities for and obstacles to civic improvement that otherwise might be ignored.

## READING THE CITY

An important aim is to make experience of the landscape more interesting to local readers by showing the often surprising and fascinating successive uses of sites and places we pass every day. Both authors have lived and worked in Poughkeepsie for over thirty years at Vassar College, giving us considerable knowledge of the city's rich history and geography. In taking students from the college on walking tours through older parts of the city, the authors have relished showing them the mix of past and present within many of the city's neighborhoods. The city can be read as a text, a palimpsest in which remnants of the past remain visible. For example, we usually stop near the little park, honoring colonial-era Governor Dongan, where the Fall Kill (often written as Fallkill Creek) begins to drop rapidly toward the Hudson. Down the slope to the west sits the railroad station and views of the river and the Mid-Hudson Bridge crossing it. Home to heavy industry in the nineteenth century, with that private property blocking access to the river, the waterfront now attracts residents and visitors to its park and Children's Museum. The route of the Fall Kill upward from the river to Dongan Park and beyond is now being developed as a greenway trail.

On the hillside to the south of Dongan Park sits a city-owned day care center once the mansion of the Pelton brothers, where these mill owners could look down upon their carpet factory on the northside of the creek. Built in the late 1830s, the mill closed in 1891, but a cigar factory later inhabited the building. In the late twentieth century, the interior of the mill was transformed into attractive condominiums fronting on Mill Street. If we stand on the bridge crossing the Fall Kill at the mill site and look westward toward the Hudson River, our view encompasses all four eras of transportation history that have been formative in Poughkeepsie's development: the river where eighteenth-century sloops and nineteenth-century steamboats carried passengers and commerce; the railroad station, where passengers arrived from New York City from the late nineteenth century to today's commuters; and the Mid-Hudson Bridge, busy with cars and trucks of the contemporary automobile age.

North of the bridge across the Fall Kill and across from the mill site stands the church building that once housed St. Peter's parish, Poughkeepsie's first Roman Catholic (and predominantly Irish) congregation. That structure now houses Mount Carmel parish that began as an entirely Italian congregation in the 1910s. The church interior contains Irish-American names on wall plaques while Italian Baroque statuary fills the sanctuary. Walking eastward up Mill Street, just beyond Dongan Park, one encounters several businesses that have served the city's Italian community for generations even as so many have moved out to suburban or exurban housing. The Aurora Café with its cannoli and other baked delicacies together with Dalleo's grocery continue to draw former residents or their children back to the area.

A little further east and north, a low-income housing project sits on the former site of Pelton's pond, one of a series of dammed-up ponds along the Fall Kill once used for manufacturing. This mosquito-breeding place spread fevers every summer among the adjacent tenement houses during the late nineteenth century. Suffering residents resorted to near-violent protests in the 1870s that led, in 1899, to the pond's succumbing to landfill. Only a few blocks eastward up Mill Street is a lovely white Greek Revival structure built for a Presbyterian congregation in the early nineteenth century. It became a Jewish synagogue during the late nineteenth century and now houses an African American congregation.

Within a few blocks, we can see this intricate patchwork of ethnicity and commerce, religious edifices and housing and social activity, constantly changing through the years. And these are but a few of the city's sites that have intriguing but now mostly forgotten histories. We hope that those that appear in our story will vivify the landscape for readers, leading them to think in new ways about Poughkeepsie's past, present, and future.

## CITY AND REGION

*Main Street to Mainframes* focuses on the city of Poughkeepsie as the primary place within the mid-Hudson region. The Poughkeepsie urban region however, consists of a number of locales where social, economic, political, and cultural forces interact in both time and space to constitute a context for the city's historical narrative. Scale matters: a walking tour of the Mount Carmel neighborhood views the changes to the urban scene at the level of a sidewalk observer; the lived experience is shared through personal stories of local workers or social activists, while the larger context of the socioeconomic landscape is found in statistics, reports, and interviews. External forces, such as immigration, the decline in manufacturing, or urban renewal shaped local and regional spatial and social relations over decades. Meanwhile, personal biographies and memories offer insights into the role of individuals in these changes.

The mid-Hudson region is composed of numerous interconnected locales and settings where people and places interact: urban downtowns, workplaces including IBM, shopping malls, churches, hospitals, educational institutions, community centers, parks, and ball fields, to name a few. Poughkeepsie's urban history is interconnected with the histories of Kingston, Hudson, Newburgh, and Beacon, while the valley is within the orbit of New York City. Over three centuries, developments in the four counties constituting the mid-Hudson region—Columbia, Dutchess, Orange, and Ulster—have mirrored those in the "Big Apple." And, over these years, the region itself has engaged in the process of globalization through flows of human and economic capital and goods and services, from Matthew Vassar's ale and IBM's mainframes to intellectual and artistic creations.

The twentieth-century history of Poughkeepsie is the focus of this work, although its urban realm frames its reference. As the economy shifted from agriculture to manufacturing to the postindustrial system, so has the urban and regional landscape evolved; as new immigrants arrived and settled, the city's streetscape sported new facades, while rural roads have increased auto and school bus traffic and the countryside has become pocked with residential and commercial sprawl. In the twenty-first century, images of city and country remain in constant flux, while social and economic relations within the New York metropolitan area's outer fringe grow ever more complex.

This book is arranged in four parts. The first three chapters focus on the pre-1900 history of the city of Poughkeepsie in its regional context, with short comparative histories of its main rival urban centers of Kingston, Hudson, Newburgh, and Beacon. Although these rivals now share the aims of benefiting from tourism, the arts, and second homes, fostering a common view of their region and its opportunities, in the nineteenth century they pursued very different strategies for urban growth, emphasizing their distinctiveness rather than what they shared.

The next six chapters consider the changes immigration, progressive reform, an improved transportation network, and the Depression, brought to Poughkeepsie and its region before World War II. In the following seven chapters, the arrival of IBM and the production of its mainframe computer drive the regional economy during the post–World War II period, while the city underwent severe problems that it attempted to address through urban renewal projects and Model Cities programs. The last five chapters examine the postindustrial changes within the urban realm, including the important economic roles of health and education services and the potential of cultural and arts activities. An epilogue brings the story into the early decades of the twenty-first century with the reopening of Main Street and post 9/11 population growth throughout the region.

# PART I

# Before 1900

ONE

# The Valley Setting

IN 1884, WALLACE BRUCE, in his handbook for tourists traveling up the Hudson River on steamboats, described the city of Poughkeepsie as having "a beautiful location, and is justly regarded the finest residence city on the river. It is not only midway between New York and Albany, but also midway between the Highlands and the Catskills, commanding a view of the mountain portals on the south and the mountain overlook on the north—the Gibraltar of Revolutionary fame and the dreamland of Rip Van Winkle."[1]

The larger context for the history of the city of Poughkeepsie and, by the twentieth century, the Poughkeepsie urban region has always been the mid-Hudson valley with its surrounding mountains, farms, and resorts, and other river towns. Our narrative begins with the valley as both physical environment and culturally significant locale. This chapter then asks what kinds of continuity, change, and adaptation occurred in the valley before the twentieth century, letting us see how they prepared residents for change during the twentieth century.

## RIVER, MOUNTAINS, VALLEY

Bruce's description in 1884 locates Poughkeepsie on a mental map that combines regional literary legend, including the writings of Washington Irving and James Fenimore Cooper, and references to the emerging historical narrative of the birth of the nation, with economic and political coordinates to the state capital upstream and the growing metropolis of New York City downriver. Romantic, perhaps, but it was a description that could appeal to tourists. The beauty of the natural environment drew most of them to the valley where they sought out the picturesque wilderness landscape painted by the artists of the Hudson River school.

Thomas Cole, founder of the Hudson River school, painted the mountains, gorges, and "kills" of the Catskills in the 1820s and 1830s, helping to establish the consciousness of wilderness and nature in the creation of an American culture. His painting of Kaaterskill Falls drew numerous other artists to sketch this landmark feature, second only as a site to search for the sublime to that of the larger Niagara Falls. The Year 1824 saw the establishment of a mountain resort, the Catskill Mountain House, where thousands of artists and tourists could more comfortably enter the mountain landscape. It was from the site of the Catskill Mountain House overlooking the Hudson River valley to the east that James Fenimore Cooper wrote in *The Pioneers* (1823) that the Leather-stocking Natty Bumppo looked out upon the vista and declared that a man could stand there and see "Creation! . . . all creation."[2] Tourists in the 1830s wrote paeans to the panoramic view of the Hudson River valley from this cliff edge, a view stretching 50 miles. As the European traveler Harriet Martineau wrote in 1835, "I shall never forget, if I live to be a hundred, how the world lay at my feet."[3]

Despite the vanished wilderness and the inroads of development since the 1820s and 1830s, the valley's beauty continues to draw tourists, one of the recurring themes in the region's history. That attraction reinforced notions that love of nature and of living close to it was a primary American attribute. Andrew Jackson Downing's writings and efforts as a landscape gardener in the 1840s would transform the American domesticated landscape and form the basis for the development of landscape design "adapted to North America," and landscape architecture as a profession. In his *Treatise on the Theory and Practice of Landscape Gardening, Adapted to North America; with a View to the Improvement of Country Residence* (1841), Downing remarked on the extensive reshaping of mid-Hudson valley landscape by the estates that fronted on the Hudson River in the rural areas separating the villages and small cities: "There is no part of the Union where the taste in Landscape Gardening is so far advanced, as on the middle portion of the Hudson."[4] During the mid-nineteenth century, the countryside was becoming domesticated, creating a more refined sense of the picturesque outside of the rugged wildness of the Hudson Highlands. In the twenty-first century, the region became hospitable to the arts once again, tourism became important for valley prosperity, and so did conserving the landscape along the river. That led to a successful push in 1997 for the U.S. Congress to designate the Hudson River valley as the "Landscape that Defines America."[5]

The Hudson remained the chief artery for the transportation of goods and people throughout the first two centuries of European settlement, but not without major change as the quality of its water declined through human pollution. In the late twentieth century, river cleanup became a regional preoccupation. The river actually is an estuary or drowned river valley, sometimes described as an arm of the Atlantic Ocean. Called by Native American Indians, the original inhabitants of the region, "great waters constantly in motion," or "the river that flows both ways," its tidal range stretches northward as far inland as Troy, while a salt front, usually in the vicinity north of Peekskill, may reach the Poughkeepsie area during summer drought conditions when the water flow is low. The river channel reaches a depth of 700 feet near West Point in the Hudson Highlands, and deepwater along the Poughkeepsie shore and the subsequent development of deepwater docking facilities has been a significant factor in the city's economic history. Dredging of shallower reaches of the river to the north of Poughkeepsie has allowed oceangoing vessels to sail up to Albany.

For most of its length, and during most months of the year, the Hudson offered fair sailing, although the winds in the narrow passage through the Hudson Highland gorge could be treacherous. Eventually, however, sailing ships, schooners, and sloops gave way to steamboats after Robert Fulton and his father-in-law Robert Livingston built their boat the *Clermont*, named after the Livingston estate, in 1807. Their attempt to monopolize steamboat traffic failed, and competition for passengers and trade exploded. Steamboats became floating palaces, and fares plummeted. By the mid-nineteenth century, travel time from Albany to New York City had decreased to a matter of many hours rather than days as steam power eliminated the reliance on wind and the difficulties of passage through the Highlands.

From the earliest days, the fishing industry held an important role in the economies of riverfront communities all along the Hudson River. Tons of shad and sturgeon were shipped downriver to the growing urban markets throughout the nineteenth century. Unfortunately, declining fish stocks due to overfishing and river pollution during the twentieth century virtually eliminated fishing as a commercial industry. Ice harvesting, which once served as a major industry during the winter months, has disappeared altogether. Ice blocks cut from the frozen river and stored in gigantic icehouses all along the shore were shipped to city dwellers to preserve their food during summer heat in the years prior to electrification and refrigeration. With this drastic change in their industries, both fishermen and ice cutters had to adapt by finding other employment.

An easily distinguishable physical region, the middle portion of the valley had the clarity of highly visible mountain boundaries and the continuity of a vast geological time scale. The Hudson Highlands are composed of one-billion-year-old crystalline igneous and metamorphic rocks, such as granites and gneisses, that are highly resistant to erosion and extend from Storm King Mountain on the west bank, just north of the military academy at West Point, across the Hudson River to Breakneck Mountain and Mount Beacon on the east bank. Northeast from the Hudson Highlands, the Taconic mountain range forms a boundary between New York and Connecticut. Its erosional remnants are generally less than 2,000 feet in height, yet their relatively unbroken mass has been a barrier to east–west movement.

The Catskill Mountains frame the western horizon. Reaching heights of 4,000 feet, the flanks of the Catskills show their sedimentary origins as layers

of sandstone and shale especially clearly in the low light of winter after a dust-
ing of snow cover. Between the Catskill front, or Wall of Manitou, and the
Hudson River lies the Shawangunk Ridge, a highly resistant formation of
quartzite conglomerate that extends more than 100 miles south to New Jersey
where it becomes the Kittatinny Mountains. The glacially scoured top of the
ridge with its exceedingly thin soil cover, the steep escarpment, and the masses
of fallen talus at its slopes are micro-ecological habitats for rare plant communities, such as the only high altitude pine barrens in eastern North America.

The regional landscape of the past thirteen to fourteen thousand years
offered early inhabitants a host of natural resources whose use and exploita-
tion have changed dramatically over time, sometimes to near extinction of a
species like the beaver. Europeans cut down chestnut-oak forests and pines for
firewood, lumber and charcoal for iron furnaces, hemlocks for tanning, and
opened up large areas for farming. Riverbank clay was formed into bricks,
limestone into cement, and sand and gravel for construction.

The soils of much of the mid-Hudson valley are fertile and friable and,
from the beginning of European settlement, the land has been a productive
agricultural region, primarily in grains and fruit orchards. After the opening
of the Erie Canal in 1825, lands in the western part of the state and eventually the Midwest supplied the wheat for the nation, while commercial agriculture in the mid-Hudson concentrated more on its dairy products for the
growing markets in Connecticut and metropolitan New York. With the
decline of dairy farming in the twentieth century, farmers have once again had
to adapt, often by leaving farming altogether or developing new agricultural
specialties and new ways of marketing,

## VALLEY PEOPLE

The ethnic and racial composition of the valley's human population has
changed periodically and dramatically since the early settlements in the seventeenth century. The Dutch and English settlers who traveled north from
New York to the mid-Hudson valley in the seventeenth century found a
region with highly visible natural boundaries, abundant natural resources, and
an indigenous population of usually friendly Indians. The European newcomers initially preferred the high, dry west bank of the Hudson with some
of the province's best agricultural land, in what is now Orange and Ulster
counties. Dutchess County on the east bank was less attractive, "thought to be
low, swampy, and heavily wooded."[6] The first European settlement in
Dutchess probably occurred near Rhinebeck, across the river from Wiltwyck
(Kingston) on the west bank that had been chartered as early as 1661.

Settlement in the Poughkeepsie area did not begin until about 1683. The
first patent in Dutchess was the Rombout in 1685, a purchase by two New
York City residents of about 85,000 acres from the Wappinger Indians

included both the Wappinger and Fishkill valleys. The Rombout encompassed the current towns of Fishkill, East Fishkill, Wappinger, the city of Beacon, and parts of Poughkeepsie and LaGrangeville. Other large patents in the county in the 1680s were the Great Nine Partners and the Beekman family's upper (Rhinebeck) and interior southeastern patents. Marked economic inequality in landholdings characterized Dutchess County in its earliest days, but would be reduced in the wake of the American Revolution.

Whereas the owners of smaller patents on the west bank moved sooner to divide and sell their lands, creating a society of mostly medium-sized and small freeholds, the larger patentees on the east bank preferred leasing to tenants, resulting in conflicts over ownership and the terms of leases in the mid-eighteenth century and slower settlement. As late as 1733, Dutchess County numbered only 389 families, half of them settled on leased lands on Henry Beekman's Rhinebeck and interior patents. By mid-century, the central precincts of Dutchess County, including Rombout, Poughkeepsie, and Amenia, had many freeholds, but to the north and south, large landlords predominated like the Livingstons and the Philipses whose tenants still owed some feudal services. Loyalist holdings provided the majority of land confiscated and sold in Dutchess as a result of the Revolution. The number of individual landholders increased twelvefold and most of the new owners came from the lower classes.

Before the Revolution, Dutch and English farms had covered the land between the Highlands and the Catskills; in 1790, Ulster County had the highest proportion of residents of Dutch descent in the mid-Hudson region, 30 percent compared to 18 percent or less in Columbia, Dutchess, and Orange counties. The west shore Dutch had been joined by Scotch-Irish immigrants in settling the western uplands. After the English conquered New Netherland in 1664, the ethnic mix of the colony had become even more complicated. Both the English and the Dutch brought African slaves to the valley.

## WHAT HAPPENED TO THE FIRST INHABITANTS?

The landscape the white newcomers preempted had not been empty, but the native Americans whom they encountered, the Algonkians, had not aggressively resisted the whites' encroachment. The natives lost their best lands during the seventeenth century. Small remuneration or trickery in the unending pressure of whites for land purchases, coupled with native lack of immunity to the Europeans' diseases, had already reduced the Indian population on both sides of the river—to about 300 by 1774, if Governor Tryon's estimation can be believed. During the eighteenth century, a wandering group of displaced Indians variously known as Wappingers, Lenape, and Pomptons eked out a marginal existence in unoccupied or thinly settled areas in the Hudson River Highlands. They were led by members of the Nimham family who served as cultural brokers, translating and negotiating for their people. Daniel Nimham learned English, became a Christian, and pressed—ultimately unsuccessfully—their claims to land with the governments in New York and London. Feeling betrayed by the British, he joined the patriot cause during the Revolution, dying in battle. Soon thereafter his people lost nearly all the land of which they still had use.

The remnant largely disappeared from public mention and historical memory until the end of the twentieth century. A notable brief exception is the guide prepared by the Federal Writers' Project, under the WPA. It notes the unhappy experience in Dutchess County of the short-lived (1740–1744) Moravian congregation of Indian converts at Shekomeko, ordered to leave after four years. The guide adds that the "compulsory emigration of the Indians of Shekomeko was but an instance of the many migrations north, south, and west in which the native population of Dutchess melted away during the eighteenth century. Large numbers wandered into Pennsylvania, Delaware, and Maryland, and many more into Ohio."[7] As they left, a new stream of white newcomers pushed into the Hudson valley from the east.

The westward push of New Englanders into Dutchess and Columbia counties during the late eighteenth century brought a burst of Yankee entrepreneurship. Movement of individuals and families among the region's localities became more frequent as did consciousness of variation within the region, especially in the population's origins and opportunities. Richard Smith, a land speculator, noted in 1768 the "divergent customs of newly arrived New Englanders, of long established 'low Dutch,' of remnants of the palatine emigration of 1708, and of the close, mercenary, and avaricious Dutch and English of Albany."[8] The Dutch tended to maintain their linguisitic and theological separateness longer, but gradually a new sense of regional identity developed as Yankees mixed and married with Yorkers of English and Dutch descent. Thus began that succession, and subsequent intermingling, of white newcomer groups in the mid-Hudson valley that has continued right down to the present, especially the great waves of Irish and German immigrants in the 1840s and 1850s and of central, southern, and eastern Europeans at the turn of the twentieth century.

More Yankees and tenant farmers on large patents held by landlords could be found in Dutchess County on the east bank of the Hudson than in Ulster County on the west bank. In Ulster, Dutch ancestry remained predominant and a majority of the farmers occupied small freeholds averaging a little less than 200 acres. But the goals of most mid-eighteenth-century farmers throughout the valley remained similar: achieve subsistence and increase comfort, add to one's land, and pass it on to the next generation. While some farmers already participated in long-distance trade, most obtained the goods and services they couldn't supply for themselves through local exchanges with a variety of partners, especially neighbors and storekeepers. "The distribution of liabilities and debts among numerous fellow villagers increased their dependence on each other as well as their security."[9] In Ulster County, swapping of products remained common until the mid-1830s when storekeepers increasingly demanded cash for the goods they sold. As local exchange diminished, market orientation increased.

## A LEVEL PLAYING FIELD?

During the American Revolution, residents of the Hudson Valley held separate allegiances to the British and American causes. In 1777, in an attempt to divide the colonists, the British forces, along with some of the valley's Loyalists, marched north, captured forts in the Highlands, and sailed up river to burn Kingston. However, the British defeat at Saratoga failed to secure the valley. The story of Benedict Arnold's capture in 1780 would later add romantic legend for nineteenth-century tourists, while General George Washington's headquarters in Newburgh from 1782 to the cessation of hostilities in 1783, and the rebuilding of Clermont, the home of Robert Livingston, after having been burned by the British, would add historic "association" to the valley landscape. After the capitol moved from Kingston to Poughkeepsie, the city played its most significant role as the site of the ratification of the Constitution by New York State. Land and people, formerly divided, became united, as many Tories fled to Canada and their lands redistributed.

Confiscation of Loyalist estates was initially a boon to speculators. But the speculators mostly sold small tracts to settlers, so that freeholders soon increased dramatically in Westchester and Dutchess counties. When the New York legislature forebade primogeniture and entail and eliminated all feudal tenures, most landlords sold rather than continue leasing, with the Van Rensselaers and Livingstons, patriots during the Revolution, holding out until the 1840s.

Sixteen miles of historic properties along the Hudson in the townships of Rhinebeck and Red Hook can be traced back to one source, Chancellor Robert R. Livingston. In 1774, he inherited the vast lands of his grandfather, father, and his mother's father, Colonel Henry Beekman, that included 17,000 acres of Clermont in Columbia County, Beekman patents and purchases in Dutchess County, and the 240,000-acre Great Hardenbergh Patent in the southern Catskills. The Livingstons' chain of great estates included Grasmere, The Pynes, Wildercliff, Montgomery Place, Rokeby, and Edgewater, each mostly having 300 acres and depending on a staff of servants and slaves. They were joined by rich businessmen from New York like the Roosevelts, collectively forming a river gentry that stretched from Fishkill to the southern border of Columbia County. Between 1742 and 1925, these families created eighty estates, half of them still in the original families in the 1920s.

The old families who made up the river gentry in the twentieth century had long before lost the entrepreneurial spirit that had made their fortunes in the late seventeenth and early eighteenth centuries. Their descendants viewed tenants as social inferiors who must be kept in their place, and as river gentry they also looked down on the citizens of nearby river towns who sought to make money in trade and other ungentlemanly callings. Martha Bayne, writing in 1937, noted one continuity in rural Dutchess over two centuries: "Just as there was a contrast between the small land owners and their wealthier neighbors before the Revolution, there is now a split between the few remaining estate owners and the 'dirt farmers.'"[10] The legacy of their landed wealth continued into the twentieth century when some of their mansions now became museums open to the local public as well as visiting tourists.

## WHY SO MANY SLAVES IN THE VALLEY?

Left out of the gradual process during the eighteenth century of white ethnic amalgamation were the African slaves brought to the Hudson River valley, first by the Dutch West India Company and later by the Royal African Company monopoly, providing forced labor for Dutch and English settlers. The first census of Poughkeepsie in 1714 enumerated thirty slaves in a population of 445. In Ulster County, slaves constituted as many as one-tenth of all inhabitants. By 1790, the Hudson valley accounted for 60 percent of all the slaves in New York State. The fertility of valley soils encouraged white farmers to look for sources of cheap agricultural labor outside their own families. They turned to slaves who could be expected to develop the needed versatility of skills as valley farms in the eighteenth century moved beyond their mainstay of grains for export to more diversified production. Advertisements for male slaves regularly included the "phrase 'understands all kinds of farm work.'"[11]

One-fourth of the households in the townships of Fishkill, Poughkeepsie, and Rhinebeck had slaves. Manumission was rare and overall the valley was the most politically and racially conservative area in the state. In 1799, the state adopted gradual abolition by freeing those born after that date, but compensated their owners by giving them the labor of these children until African American males reached the age of twenty-eight and females, the age of twenty-five. So the legal end of slavery became 1827. Moreover, the slave owners successfully insisted on limiting the rights of free blacks. African Americans contributed to the early development of the valley as involuntary members of its labor force.

Yorkers and Yankees made the economic decisions that set the character and future direction of the mid-Hudson region. White male residents of the mid-Hudson valley's four major river towns by 1800—Hudson, Kingston, Newburgh, and Poughkeepsie—soon exploited new opportunities for growth.

## RIVER TOWNS TAP THEIR HINTERLANDS

Commercial access by water to a larger regional market extending from Long Island to Albany fostered the growth of the river towns after 1800, spurring them to build transportation networks to exploit their overlapping hinterlands. The city of Hudson in Columbia County led the way in tapping its hinterland for agricultural produce to supply New York City. By 1807, it had built three turnpikes to reach the western Connecticut and Massachusetts trade.

By the early nineteenth century, farmers had thickly settled all the good arable land of Dutchess, Orange, and Ulster counties, with wheat as their primary crop. Newburgh had built its first turnpike in 1801 and, by 1820, the village had established in distant Ithaca a branch office of the Bank of Newburgh. In 1808, Poughkeepsians built Dutchess Turnpike eastward to Sharon, Connecticut, connecting it with an existing turnpike to Litchfield. By that year, only Kingston had failed to push a major turnpike into its hinterland. All four towns embraced improvements in river transportation. First sailing vessels, then steamboats, carried produce that had been brought from the interior to urban markets. From Poughkeepsie's river landings in 1813, sloops sailed for New York City; the next year the village became a steamboat terminal.

However, by 1825, the opening of "Clinton's folly," the state-constructed Erie Canal from Albany to Buffalo, dashed any ambitions of Hudson river towns to capture trade west of the Catskills. The great population shift within New York State between 1785 and 1820 also favored use of the canal. In the earlier year, three-quarters of New Yorkers lived in the Hudson valley or along the Atlantic coast. By 1820, three-quarters lived in the newer counties to the north and west of Albany. Farmers in the more fertile land of the Mohawk valley and Genesee regions now preferred traveling the shorter distance north to the canal.

So, needing to adapt their production in order to survive economically, Hudson valley farmers began experimenting with a variety of other grain crops, like barley, along with raising sheep and cattle. Commercial agriculture in the valley also turned to fresh vegetables, fruits, and juice for urban markets in Connecticut and metropolitan New York. In the end, most farmers in the region chose a new specialization in dairying, at first supplying butter and cheese. Many farmers in Ulster County supplemented their dairy products with domestic manufacture of barrel staves. Both kinds of production remained firmly in the household's control, unlike the putting-out system in New England where the merchant providing materials and selling the finished product set the terms. With the coming of railroads by mid-century, fresh milk would be added to valley specialization in dairying. Together with improved transportation and the growing interest in a more businesslike and "scientific" agriculture would gradually modify valley farmers' daily round of life, increasing the trend to a market-oriented family. As late as the 1830s, a young farmhand in LaGrange illustrated the mix of simple methods of production with the ambition, the literacy, and the sociability of a self-consciously proud and independent rural white population, especially those of Yankee descent.

The day after Christmas 1833, Vincent Morgan Townsend, still a bachelor at age twenty-one on his family's farm in what is now the outer suburb, LaGrangeville, told his diary that "Pap" let him have a horse for an evening social if he would take a load to the river landing at Poughkeepsie [about 10 miles from the farm], which he did. "Smoked 2 segars, drank a glass of beer and cut for hop. . . . Stopped at the mill and got a grist of buckwheat," hoping for buckwheat cakes every morning that winter. Next day, Townsend had "company in the evening. Talked mostly about how to get rich, regaled with nuts and apples til 10."[12] The next night he read the newspaper and a chapter in Scott's biography of Napoleon. Twice he reported participating in debates at the Nelson House in Poughkeepsie, once successfully on the question: Is Novel Reading Beneficial?

In the mid-Hudson region, towns along the river, settled as economic ventures, vied for supremacy as the major population center between New York City and Albany. At first glance, considering their remarkably similar size, rates of growth, and ethnic composition, Hudson, Kingston, Newburgh, and Poughkeepsie seem sufficiently alike to be easily generalized. But they took very different paths to prosperity, partly as a result of their differing ability to capture the trade of their hinterlands. They also had varying degrees of success in establishing strategies for economic development. Their histories up to the end of the nineteenth century indicate why Poughkeepsie with its more diversified manufacturing began the twentieth century as the leading urban center in the region.

## HUDSON, KINGSTON, AND NEWBURGH BEFORE 1900

An infusion of New Englanders into Columbia County created a new river community almost overnight after 1785. Quaker whaling families from Nantucket established the city of Hudson. Within three years, Hudson had fifteen hundred inhabitants, shipbuilding yards, a sperm oil works, and many shops. With twenty-five seagoing boats, it became one of the busiest ports on the river. For its well-planned layout of streets, enterprising Hudson adopted the grid system, well before New York City's 1811 choice of the grid. The Hudson plan included a parade ground at the city's western end on a rock promontory rising above the river where residents enjoyed the spectacular views at sunset with the Catskill Mountains in the distance. The whalers experienced ups and downs in prosperity, until the bottom dropped out of the market for sperm oil by the 1840s. Farming in Columbia only partially compensated for that economic loss. Enjoying moderate prosperity subsequently, Hudson by 1870 had less than half the population of the valley's other three major river towns. However, in the late twentieth century, the city's siting would lend itself nicely to becoming a center for antique dealers serving second-home owners and visitors from New York City to Columbia County.

In contrast to the sudden burst of entrepreneurial energy that created Hudson in the late eighteenth century, Kingston remained a quiet, largely Dutch farming trade center in 1820. An unexpected project begun by outside investors during the mid-1820s radically transformed Kingston's economy, population, and orientation to Rondout Creek. Many of the old Dutch families reacted to the impact of the construction—completed in 1828—of the Delaware and Hudson Canal with a shock like that of Rip Van Winkle waking up from his long sleep. The canal connected the anthracite coal fields of Pennsylvania by water with the Hudson River at Kingston and thus to river towns and ports throughout the Northeast. In addition to coal export, the demand for canal building materials spurred a major cement, limestone, and bluestone industry, located not in the old hilltop village but along previously undeveloped Rondout Creek. In Rondout, lots of backbreaking "dollar-a-day" jobs moving coal and stone and lots of heavy, dusty work in the lime and cement plants required lots of unskilled or semiskilled workers.

These poorly paid workers constituted half of Kingston's labor force by 1860 whereas they accounted for only one-third in Poughkeepsie and other cities with more diversified economies. More than one-third of Kingston's population was Irish-born compared to one-fifth of Poughkeepsie's. Squeezed together in the shanties of Rondout's "New Dublin," they competed with native firemen or less skilled natives and together rioted with a group violence unknown to the village. Soon the river town came to seem very different from its hinterland where Dutch-descended farming families continued to pride themselves on the stability and relative quiet of their households and hamlets.

By the 1840s, Newburgh faced a different threat. Like all the region's river ports at the beginning of the steamboat era, the village quickly built turnpikes to gather agricultural exports from its hinterland. In the 1810s, Newburgh's freighters invested in the ambitious project of linking Newburgh with Ithaca, hoping to bring produce overland from the Finger Lakes and Genesee country for transshipment to the New York City region and beyond. But the Erie Canal had ended that dream and by 1841 the Erie Railroad posed a new challenge by laying track from New York City to Goshen about 20 miles away from Newburgh. Goshen's new ability to bypass its rival in shipping butter and pork had a calamitous effect on Newburgh's freighting business, resulting in loss of population, shop closing, and plummeting real estate values. For rich freighting families who had put their profits in local real estate as a secure investment, the choice now was to leave town or innovate.

In sharp contrast to Poughkeepsie's diversified manufacturers and Kingston's businesses dependent on the canal built by outsiders, Newburgh's

freighters chose united and bold innovation. Following the example of
Boston's merchant princes who abandoned overseas trade to build cotton textile factories, the freighters established in 1844 the Newburgh steam mills
employing three hundred workers, mostly women. They constructed their
huge factory building, still standing, at riverside, facilitating river transport of
raw materials and finished product. Soon an industrial complex grew up, with
mills and nearby iron foundries to create textile machinery.

### SLOWING URBAN GROWTH

The next century would see major changes and differences between the four
major river towns, but their relative size would remain remarkably similar. In
1850, Poughkeepsie numbered 13,944 inhabitants; Newburgh, 11,415; and
Kingston and Rondout combined, 10,232 while Hudson lagged well behind
with 6,286. The towns continued to compete for advantage in attracting customers, new businesses, transportation facilities, and large public employers,
like state hospitals. But the towns' relative sizes remained similar in 1870; by
1900, the differences of the larger three narrowed to hover around 24,000 with
Newburgh and Kingston slightly ahead of Poughkeepsie. Over the next few
decades of the twentieth century, Poughkeepsie nearly doubled in size as it
gained far more than any of the others. Overlapping hinterlands brought continuing competition and rivalry.

Sharing the lower part of the continuous waterway from New York City
to Buffalo, the four river towns also shared in the flow of immigrants northward up the Hudson from the 1830s onward. Some came for specific job
opportunities like Irish immigrants taking unskilled work near the Delaware
and Hudson Canal or constructing the Hudson River Railroad to Poughkeepsie in the late 1840s. Others, like some German craftsmen, stopped short
of intended westward destinations to try practicing their trades in the valley.
By 1870, Kingston had nearly 27 percent foreign-born, Newburgh, 26 percent, Poughkeepsie, 22 percent, and Hudson 19 percent. Proportions of colored residents ranged between 2.4 percent in Kingston and 4 percent in Hudson. The arrival of so many immigrants with alien cultures unsettled older
native residents, making them more conscious of what they shared with each
other. They became less concerned with "lingering Yankee-Yorker antagonisms. In this way the deep-rooted cultural distinctiveness of the Hudson-
Mohawk region tended to fade in significance."[13]

Also fading during the late nineteenth century was the region's economic
importance and relative population growth within New York State. The four
river towns continued to be centers for local trade, depending on manufacturing for further growth, but they did not develop strong specialized industries
comparable to those of the upstate cities they had once hoped to surpass, like
Utica, Syracuse, and Rochester.

## KNOCKOUTS IN THE 1890s

All three of the mid-Hudson region's larger river towns, now small cities of more than twenty thousand inhabitants, entered the 1890s in a mood of pride and prosperity. But that decade saw dramatic reversals in fortune for both Newburgh and Kingston. In Newburgh, the steam mills closed in 1892. Then the Panic of 1893 bankrupted several machinery factories. This time the city's moneyed class did not invest in any bold new venture, let alone help struggling manufacturers stay in business. Recovery in Newburgh came inadvertently. The national panic in 1893 lowered rents enough to create inexpensive housing. That made Newburgh attractive for garment factories and sweatshops that required little capital but ample cheap labor, usually of immigrants. Several clothing companies moved to Newburgh, often occupying vacated premises of the former iron and engine works. Old-timers might deplore these alien newcomers, but the new industry thrived in Newburgh until the 1930s.

The 1890s punished Kingston more severely. Unable to compete with the low rates and the speed of railroad transportation, the Delaware and Hudson Canal ceased operation in 1898. The city's waterfront section, previously the center of business and population, now became a rundown neighborhood on the edge of the city. Almost all of the industries that had helped fuel Kingston's growth during the late nineteenth century either disappeared or suffered badly, including ice, textiles, tanning, and cement. Local cement production had been hurt by the new Portland cement process, but some production continued at Hudson and Cementon.

By the end of the century, all the river towns had embraced the railroad and turned away from the river traffic that once made their waterfronts so lively. The transition came earliest in Poughkeepsie. The village, soon to become incorporated as a city, had through service to Albany by 1851, linking up with lines to Buffalo that became the New York Central system. The west shore towns initially had high hopes of achieving competitive railroad connections, but only got their own line to New York City in 1884. It never became a major trunk line and soon was absorbed by the New York Central system. The last railroad competition between the river towns centered on their rivalry in trying to become a gateway city linking New England and Mid-Atlantic railroad systems; the aim was to bypass metropolitan New York's traffic congestion. Poughkeepsie triumphed over Newburgh and Kingston by bridging the Hudson in 1889, though the triumph brought much less economic benefit to the city than had been anticipated.

Although Poughkeepsie generally resembled its three neighbors along the Hudson in many particulars—size, ethnic composition, and economic booms and busts—its development during the nineteenth century differed in its railroad connections, the diversification of its manufacturing, and its greater ability correspondingly to weather economic downturns. Like its rivals, Poughkeepsie continued to depend on its surrounding agricultural hinterland throughout the nineteenth century. The urban nodes of the mid-Hudson valley knew the importance of farm prosperity to their own prosperity and constantly talked about the ebbs and flows of farmers coming to market.

# TWO

# Poughkeepsie Grows from Village to City

POUGHKEEPSIE BEGAN in the 1680s on the plateau above a highly irregular slope running down to the river. A turning point in the Post Road, begun in 1703, from Manhattan to Albany fixed the village's center at the intersection of roads running toward the farms and small marketplaces in the east and roads connecting the communities north and south along the Hudson River. Taverns, shops, homes, and churches began to cluster close at this turning point along the hilltop. The most built-up area as late as 1790 was today's six blocks bounded by Main Street to the north, Market Street to the west, Church Street to the south, and Academy Street—once known as "Ragged Lane"—to the east. The village had no initial orientation to the river. Not until the 1770s did a lane straggle down from the hilltop to a warehouse at what became the Union Street river landing. Soon docks were constructed along the Hudson's riverfront to load sloops with farm produce from the hinterland as the waterfront emerged as a regional shipping port. The Main Street Landing became the main public dock for the city in 1811, when steamboats began to stop at this central docking site. The ferry to Highland on the west shore was berthed in its slip at this landing, and the Exchange House hotel was built next to this dock.

Poughkeepsie's manufacturing first grew up along a tributary to the Hudson River, known as the Fall Kill, that enters the Hudson after passing over a small, yet quite romantically dramatic waterfall. The "kill" (the suffix "-kill" is Dutch for stream or brook) drained the farmlands to the north and northeast of the settlement and was dammed in small ponds for waterpower to drive the mills along its banks. Poughkeepsie's mills ground corn and wheat, sawed timber, and produced felts and woolen cloth throughout the eighteenth and nineteenth centuries, but its manufacturing diversified to very different kinds of production like a brewery, a dyewood mill, and a carpet factory. The settlement of the countryside surrounding the village continued. By the mid-eighteenth

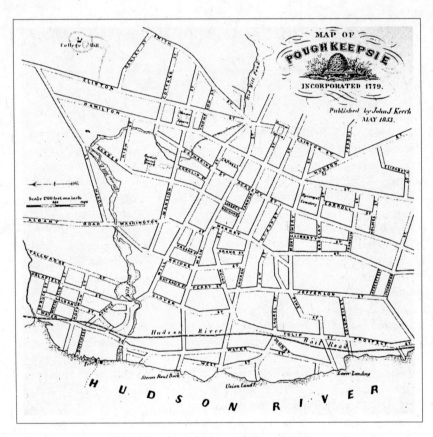

FIGURE 2.1. 1853 map of Poughkeepsie

century, smaller clusters of homes, shops, and mills began appearing at intervals of 5 to 10 miles in the vicinity of the county seat.

With popular participation in politics increasing and deference to your "betters" decreasing in the wake of the American Revolution, the Livingstons who resided along the river north of Hyde Park retreated to their land. Abandoning their family's expectation of and creativity in state and national leadership, they had for several decades been "shaping a distinctive class culture of genteel sociability"[1] and noblesse oblige while continuing, like their more entrepreneurial forebears, to reject frivolity and idleness. Like members and descendants of the colonial elite elsewhere, they took up family history and genealogy, glorifying themselves through their ancestors. While maintaining their interests in land and trade, they created a private aristocratic world apart from what they saw—and shunned—as the rude hustle and bustle of Jacksonian America exemplified by nearby towns like Poughkeepsie and Newburgh and rural hamlets eager to experiment with manufactures.

## WATERFRONT DEVELOPMENTS

Confirmation of the increasing importance of the river to the city's economy came when one of its richest citizens, Matthew Vassar, moved his brewery in the 1830s from Vassar Street, near the top of the hill, to the waterfront. His oceangoing sloops could be loaded more easily there with ale and porterhouse for the West Indies. The growth of manufacturing along the waterfront mostly came later, however. Poughkeepsie's early textile factories located along the descent of the Fall Kill in order to exploit its waterpower. So did silk and carpet factories in the 1830s. Gas works, a hot-air furnace casting ironware, and another tannery also located well up the river slope. The offensive odors from the tannery led before long to its removal to the village's eastern outskirts where a number of factories located around the easternmost pond along the Fall Kill.

Commerce continued to balance manufacturing in importance in Poughkeepsie's economy before the Civil War and transshipment of bulky commodities depended on river access. Antebellum freighters and commission merchants whose businesses depended on the river not only located, but also lived there before the Civil War in order to be close to their places of work. North Water Street then had a remarkable mixture of residents from different social classes, ranging from poor day laborers to ship captains and rich lumber and grain merchants like the Reynolds and Arnolds. Professional and business people also lived above or near their stores before mid-century. That proximity probably reinforced the already strong sense of connection among the city's business leaders between their business success and their civic responsibility.

Not until the coming of the railroad cut off a strip of land next to the Hudson from the rest of the river slope would much larger factories begin to take over that strip and its waterfront. The later larger newcomers to Pough-keepsie's manufacturing during the nineteenth century would be as diverse in products and character as their predecessors. The city did not develop any pre-dominant industry or specialty, unlike upstate Rome that specialized in cop-per manufacture as Cohoes did in collars and Troy in cast iron.

## IMPROVEMENT PARTY DREAMS

Matthew Vassar, successful Baptist brewer of English birth, was willing to take financial risks for his vision of how Poughkeepsie and his own fortune could be bettered. In collaboration with other leading citizens, including bankers, lawyers, two big winners in the lottery business, and bookseller and publisher Paraclete Potter, Vassar played a major role in creating the Improve-ment Party of the 1830s and was elected mayor of the village on its ticket. A practical visionary, ready to try new experiments, Vassar embodied the "can-do" postrevolutionary mood that fueled so many ambitious urban dreams in America in that decade.

The Improvement Party promoted creation of new industries, new streets, pavements and brick sidewalks, and private academies for young men and seminaries for young women. One estimate in 1841 claimed that these boarding schools infused $70,000 per year into the local economy. By contrast, the village provided a meager start in 1840 to the education of poor children with a public school system approved by a small majority of voters. Instruc-tion began in rented rooms in an old theater and a coach factory.

The Improvement Party members of the 1830s had different priorities, as their emphasis on private academies and seminaries suggests. Hoping to attract more families of substantial means and new businesses, they talked up their town endlessly, proclaiming its many virtues as a place of work and res-idence. They became the first of a succession of "boosters," trying like their counterparts across the nation to inflate their towns' chances of becoming big-ger and richer. Boosterism continues down to the present, though optimism has risen and fallen frequently. The aspirations of these early boosters of the 1830s did go beyond that goal, however, in desiring a wider uplifting of the local population in morals and personal cultivation.

Matthew Vassar and his colleagues envisioned a society in which masters and artisans alike shared in the benefits of adult education through the libraries of mechanics' institutes, lectures on the Lyceum circuit, and informal discussions in bookstores. Their vision foreshadows the democratic vision that inspired the first president of Dutchess Community College in the 1950s. The Improvement Party never forgot the bottom line of potential profit in their ventures and saw no contradiction between that and their more generous aspi-rations for their city. Expecting Poughkeepsie to grow rapidly, these specula-tive promoters laid out residential lots for sale on streets that, as it turned out, wouldn't be occupied for years. In some areas, their subdivisions approximated a grid, but the highly irregular thoroughfares that the village had inherited from colonial times made any coherent design impossible, unlike the village of Hudson that had begun with a plan. The real estate boom that the promoters launched collapsed, bankrupting some of them. A few migrated to Wisconsin to start afresh in the early 1840s.

The promoters had tried to create something new to Poughkeepsie: distinct upper-class residential sections. Least successful was their plan to make Delafield Street, close to the Upper Landing, an avenue of handsome homes, set back 50 feet or more with lawns in front. Somewhat more successful was the promoters' attempt to create an elite residential square uptown—copying upper-class precedents in England—around what became Mansion Square Park. St. Paul's Episcopal Church was established on one side of the park to be its gathering place. By the late twentieth century, however, the neighborhood had become much less fashionable, as the large houses were divided into apartments and rooming houses.

The promoters also tried several novel ventures that they located near the Upper Landing. They embarked on whaling, growing silk, and manufacturing locomotives—even though no railroad had yet reached Poughkeepsie. The whaling venture gained some unpleasant notoriety when Richard Henry Dana's *Two Years Before the Mast* recorded encountering "the whale-ship New England of Poughkeepsie" with a crew who seemed to Dana "a pretty raw set, just out of the bush, and as the sailor's phrase is, 'hadn't got the hayseed out of their hair.'"[2] These innovating Improvement Party industries failed in the early 1840s, but the village's diversified production survived and some businesses expanded. The energy and civic vision of the promoters, the educational institutions they founded, and, not least, their improvement of city streets and sidewalks had made a difference as would the civic "do-goodism" of members of the Chamber of Commerce early in the next century.

Most Poughkeepsians did not welcome controversial reforms, however. Visitors and local citizens who promoted the abolition of slavery suffered the wrath of this conservative city, including assaults from local mobs. When Samuel Gould, an agent of the American Anti-Slavery Society, tried to give a lecture at the First Presbyterian Church, the gathering stormed the pulpit "crying 'hustle him out,' 'ride him on the rail,' 'tar and feather him,' and 'out with the nigger.'" Gould fled, but the mob followed, "tearing his clothes and pelting him with snowballs" until he reached the home where he was staying.[3] When a state constitutional convention in 1846 submitted a proposal for African American suffrage to the electorate, voters in Dutchess County rejected it by a ratio of 8 to 1, a margin almost three times greater than in New York State as a whole.

The withdrawal of the now silenced white reformers from public protest had the ironic effect of pushing the city's most frequently humiliated residents to the forefront of agitation. Local black abolitionists like barber Uriah Boston continued to speak clearly and vigorously for racial equality, occasionally supported by a powerful outside voice like that of ex-slave Frederick Douglass. In the 1850s, antislavery advocates did raise sufficient money to pay a southern planter to free a returned fugitive slave, John Bolding, who previously had lived and worked as a tailor for some years in Poughkeepsie.

The city's white population, hitherto Protestant English or Dutch-descended Yorkers and Yankees, became more complex through a stream of Catholic Irish immigrants in the 1830s attracted by work on this boom decade's new construction projects. Finding themselves also at the social and occupational bottom of their new home, the new immigrants generally had little sympathy with Poughkeepsie's African Americans or with abolitionism.

## IMMIGRANTS BUILD A RAILROAD

A new provocation in the 1840s to activism by businessmen in Poughkeepsie was similar to the stimulus in Newburgh, but their choice of solutions differed. The completion of the Harlem Railroad linked eastern Dutchess County directly with New York City; its plan to extend the line to Albany threatened Poughkeepsie's primacy as transshipment center for county agriculture. Matthew Vassar mobilized businessmen in the western part of Dutchess to promote, successfully, the creation of a competing link to the city along the Hudson River. Upon completion, trains were "streaking some 40 miles per hour along the river."[4]

By 1851, the Hudson River Railroad reached Albany. Just as canal construction brought poor immigrant Irish laborers to Kingston, building the railroad brought them to Poughkeepsie. After watching the dangerous blasting and clearing of rock along the railroad route, one local boy at the Collegiate School observed: "Don't the paddies have to work."[5] The "paddies" sporadically struck over wages, sometimes bitterly, to the distress of respectable Poughkeepsie. Bouts of drunken brawling and rioting among these Irish laborers confirmed natives' unhappy sense of being invaded by an alien culture, although in the 1850s heavy drinking was not confined to newcomers.

The influx of immigrants did not end with the completion of the railroad in 1851. During the 1850s, refugees from overpopulation in the German states and from the Revolutions of 1848 swelled the tide still fleeing the aftermath of the terrible potato famine in Ireland. The impact on Poughkeepsie of several thousand newcomers was profound. By 1860, the Irish-born alone composed almost 20 percent of the city's male labor force and the German-born nearly 12 percent, or together almost one-third of the total. One of every three male workers came from a foreign land, bringing unfamiliar speech to the city.

Some native workers saw the immigrants as a potential threat to their own employment and living standard. The Catholicism and the frequency of illiteracy and destitution—so that 46 percent of the public charges at the poorhouse were Irish in 1850—alarmed members of the city's middle and upper class, too. Even before he moved from New York City to the Locust Grove estate near Poughkeepsie, Samuel F. B. Morse had published as "Brutus" a series of letters entitled *Foreign Conspiracy* in which he projected a papal design to destroy American liberty.

By 1846, nativists in Dutchess County had founded a Native American Party and a newpaper *The Poughkeepsie American* that cried out against Roman Catholics "thus grasping at political power, and attempting to gain ascendancy in the States." In 1847, it asked citizens editorially: "Are you aware that almost nightly there are landed on our docks, from the steamboats, numbers of destitute emigrants, many of them sickly: that our poor house is at present full to overflowing, a great portion of the inmates being foreigners. Awake! Awake! ere it be too late."[6] Despite these fears, the Native American Party at the peak of its popularity in the election of 1846 only attracted 11 percent of the vote in Dutchess County and 9 percent in the *town* of Poughkeepsie. Its appeal declined sharply after that, dropping to 4 percent of the total *town* vote in the election of 1847. By 1848, the party had become largely inactive and soon disappeared. But nativism and anti-Catholicism continued to have followers, becoming active again in the 1890s and in the 1920s.

## AVENUES TO ACCEPTANCE

The process of accommodation between immigrants and natives began, although prejudice against the immigrants remained blatantly in advertisements specifying "No Irish Need Apply." The newcomers, lacking the skills for regular employment, hungered for whatever stability and security they could find in their precarious struggle for survival. They found them most often by owning a small lot with a shack or cottage to assure themselves shelter in bad times. So strong was their motivation that Irish laborers in Poughkeepsie, as they did in other northeastern localities, soon achieved higher rates of home ownership than families of native parentage.

The Civil War provided a different avenue to immigrant respectability. Both Irish and German immigrants demonstrated their patriotism by volunteering in large numbers for service in the Union army. Wartime events and ceremonial occasions added to a sense of shared purpose among natives and newcomers as it would again in World War I. Father Riordan, pastor of St. Peter's in the 1860s, reassured the city leadership by a patriotic speech and the raising of the flag in front of his church. After the war, Riordan led many of his parishioners to join the temperance cause, a further adaptation to dominant social norms in their new world. St. Peter's Total Abstinence and Benevolent Society stood second to no Protestant society in membership and local publicity.

Riordan's leadership helps explain why the city's Protestant-dominated Board of Education took two controversial steps in 1873, abandoning opening religious services and Bible reading at the high school and permitting St. Peter's Church to become the site of a remarkable experiment in elementary education in 1873, unique at the time in the United States. Accepting a proposal from St. Peter's, the board leased two parochial schools from the parish. The pastor would nominate the teachers for the schools, with the proviso that no religious instruction or activity take place during school hours. The parish retained unrestricted control of school use after those hours. The board's action mixed prejudice, principle, and practicality, judging by the explanation that its president, Dr. Bolton, gave privately to historian Benson Lossing, a bitter opponent of this accommodation of Catholic newcomers.

Bolton argued, "Resistance to ecclesiastical tyranny is as much of an Americanism as is a desire to have the 'Bible in the Public Schools.' If you read the children of immigrants out of the public schools by sectarian practices, what have you got? an alien race, opposed to a government that will not protect them, denationalized by popular antipathy, and devotees of a hierarchy that satisfies all their wants both in life and death. But bring them out and scatter them among our own, and what will be the result? we will not proselytize them—oh no! but they will proselytize themselves."[7] This experiment of parochial-public cooperation lasted until the 1890s when a revived nativist and anti-Catholic American Protestant Association persuaded the Board of Education to abandon it.

Because German immigrants more often came as masters or journeymen in their trades, their reception in Poughkeepsie generally proved easier. Many of them soon set up shops, mostly in the working-class shopping area along lower Main Street on the river slope. The Protestants and Jews among them tended to move uptown sooner. Catholic Germans continued to cluster residentially around their Nativity parish on Union Street. But their pastor admonished them at the parish jubilee in 1896 to "count and calculate their dollars in English"[8] even as they maintained their mother tongue at home and in church.

## INDUSTRY TAKES THE RIVERFRONT

The unexpected alteration of Poughkeepsie's labor force by immigration at mid-century, bringing the proportion of foreign-born to more than one-fifth of the population, coincided with the even more dramatic revolution in transportation that would profoundly alter the waterfront and the city's relation to the river. Because the iron horse took only two hours to travel from Poughkeepsie to New York any time of year, the river steamers and stage lines north to Albany quickly lost passenger business. Freight transportation left the waterways gradually.

The use of coal, in turn, removed any need to locate mills and factories near waterfalls. Instead, industries relocated next to the railroad, for easier reception of coal and raw materials and distribution of finished products. In 1871, grain merchants W. W. Reynolds & Son gave up running a steamboat to Albany, abandoned the river as a means of obtaining western grain and flour, and built their new brick warehouse and elevator opposite the railroad station.

In the 1850s, iron furnaces created by outside investors sprang up along the riverfront and the locally resident Adriance family's Buckeye Mower and Reaper Works moved from Massachusetts to the riverfront in the 1850s. Since the railroad ran so close to the Hudson, the river now was largely cut off from the city. Gone were the days of easy access to swimming, boating, skating, sledding, and other recreations along the river. The waterfront became associated with noise, smoke, grime, and other unpleasant industrial by-products. Edmund Platt remembered, "without the snorting of the blowing engine at the 'Lower Furnace' residents of the southern section of Poughkeepsie scarcely knew how to go to sleep at night."[9] Families who once had enjoyed living nearer smaller businesses at waterside disappeared. A fundamental

FIGURE 2.2. Poughkeepsie waterfront, 1889

FIGURE 2.3. Reynolds mansion, 229 Mill Street, 1881

urban reorientation was under way, just as it was in other cities where large industry took over riverfronts.

In 1854, the village, now numbering more than 12,000 inhabitants, applied to the state for incorporation as a city. Yet, as late as 1860, much of the area within the city limits remained undeveloped, even on the river slope. The Upper and Lower Landings continued to be somewhat separate clusters of business and residence connected with the main business area on the hilltop by a fringe of houses along Union and Mill streets. Poughkeepsie was a community in transition. It had begun moving like so many other American cities at mid-century toward an industrialized and more socially segregated future. But, in 1860, both open spaces and socially mixed residential areas remained as reminders of a less congested village past where an ideal of artisan citizenship had not yet become an anachronism. In its many smaller shops, employers still interacted with their workers. Mill Street just east of the river slope and only a block away from the shops of the city's Main Street remained the most fashionable address with its comfortable brownstones. The conspicuous consumption of the Gilded Age's southside Victorian mansions lay in the future as did the deterioration of much older housing on the river slope.

## LOCATING SOCIAL CLASSES
## IN THE NEW SHAPE OF THE CITY

The last half of the nineteenth century saw expansion and further diversification in Poughkeepsie of opportunities in both education and factory employment, especially for women and for the mid-century influx of immigrants and their children. But the frequent residential mixing or proximity of different social groups of a village becoming a small city gave way gradually to increased separation of class and ethnic groups. With industry increasingly dominating the riverfront, wealthier families moved uptown in the Gilded Age. The city's richer families increasingly chose instead to reside in brownstones at the very center of the city, on streets adjacent to the fashionable part of the shopping district from Market to Hamilton on Main Street. Or they built much larger mansions in new enclaves along the highest ridges on the outskirts, like Garfield and Academy streets to the south and North Avenue.

Poughkeepsie assumed the form with which many cities would begin the twentieth century, moving away from earlier upper-class concentration near the center to middle class and then to lower class toward the outskirts. In Poughkeepsie's remarkably uneven topography, the affluent ridges defied this pattern and increasingly drew the rich away from the center. But even beyond 1900, Mill Street between Market and Hamilton remained fashionable, a world unto itself. At the other social extreme, the presence of the City Home, previously known as the Alms House, at the eastern outskirts would be followed mostly by housing for working- and lower-middle-class families.

By 1867, with diminished river traffic, the consolidation of the four river landings along Poughkeepsie's waterfront began. By 1873, steamboats ran only to one, the Main Street landing. By the 1890s, the venerable Exchange House hotel there had been demolished, replaced by a waiting room. A new railroad constructed between 1869 and 1873, the Poughkeepsie and Eastern, brought iron to the furnaces that had sprung up along the river, and the expanded railroad network throughout the county preserved Poughkeepsie's status as a transshipment and retailing center. Even before that improvement, the *Eagle* had exulted in 1865 that trade with eastern towns in Dutchess County had greatly increased despite those towns' easier access to New York City through the Harlem Railroad.

In a bid for the Poughkeepsie and Eastern Railroad to span the Hudson River, Harvey Eastman and other business leaders in 1873 began efforts to build a bridge to link the coalfields of Pennsylvania to the manufacturing cities of New England. The American Bridge Company began the construction of timber cribs, or caissons, three years later, but work stalled for another decade. Finally, in 1886 the Union Bridge Company undertook construction. When it was completed two years later with a total length of 6,768 feet of both span and approaches, Poughkeepsians claimed it to be "the world's longest bridge" as the first train crossed on December 29, 1888. Although never as famous as the Brooklyn Bridge constructed in the same era, the Poughkeepsie Bridge served as an important link for east–west rail travel into the first half of the twentieth century, and as a significant landmark on the river, especially during rowing regattas.

To optimistic civic "boosters," the city's status was also enhanced by new manufactures from the 1850s onward. They included the iron furnaces, the big mower and reaper works, by 1870 a shoe factory, and by 1880 a glass factory, collectively adding to the city's remarkably diversified manufacturing sector. Adverse times or seasonal rhythms in one industry did not have the impact on overall employment and prosperity in Poughkeepsie that they did in cities dominated by one or two industries.

## POST–CIVIL WAR ECONOMIC INEQUALITY IN POUGHKEEPSIE

Although the city did not suffer such swings in fortune as more specialized urban economies, it did not differ from them in the relative economic rewards received by those on different rungs of Poughkeepsie's occupational ladder. Under the federal income tax levied in the North for the War for the Union, all those who received annual incomes of $600 had to report them. At the bottom, ordinary day laborers earned less than $400 a year. Yet they composed one-fourth of the male labor force and rarely received more than a dollar a day. Just like today, inequality in assets was much greater. John Whitehouse, for example, reported owning $150,000 in real estate and $475,000 in personal property at the 1870 census whereas the real estate owned by day laborers rarely amounted to more than a few hundred dollars. Many had none. The sharp contrast between the rich and wage earners in Gilded Age Poughkeepsie could be seen in their housing, becoming more extreme by the 1880s and 1890s as some of the rich moved from town houses to great mansions on the ridges.

Poughkeepsie's newspapers did not concern themselves with poverty in the local population except when hardship became extreme, as in periods of high unemployment in winter. On New Year's Day 1877, after heavy snows, the *Eagle* reported that the Alms House gave temporary relief to eighty-seven families and the mayor called upon citizens to find employment for the poor. Again, in 1879, the paper reported that a "great deal of suffering and want has been alleviated during the past winter" through the Alms House, adding that "fair weather is a great assistant to taxpayers.[10] Citizens took for granted families struggling for subsistence at the bottom of their society.

A local boy, John Adriance first became involved with the manufacture of agricultural machinery in 1854 in the already well-developed industrial town of Worcester, Massachusetts. But, in 1859, he brought a newly patented mower home to Poughkeepsie to produce. His large Buckeye plant employed nearly twice as many skilled as unskilled workers, drawing many from outside the region. Census reports in the next decade show numerous machinists born in New England states. As late as 1879, 65 percent of Buckeye's craftsmen were still men of native parentage. But the proportion of immigrants and their native children was increasing over time. Unskilled laborers generally succeeded as often as the skilled workers in persuading Buckeye's foremen to train their boys to become well-paid machinists and molders.

The new Whitehouse shoe factory of 1870 illustrates even better than Buckeye a general tendency of the city's factories to level differences in occupational opportunity among their manual workers. The advancing sons of Irish laborers met the less fortunate sons of native skilled workers among the plant's 253 semiskilled operatives who worked on various machines for sewing the leather, burnishing and trimming, heeling, tacking, and breasting. The factory also employed women and children under fifteen years of age for some tasks; by 1880, it reported a ten-hour day all year long for 140 men, 80 women, and 76 children. Whitehouse paid $1.17 a day to ordinary operatives—little more than the wage for day labor—and a mere $1.50 for skilled mechanics. A few women previously had done the light sewing in shoemaking for several local shoe merchants, but the factory represented a large increase in jobs for them in that industry.

## EMPLOYMENT FOR WOMEN
## AND AFRICAN AMERICANS

In some other manufactures, like tailoring, opportunity for one group came partly at the expense of another. Competition from ready-made clothing manufactured elsewhere and from men born in the German states displaced skilled native women tailoresses at mid-century. By the 1870s, alternative jobs for mostly younger women would be provided by new garment factories making shirts and skirts. In 1880, one manufacturer of shirts, skirts, and overalls reported a workforce of eight men, ninety women, and seven children, with skilled workers receiving $1.50 for a ten-hour day and ordinary workers 75 cents.

Displacement of some native workers by immigrants affected more than women. German immigrants also moved into barbering where a few of Poughkeepsie's African Americans—descended from slave families in the valley since Yorker times—had long found self-employment. In other personal-service occupations, such as coachman, porter, and gardener, black Americans now faced competition from Irish newcomers. Abraham Bolin appeared in the 1850 census as a gardener and by 1870 as a missionary. Breaking free of contemporary expectation, however, his son Gaius made an exceptional rise as the first black graduate of Williams College and then as a lawyer in Poughkeepsie.

African Americans continued to predominate among waiters in hotels. But, overall, the influx of immigrants adversely affected opportunities for black Americans in the limited kinds of better-rewarded service work open to a minority among them. The majority depended on unsteady employment as day laborers and, as was true elsewhere in northern cities, none found jobs in manufacturing. Correspondingly, African American women were much more likely to seek employment than white women, but had far fewer choices. Over half held jobs, but well over 90 percent of these at every census worked as domestic servants.

While native white women had more choices, almost all (except some business proprietorships left to widows by their husbands) involved activities regarded as feminine or appropriate for women. And the rewards often were meager. Women principals received little more than teachers and sometimes less than male janitors in the school system. Even the better-paid found laying away enough for their old age difficult, sometimes impossible, ending up on public charity in the Old Ladies' Home. Other female professionals faced limitations in reward and what they could do. Women who had earned medical degrees at major universities found their practices confined to women and professional recognition by local male doctors given grudgingly, if at all. However, the County Medical Society did admit two women members and Vassar Brothers Hospital did appoint Dr. Elizabeth Gerow to its medical board. She and a male doctor cooperated to provide some medical service for the poor. Like other hospitals, Vassar Brothers, founded in 1884, relied on female nurses trained in hospital-sponsored nursing schools; the women were expected to cook meals for their patients as well as to nurse them.

## TRADITIONAL HANDICRAFTS DECLINE

Traditional crafts flourished in Poughkeepsie as late as the 1850s, allowing German newcomers to open their own shops in cabinetmaking, shoemaking, tailoring, cigarmaking, butchering, baking, and other trades. Although they tended to locate first near their fellow countrymen on the river slope, some prospered sufficiently to move their shops to the hilltop. A few became major landlords and moneylenders, like butchers Charles Kirchner and Jacob Petillon, or employers on a larger scale like cigar manufacturer John Schwartz.

In 1868, Schwartz fired all the workers in his large shop who belonged to the Journeymen Cigar Makers' International Union. But, by 1889, all of the city's cigar makers belonged to the union that reported "no difficulty with our employers, save one, who has grossly violated the apprentice law."[11] This unionized industry remained exceptional, however. Poughkeepsie had little labor organization outside the construction trades before the 1890s, although the Knights of Labor claimed a small membership and newspapers reported occasional strikes. Cigarmaking remained an exception to the undercutting of handicrafts by industrialization after mid-century. At the opposite extreme, predominantly British weavers at the Pelton carpet factory engaged in a nomadic search for the poorly paid work in their trade, judged by the multiple birthplaces of their children. And during the boom in the carpet industry in the 1870s, children constituted one-sixth of the Peltons' workforce.

What a far cry even the better factory employments were from antebellum handicraft traditions. Even during the 1850s, some Poughkeepsie employers, like Egbert Killey, master printer and publisher of the *Telegraph*, preferred an older ideal to calculating business practices. His obituary noted that no Killey apprentice "who had conducted himself creditably was ever discharged at the expiration of his time, but furnished with employment until an opportunity offered for good and permanent business, and the necessary aid in many cases furnished to enable them to go into business for themselves."[12] Killey's efforts "for the leveling up, as he used to say, of the masses" included successful campaigns to establish free public grammar schools in his city, a free library for young mechanics, and a program of adult education, the Poughkeepsie Lyceum.

## DAIRY PROCESSING BECOMES AN INDUSTRY

By the middle of the nineteenth century, the now dominant form of farming in Dutchess County, dairying, also participated in the progress of industrialization with the factory processing of milk. Gail Borden, an inventive man with a varied history of employment, turned to experimenting with methods of condensing milk. Having seen three children die of spoiled milk on a transatlantic voyage from London, he sought to create an uncontaminated, nonperishable, and tasty product. He succeeded, using a vacuum pan and low heat, in creating a powder that could be turned into liquid milk again just by mixing with water. During the Civil War, the Union army bought all he could produce. He chose Wassaic in eastern Dutchess as the site of his first factory in 1861; in 1863, he opened two more factories in Brewster, not far away.

Farmers now brought their milk to the factories in large cans that Borden cleaned and steamed for them, free of charge. But Borden demanded that his farm providers follow fifteen rules that he tried to enforce rigidly. They included drawing milk from their cows "cleanly" and passing it through wire cloth strainers, then cooling it immediately. Farmers must also avoid letting their cattle feed on plants, like turnips, that might adversely affect their milk's taste. At Borden's factories, inspectors constantly examined every farmer's milk, taking samples for testing, and the final product was hermetically sealed in cans. One of Borden's friends described the entire process of manufacture as governed by an ideal of "absurdly fastidious neatness."[13] But the Gail Borden Eagle Brand of condensed milk became the gold standard, and set one sector of agriculture, dairying, on the road to becoming an industry with the standardization that entailed.

# THREE

# Improvements and Conflicts
# in the Late Nineteenth Century

EXPANSION OF educational opportunities had been a staple of civic ambition since the days of the Improvement Party. In the late 1850s, Matthew Vassar, once again the innovator, decided to stake his claims to future recognition as philanthropist, not on the grand hospital he had previously envisioned, but on a well-endowed institution for higher learning with a special mission. A Baptist minister, Milo Jewett, who had purchased his stepniece Lydia Booth's female seminary, exhorted Matthew to create "a College for Young Women which shall be to them, what Yale and Harvard are to young men" with "a full course of liberal studies in an institution fully equipped." Jewett, who would become the college's first president, recalled that he "frequently had urged upon [Vassar] the obligations of rich men to use their property for the glory of God, remembering that they must hereafter give an account of their stewardship."[1]

## PIONEERING IN HIGHER EDUCATION

Vassar's decision to build his college outside the city in the town of Poughkeepsie on a site formerly occupied by the Dutchess County race course would result in an early extension of the horse-drawn trolley in 1872 to what would become suburban Arlington. Vassar chose James Renwick, who had designed New York's St. Patrick's Cathedral, to create a college under one roof that at the time of its completion had the largest interior space of any building in the United States. Construction began in 1861 and the school opened with 353 students in 1865.

By their physical location, Vassar women during the late nineteenth century were cloistered compared to the male students of another new school in

FIGURE 3.1. Main Street, c. 1890

Poughkeepsie. The young men who came to Eastman Business College boarded throughout the city. Harvey Eastman, a young educational entrepreneur from western New York, began in 1859 with great pretensions—and advertising—on a shoestring. A master at publicity, Harvey Eastman created a lively marching band that traveled around the country advertising the school. At Lincoln's second inauguration, the Eastman band immediately preceded the president's carriage down Pennsylvania Avenue. By 1862, Eastman claimed to have attracted 1,200 young men to his college, and by 1864 he reported 1,700. Eastman himself went on to become mayor of the city, joining a roster of prominent local residents, and served as an example of how successful newcomers could fairly quickly become members of the city's elite.

Late in the Civil War, many ladies of Poughkeepsie's comfortable classes received a different kind of education, indirect and informal, from their collective effort to raise money for the U.S. Sanitary Commission. Deemed a worthy cause for women to support, the commission inspected army camps for unsanitary conditions and provided food, ambulances, nurses, and field hospitals. In an era when respectable women normally avoided public attention, wives of locally prominent men initiated, organized, and ran a giant fair. They redecorated a coach factory to be a fairyland where they sold refreshments and gifts from contributors throughout the county. Thousands came to the fair. The *Eagle* reported that the "crush of crinoline and the smash of hats was terrible," but all appeared happy. "You could hardly turn about without meeting the glance of a pair of eyes that would make any person hand out any amount for anything for sale."[2] The crowds also consumed 917 quarts of ice cream, 50 gallons of lemonade, and 46,000 oysters. The greater involvement of women in public life in Poughkeepsie, as in other localities during the late nineteenth century, built upon empowering experiences like this one.

## THE POST-CIVIL WAR BOOM
### BRINGS PUBLIC IMPROVEMENTS

Rents rose, construction increased, and postwar Poughkeepsie surged in both population growth and prosperity. In 1867, the city had won a hot competition with Newburgh for the state's location of a large hospital for the "insane." Only a hair-raising sleigh ride at night through a "hurricane" of snow to Newburgh to present Poughkeepsie's final offer netted this major institution for the city.[3] The state chose the distinguished architectural firm of Vaux, Withers and Company of New York to design the hospital. Its construction added many new jobs after 1868; by the turn of the century, the hospital had two thousand patients and a large staff.

So buoyant was the civic mood by the late 1860s that the city's first daguerreotype artist, S. L. Walker, wrote to historian Benson Lossing that "I am about to write up (in pamphlet form) a brief Puff for Poughkeepsie. This I have been requested to do by a party of gentlemen associated for the purpose of adding to the character and population of our ideal city."[4] Harvey Eastman, ever the optimist, predicted that Poughkeepsie would reach 80,000 population, perhaps even 100,000, becoming bigger than Syracuse.

Eastman, of course, was far from alone in his overreaching predictions, resembling members of the Improvement Party before him and American boosters generally. But, like them, he also undertook big new projects. Elected mayor of the city in 1871, he helped implement an ambitious program of municipal improvements. He observed that Poughkeepsie had a bad reputation for fevers; when he talked to New Yorkers about Poughkeepsie's virtues, they frequently responded, yes, his city had fine schools, "but, oh, how sickly!"[5] His solution was to go into debt to achieve state-of-the-art sewage and water systems.

Street lighting provided one of the most important modern improvements of the late nineteenth and early twentieth centuries. Introduced in the 1880s, the first electric lights in Poughkeepsie received their power from a new dynamo at Bullard's foundry on Main Street in 1884. That beginning led to the incorporation of the Poughkeepsie Light and Power Company in 1885, which built a larger plant on Winnikee Avenue a year later. Gas, produced by the Poughkeepsie Gas Company since 1851, continued to supply lighting to houses and residential streets through the end of the century.

From 1886 through the first decade of the twentieth century, electric arc lights lit the city's major thoroughfares. Electric lighting symbolized the emergence of urban modernity: dark nights no longer seemed unsafe as pedestrians could walk along downtown streets and "window shop" in the brightly lit large glass windows of retail shops or attend the theater with its brightly lit marquee. Edison's development of incandescent electric light encouraged creation of better-lit indoor spaces. This important technological development, along with the adoption of alternating current, began to reorganize the workday and home life. As eight-hour days became the standard, workers had more leisure time to enjoy evening activities in a well-lit downtown. Some shops even began to remain open after dark on specified evenings to lure shoppers. Poughkeepsie's Main Street became an attraction at night as well as during the day.

The growth of the communications industry is similarly symbolic of the advent of modernism, anticipating the twentieth century. In Poughkeepsie, a telephone exchange begun in 1878 may have been the third one built in America, "having been preceded by New Haven and Albany."[6] The first telephones to be connected to the exchange were the office of the *Eagle*, Poughkeepsie's major newspaper, the home of John I. Platt, the *Eagle*'s publisher and a stockholder of the telephone company, the office of the city water board, and the pumping station. By May 1880, the exchange had 106 subscribers.

Poughkeepsie developed the first slow sand filtering system for its water supply in America, a notable achievement. During the eighteenth and early nineteenth centuries, the water supply had been a combination of shallow wells, cisterns, and surface streams and ponds, such as Vassar Lake. However, these resources became increasingly unhealthy and insufficient as the population grew during the post–Civil War years. In 1870, the city employed James P. Kirkwood, a water engineer who had studied sand filtering systems in Europe, to develop a system for the city using water from the Hudson River. Two years later, John Sutcliffe constructed filters on land a mile north of the city line. Clean water began to flow to houses and businesses in the city.

## THE BOOSTER AS PHILANTHROPIST

Like Matthew Vassar and other local businessmen during the nineteenth century, Harvey Eastman saw his civic and business activities as integrally related. What improved the city increased the likelihood of success in his own enterprise, and Eastman went much further than most in setting a personal example. With his usual flair, he surrounded his own residence with a private park where the YMCA now stands. The 11-acre privately owned Eastman Park extended southwest from the corner of South Avenue and Montgomery Street. Eastman created his park out of swampland. It featured a fountain, aviary, terraced walks, deer park, flower gardens, and plantings of evergreens and exotic and rare trees. The park provided a baseball diamond, tennis courts, and a playing field that he flooded in winter for ice skating open to the public. The park also had a lake with an island bandstand where Poughkeepsians could come for free band concerts. The Volunteer Baseball Club played on the part of Eastman's grounds that became Riverview field.

Another philanthropist's nephews extended their uncle's contributions to Poughkeepsie. On the site where Matthew Vassar's home stood in the mid-nineteenth century, at the intersection of lower Main Street with Vassar Street, the nephews built the Vassar Brothers Home for Aged Men in 1880. Across Vassar Street from the home and designed a year later by the same architect, A. J. Wood, was the Vassar Institute. Matthew Vassar, Jr. established the Institute as a free academy for scientific and literary work to "promote useful knowledge"[7] for the citizens of the city. It has remained as a venue for artistic events, scholarly gatherings, and dramatic presentations into the twenty-first century. The oldest church building in the city is a relatively small Greek Revival style structure on the corner of Vassar and Mill streets. Constructed in 1835 as a Presbyterian church, reorganized as a Congregational church two years later, and in 1860 as a Jewish synagogue, it became the Second Baptist Church later in the twentieth century.

Public buildings added to the importance of the city's center. At the top of the river slope, the intersection of Main and Market (also known variously as the Albany Post Road or South Avenue) clustered many of the civic buildings for the city and surrounding county. In the block prior to the intersection stood City Hall. The oldest public building in the city or in the county had been built in 1831 in a rather small-scale, symmetrical federal style, with several Greek Revival elements. Initially constructed with fish stalls and an open-air market on the ground floor and public rooms above, it housed more of the city's administrative functions by the first decade of the twentieth century, including the city's post office, police station, and jail.

Nearby Union Street preceded Main Street as one of three footpaths or wagon roads that provided the main routes in the eighteenth century from the village to the Hudson River. Main Street did not reach the river until 1800, while the winding roads eventually were straightened. During the mid-nineteenth century, owners of the land between Union and Main streets divided it into lots for sale. Side streets such as Perry and South Clover connected them. By the end of the nineteenth century, Union Street had been densely built-up. Its buildings fronted directly onto the sidewalk, with little space between them. They consisted primarily of two-story clapboard and brick residences with a few groceries, butcher shops, shoemaking and repair shops, saloons, and churches that catered to the mostly German and Irish immigrants who lived in the neighborhood. What the Union Street area did not have much of, except on poorer Jay Street straggling down the river slope from Market Street, was a significant African American presence.

## AFRICAN AMERICANS OPEN UP WHITE SCHOOLS

By 1873, Poughkeepsie's second boom of the nineteenth century had ended, once again with both realized public improvements and unrealized dreams of surpassing larger cities upstate. That year also saw a major step toward better educational opportunity for a group long left behind, the city's African Americans. But this happened not through any generous initiative from whites even in this era of Reconstruction in the South. Black children could attend the colored school for elementary schooling, but none attended the high school before 1870 and neither Vassar College nor Eastman Business College would admit Negroes.

In the fall of 1873, Joseph Rhodes, owner of the Eagle Dyeing Establishment, tried to enroll his two daughters in an all-white primary school. The principal seated them reluctantly. The ensuing struggle would occupy the Board of Education throughout the school year without the board finally accepting or rejecting the fait accompli. (That year the same board approved the almost equally controversial plan to allow St. Peter's two parochial schools to be run with Catholic teachers as a public school, paid for by all taxpayers.) Colored students in other localities made similar attempts. In 1874, the state legislature abolished segregation in public schools, making these civil rights cases moot. In 1879, Josephine Rhodes became the first black graduate of Poughkeepsie High School.

Because the Board of Education had made it easier for Catholic students to attend the high school by abandoning readings from the King James Bible, the Irish, poorest of the immigrant groups, now took the most advantage of this new educational opportunity. Ten sons of Irish immigrants compared to only two sons each of German and of British parentage received diplomas from the high school among the thirty-four graduates of the classes of 1879 through 1882. The eight Irish-American male graduates who stayed in Poughkeepsie found better occupations than the vast majority of native-born sons of Irish parentage, becoming clerks, lawyers, bookkeeper, street superintendent, master plumber, and civil engineer. Sons in German households more often entered skilled crafts, like their fathers; unfortunately, at a time when traditional handicrafts lost ground to industrially made products, that choice could become a poorly rewarded cul de sac.

Not surprisingly, Irish fathers of male high school graduates tended to be among the more enterprising, whether as teamsters, junk dealers, contractors, bosses in the building trades, or laborers who had acquired some property. Seeing how more education gave a "leg up" to better occupations and reward, these fathers seized the opportunity, adapting to their new world's expectations and conditions. A similar pattern appears among all ethnic groups, including boys of native parentage whose fathers usually appear as professionals or proprietors at the time the boys entered high school. Most of these parents enjoyed middling success; had they been richer, they normally would have sent their children to private academies. The public school facilitated upward mobility for children whose families already were improving their situation; it also helped other families maintain advantages they otherwise might lose. In theory of course, students from the poorest homes could have climbed the educational ladder through high school, but few did.

The gap between white-collar and manual workers widened in other ways. Early fire companies in Poughkeepsie, as elsewhere, attracted shop owners and employers concerned to protect their properties as well as artisans and laborers. But as fire companies improved their equipment and firehouses in the late 1850s and early 1860s, they seem to have become more attractive to wage earners without a future of economic advancement and less attractive to the largest merchants and manufacturers. Individual firehouses became more sharply differentiated by class as the city grew larger and its neighborhoods more sharply differentiated, too. Two companies nearest the central business district numbered primarily businessmen and clerical and sales workers whereas a company near the river had many unskilled workers, mostly boatmen.

Men with poor future prospects appear to be compensating through a more intense social life in their fire companies, frequently making convivial excursions to visit firehouses in other cities. The *Daily Press* deplored the amount of newspaper coverage of "firemen's visits abroad, including tar-barrels, torchlights, collations, speeches, beautiful bouquets, pretty girls and all that sort of thing."[8] But for those whose work brought little reward and less attention, their fire companies offered some recognition in life, a dignified burial, and support for survivors.

## A MOBILE POPULATION IN A CHANGING ECONOMY

The national economic depression after 1873 financially overburdened a municipality already deep in debt from its big investment in the new water and sanitation systems. Retrenchment followed. The city also experienced a sharp increase in bankruptcies of businesses large and small from 1875 to 1879. Not that failure of firms had ever been uncommon, especially little ones like the shoemaker whose shop was "a very small affair, works at bench only, just lives from hand to mouth."[9] Of the 1,530 Poughkeepsie firms reported on by the Mercantile Agency and R. G. Dun and Company between 1845 and 1880, 32 percent lasted three years or less and only 14 percent survived twenty years or more.

Only thirteen years after recovery from the depression of the 1870s, another and worse national downturn began in 1893. Although not as devastating to Poughkeepsie as it was to Newburgh and Kingston, this depression would see the abandoning of some major older enterprises for a variety of reasons. Many of these businesses' problems had been in the making for some time like the Vassar brewery's poor management and the change in taste preferences from porter to lager beer, the obsolescence of the dyewood factory, and the depletion of local ores for the iron furnaces.

The Buckeye agricultural machinery works remained at riverside, yet soon would become Moline Plow, a branch of a national corporation located elsewhere. Offsetting these changes, Poughkeepsie welcomed the creation of a glass factory in 1880 and, in the 1890s, a major new employer, Sweden's De Laval Separator Co. that manufactured machines to separate the cream from the warm milk as it left the cow. That decade also saw the opening of a variety of machine shops, some aggressively recruited by the city government that offered them incentives. The city's manufacturers continued to be diversified, and the proportion of skilled metal workers increased.

The city's importance as a regional retailing center increased with the expansion of the Luckey, Platt department store. In 1874, it had been a more traditional dry goods firm that occupied one floor of 1,280 square feet. By 1903, it had been transformed into a store with twenty-three departments selling everything from carpets and furniture to millinery and boys' clothing. Luckey's advertised that its "goods are sold at one price to everyone, [so] a small child can deal as well as the oldest shopper."[10] No longer needed was the antebellum versatile clerk, preparing to become a partner, who had apprenticed to a firm in order to learn all aspects of its business. Now a high proportion of Poughkeepsie's sales and clerical workers adapted to the less promising status of remaining employees for life, with only a small minority subsequently becoming proprietors. At the same time, they had to adapt to the increasing presence of young women as sales clerks.

The commercial world had changed fundamentally since Edmund Platt had clerked for the Candee brothers in dry goods in the early 1860s. Platt could take time off to attend weddings, visit relatives, collaborate with the Candee brothers in church and YMCA work, and make New Year's Day social calls with brother Will. Running Luckey's later, Platt did not normally attend his clerks' weddings and his diary records no occasion of socializing with them after hours.

## VALLEY PEOPLE ON THE MOVE

Migration within the mid-Hudson valley could lay a strong foundation for later success through understanding of regional business needs, as it did for English-born James Collingwood. Coming directly to Newburgh in 1832, he worked at his trade of shoemaking for several years before pursuing it next in Fishkill across the river in Dutchess County and also building some houses there. From Fishkill, he moved to West Park back across the river in Ulster to farm. Finally, he resettled in Poughkeepsie, starting up a lumber business. He became one of the largest dealers along the river, and in 1867 he built the Collingwood Opera House that would become the Bardavon movie theater in the twentieth century.

Looking back nostalgically from the mobility of our own time, we sometimes erroneously presume a stability in the cities of our past. Poughkeepsie did, in fact, have higher rates of persistence among its population than some other cities at mid-century. Nevertheless, half of its adult residents disappeared from the federal census here during a decade, both in 1860–1870 and in 1870–1880. Deaths account for only a small minority of those disappearing. So newcomers to city neighborhoods were usual, and at least limited accommodation to them, habitual. How quickly and how often new arrivals interacted with older residents is largely speculative, but anecdotal evidence suggests that some new arrivals, including immigrants, found relatives, friends, or people from the same locality already here. Others had been in the city at some previous time and so knew their way around and had old acquaintances. Unskilled workers left the city most frequently; owners of larger businesses moved on less often, giving them a disproportionate influence on public discussion and memory.

The organization of civic occasions after the Civil War played down the obvious antagonisms in the 1850s between immigrant newcomers and nativists. In preparing to celebrate the centennial of American independence in 1876, the seventeen-member committee included not only prominent Protestants but also Michael Plunkett, John Dooley, and the German Andrew King. More than a third of the fire and military company officers marching had Irish and German birth or parentage. A Roman Catholic temperance organization, St. Peter's Total Abstinence and Benevolent Society, preceded a Knights of Pythias lodge led by a German Jew, Adolph Ascher. The nativist order of United American Mechanics—which had led the cry against immigrant newcomers in the 1850s—brought up the rear.

Missing from the planning for this event were Poughkeepsie's African Americans, although probably not for lack of seeking recognition. In the years of national Reconstruction, they had become more aggressive in asserting their needs and rights. The very next year, 1877, Abraham Bolin petitioned the City Council for police protection for a large camp meeting that the "colored people" were preparing to hold in Livingston's woods. The *Eagle* reported a week later that about "1,500 people attended . . . and the utmost order prevailed. The services were full of interest and conducted with order and decorum. About two-thirds of the people assembled were white."[11]

Do such ceremonial occasions mean that social antagonism and conflict were rare? Hard to say from newspaper coverage. But differences between newspapers at mid-century suggest that some papers, like the *Eagle* (later renamed the *Journal*) tended to play down or omit unpleasant news except when it concerned those they disliked, notably the Irish or labor activists. The *Eagle* breathed a public sigh of relief in 1877 when New York Central railroad workers in Poughkeepsie, unlike their counterparts in some other cities, did not go out on strike against Cornelius Vanderbilt after he cut their pay sharply. By contrast, the *Daily Press* more often reported protests or strikes by groups of workers as well as nastier crimes like a gang rape in a north side brothel. The *Press* also had kinder things to say about immigrants, but made unflattering comments about the activities of local African Americans.

In newspaper accounts of local disputes, workers rarely resorted to violent action or threats of it after the Civil War. But on at least one occasion they expressed their anger effectively to make local government deal with their grievance. Mosquitoes breeding in ponds along the Fall Kill—dammed for use by some of Poughkeepsie's leading manufacturers including the Peltons—had become the source every summer of fevers and agues, sometimes diagnosed as malarial, for the families of workers living near the ponds.

A huge crowd of workingmen gathered in 1870 to demand that the ponds be drained and filled. Their spokesman, Irish laborer John Kearney, insisted: "We have been lying sick over there by the dozens, yes hundreds. We want this dam and we'll take it down and run the risk of the law." Another voice repeated the threat: "There is an aristocratic party at work. The poor laboring man can die.... If the Water Commissioners can't do this thing, we'll do it."[12] The city yielded, ordering that the ponds be filled, although that project would not be completed until the end of the century.

## WHERE DIFFERENT CLASSES AND
## ETHNIC GROUPS LIVED AND WHY

The residential pattern in Poughkeepsie by 1900 remained broadly similar to 1850, partly because initial uses of land in any area more often than not influenced subsequent kinds of use despite turnover in individual firms and families. However, as the more easily traversed city of 1850 more than doubled in population and spread spatially, the greater distances probably reduced frequency and intimacy of acquaintance between neighborhoods. At mid-century, young Edmund P. Platt, son of publisher Isaac Platt, lived in his family's new brick home on South Hamilton Street between Church and Montgomery streets where only a few houses had previously been built. Edmund could walk down to the river after dinner, then go on to look at the furnace on South Water and inspect the chair factory. Some evenings he walked in the opposite direction to the then eastern outskirts of town to visit the Alms House. This former home for the destitute has been renovated in the late twentieth century to become attractive housing on Maple Street for senior citizens. Before the coming of the Main Street horse car railway in 1870, businessmen as well as workers often had long daily walks to and from their places of work.

Generally, the frequency of manufacturing on the city's north side, due to the falls and ponds along the Fall Kill, would attract more working- or lower-middle-class housing than did the south side, with its high ground east of South Avenue. Even Mansion Square—which numbered some elite citizens, like bank president Thomas Davies—soon had near neighbors of very different status. In 1840, African Americans purchased a building there for the African Methodist Episcopal (A.M.E.) Zion Church. Just a block west of Mansion Square, the congregation had come to an area where a laborer, carpenter, two painters, glove sewer, and chairmaker already resided. That neighborhood became one of the city's four small residential concentrations of African Americans; the others were the Old Long Row on the outskirts, Jay Street, and Mechanics' Alley (built over in the twentieth century) downtown off Main Street.

On upper North Hamilton Street, a German carpenter set up a brewery in the 1860s and by 1873 five German breweries operated there. Rapid growth on nearby Cottage Street brought a gradual increase in the proportion of skilled and white-collar workers. But it retained the northeastern outskirts' early character as a less desirable neighborhood, attracting a disproportionate number of laborers, teamsters, and members of the building trades. The Poughkeepsie and Eastern Railroad reinforced that lesser desirability when it pushed through the area in the late 1860s and placed a station at Cottage Street.

Further east on the city's outskirts, poor blacks mixed with poor native whites and immigrant newcomers on the southward extension of Mansion Street to Main Street behind the as yet unfilled Red Mills pond. Separated by water from the rest of the city and close to the Alms House, the Old Long Row, today's Pershing Avenue, had some of the cheapest and smallest houses in Poughkeepsie. As late as the 1950s, one could still see many tiny cottages there, some of which had been built by the residents themselves.

Applications for charitable relief flesh out portraits of the city's poorest areas. They often came from streets near the northeastern outskirts like the Long Row and North Clinton and also from Albany, Spruce, and Dutchess Avenue at the northwestern edge. But the largest number came from streets toward the center of the river slope like North Bridge, Jay, and Church below Market. At the opposite extreme, almost no requests for relief came from the central business district.

The city's poorest neighborhoods invited disreputable activities as they do in most urban areas. In 1862, the *Eagle* reported that the Long Row "is going to be cleaned out of the brothels and other dens of iniquity."[13] The intended cleanup followed a notorious crime that winter in which twelve or more "young rowdies" conspired in a gang rape of a brothel owner. For impoverished newcomers struggling to survive in a new and often alien environment, however, such areas on the outskirts provided a temporary haven with cheap shelter. At the time of the potato famine, Irish families appeared on the Long Row who subsequently would relocate in the area of Irish concentration in Ward I in the northwestern part of Poughkeepsie.

## RESIDENTIAL CLUSTERING OF IRISH, GERMANS, AND AFRICAN AMERICANS

The new jobs created near the Upper Landing by the Improvement Party's industries in the 1830s had immediately attracted Irish newcomers and would continue to do so during the famine influx after 1845. Ward I became a political stronghold of the Irish who, unlike German immigrants, stayed nearer their poor countrymen and St. Peter's Church after they prospered. In the area immediately north of the church, the proportion of residents of Irish birth or parentage rose from two-thirds in 1850 to three-fourths in 1870. Here ethnic residential concentration increased as Irish newcomers who dispersed initially in search of cheaper housing subsequently found it possible economically to rejoin their kindred.

The area of greatest German concentration by 1880 around Union, Perry, and South Bridge streets on the upper river slope also had a cross-class character. It differed from the Irish pattern in that some more prosperous Germans already had left the area, moving uptown to streets populated by mid-

FIGURE 3.2. Flanagan's saloon, 267 Main Street, c. 1890

dle-class natives. Nothing like a ghetto, even a self-created one, ever developed in the neighborhood despite the visible clustering of German businesses and institutions. Even though the German Catholic, Methodist, and Lutheran churches sat within a block or so of each other, nevertheless, the Irish, English, and families of native parentage shared the surrounding streets with the Germans. Poughkeepsie did not develop the great concentrations to be found in a more heavily German city like Milwaukee.

Germans fleeing the Rhineland in the 1840s had shared some of the same entry streets with other immigrants, notably Jay Street, which straggled down the hill from Market—across from where Adriance Library would be built—to Jefferson Street. By 1850, nearly one-fifth of the city's 144 male German workers, many of them craftsmen, lived on or near Jay that they shared with African Americans, poor whites, and other immigrants. They mostly moved to the Union Street area as soon as they could. German Jewish businessmen, in contrast to their Catholic and Protestant counterparts, tended from the beginning to reside above or near their shops on Main Street. Successful clothiers like M. Shwartz lived there as late as 1880.

At the opposite extreme, the city's African Americans became more concentrated over time in their four pockets. As blacks increased in the poor entry streets of Jay and the Long Row, the proportions of Irish and Germans decreased over time. Some self-employed blacks lived at their businesses in white neighborhoods and the black pockets did have white residences around them. But segregation was the rule, as the city's reluctance to desegregate public schools even in 1873 had suggested.

Clustering in pockets surely limited interaction, but did not preclude interracial and inter-ethnic conversations on the street. On the south side where Irish families moved into neighborhoods already populated by other immigrants and by natives, white and black, they made a virtue of necessity, talking with those they might otherwise have avoided. Living midway between Church and Jay on Jefferson Street, Genevieve Carroll O'Brien got to know some of the African Americans on Jay Street. She remembered the garbage collector, Jesse Ford, as a "character" who always wore his stovepipe hat. When the Carroll's doctor proposed amputating her grandfather's leg, Jesse urged instead the use of a hot poultice of red cabbage soaked in hog fat to reduce the swelling.[14] Jefferson Street would remain working class at the turn of the century as new residential developments in Poughkeepsie between 1880 and 1900 largely followed scripts previously enacted.

## A NEW INFLUX OF IMMIGRANTS
## AT THE TURN OF THE CENTURY

Another old residential script had reappeared by 1900: a new influx of immigrants who would once again transform some neighborhoods. The new influx, this time from central, southern, and eastern rather than northwestern

Europe, would bring the proportion of foreign-born in the city's population to a height not seen since mid-century. In the streets north of St. Peter's Church, the census enumerator in 1900 found the newcomers intermingled with the much more numerous earlier arrivals from Ireland. Although the enumerator often misspelled names, he did at least attempt to record them, unlike the city directory compilers who for several years simply reported some addresses as housing Italians, Poles, Hungarians, or "foreigners."

The arrival of these "new immigrants" was gradual. As the Americanization campaigns and the movement to restrict immigration during the early twentieth century showed, however, worries persisted about whether and how easily the newcomers could be assimilated. The process of mutual accommodation had to start over. Once again, churches and synagogues played an important role, maintaining separate religious and national identities while their congregations learned how to make their way in America. In 1902, Polish families incorporated St. Joseph's Church and in 1908 Italians incorporated Mount Carmel Church. Russian Jews coming to Poughkeepsie at the turn of the century generally preferred the orthodox Congregation Schomre Hadath, incorporated in 1888, to the Vassar Temple that German Jews had organized at mid-century. Hungarian Jews would create their own Congregation Schomre Israel by 1913.

One major new script foretold Poughkeepsie's future: the migration toward the end of the century of more affluent families to new Victorian mansions south of Montgomery along Academy and South Hamilton streets. This movement ran counter to the post–Civil War tendency for the rich to concentrate residentially at the physical center of the city, on streets closest to the best Main Street shopping. But in the desire for more spacious homes and grounds, the movement had much older precedents in the valley's country estates. A dramatic example was the 1847 acquisition and renovation of a former Livingston estate, Locust Grove, by inventor and painter Samuel F. B. Morse. Then, in 1850, Matthew Vassar hired Andrew Jackson Downing, a nationally influential landscape designer whose home and studio were across the Hudson in Newburgh, to design property on lower Academy Street to be his summer home Springside. Downing and his partner Calvert Vaux created a romantic setting that Vassar opened up to visitors and fellow Poughkeepsians in the manner of a private park.

By the early 1890s, two great mansions built for Adriance families appeared on lower Academy not far from Vassar's Springside. During the same decade, J. W. Hinkley's Irish-Catholic family joined the Protestant establishment on Academy Street by purchasing and renovating Eden Hill. In the 1900 census, the household listed five servants and a coachman. Barbara Hinkley Shultz remembered four summer houses, winding paths and terraces, a veranda wrapped around both the first and second floors overlooking the Hudson and the Catskills, seven bedrooms on the second floor, and five bedrooms on the third where the large center hall served as an amphitheater for performing plays.

## A PLURALISTIC SOCIETY

Opportunities for recreation, sociability, and mutual benefit increased in the city during the late nineteenth century and so did organizations pursuing them. Did they result in increased acquaintance between members of different social groups? On certain occasions, such as sporting contests, they probably did. The Volunteer Baseball Club had a mixed membership by the mid-1870s with players of native, Irish, and German parentage, ranging from city editor and dry goods merchant to clerk, painter, and conductor on the city railroad.

But most fraternal organizations tended disproportionately to attract members of a particular ethnic group. Second- and third-generation Irish-Americans predominated in the Knights of Columbus. The name of the Germania Singing Society described its membership. Announcing the annual ball of the Turners' Society in 1877, the *Eagle* observed that "our German friends never undertake anything but what they carry out in a first class manner."[15] Two of the three lodges of the Odd Fellows were led mostly by men of native parentage, but, as early as the 1870s, had some officers of German descent like Jacob Rosenbaum and William Haubennestel. However, all the officers of the third lodge, Adler, had German surnames. Officers of the Knights of Pythias lodges tended to be more mixed in ethnic derivation and occupational status as did local military organizations. Lodge No. 43 had mostly Jewish officers.

Some kinds of outdoor clubs had more restricted memberships. Poughkeepsie's elite native Protestant families initiated and controlled both the Tennis and the Golf clubs. Following the much earlier exclusive Apokeepsing Boat Club, men of German derivation did organize the more inclusive Poughkeepsie Yacht Club. However, no sports club by the 1890s had the importance in the city's civic and economic life of the first social club in Poughkeepsie to survive for any length of time, the Amrita Club. Organized in 1873 by native businessmen, it initially rented quarters, but, by 1894, Amrita had purchased its own clubhouse,

Did the tendency to ethnic and class separation in the city's organized social and recreational life create an acute consciousness of social distance and stratification by the 1890s? Probably not. Many of Poughkeepsie's businessmen owned relatively small shops where they knew both their employees and customers. Suburbanization had not yet moved most of the more affluent and educated away from city center where people of every description came to shop. The city had long brought together representatives of its various social groups to celebrate major civic and patriotic occasions.

By the 1890s, the children and grandchildren of the great mid-century influx of immigrants also had begun to appear as elected or appointed city officers. Leading the way, Peter Shields, first reported at the Alms House in the 1850 census and later as laborer, had become deputy sheriff of Dutchess County by 1880. A little later, natives of Irish and German parentage won election as city chamberlain and recorder and, by 1903, Joseph Morschauser became city judge. They joined officeholders traditionally drawn from local businessmen, some from old county families, but others like Harvey Eastman or shoe manufacturer John O. Whitehouse, were gifted or rich newcomers.

At the turn of the century, Poughkeepsie remained a stable community with social and political mobility for the most talented descendants of earlier immigration. Continuing economic growth also provided jobs for the new influx of newcomers from eastern and southern Europe. Despite the local hardships created by national depression after 1893, the city did not suffer as much economic disruption as its valley neighbors, Newburgh and Kingston.

## RIVER GENTRY IN THE LATE NINETEENTH CENTURY

North of the city, the hills with commanding views above the river continued to attract wealthy families for residence for at least part of the year. But the scale and the grandeur of their houses increased steadily, and, by the 1890s, dramatically, inadvertently setting the stage for attracting tourists to the region in the twenty-first century. The progression can be seen in the careers of the sites for the Roosevelt, Vanderbilt, and Mills mansions. Hyde Park's Springwood began with an eight-room farmhouse to which a new owner in 1845 added a service wing and a three-story tower. James Roosevelt, who purchased it in 1867, turned the house into an Italianate villa of seventeen rooms in 1887 and his widow Sara Delano Roosevelt, mother of Franklin, commissioned a New York firm to transform the villa into a Georgian Revival mansion with thirty-five rooms, twenty-two bedrooms, and nine baths.

But James and Sara Roosevelt were pikers by comparison with another parvenu, Frederick W. Vanderbilt, whose chosen Hyde Park site also had a longer history as a residence. Noted physician John Bard had built first in 1764 and his son followed with a large new mansion where the current Vanderbilt manse sits. The next owner hired a landscape designer for the gardens in 1818 and made the mansion larger in 1829. It burned down, to be replaced by a grandson of John Jacob Astor with a "pink" forty-room Greek Revival villa. The grandson Walter Langdon lived there until 1895 when he sold to Frederick W. Vanderbilt who hired McKim, Mead, and White to build him what turned out to be a fifty-four-room Renaissance palace in 1898.

Far from being outdone, Ruth Livingston and her husband Ogden Mills had already engaged the same firm in 1895 to transform a long-time Livingston residence into Staatsburgh. The result: on 212 acres sixty-five rooms, with decoration in the styles of Louis XV and XVI. Ever since the donation of the Mills, Vanderbilt, and Roosevelt houses to the national and state governments in the mid-twentieth century, the valley has benefited economically from the fascination Americans have with the homes of their Gilded Age aristocracy. Local visitors to the grounds who do not choose to enter the houses enjoy the free access to open space with spectacular views of the Hudson. The most dramatic view of the river, however, can be seen from the picturesque "Moorish" residence created in the 1870s by the celebrated landscape painter, Frederic Church "in his grandly sited Olana above the Hudson."[16] Church designed the Olana landscape in the manner of Downing and Vaux, and would declare that he had made "more and better landscapes in this way than by tampering with canvas and paint in the studio."[17]

## ACQUAINTANCE AND COMPETITION IN THE VALLEY

Late nineteenth-century improvements in transportation simply made easier the already high frequency of visiting around the mid-Hudson valley by residents. Despite the difficulties of travel, compared to today, families kept in touch not only with relatives but with friends in other localities in the region where they had lived previously. Old-timers frequently visited relatives in other counties. Edmund Platt of the department store remembered his family taking the steamboat in summertime to stay with cousins in Orange County. Phoebe Collins in Poughkeepsie had frequent visits from the family of Daniel Griffen, a farmer and relative from Westchester County. In the 1880s, Griffen also visited his cousin Alice Smiley at the new Mohonk Mountain House resort near New Paltz in Ulster County. With an already obsolete perspective, he commented later that he couldn't understand why anyone would buy a mountain lake for a resort when good farmland could still be purchased in Westchester.

Residents of valley towns could not afford to be insular during the nineteenth century. At the lowest occupational level, laborers who spent winter hunting employment in the city often found work on farms during the summer. Some moved in and out of the city for longer periods several times, like car man Elias York who left Poughkeepsie at age forty-eight. He reappeared in the city at age fifty-four to work in a furnace, then disappeared once more for a few years only to crop up again at age fifty-eight, listing himself as a farmer, presumably a farm worker. At the other end of the social ladder, leading businessmen in every locality jealously watched new transportation and other economic developments elsewhere to estimate the effect on their own competitiveness.

Did the principal towns in the mid-Hudson valley look for ways to cooperate, to pool their resources in projects that might benefit the region? No. Although individual citizens might invest in projects outside their towns, the towns themselves behaved like bitter rivals in their separate quests for economic advantage. When New York State entertained bids for the location of new institutions that could become major employers and purchasers, fierce competition ensued. Poughkeepsie fought tooth and nail in the 1860s to successfully attract its new hospital for the mentally ill.

In the coming age of the automobile, the city and its surrounding suburban development would become an urban region. This expansion would reinforce the unchanging desire of its residents to be "up-to-date" and competitive with neighboring localities. Poughkeepsians in the nineteenth century
had not inhabited an insular world. Their connections with the rest of the
mid-Hudson valley would increase in the twentieth century.

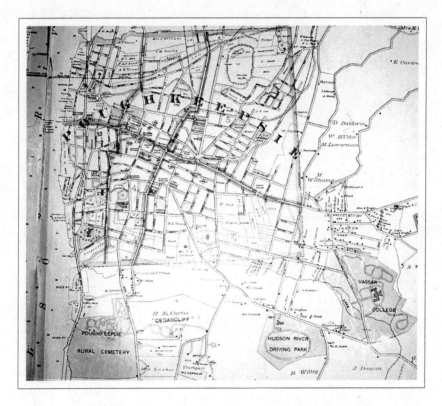

FIGURE 3.3. 1891 map of City of Poughkeepsie and environs

PART II

# A Diversified Industrial Economy and Society

FOUR

# The Cityscape at the
# Turn of the Twentieth Century

AS THE TWENTIETH CENTURY began, public officials praised Pough-keepsie's strong economy and its energetic and diverse populace. Still com-peting with other river towns in its hope of being biggest and best, Pough-keepsie's leadership rejoiced in the opportunity to put on a grand show in the valley's celebration of the 300th anniversary of Henry Hudson sailing up the river and the 100th anniversary of Fulton's first steamboat excursion. The city's largest civic celebration of the early twentieth century emphasized the great technological progress in transportation, fueling optimism about future improvement. A richly decorated downtown and parade route with enthusi-astic crowds created temporarily a colorful cityscape expressing civic pride and unity, ignoring the highly varied actual cityscape of Poughkeepsie's diverse and unequal neighborhoods. Poughkeepsie's performance drew gratifying plaudits from outsiders.

## HUDSON-FULTON CELEBRATION

Commenting on the festive commemorative event held in Poughkeepsie dur-ing the first days of October 1909, New York's governor, Charles Evans Hughes, rhapsodized about the city's efforts: "It is not a disparagement to any other place along the beautiful Hudson River, that I say here what I have said before, that the recent Hudson-Fulton Celebration reached its climax in beauty and completeness in Poughkeepsie. . . . I saw the patriotic and public spirit with which Poughkeepsie seemed filled and with which its people were truly imbued."[1]

The two-day celebration consisted of parades, historical tableaux, ban-quets, speeches, band concerts, songfests, prayerful commentaries, and "a brilliant display of pyrotechnics at the river front . . . the exhibition included set pieces and a dazzling variety of aerial bombs."[2] The official report of the celebration to the New York state legislature noted: "the city put on holiday dress and became a gala scene of fluttering flags and bunting by day and scintillating lights at night. In addition to the general decorations of public and private buildings, the Decorations Committee converted Market Street into a magnificent Court of Honor by the use of the decorations used in Washington at the inauguration of President Taft."

The Hudson-Fulton Celebration began in New York City on September 25, 1909, ending sixteen days later in Cohoes, a few miles north of the state capital in Albany. Cities all along the river sponsored events with thousands of participants. The arrival of replicas of Hudson's ship *Half Moon* and Fulton's *Clermont* at each of their waterfronts provided the centerpiece for the cities' celebrations. While the *Half Moon* represented the earlier role of sailing ships in European expansion, the *Clermont* symbolized the globalization of trade through steam power.

## TROLLEYS REFOCUS POUGHKEEPSIE

Most commercial traffic, however, had left the river for the railroads that spread like spiderwebs across the land. Steam engines on rail lines now moved the people and freight. With the *Half Moon* and the *Clermont* only historical artifacts by 1909, waterfront docks lost their importance as commercial hubs. The new age of the trolleys reshaped Poughkeepsie's highly irregular spatial layout toward the more usual radial pattern focused on the city center of the early twentieth century. J. W. Hinkley's trolleys, beginning in 1894, extended the city's reach into surrounding areas with shoppers ready to come to downtown as the trip became easier.

Hinkley purchased the City Railroad, changing its motive power from horses to electricity. New franchises from the City Council enabled him to build north and south loop lines and a much longer line running about 10 miles down South Road to Wappingers Falls. As they did throughout urban America at the turn of the century, the trolley lines brought shoppers as well as workers to the central business district, all lines converging on the intersection of Main and Market. Now quite literally the hub of Poughkeepsie, that intersection and its immediate surroundings became the city's major meeting place.

On October 1, 1894, the first electric car of the Poughkeepsie City and Wappingers Falls Electric Railway rode out of the powerhouse on upper Main Street. "It was Car No. 8, painted a London smoke color with stripes of silver, and was handsomely upholstered."[3] The trolley line brought public transit throughout the city, from the ferry landing at the foot of Main Street east as far as Vassar College, and in loops along Grand, Hooker, and Montgomery streets on the south side and Parker, Clinton, Cottage, and Washington streets on the north side, with an extension to the Hudson River State Hospital, which had been established north of the city in 1871–1872.

Within the city, the new "flashy orange" south end trolley running out Hooker Avenue to Grand made it easier to consider building a suburban park settlement. In 1895–1896 an architect with experience in Philadelphia suburbs designed similar houses for new Dwight Street. The project failed, but the spread outward from the city continued. Except for new houses in Arlington and Fairview, residential development in Poughkeepsie in 1900 remained mostly within the boundaries of the city and, before that, of the village at its incorporation in 1799. Open space remained in various places within the city limits. The most dramatic undeveloped property, formerly the site of the College Hill School and then a hotel of that name, was purchased in 1893 by W. W. Smith of Smith Brothers Cough Drops. Smith, perhaps Poughkeepsie's most generous philanthropist after the Vassar family and a leader in the Prohibition Party, gave the land to the city to be used as a public park. The trolley up North Clinton made the park with its commanding elevation more accessible.

For Poughkeepsie's retailers, a trolley southward to the village of Wappingers had more promise for attracting shoppers than extensions in any other direction. As late as 1937, Hyde Park village, a similar distance to the north,

FIGURE 4.1. Main Street, c. 1900

counted only 738 residents. New Hackensack to the southeast had a mere 110 whereas as early as 1870 the textile and garment factories of Wappingers already supported a population of 2,263. English immigrants predominated in the leadership and skilled work of the factories, giving them more importance in village affairs than older native residents. Although the Scotch claimed many skilled jobs, they had a larger proportion in less skilled manual work than the English. The Irish mostly worked as operatives and laborers. Correspondingly more Irish women worked in the factories than young unmarried women of any other ethnic group. By the 1890s, they could go beyond the village to shop. Wappingers' small businesses offered nothing like the variety of consumer goods available near the new trolley's terminal in downtown Poughkeepsie.

Workers could commute to their jobs using the trolley system, whether they performed white-collar jobs in retail, finance, or commerce in the busy central business district, or jobs in the factories and warehouses along Cottage and Smith streets and elsewhere on the north side. David Lumb, great-grandson of the founder of Lumb Woodworking, believes that all social classes rode the trolley. The Lumb family lived on Hooker Avenue, and David, as a young boy in the early 1930s, recalled his father going to work and returning home for lunch each day on the trolley. The frequency with which members of different classes took the trolley no doubt varied substantially in this relatively small city. Laborers and other less skilled workers unable to afford the fares would have walked to and from work.

Some people rode the trolley for amusement and to see the sights of the city and town. One tourist wrote of her impressions in 1932:

Perhaps the pleasantest approach from New York to a tour of the Poughkeepsie trolley lines was by the steamers on the river. If you left the city on the Albany boat, you got to Poughkeepsie in time for lunch. As the "Hendrick Hudson" or "Alexander Hamilton" moved slowly to the pier, close by the New York Central Station, you could see a car or two at the end of the line at the foot of Main St. or on the big hill. It was only a walk of a few feet to the trolley.

Boarding the car, you'd buy three tokens from the operator for a quarter, put one in the fare box, get your transfer and take a seat. With the car loaded, the ride up the hill began. There are steeper hills near the river in Yonkers, and possibly longer ones in other river towns, but the ride up the Main St. hill on a single truck Birney was something to remember for a long time. It wasn't quite straight, as the street curved a little.

At the top of the hill, you crossed Market St. . . . The line continued through the main shopping area of the city, past the junction at Washington St., where the North Side Loop branched off and the State Hospital route began, and then past Luckey-Platt's and all the rest of the stores. . . . After perhaps a mile, the stores gave way to a mixed area of homes and small neighborhood shops, meanwhile having passed the car barn. In a few minutes more, the car crossed the city line and you were in Arlington . . . finally ending at the gate of Vassar College. . . . The whole ride from the ferry house at the river hadn't taken half an hour. . . . In the afternoon, you could get swell pictures out at Vassar. The sun hit the cars just right.[4]

Many people took the trolley on excursions to connect with other rail lines west and south. As the name implied, the trolley line extended south as far as Wappingers Falls, 15 miles distant. Some who rode the trolley from Poughkeepsie worked at various industries located at the falls, such as the Dutchess Bleachery and the Sweet-Orr Company, which produced over a thousand pairs of overalls weekly. Others enjoyed a trip into the countryside. For example, some would stop at the rural cemetery just south of the Poughkeepsie city line to visit family graves or simply to enjoy a picnic on the lawn or under the trees in a romantic and picturesque setting. The trolley stop at the Poughkeepsie Rural Cemetery still exists. To the west, the line connected with the rail line over the Hudson River, by way of the Poughkeepsie Railroad Bridge, to the New Paltz and Wallkill Valley Railroad for trips to Highland,

FIGURE 4.2. South Road, 1919

New Paltz, or the resorts at Lake Mohonk or Minnewaska. In 1897, over one hundred "Vassar girls" took a ride on these rail lines across the railroad bridge to New Paltz and Lake Mohonk. On a national holiday, July 4, 1898, 2,198 excursionists crossed the bridge, according to a contemporary report.

At the height of operations, twenty-five trolley cars seated thirty to fifty people each. During the forty-one years of running on the city rails, the trolleys were involved in numerous incidents, especially if they lost their brakes on the Main Street hill that led down to the steamboat dock on the riverfront. In one such incident, the car went into the river carrying a prisoner being taken to Sing Sing prison. The son of the guard reported the prisoner's reaction, as follows, "Climbing quickly out of the water he escaped. He ran as fast as he could back to the county jail where he had been. It was safer there."[5]

The Wappingers Falls line ended in 1928 due to the widening of the Albany Post Road as Route 9, while the city trolley, struggling with declining fares during the depression, continued until 1935. At that time the Poughkeepsie and Wappingers Electric Railway Co. retained its urban transit status as a bus line, owned and operated by the same Hinkley family. Eventually the city removed or covered over most of the rail lines with macadam when repairing the city streets. Automobiles, trucks, and buses took over the streets.

## URBAN INFRASTRUCTURE IMPROVEMENTS

In Poughkeepsie, major streets began to be macadamized by the turn of the century, and curbs, gutters, and a shift from brick to bluestone or flagstone for sidewalks spread throughout the city. Other city streets were improved over the next few decades, along with street lighting. Increasingly the urban landscape reflected the impact of the automobile. As the city expanded, many of the new houses built driveways and separate garages. Traffic on Main Street and parking in the central business district became significant civic concerns that underscored urban planning developments throughout the rest of the century.

In 1901, the companies that produced and distributed gas and electricity, and held the contracts for lighting the city's streets, consolidated into one company. This business reorganization followed by only one year the consolidation of electric and gas companies in New York City to create Con Edison in 1900. Central Hudson Gas and Electric Company became one of the largest enterprises in the mid-Hudson valley in the twentieth century as it reached beyond Poughkeepsie to include villages and counties on both sides of the river. It became a model twentieth-century corporation by virtue of its concentration of financial capital and number of employees.

Telegraph and telephone wires strung along the city's main streets formed a web that suggested progress and modernism, but the wires also became a visual blight on the streetscape. After 1900, the streetscape gradually began to be clear of clutter as city government required that telephone wires be laid in underground conduits. The municipality's water and sewer systems also lay under its streets.

Poughkeepsie also improved its ability to fight fires that in the nineteenth century had devastated a number of areas of the city, especially the blocks of commercial buildings along Main Street. In 1908–1909, the city built three firehouses scattered throughout the business district: Lady Washington Hose, O. H. Booth, and Niagara Engine Company.

Improvements to the city's infrastructure, such as water and sewer systems, electric power and telephone lines, the alignment and paving of streets, and the extension of the street railway and trolley system exemplified the city's growth and development over the latter part of the nineteenth century and the first decades of the twentieth century and also Poughkeepsie's participation in a nationwide urban trend. These changes could be seen most easily on the riverfront and along the major downtown thoroughfares of Main and Market streets.

## CHANGES TO THE ECONOMIC LANDSCAPE

By the first decade of the twentieth century, most of the earlier industries on the riverfront, especially those that relied on the river for transport, disappeared. George Polk's shipyard, the Poughkeepsie Whaling Company, various storehouses, a tanning yard, chair and sash factories, a grain elevator, the Gifford, Sherman & Innis dyewood mills, Poughkeepsie Iron Works, Pelton's carpet factory, and the Vassar Brewery had gone out of business. Some of the factory buildings continued to be used for other kinds of production; a manufacturer of parts for pianos purchased the inactive Innis Dye Works in 1913. Meanwhile, other industries continued to occupy the land along the river and the rail line.

New and expanded industries stood out, including several large employers that depended primarily upon outside capital whose owners lived elsewhere. Outside investors established the Poughkeepsie Glass Corporation in 1880 on the site of the former whaling dock and remained into the mid-twentieth century. The De Laval Separator Company, of Stockholm, Sweden, manufactured and distributed pumps and milking machinery to the dairy industry throughout the eastern United States. The company built a factory south of the Lower Landing, incorporating Polk's boatyard, in 1892 and continued at that site as a major employer for half a century.

Lane Brothers manufactured various hardware specialties and, for a short while, built steam automobiles at their plant. The Dutton Lumber Company encompassed many acres to the north of the railroad bridge. The company, largest of its kind in the eastern United States, distributed both domestic and foreign lumber, brought by oceangoing ships to its deepwater dock. Meanwhile, both the Upper and Lower Landings had lost their former importance as the ferry slip and the dock of the Hudson River Day Line now concentrated at the foot of Main Street.

Numerous other industries, small factories, and warehouses intermingled with retail establishments up Main Street and along the east–west rail line on the north side. Wagon and carriage making, which once occupied a number of small firms along Main Street, declined as a result of the introduction of bicycles and automobiles. Sales and repair shops for the latter took over some of those buildings.

The manufacture of shoes and clothing, begun in the nineteenth century, continued into the twentieth century, often changing ownership and type of clothing. The Poughkeepsie Underwear Company on Cherry Street shifted its production from shirts to trousers and overalls, to underwear. A Brooklyn shoe manufacturer had built this very large three-and-a-half story brick factory in the mid-1870s to produce shoes in Poughkeepsie. Before long, that production ceased and a new proprietor converted the building to manufacture skirts; after standing idle in the last decade of the nineteenth century, it reopened to manufacture underwear in 1902. In 1906, the company employed 175 workers and produced over 60,000 dozen undergarments a year.

From the ferry slip and steamboat dock, Main Street went up the hill toward the center of downtown, past the intersection with Water Street and W. T. Reynolds's wholesale groceries, later to become the sales office for J. D. Johnson's plumbing supplies, where it crossed the main tracks of the New York Central Railroad. Immediately to the north, the railroad erected an impressive station building in 1918. Modeled after New York City's Grand Central Station (1903–1913), it has been the main transit center throughout the railroad and automobile transportation eras for the Poughkeepsie region.

Lower Main Street had become a mix of residences and small shops and commercial structures. A number of commercial buildings sprang up when the city paved Main Street from Washington Street westward down the slope to the Hudson River. On the slope at 186 Main Street, Harris Canter constructed a building in 1893 with a store on the first floor and apartments on the upper floors. From 1893 to 1921, F. H. Grobe sold slate and hardwoods, tile, wrought iron, and brass goods there. In 1921, Harris Canter established a dry goods and department store that specialized in "men's furnishings" from 1922 to 1955. From its construction in 1893 until 1966, the owners rented apartments to people who worked in various occupations in the city, such as a butcher, clerk, nurse, carpenter, druggist, and policeman. A decade later, the current owners boarded the building up and sold it to the Poughkeepsie Urban Renewal Agency to be torn down during the agency's clearing of much of lower Main Street.

Between City Hall and the Dutchess County Court House sat a bank, the Poughkeepsie Trust Company. Built in 1906 as a modern fireproof office building of stone, brick, steel, and concrete, it provided a separate hallway that "allowed ladies to transact their business discreetly without having to enter the main corridor."[6] At the corner of Main and Market stood the massive Dutchess County Court House. Constructed in 1903 with five stories of alternating courses of red brick and grey granite, it stands on the site of the original courthouse built in 1720 and where, in a subsequent courthouse on the same site, state legislators debated and eventually ratified the federal Constitution in 1788. From the vicinity of the intersection of Main and Market streets, three other streets parallel to lower Main, Union, Church and Mill, created a dense urban fabric from the village center down to the waterfront in the early 1900s.

## THE CENTER OF THE URBAN REGION: MAIN AND MARKET STREETS

The political and economic hub of the city and the county centered along Market and Main streets. At the turn of the century, Poughkeepsie, like many small and energetic cities, sought to enhance its image by promoting the architectural and planning ideals that emerged from the "White City" designs of the World Columbian Exposition in Chicago in 1893. Public and semipublic architecture of the period sought to advance civic virtues.

The designs for Adriance Memorial Library in 1898 and the YMCA in 1909 exemplified the city's interest in civic improvement through urban architecture of classical beauty and form. Their donors established both institutions to promote civic education and health. Built south of Main Street along Market Street, the classical structures articulated both civic pride and progress. The white marble French Renaissance facade of the library welcomed the public into richly paneled reading rooms. A description of the library in its opening year praised it as "not only a thing of beauty, but a substantial and permanent building."[7] The YMCA with its white marble and red terra cotta Renaissance facade received hyperbolic description as a "great city palace" of civic improvement.

Other private and semiprivate buildings along Market Street from the library to Main Street built in the first decades of the twentieth century also projected a classical progressivism. The Amrita Club in 1912 suggested its elite status through its design in brick Colonial Revival, while two banks, the Poughkeepsie Trust Company in 1906–1907 and the Poughkeepsie Savings Bank in 1911–1912, both presented facades that symbolized the solidity and economic progress of their respective institutions. Inside the latter, above the vault, a stained glass panel picturing Hendrik Hudson's ship *Half Moon* reflected the bank's interest in both regional history and civic beauty. The brilliant panel was designed and installed just two years after the city's involvement in the Hudson-Fulton celebrations when banners and classical columns festooned the streets.

Along Main Street, Luckey, Platt & Company created the "first modern department store in the Hudson Valley"[8] by incorporating a number of former storefronts, initially constructed in 1865–1875 from 336–346 Main Street, into one business. The firm tore down the older structures in 1901, replacing them with a large building in an ornamented Beaux-Arts style with salesrooms on all four floors. Luckey, Platt advertised its thirty different stores under one roof, with over a mile and three-quarters of counters and shelves, about 60,000 square feet of floor space, and a staff of 175 clerks in 1906. The store drew customers from as far as the eastern border with Connecticut and elsewhere throughout the Hudson valley. It brought modern shopping to Poughkeepsie, especially for women, and was the first store to install plate glass windows to encourage "window shopping" along the street during the day and night.

The modernization of downtown Poughkeepsie at the beginning of the twentieth century did not erase the earlier streetscape, however. The late nineteenth-century commercial architecture of wood, brick, and cast iron continued to be well represented from the riverfront east toward the city line. The diversity of structures was described in a 1919 survey of Lower Main Street:

> For the most part, each building is different from its neighbor in type. High and low, old and new, brick and frame, dwelling and store front, clean and dirty, stand side by side, or separated here and there by an old-time yard or vacant lot. Country conditions still persist. Not far from a crowded moving picture theatre a cow was found, placidly munching her cud. Progress, however had reached the old frame dwelling in front of her, for it housed three families and a bakery.[9]

Most structures along Main Street housed small shops on the first floor and apartments above. The shops sold all manner of goods, from clothing to jewelry, and furniture, carpets, and glassware; they also contained places to eat and drink. At the turn of the century, a number of millinery and dressmaking operations were run by single women, notably widows; almost all were gone by the 1920s as ready-made clothing, hats, and gloves were sold by the department stores.

The shops along Main Street, especially in the 200 and 300 blocks, constituted the main central business district. In the core area of downtown, many of the buildings had been built after the Civil War in the aftermath of devastating fires that ripped through the antebellum wooden structures. Cast-iron facades with dates 1871 and 1872 graced the north side of Main Street while the Elting Building, erected in 1892 on the corner of Liberty and Main, offered an unusual small tower for Elting's clothing store and later Whelan Drug. Modernization of store facades along Main Street would continue throughout the early decades of the twentieth century.

Shoppers crowded the sidewalks throughout the week, but especially on weekends and during holidays. The heart of downtown included a few places to eat or enjoy an ice cream soda, such as the Boston Candy Kitchen with a modern soda fountain, marble front, and marble countertop. Smith Brothers Restaurant at 13 Market Street, on the corner of Main and Market streets, became a Poughkeepsie landmark; indeed, travelers who had arrived on Hudson River steamboats or the railroad often made it their first stop in the city. The luncheonette had another claim to fame as the home of Smith Brothers' nationally famous cough drops, originally made in a small factory on Church Street and later relocated on North Hamilton.

Downtown places of entertainment included the Collingwood Opera House that had opened in 1869 as an active theater in the late nineteenth century with vaudeville shows. "Poughkeepsie was one of the favorite one night stands for the showmen," according to a famous vaudevillian, while another "old time minstrel" reminisced that the city "always was a good minstrel town."[10] The Collingwood reopened as a cinema in 1923, renamed the Bardavon Opera House. Close by, two hotels commanded the space near the intersection of Main and Market: the Nelson House and the Poughkeepsie Hotel. The latter, standing at the north end of Market, had to be torn down in 1917. Between 1917 and 1928, the city pushed New Market Street north through the hotel's site to connect with Washington Street.

## UNION STREET: A WORKING-CLASS NEIGHBORHOOD

A description of the neighborhood along Union Street, written in 1912 by a Vassar College student for the college newspaper, offers a glimpse into the area's diversity and social dynamics. Anything but a casual observer, this student with her well-trained eye and prose may well have benefited from tutelage by Professor Lucy Salmon, the shrewdest and most imaginative writer about Poughkeepsie at that time.

> What a curious mingling of antagonistic conditions confronts us! Within the radius of a few hundred yards are Post Office, police station, fire house, law offices, Jewish barber and shoe-mending shops, an Irish smithy, a colored dyeing establishment, two saloons, a German tavern. . . .
>
> A crowd of happy boys and girls are returning from the German Lutheran Church. In this neighborhood we find the homes of English, German and Irish immigrants of yesterday. . . . Noticeable is the absence of the front yard, but often there are large yards to the rear of the houses. Yonder in a yard partially devoted to family gardening, an industrious Hausfrau is picking greens for dinner while her neighbor, in the act of cleaning various rugs and carpets, stops now and then to chat or call to the children playing in the next yard not to get too near the fence and destroy her rose bushes and dahlia plants.
>
> Prosperous business places have been established here also, particularly by the Germans. There are three German butcher markets. A few doors

below is Lash's German Bakery. Among the 30,000 odd inhabitants of Poughkeepsie, there are represented 40 nationalities, of which the Germans, Irish, Jews, Italians and Slavs alone have been numerous enough to characterize certain neighborhoods.[11]

A survey of local housing conditions in 1919 characterized the river slope neighborhoods in less romantic prose. Investigator Helen Thompson of the New York City Tenement Department wrote:

> On either side of Main Street, as it leaves the river and climbs to North Bridge and South Perry Streets, lie the First and Second Wards. In that strip of hillside and valley are water front and railroad tracks, factories and lumber yards, a park and extensive stretches of waste space, more or less dumping ground for ashes, tin cans and refuse. The church, well up on the hillside with its well-kept green, the junk yards sprawling over the larger part of a block and facing the school house, the graceful Fallkill and its refuse-strewn banks enter into the picture. The river and spanning bridge and the purple highlands may be considered as background.
>
> There are similar contrasts in the dwellings and their surroundings. Here one sees a trim little home, and there a squalid shanty; here a row of tenements flaunting all the ugliness of their cluttered back porches, there a row of modest dwellings set off by neat front yards; here a sodden and gloomy structure of failing bricks and broken glass, housing a few insensitive tenants in the still somewhat intact portions; here a one-time stately residence, turned tenement, falling into decay and dilapidation; here a row of newer brick tenements, pretentious in front, and in the rear litter and dirt and unpaved muddy surface. There are the long black yards, either clambering up the hill, or irregularly descending towards refuse-strewn hollow, with their stables and chicken coops, the one-time privy structure made into a toolroom or rabbit house. The neat lawn and admirable garden of one are flanked by the refuse heap and manure pile of the other.[12]

Helen Thompson inspected over four hundred buildings along Main Street and in the river slope neighborhoods. She intruded into the interiors of the tenements and provided information on how landlords, eager for more rent, had partitioned apartments into smaller living quarters, extended their buildings to largely fill a previous backyard, and substituted narrow, steep front stairways for formerly spacious halls. Interior bedrooms without windows and with doors closed became dark and airless, and water closets were also unventilated and often unsanitary. Thompson's report led to building code changes in the 1920s.

## MILL STREET: LOWER TO UPPER IN SOCIAL SPACE

Known as Upper Landing Road, Mill Street in the nineteenth century provided another of the winding routes from the top of the river bluff down to the Hudson River. In the early twentieth century, the city straightened the street that had two-story brick houses on narrow lots. The neighborhood encompassing this area of Mill Street and the cross streets of Clover, Perry, Bridge, and Vassar streets accommodated a vibrant community composed of English, Irish, Italian, Polish, and Slavic immigrants. Residential proximity, however, did not preclude a tendency to socialize largely with one's own kind.

Residential properties mingled with Jewish temples and Christian churches of various denominations, as well as bakeries, groceries, and butcher shops. Religious buildings often reflected the changing social scene. For example, while the German-speaking Poles attended the Church of the Nativity, with Catholic mass said in German, other Poles attended mass at St. Peter's; in 1901, both groups united to form a new Polish Catholic parish, St. Joseph's.

Following an earlier Jewish congregation, two other synagogues chose to locate in the riverfront area in the early twentieth century: Congregation Schomre Hadath on South Bridge Street (1923–1924) and another congregation on Clover Street, between Main and Union streets. Later in the twentieth century, the temples moved to new locations eastward on Hooker Avenue and Park Street as the Jewish population spread out from the riverfront area into newer housing in the eastern and southern districts of the city and town.

Greeks began arriving in Poughkeepsie in 1900, many from the same village in Greece, starting candy stores, restaurants, and wholesale groceries. By 1924, Greek families in the city became numerous enough to open their own Greek Orthodox church, school, and community club on Academy Street. Later in the century, this congregation also migrated out to Park Avenue, just off Hooker Avenue on the city's south side. All of the former churches and synagogues whose congregations had left the river slope became the homes to various Christian denominations with predominantly African American congregations.

Lower Mill Street, as it crossed the Fall Kill, encompassed a mixture of industrial, commercial, and residential land uses. By the early twentieth century, Pelton's mill pond was a thing of the past and the felt and carpet factory on the creek just upstream from the waterfall had closed. The Pelton brothers' large home became part of the city's Wheaton Park, just uphill from the railroad station. Close by stood Holy Comforter Church, designed by the famous nineteenth-century architect Richard Upjohn in 1860. Two Roman Catholic churches served as landmarks in the neighborhood surrounding Dongan Square, just to the north of the Fall Kill at the western end of Mill Street. Our Lady of Mount Carmel (1910) and St. Peter's (1853) church steeples dominate the sky over the riverfront and offer an ethnic character to the neighborhood of Irish and Italian immigrant families. Primarily residential, Albany, Delafield, and Tallmadge streets to the north included a few relics of the Improvement Party's dream of creating a fashionable area on the heights above the Upper

Landing, but more modest houses predominated. Industrial and commercial businesses ran east along the Fall Kill to Washington Street and beyond.

Sandra Piotti Ponte grew up in her Sicilian immigrant parents' house on Duane Street, one block from Our Lady of Mount Carmel parish parochial school. Sandy worked for many years as a legal secretary to a local judge and for three decades at Vassar College. While working at the college, she wrote a senior thesis on the role of the Roman Catholic church in acculturating and eventually assimilating southern Italian immigrants during the first decades of the twentieth century.

> The church became the center for ethnic and religious life for the southern Italian. The church not only preserved some of the southern Italians' cultural values, but slowly incorporated and fused them into one community, a single institution that transcended place and locale which had been very important in peasant life. Although there were regional concentrations in the nationality parishes, mixtures of Old World villages were inevitable.[13]

Leaving Mount Carmel Church and walking eastward uphill on Mill Street, we see how the houses increase in size and elegance, with some striking mansard roofs. At the upper end of Mill Street, from Clover Street to the top of the bluff and the main business area of the city at the intersection with Washington Street, the streetscape suggested a neighborhood of more skilled and professional workers and proprietors. For example, the Reynolds family, a successful business family in Poughkeepsie since the early nineteenth century, lived at number 227, at the ridge top, in an impressive brick mansion that became the Italian Center in the 1920s. The Polish community created its social center on Bridge Street between Main and Mill streets during the same decade.

The elite or fashionable neighborhood on Mill Street extended eastward from Washington Street to Garden and Catherine streets. In the late nineteenth century, according to one resident, "The look of the area included cobblestone streets, wide-branched maples, well-kept homes, big gardens stretching 150 feet back of each house, separated from each other by grape trellises."[14]

The Wilkinson family lived at 297 Mill, a Greek Revival house with a large back parlor often used for parties and dancing. Edith Wilkinson recalled the pleasures of living in a big house with servants and hosting neighborhood entertainments in the latter decades of the nineteenth century. "Mill Street was a homogeneous place, just like a village." Neighbors visited neighbors. "Every woman resident of Mill Street each spring and fall called formally on every other woman, called with gloves and cards, even if each saw the other frequently. Two weeks each season were required to complete the calls."[15]

Historian Helen Wilkinson Reynolds also wrote of her life in the Mill Street neighborhood during that period. In 1911, she described how residential areas became separated from the earlier mixture of commercial and industrial land uses during the nineteenth century:

Main street ceased to be a combined business and residence street. Here and there, at scattered points in the town, occasional substantial dwellings were built, but the compacted residence quarter was Mill street, which became the scene of a network of the ties of blood and friendship. Some unconscious bias toward city development placed the houses close to the sidewalk. But the deep rear lots were full of fruit trees and garden vegetables, and bright with flowers which are tended by their owners' hands.

Deeper rooted family life, and many inter-relationships, created a family esprit de corps in the town. Articles that now pour forth from factories were slowly and laboriously made by hand, household duties were numerous, and there was little travel. Recreation was found in the interchange of simple entertainment; mid-day dinner was the universal rule, and the canonical, two-course "party supper" consisted of fried oysters and chicken salad, syllabub and homemade cake and preserves in variety. A great deal of solid reading was done; people were familiar with standard novels, history and biography, little trash finding its way into print. There was not much extreme poverty; but the poorer people were personally known to those in better estate, and most families had their particular pensioners, whose needs they watched over, out of which relations grew life-long attachments and allegiances.[16]

The close interrelationships that created a "family esprit de corps in the town" might be viewed by a skeptical observer as the way an elite achieves the degree of unity essential to its local influence and perpetuation. Certainly that observer would find suspect the claim that in a city with a population of 20,000 by 1870 an affluent minority knew personally most of its poorer citizens. That most "better estate" families treated their aging former servants as pensioners may have been true, but again a skeptical observer would find the emphasis on resulting cross-class attachments misleading as an indicator of the state of social relations in Poughkeepsie.

## NEIGHBORHOOD EXPANSION SOUTH OF MAIN STREET

After the turn of the century, the "homogeneous village" of Mill Street began to dissolve. Developers and fashionable families increasingly settled streets south of Main Street like South Hamilton, Academy, and Garfield streets as an elite neighborhood. The owners of many of the houses built in this south side area during the latter decades of the nineteenth century clearly intended them to be showpieces of elegance and wealth. For example, in recognition of his ownership of the most famous Hudson River steamboat of the era, the *Mary Powell*, Captain John H. Brinckerhoff built his enormous house on South Hamilton Street with a sweeping porch that suggests the deck of a steamboat. Also on South Hamilton, James Reynolds, owner of an elevator factory, built one of Poughkeepsie's first shingle style houses.

During this period, a number of Protestant congregations erected imposing new churches south of Main Street. Trinity Methodist, built in 1892, occupied the corner of Hooker Avenue and South Hamilton. The new First Presbyterian Church rose on South Hamilton between Church and Cannon streets. Built of stone in a Romanesque style with Gothic Revival influences and with interior decoration by Tiffany & Company, one observer hailed it as "the finest church edifice in the Hudson Valley."[17]

The Academy and Garfield area south of Montgomery Street began to be opened up to elite residential development in the late nineteenth century, far enough away from the traffic of the central business district to be a quieter district. The area attracted many of the people influential in the development of the city, including bankers, lawyers, merchants, and other businessmen and professionals. Much more spacious lots could be found toward its southern end on Academy Street where the Adriance family built two imposing residences.

Many of the houses boasted over 4,000 square feet of interior space including rooms for servants on third or fourth floors as well as towers topping rooflines with views of the Hudson River to the west. Numerous bay windows and front and side porches offer variety and interest to each individual structure. The houses provide excellent examples of the design fashions of the time, such as the Queen Anne style, with its half-timbering, asymmetric peaked gables, slate roofs with wooden "Hudson River" brackets, variegated brick chimneys, stained glass window treatments, and carved and painted sunbursts. Unlike Mill Street's homes abutting the street, most Garfield Place residences sat well back from the street on large lots, some having terraced gardens and gazebos in the back yard. Sidewalks of slate or bluestone along tree-lined streets offered comfortable shelter and a domestic resonance to the Victorian-era neighborhood.

Christ Episcopal Church became a neighborhood landmark by the end of the nineteenth century. Begun in 1887 and consecrated in 1888, the neo-Gothic structure possessed a 120-foot high tower, raised the following year. Albert Tower, president of the Poughkeepsie Iron Works, gave the initial funds. Built on the old English burying ground in the block bounded by Montgomery, Carroll, Barclay, and Academy streets, the imposing red sandstone edifice marked the developing elite status of the neighborhood as the twentieth century began. The parish added a rectory, in Tudor style, in 1903. During the first decades of the twentieth century, the church served as a central gathering place for the social elite and politically powerful who filled the pews to listen to the sermons of the Reverend Alexander Griswold Cummins, rector from 1900 to 1945.

During the first decades of the twentieth century, many middle- and upper-middle-class residents moved further south and east to substantial houses built on lots between and along South Hamilton and Hooker Avenue, including the area between Dwight, Adriance, and Whitehouse avenues. As one example of the emerging status of the area, the First (Dutch) Reformed Church relocated from the center of downtown to Hooker Avenue opposite Dwight Street and built an imposing stone edifice in 1919–1923, to be near many of its middle-class and upper-middle-class parishioners who had migrated to the south side.

The Dwight Street lots had been opened up in 1895–1896 to be an "extensive suburban park settlement" of architecturally distinguished homes on large landscaped lots far from the busy factories and shops of the waterfront or Main Street.[18] Construction of most of the houses did not occur until 1908–1911. Architecturally quite eclectic, some had Mediterranean flourishes with tile roofs. Others followed the fashionable mode of the Arts and Crafts movement. The Samuel Moore house on Adriance Avenue, built in the Craftsman style in 1909–1910, used a design by Gustav Stickley. Andre Reid of Poughkeepsie designed two Craftsman-style bungalows built side-by-side on Hooker Avenue in 1910.

Other houses included good-sized bungalows with sweeping roofs and porches. Set back from the tree-lined street and sidewalk, all had landscaped lawns and driveways. In contrast to earlier elite neighborhoods where some, but not all, house lots possessed an additional building for a horse and carriage, by the early twentieth century, most lots in the newer areas also included a detached garage, as the automobile began to make its mark on the residential landscape.

FIGURE 4.3. Manitou Street, 1912–14

## DEVELOPMENTS NORTH AND EAST

Residential neighborhoods, particularly for working- and middle-class home owners, opened up to the north and northeast along Balding Avenue and Marshall Street. Winnikee Avenue developed on land that had been created by filling in one of the old mill ponds that had existed for a century along the course of the Fall Kill. In antebellum Poughkeepsie, this area had been the eastern edge of the city with a cluster of manufacturers around this pond, collectively known as the Red Mills. This initial land use coupled with the low-lying terrain made it unlikely that more affluent citizens would ever choose to settle there. Instead, two-family duplexes on rather narrow lots comprised the majority of houses to the north of North Clinton Street and in the blocks adjacent to Smith Street and Cottage Avenue along the tracks of the Poughkeepsie and Eastern Railroad. This mixed neighborhood included African American and European ethnic working-class families as well as poor rural families from the farmlands of eastern Dutchess County. The black congregation of the Smith Metropolitan A.M.E. Zion Church built their house of worship on the corner of Smith and Mansion streets in 1910–1911.

Meanwhile, the city expanded east of South Clinton and South Cherry streets toward Worrall Avenue. Relatively modest single-family dwellings filled in along Virginia and Hammersley avenues. Between 1912 and 1914, developers built duplexes in a variant of the Queen Anne style on narrow lots along Fox Terrace, Lexington, and Manitou avenues as part of a "trolley suburb." Residents could take the trolley down Main Street to work or to shop.

Corlies and Innis avenues and King and Maple streets opened up a neighborhood of single-family homes to the northeast of Main Street. The houses include a mix of Colonial Revival and bungalow styles. The one-and-a-half-story large bungalow in pink-painted stucco at 101 Corlies Avenue built by Frank Mader of the Arrow Head Garage remains a classic middle-class residence of the 1920–1930 period that reveals the interest in modernist design during the 1920s. When the urbanized boundary began to expand south of Hooker Avenue, some builders tried new construction techniques, such as the use of concrete block in a 1911 house on Ferris Lane and a 1919 house on Cedar Avenue. New styles, new methods in construction, more spacious lots, and increasing dependence on transportation, initially by trolley, signaled the end of the old, closely built-up walking city. Suburbanization, already crossing from the city into the town of Poughkeepsie, had begun.

FIVE

# A New Wave of Immigrants
# Changes the Citizenry

FROM 1900 TO 1920, the population of the city of Poughkeepsie grew by a
third, from 24,000 to 35,000, and by 1930 it would reach over 40,000. To the
mid-Hudson cities' longer-term residents, the increase in the number of city
inhabitants posed fewer surprises and less concerns than did their composition. A recurring process in the valley's and the nation's history brought at the
turn of the century a huge new influx of newcomers with alien languages, customs, and cultures. As noted earlier, compilers of city directories around 1900,
finding themselves unable to grasp the names of some of these newcomers,
recorded them simply as Hungarians, Italians, Russians, and Poles. By the
1900s, a minority of the earlier wave of Irish and German immigrants had
achieved positions of public prominence and had moved into better residential neighborhoods. The Germans more often continued to move eastward
south of Main Street. The more prosperous Irish joined them in that area, creating a new parish, St. Mary's. Working-class Irish tended to remain closer to
the industrial areas northeast of Main Street as they pushed out from their
Ward I stronghold. A continuing influx of immigrants from the Emerald Isle
made the Irish the largest foreign-born group in the city as late as 1910. These
later-comers dispersed residentially throughout the city.

The new influx of foreign-born newcomers composed between 13 and 17
percent of the populations of Kingston, Newburgh, and Poughkeepsie by
1910. They did not immediately arouse in the Hudson valley as much fear
among white citizens of native parentage as had the mid-century influx that
provoked creation of a nativist political party. But whether spoken or not,
there were worries about being swamped and overwhelmed by foreigners.
Among writers for a national audience, Madison Grant vividly expressed
these fears in his book *The Passing of the Great Race* (1916) just as Samuel F.

B. Morse had done in the 1850s. Reassuring signs of intended stability and respectability among the newcomers were not long in appearing, however, notably in their hunger for home ownership. By the 1930s, 47 percent of the city's foreign-born owned their homes compared to 38 percent of natives of foreign parentage and 36 percent of whites of native parentage.

Censuses enumerating "foreign stock"—the native born of foreign and mixed parentage as well as the foreign-born—make clear how large a proportion of the river towns' populations were not long removed from their Old World origins. In the 1930 census, "foreign stock" comprised 40 percent of Kingston, 43 percent of Poughkeepsie, and 47 percent of Newburgh. The local impact of the so-called new immigration from southern, central, and eastern Europe proved to be gradual. In Poughkeepsie, the largest number of foreign-born as late as 1910 came from Ireland, followed by Germany. Not until 1920 would the Italian-born be the most numerous in the city, slightly more than the Polish and Russian-born combined. By 1930, the foreign-born in Poughkeepsie included 1,642 Italians, 691 Poles, 656 Germans, 465 Irish, 344 English, 269 Hungarians, and 233 Austrians. By that year, the Italian-born and native-born of Italian parentage alone comprised 10 percent of Poughkeepsie's population compared to 6 percent for German stock, 5.5 percent for Irish stock, and 4.5 percent for Polish stock. Italians also became the largest group in Newburgh, but Germans were the most numerous in slower-growing Kingston.

## NEWCOMERS FROM ITALY

For Italians, frequent demand for hard labor in construction drew them from ports of debarkation, like New York City. Often hearing from fellow countrymen about jobs laying track for railroads, they moved north from the metropolis to Harmon, Peekskill, Poughkeepsie, and Tivoli. The *News-Telegraph* in 1887 claimed, "None but the Italians could or would do the sort of work given to them. The best of them do not get more than $1.50 a day."[1] Other kinds of mostly physical labor were open to them in the valley from the outset, like stone masonry. Some Italians became stevedores on Hudson River lumber boats. Many grew grapes and apples in Dutchess and Ulster counties, with a large settlement in the town of Highland across the river from Poughkeepsie. In the early years, men often came alone to work in the United States, but later returned to wives and families in Italy. By the turn of the century, young men more frequently arrived with their families.

A few arrived long before their countrymen came to the city in large numbers. The first four Italian men came from Cosenza in the southern toe of Italy to lower Mill Street in 1888. They included a fisherman, a tailor, and a winemaker, but all of them now took jobs on the Central New England Railroad. They sent for their families in 1890 and soon their children and more families joined the rapidly expanding Italian community. One example of an immigrant who rose rapidly both socially and economically in the community was Charles Mansollilo. In 1907, he and his wife took a boat up the Hudson to Poughkeepsie to attend a christening, liked the city they saw, and moved. He became a barber, a health inspector, the city's first Italian alderman, and finally an insurance agent.

Whenever they could afford to do so, other newcomers started grocery, candy, variety, and other small stores as well as barbershops. A few individuals and families gained unusual importance in the Italian community. Bartolo and Carmelo Barone could read and write English. Bartolo became the grocer and banker who handled remittances to immigrants' families in the mother country and made loans to his countrymen. Everyone knew the Torsone family's funeral home and the Dalleos' store with all the needed ingredients for a proper meal for *paisanos*.

Only a minority of the first generation became shop owners or found white-collar jobs, however. Some became teamsters and pressers or took jobs as tailors and butchers. But the majority of Italian-Americans held low blue-collar jobs until 1940. During the big influx of immigrant newcomers to the city after 1907, the largest number continued to find jobs on the railroads or in construction. William Rinaldi, assistant supervisor of track on the New York Central Railroad, attracted newcomers by providing access to jobs at $1.30 per day for a ten-hour day, six days a week. While working for the railroad in Yonkers for $1.25 a day, Sam Cassetta heard that you could make $1.30 in Poughkeepsie. So he moved in 1915. By 1922, he found work with Scott Construction Co. digging the first and last holes for the new Mid-Hudson Bridge.

By 1920, Italian-Americans had made major inroads or already predominated in certain skilled and semiskilled crafts. They constituted 41 percent of the city's barbers, a trade in which African Americans and Germans had preceded them. In that year, they provided 28 percent of the city's bakers, 33 percent of its tailors, and 60 percent of its shoemakers, now largely confined to repairing ready-made shoes. They did not find employment in large numbers until much later in the generally higher-paid metal or building trades where machinists and molders, carpenters, plumbers, electricians, masons, and painters remained predominantly of native parentage or Irish stock.

One immigrant who had been trained as an iron molder could not find work in Poughkeepsie after the old Buckeye agricultural machinery works closed in the mid-1920s. So James Feione bought a two-family house near the Smith Brothers Cough Drop factory on North Hamilton Street, renting out the upstairs apartment. With two children already, the Feiones set up a grocery in their front room, selling to the neighborhood and Smith Brothers workers. Mrs. Feione cooked suppers for the workers. In the Depression of the 1930s, they had to carry many customers on credit, but the repeal of prohibition let them make over the grocery into a restaurant. There Mr. Feione proudly presided as bartender and the entire family participated in running the business.

Following Old World custom, women in immigrant families in Pough-keepsie, as elsewhere, worked outside the home less often than native women. Females composed only 16 percent of all foreign-born employees, compared to 32 percent of native employees. But, over time, employment in well-super-vised garment factories became more respectable. By the 1920s, a large num-ber of Italian women and young girls made trousers for the Dutchess Manu-facturing Company. Starting as a floor girl making $2.78 for a forty-five-hour week, a worker could rise to earn $5.00 a week as a machine operator. That became the largest category of employment for Italian women.

Greater numbers at work carried the community beyond economic sur-vival to be able to afford cherished special occasions. By 1912, a newspaper reported that the Italian population of Poughkeepsie, now about 1,700 resi-dents and one-fifth of them citizens, "will celebrate the feast of Our Lady of Mount Carmel July 16, on a larger and more elaborate scale than ever before." Previously Hudson valley Italian-Americans had traveled to New York to cel-ebrate the feast day, but they expected now that those living as far north as Peekskill would journey to Poughkeepsie instead. Sandra Ponte described the *festa* as central to the Italian celebration of community through the rituals of the church. The annual procession of the parishioners carrying the statue of Our Lady of Mount Carmel through the streets of the neighborhood sur-rounding the church provided "the most eventful manifestation of social life in the Italian community."[2]

Ponte added that the event was "resented most by the surrounding com-munities." Viewing the festival as a core event that gave meaning to her par-ents' generation and consolidated the ethnic community, she emphasized that although "outsiders were unable to grasp the implications of these religious occasions, they were all the immigrants had to express their social life. . . . The southern Italian immigrant did not distinguish between the religious aspects of their *festa* (the praying and devotions) and what the American people saw as inappropriate, profane characteristics of their celebration—the noise, food and dancing."[3]

## HOW COUNTRYMEN HELPED A TEENAGE NEWCOMER

Newcomers who came first as strangers to Poughkeepsie usually could find fellow countrymen to help them out in various ways. Not infrequently they discovered families who had come from the same village in Italy or even rel-atives. Tony di Rosa first migrated to Buenos Aires, then came to the United States by himself, at age sixteen in 1927, to New York City where he had relatives. Seeking a job on the railroad, he altered his passport to become "eighteen." His persistence impressed a railroad boss who told him to take the 7 A.M. work train to Poughkeepsie, a city he did not know. Hungry, after working on the tracks, Tony was told to go to the Barones' grocery. (Before long, the Barones credited him with food before he got his weekly pay, and later opened an account for him.)

Lacking a place to stay in Poughkeepsie, Tony was relieved when a kind fellow Italian worker took him home. Shortly he discovered the Modica family from his own village in Sicily. The Modicas made him feel like one of their family, even celebrating his birthday with a surprise party with the special treats of a big *scaccia* and wine. On weekends, to make extra money, Mrs. Modica brought home coats to prepare for the garment factory that employed her; Mr. Modica played his clarinet when he could. Tony soon found an aunt with whom he lived on Gifford Street until her favoritism toward her sons led to a parting. Then the Coccono family took him in with great warmth. At times, Tony worried about which of his fostering families he should be eating or spending time with since they all seemed to think he belonged to them.

Adapting like other newcomers to available employment, di Rosa worked at a number of jobs with long hours and low pay. He found that the New York Central Railroad hired many Italians, some of them as foremen of work gangs. He became a water boy on the railroad several times, sometimes walking a mile with two pails of water that the men working on the tracks on hot days drank quickly. He also found employment as a water boy in the Highland orchards at harvest time. In the winter, a time of scarce employment, he got a job with the city's night snow removal crew, loading snow onto trucks to be dumped at the river. Another time, cousins who owned a sand and gravel business hired him to help remove soil from a big gravel bank out in Pleasant Valley. When he was employed, Tony would send $10 a week to his mother still in Argentina.

When Tony first came to Poughkeepsie, some men on the job called him "Grease Ball" because he wasn't fluent in English. So he set about learning the language as fast as he could in his first major step toward becoming American. When he didn't have a job, he would walk down Gifford Street "picking old newspapers and magazines from trash bins, looking at the pictures to see what the words were saying. Young boys on the street would call him 'wop,' 'guinea,' but none came to fight him."[4] He would walk all the way across the city, out to Vassar College, looking in the windows of Main Street shops and enjoying the posters at movie theaters like the Bardavon.

When he was working six days a week, he longed for Sunday when he could go swimming with friends in nearby creeks. On Saturday night, he, like many Poughkeepsians, would head to Woodcliff Park a few miles north of the city to enjoy the games and girl watching. On Labor Day he went to a Moose Club clambake; on the 4th of July he enjoyed the parade from Eastman Park up Market Street to Main Street.

In 1929, he bought a car at auction while still working for low pay. Then, at the beginning of the Depression, he was laid off, unable to find work or send money to his mother. Earlier that year he had another shock. Mrs. Coccono told him that he could no longer room with her family because her three daughters—his friends—were growing up, becoming young ladies. A decade later, Tony di Rosa's circumstances had changed for the better. Self-employed, he owned the Independent Coal Company and had even received a gift from President Roosevelt.

But, as Sandra Ponte notes, attitudes toward the Italian community and its celebrations in Poughkeepsie changed slowly. The Reverend Monsignor Cajetan J. Troy reported that:

> When WWII broke out, Italians in Poughkeepsie were being ridiculed. When the first contingent left for army training, many of them were Italian boys from our parish. They left at 3 AM. The only persons who saw them off were two Italian priests from Mt. Carmel. People's attitudes soon changed for the better. A secret service agent came to our rectory to tell Fr. Pernicone that he didn't find a single group or person against the U.S. We simply rolled up the Italian flag and put it away when it could be unfurled with honor. Our ethnic Church was the center of all this.[5]

Ponte recalled from personal experience the attitudinal changes that occurred after World War II when the Irish nuns at the parochial school began to be replaced by other teachers. Changes began to happen within the ethnic parish as well. Beginning in the late twentieth century, Ponte and a few other women parishioners carried the statue of Our Lady during the *festa* procession. The neighborhood, meanwhile, persisted as an ethnic enclave, with many businesses such as delis, bakeries, and restaurants offering Italian delicacies, while a number of Italian-Americans continued to reside in the area. The large majority who had moved elsewhere in the city and suburbs returned to shop and celebrate special occasions.

Italians, like other Catholic immigrants, had quickly desired a parish of their own. That tendency had first been acted on in Poughkeepsie by Catholic German-born newcomers in the 1850s. They insisted on separating from predominantly Irish St. Peter's Church, although they fell within its territorial jurisdiction. Father Nilan, pastor of St. Peter's, opposed the German pattern of cultural separation.

As one of the leading advocates of "Americanization" within the church, Nilan believed "that immigrant Catholics should make strong efforts to become more American and that the practices of the Catholic Church should reconcile fundamental traditional beliefs with the uniqueness of the American experience."[6] Accordingly, he protested when the Archbishop of New York agreed to the creation of a separate German Catholic cemetery next to Vassar College, and he was sorry to see new groups like the Italians and the Poles follow the German pattern.

Since the Italians at first settled largely in the vicinity of St. Peter's, they worshiped initially in that church's basement. Nilan spoke Italian, but that did not satisfy the newcomers. They had to wait until 1904 to have their masses celebrated by an Italian priest associated with Mother Cabrini School across the river in West Park. By 1908, now with an Italian population of more than 1,000, they incorporated Our Lady of Mount Carmel Church, dedicating it in 1910.

## A NEW POLISH WORLD IN POUGHKEEPSIE

Similarities in the experience of Poughkeepsie's newer immigrant groups at the turn of the century were more the rule than the exception. Like the Italians, Polish newcomers often first tried work elsewhere before settling in the Queen City on the Hudson. Stanley Waryas's father "originally headed for the coal mines in Pennsylvania,"[7] where he worked for three months. Not liking the mines, he and a friend found employment in some mills in Vermont before the two traveled to Poughkeepsie where the friend's uncle had a butcher shop on Main Street. Waryas found poorly paid work as a molder in local foundries where two Polish foremen sought fellow countrymen to work for them. By the 1920s, Waryas's five sons imported Polish-language newspapers from Milwaukee and Toledo, making more money than their "father made all week long working in the factory."[8]

Ten to fifteen dollars a week—not much more than day laborers earned—made any saving difficult. But Waryas, like so many other ambitious immigrants of all nationalities, managed to start a small business after awhile. As his son Stanley recalled, his father "bought a small neighborhood grocery store [where] there were a good many Polish people living in that area. He used to import Polish kielbasy from out of town. He was known as Grandpa to everyone. The kids were the luckiest customers because every time they came they knew they were going to go out with a cookie or something."[9]

Immigrants who didn't have relatives locally might learn of employment from fellow villagers, as Ana Kotlartz did. Coming first to Perth Amboy, New Jersey, in 1905, she moved to Poughkeepsie two years later where other Poles from her village had found jobs. Shortly, she married a fellow countryman, Stanley Kardas, in St. Joseph's Church. The two worked in the city's glass factory that employed twenty-five Poles amid a majority of Irish and German workers. Like other newcomers, they struggled with the low wages of $7.25 a week. Later Mr. Kardas worked at a button factory for $18 a week and Mrs. Kardas worked at Schatz Federal Bearing until she retired at age seventy-five in 1964.

Like most immigrants, the Kardas family socialized with their own countrymen, creating their own organizations, with their church foremost. By 1927, however, their daughter Theodora, third of ten children and now sixteen years old, temporarily unsettled them by her independence. They had not forced her to continue high school when she left after a year and a half to take a job at the button factory. But her father strongly disapproved when she began dating a fellow Catholic worker, Paul Becchetti. Mr. Kardas "was a friend of Paul's because they worked together at the button shop. But when Paul went out with his daughter—this Italian man going out with his daughter—my father forbid me to go out with him. But I snuck out and went with him."[10] When she reached nineteen, Theodora and Paul married. Later, three of their four children graduated from college and their grandsons—the fourth generation in the United States—all became professional or managerial-level workers.

## EASTERN EUROPEAN JEWS
## AND THE LADDER OF MOBILITY

One stream of immigrants to Poughkeepsie at the turn of the century proved exceptional in the relative speed of their upward mobility. They rose quickly in occupational level and wealth, if not in social status, in the New World. Fleeing from persecution, or fear of it, in Eastern Europe, they drew upon prior experience in the Old World as a trading people to start small businesses in America and gradually built them up. As they prospered, they emphasized education for their children, resulting in frequent success stories in the professions in the next generation. But, like other immigrant groups, they tended initially to maintain ethnic differences in their religious and social organizations, remaining largely separate from the earlier German Jewish community in Poughkeepsie.

As early as the late 1880s, some Orthodox Jewish Hungarian families began meeting for worship in Michael Weiss's home on Main Street at the eastern edge of the city. Soon numbering twenty-five males, they incorporated Congregation Schomre Hadath in 1888, which in the early twentieth century maintained a Hebrew school after regular school hours. In 1912, a group of mostly earlier Hungarian immigrants decided to withdraw and create a new congregation, Children of Israel. By that date, newcomers from Russia had come to predominate in the membership of Schomre Hadath. Whether religious or cultural differences motivated the withdrawal is unknown.

Among the increasingly numerous Russian and Polish Jews were the progenitors of a large family from Grodno in Russian Poland. David Effron came to America first, to Kingston in the early 1890s, but soon moved to Poughkeepsie. Helped by the Jewish Colonization Society, his parents and siblings soon afterward emigrated from Russia to Argentina where they created farms in a relatively wild inland area. Unhappy with their harsh life in Argentina, they moved again and joined David's family in Poughkeepsie. Knowing little English, they first took up peddling, but shifted to businesses with fixed locations as soon as they could afford them.

David's brother Samuel moved from peddling to a grocery on eastern Main Street, and later changed again to a wholesale business. Brother Charles and a cousin shifted from peddling to collecting rags and scrap metal. Then, with David, they turned to buying their scrap from other peddlers, operating their own junkyards. Doing well, they began investing in real estate. David also brought his wife's brothers to America and Poughkeepsie where Morris Effron sold dry goods and Jacob, coal. By the 1920s, so many children of the emigrating brothers attended Poughkeepsie High School that teachers often found themselves confused about the relationships between the Effron cousins.

An entrepreneurial spirit spurred other Jewish newcomers from Eastern Europe into peddling, and then small retailing. Ruben Rosenthal began with hot dogs and fruit. When he and Simon King, subsequently owner of Kings' Court Hotel on Cannon Street, heard that a circus had come to Kingston they caught a milk train north, found some empty barrels, scrubbed them out, and made a good profit selling a drink they made up with a hint of lemon.

Small proprietors, artisans with their own shops, and peddlers had a surprisingly high persistence in the city, but the proportion of skilled workers declined over time as the second generation avoided even newer crafts like electrician or auto mechanic in favor of white-collar and professional work. The three sons of Ruben Rosenthal, who moved from retailing to wholesaling, became a doctor, a lawyer, and a dentist, all pursuing their practices in Poughkeepsie. But their success did not make them welcome at the prestigious Tennis, Golf and Country, and Amrita clubs, although some of their member friends said, "The time is coming."[11] Lawyer Lloyd Rosenthal recalled that in his youth the YMCA had a quota system allowing Jews to become a certain percentage of the membership. He had a vivid memory of going on the waiting list because the Y had the city's only good recreation facilities.

Meanwhile, two Jewish organizations for young men met in the 1920s to form the Poughkeepsie Jewish Community Center. For nearly forty years it would occupy a building facing Mansion Square on the north side. In 1929, Samuel Effron, a founder of the city's Hebrew School, negotiated an amalgamation of the school with the center that emphasized programs for children. Later in the twentieth century, following the movement of many middle-class Jews toward the south side, the center moved to a new building on Park Avenue on the eastern border of the city with the town. For Jews, the common center providing social, educational, recreational, and religious activities was one means of lessening differences due to national origins, especially between the earlier German and later Eastern European migrations.

For other new immigrants, a shared gathering place like the Italian Center and the Polish Club, both founded in the 1920s, also played an important role in the process of their coming to see themselves as having a shared national origin in addition to their former identifications with localities and regions. They were from Poland as well as from the Galicia region or from the city of Krakow, or from Italy as well as from Sicily or from the city of Palermo. They had moved as quickly as they could to create their own New World in the form of religious institutions like St. Joseph's Church and voluntary associations like the Italian Center where they could perpetuate their native language and customs. These centers served two, seemingly paradoxical purposes: on the one hand, they encouraged an inward-turning emphasis on the religious or ethnic group that could foster in the short run an insular or parochial outlook. On the other hand, they facilitated assimilation in the long run. They not only adopted the practices, including the organizational structure and parliamentary rules of American voluntary associations, but soon cooperated with other groups in sporting and other events.

The Star of Italy and Prince of Piedmont societies combined to become the Progressive Society. The leading Polish society became the Polish-American Citizens Club. Gradually, the sense of boundaries separating them from other ethnic groups diminished. By 1929, the Italian lodge and the Jewish Center held a pinochle tournament in which the losing side provided dinner for both groups, a sign of developing interaction with other groups, especially in sporting events. Increasingly in the 1920s and 1930s, the second generation, taught in English in American public schools and sometimes participating in organizations like the Girl and Boy Scouts, moved in varying degrees to mainstream tastes, interests, and attitudes disseminated by national media.

## AMERICANIZATION AND NATIVISM IN THE 1920s

Native white Protestants generally welcomed the process of adaptation and some of their charitable and reform organizations actively sought to encourage it. In the wake of anti-foreign agitation during the "Red Scare" after World War I, Dutchess County's new Women's City and County Club discussed in 1921 how they could help Americanization. They created a committee to cooperate "with the Board of Education to obtain members for the classes for training teachers in Americanization work."[12] They also cooperated with a committee of Vassar students working at the Lincoln Center settlement house that served an immigrant neighborhood on the river slope.[13] The center held community singing and dancing gatherings for a number of weeks in the school buildings of the now defunct Riverview military academy, climaxing in a first for Poughkeepsie: a community ball at the state armory.

Meanwhile, nativism, especially hostility toward other religions, ethnic groups, and races, was mostly sleeping but not dead in the mid-Hudson valley. Its continuing presence had been evident in Poughkeepsie in the 1890s when the anti-Catholic American Protective Association succeeded in its campaign to abolish the city's twenty-year-old experiment in cooperation between public and parochial education, known as the Poughkeepsie Plan. During World War I in Poughkeepsie, as in so many localities across the United States, public anger at our wartime enemy was taken out on persons of German birth or descent. The Dutchess County Defense League, organized in 1917 to assist mobilization, established a Committee on Aliens to investigate foreign influence (by now presumed to be unpatriotic), circulate anti-German propaganda, and promote Americanization. The league's president and Hyde Park neighbor of the Roosevelts, Archibald Rogers, wrote university presidents urging them to stop teaching the German language and insisted that it should no longer be taught in high schools. When Vassar Professor Lucy Salmon visited Rogers to support a German teacher she greatly admired, she observed later that Rogers was brutal in the interview and that she had never been treated with such disrespect.

Others in the Defense League had different priorities and did not share Rogers' rage. Dr. Grace Kimball, long president of the local YWCA and now of the new National League for Women's Services, chaired the league's subcommittee conducting a census of the resources that local citizens of both sexes could bring to the mobilization and training of women to do men's tasks. The publicity committee emphasized preparedness and devised pamphlets for housewives on how to economize and avoid waste in food. Vassar students helped write "Cheese Parings and Candle Ends—Save your Bit for Uncle Sam" which included their poem, "Mother Goose's Wisdom."

> Little Boy Blue, come blow your horn!
> The cook's using wheat where she ought to use corn!
> And terrible famine our country will sweep.
> If the cooks and the housewives remain fast asleep.
> Go wake them! Go wake them! It's up to you!
> Be a loyal American, Little Boy Blue![14]

This variety of "loyal Americanism" had little in common with the anti-foreign 100 percent Americanism promoted by Rogers, the American Legion, and others.

The year 1924 witnessed an ugly form of ethno-religious hatred in the resurgence of the Ku Klux Klan, locally as well as nationally. Catholics and Jews as much as African Americans were targets of intimidation. The first Klan meeting took place across the river in Ellenville, but parades and cross-burnings followed on College Hill, South Road, and other places in the region. A local headquarters soon appeared on Poughkeepsie's Market Street near the YMCA, and there were reports of two Klaverns in the city and one each in Rhinebeck, Beacon, and Pine Plains. On August 6, a giant membership rally organized by the Klan at the old site of the Dutchess County fair in Ruppert Park in the town of Poughkeepsie drew a crowd, estimated by the *Evening Star* at 3,000, with hundreds more trying to get in without invitations.

Occasionally public authorities intervened to prohibit a public meeting like one planned for Mansion Square in the city. But rallies were held in Eastman Park and in the Arlington area in the town of Poughkeepsie. A Jamaican black newcomer recalled watching a Klan parade of white-robed and masked members that included the Imperial Wizard. Gaius Bolin, Jr., lawyer son of Poughkeepsie's first African American attorney, remembered a gathering just behind Holy Trinity Catholic Church in Arlington. The pastor avoided any trouble by opening a church lot for the Klansmen to party on. One prominent descendant of the previous century's Irish Catholic emigration, John Mack, now Justice of the Peace in the town, spoke out publicly in a widely reported denunciation of the Klan and its terrorizing activities. The Klan's "charitable visits" extended to African Americans in the valley's rural areas. In fully costumed and hooded disguise, they burst into a black church in the rural eastern part of the county during Sunday service, marched down the aisle and back, leaving $50 in the collection plate.

How many supporters the Klan had in the Hudson valley and who they were is unclear. Studies of the Klan in some Midwestern and Western states suggest that they included part of the comfortable native white Protestant middle class who felt their country was being taken over by "foreigners." That particular form of social fragmentation faded in the valley when the Klan suffered damaging scandals elsewhere. But even before that a local clergyman observed: "It is a tricky thing to say anything good of the Klan these days. They see themselves as standing firm for older American ideals of church and state."[15] Neither the Poughkeepsie *Eagle-News* nor the *Sunday Courier* devoted much space to Klan activities in New York State that summer. One report noted that a Klavern held in Binghamton drew only 1,500, despite the 50,000 expected and the presence as speaker of Imperial Wizard Hiram Wesley Evans. In late July, more than 2,000 Klansmen marched through Highland in their white robes, but unmasked, to a rural field where they gathered in a circle for the initiation of 250 new members. The *Eagle-News* found the circle "impressive," adding that outbursts of applause followed denunciations by the speaker, a Baptist minister. A cross was burned. The newspaper chose to note that placards announcing the meeting had been scattered throughout the county for a week before. The result: motorists from miles around drove to the area to sit in their cars to watch. The Klan was a show that day, but a source of tension in the valley in the mid-1920s.

## THE BOTTOM RUNG

The Klan's humiliating intrusion into a black congregation's service reflected the expectation among whites, in the valley as elsewhere in America, that blacks would mostly remain submissive and deferential. African Americans occupied the bottom of the social and, with rare exceptions, the occupational ladder, kept behind and left behind. From the seventeenth to the early nineteenth century, they had lived and worked as slaves in the Hudson valley. In Poughkeepsie before the 1930s, they continued to work mostly as day laborers. Some men served as janitors, porters, and waiters in local restaurants and hotels or worked on riverboats or in lumberyards. Labor unions would not accept them as members. A few found employment in the cigar and glass factories, as cooks or servants for the rich, or as owners of small businesses. Mrs. Unetta Patrice recalled: "Like many black men then, her father held two jobs." (She thought Poughkeepsie was a "very, very good town . . . for colored people to live.")[16] More than one-third of African American women worked for others, a higher proportion than for any other ethnic or racial group, mostly doing "day work" like cleaning house, or laundering for white families. As Mrs. Leila Jackson Lowe recalled, "Everybody had a rubbing board and tubs at that time, and she had a big laundry and did laundry work for whoever wanted it done around the city. All those rich wealthy people."[17]

Like other northern towns in the early twentieth century, Poughkeepsie practiced de facto racial segregation. No signs labeled facilities as being for whites only, but the "colored" knew which spaces they should not enter. An attorney like Bolin would be treated as an exception in certain restaurants where he was well known. But even he suffered a brief beating from a southern white boy, a student at Eastman Business College, after he refused the boy's insistence that he give up his seat on a trolley to a white woman.

Visiting African American celebrities could not spend the night in the city's hotels; if they remained in the city after their scheduled events, they had to depend upon the hospitality of local black families. When Booker T. Washington lectured on "The Negro Race" at Vassar Institute in 1910, he probably stayed with a fellow Baptist clergyman, pastor of Ebeneezer Church. After a reading of his poetry in Poughkeepsie in the early 1920s, Langston Hughes spent the night at the home of the A.M.E. Zion Church's pastor. Local African Americans fared no better. Bessie Payne's father served as headwaiter at the Nelson House for thirty years, but could not be a guest there.

In the first three decades of the twentieth century, the city's African Americans had a stable leadership, mostly born in the valley. Black newcomers to the city came largely from the upper rather than the lower South. They were most numerous during the absence of white workers serving in World War I. Unwelcome in most white voluntary associations, Poughkeepsie's blacks created a parallel social structure of their own as black families did in other northern towns. Their churches became the chief social centers; Mrs. Lowe recalled clambakes, suppers, concerts, and plays at the A.M.E. Zion Church. But she and other women and men also belonged to Negro fraternal orders, in her case, the Order of the Eastern Star. Black women created their own civic organizations, such as the Poughkeepsie Neighborhood Club in 1912. The club brought prominent Negro speakers to lecture, promoted Negro History Sunday and Negro Health Week, and became a member of the national United Federation of Negro Women.

In 1924, the Empire State Federation of Women's Clubs expected 150 delegates to come to their meeting at the A.M.E. Zion Church. Mayor Lovelace would welcome them on behalf of the city of Poughkeepsie. At the end of that meeting, a black veteran urged mass action by Negroes to right the wrongs done them through voting. In the same year, a schoolteacher, Mrs. Georgine Smith of the Colored Community House, addressed a Rotary Club meeting, appealing for more understanding of Negroes' problems. She received a standing ovation.

Although Poughkeepsie's African Americans had developed their own respectable middle class, their rank and file remained more vulnerable to job loss than other groups. Last hired, first fired. But for workers of every race and ethnicity before the New Deal creation of a partial safety net, the possibility of sustained unemployment leading to destitution remained a nagging fear. Turning to relatives and friends for support might work for a while and resort to churches and private charitable agencies like the Rescue Mission, the Salvation Army, and the House of Industry could help.

## DESTITUTION

Public relief always had been the social agency of last resort, either in the form of assistance given to families at their places of residence or by admission to the poorhouse constructed in the 1860s on the city's poorer northeastern outskirt. Called the Alms House in the nineteenth century, it later was renamed the City Home. Before 1904, Irish-born inmates were the most numerous, followed by the native-born, German, and the "colored." Between 1904 and 1910, the native-born (including those of foreign parentage) exceeded the foreign-born Irish and the "colored" slightly exceeded the Germans, although African Americans accounted for less than 3 percent of the city's population.

Over time, the proportion of those receiving "indoor relief" in the Alms House declined and those receiving "outdoor relief" where they resided increased. Between 1875 and 1908, Alms House inmates ranged from a low of 62 in 1892 to a high of 99 in 1906, with the average falling around 70. By contrast, the highest number of individuals aided at home was 1,073 in 1880, at the end of a national depression, and the lowest was 418 in 1908. Poughkeepsie transported vagrants away from the city whenever possible to prevent their hanging around long enough to establish residence and hence eligibility for relief. The city's commissioners constantly worried that relief given temporarily would become permanent, resulting in dependent families over several generations. They also worried that too favorable conditions would encourage newcomers who might be able to find work to apply instead for relief or admission.

Not surprisingly, a fear of too great luxury for residents had long predominated at the Alms House where superintendents had prided themselves on an "economical" administration creating less of a burden for taxpayers. Inmates did much of the work, with men taking care of vegetable growing and animals, women doing the laundry and cleaning. In 1910, meals consisted of cereal for breakfast and lunch, together with bread, gravy (used instead of butter), and tea or coffee. Dinner brought meat and one or two vegetables. To ease the "dullness" of existence at the renamed City Home, some Vassar College students in that year made periodic trips for conversation with the more respectable inmates, an alternative to volunteering for settlement house work at Lincoln Center.

## A FRAGMENTED CITY

The separation of City Home residents from the rest of their fellow Poughkeepsians encouraged stereotyping of the destitute poor as a group apart, viewing them collectively rather than as individual fellow citizens. The fact that on their one-day-a-week freedom to visit downtown Poughkeepsie some returned in drunken condition reinforced that perception. Were these inmates

FIGURE 5.1. World War I soldiers parade, Market Street, 1917

the rare exception in an urban population where members of different social groups interacted easily and frequently? Or were varying degrees of separation and fragmentation the rule in Poughkeepsie rather than the exception? Was shared civic participation usual, or largely confined to those with more education, income, and leisure?

Religious organizations remained the single most common form of membership throughout the early twentieth century. The census of Religious Bodies in 1936 found that their members comprised two-thirds of the city's population, although in the two largest denominations, Roman Catholic and Episcopalian, children less than thirteen years old comprised 27 and 21 percent, respectively. Catholics alone accounted for 53 percent of all church members, and some of their congregations remained identified with a particular nationality, like Mount Carmel with Italians, St. Joseph's with Poles, and Nativity with Germans. Suburban migration, however, would favor territorial parishes with ethnically mixed congregations, like Arlington's Holy Trinity founded in 1920. Jews composed 8 percent of Poughkeepsie's members of religious bodies, and individual Protestant denominations' share ranged from 11 percent for the Episcopalians to 5 percent for Methodists, 4 percent for both the Reformed and Presbyterians, and 2 percent for Baptists. Although these primarily native-born of native parentage church members sometimes participated in interdenominational gatherings and listened to the exhortations to brotherly love in most churches and synagogues, ecumenicalism was not as frequent as it would become after World War II. Religion did not do much during this period to bring together people from different ethno-religious and class backgrounds.

Poughkeepsians from diverse backgrounds came together most often and visibly as spectators at patriotic, festival, and sporting events. The active participants in those events sometimes had mixed ethnic or racial origins, but often seemed predominantly from one group. Mixing with whites of native parentage did characterize the Poughkeepsie Yacht Club where native-born men of German parentage predominated among officers as early as the 1890s. Amateur teams sponsored by local businesses, churches, and other voluntary associations may well have entailed some social mixing, whether within the teams themselves or at their contests—as when St. Peter's beat Beckwith Cleaners 4-3 at Riverview Field in 1924, thereby tying for first place with the M. Shwartz Co.

By the 1900s, Irish-Americans predominated in Poughkeepsie's professional baseball teams. Team manager William McCabe revived the Hudson River League in 1903, calling his boys choice names, then patting them on the back with a gusto less likely among the white Protestant teams predominant in the valley before the 1870s. The small minority of African Americans in the city had to act alone to create their own teams to play baseball against white teams in Riverview Park in the 1920s. First admitted to the Twilight League were the all-black Nelson House Waiters, followed in 1921 by the Dutton Lumber Colored Giants who also dropped from the League, unable to field a team strong enough to compete. The year 1922 saw the Poughkeepsie Colored Giants team that survived only by combining with the Newburgh Colored Giants.

A usual and expected expression of social segregation and fragmentation appeared in certain exclusive social clubs, notably the Tennis Club organized in 1888 and the Dutchess Golf and Country Club, organized by "men of influence" in 1897.[18] The expected dress for playing golf expressed the social standing of the new country club's members: red coats, white flannel trousers, white shoes, and formal hats. Ladies could participate in some of the other club activities that included croquet, lawn bowling, and archery. When the club's baseball team began playing a series of annual games with the Tennis Club, they followed their games with evening fireworks and a "delightful dance" in the elegant clubhouse designed by the city's most distinguished architect, Percival Lloyd.[19] The ritual of application for membership in the Tennis Club made clear its intention to remain a distinct social world. Recommendation by two club members preceded consideration by the Executive Committee, with nine favorable votes required for admission. Three negative votes meant exclusion. The membership for both the Tennis and Golf clubs was native white Protestant, although by the mid-1890s members of the wealthy Catholic Hinkley family appeared in the Tennis Club list.

Initially the Tennis Club emphasized propriety in the musical plays it performed as fund-raisers at the Collingwood Opera House. But, by World War I, its Vaudeville Night, a fund-raiser at the Masonic Temple open to the general public, advertised a "Marvellous melange of music and mirth. . . . Dancing with all the cranky, bangy, jazz of a Thankful Thanksgiving Orchestra—one-steps that would have awakened Rip Van Winkle in the third year of his snooze; waltzes that would have wafted him back to the arms of Morpheus."[20] You could have all this for $1.65, including war tax. However, it was not a price or a program likely to attract the city's workers, let alone immigrants.

As the city expanded southward beyond Hooker Avenue, residents in recently settled areas sometimes formed neighborhood associations to secure or keep an eye on communal services. The Southeast Parkway and Ferris Heights associations discussed sidewalks, lighting, garbage collection, and other needs at their monthly meetings. They also enjoyed entertainments provided by fellow members of a comfortable "suburbanizing" middle class. One of their desires was to secure a "small" public school for area children. Krieger elementary school was constructed on the old fairgrounds along Hooker Avenue in 1929.

So where did city residents from different social groups come together and with what likelihood of interaction among them? On one occasion a local newspaper reported an episode in which formerly antagonistic groups found themselves enjoying, to their surprise, each others' company. In 1924, the

*Eagle-News* reported growing fellowship between fraternal organizations, especially increasing tolerance for their differing religious beliefs. Their example was the chance coming together that both reported enjoying of 400 members of the largely Catholic Hibernians with 200 members of the Junior Order of United American Mechanics, Protestant and previously nativist, on the steamer *Homer Ramsdell* on a weekend jaunt to New York. They also widened their acquaintance with other valley citizens since passengers included a delegation from a Kingston lodge, 350 Maccabees from Newburgh, and many Pythians from Beacon. Dancing and games on board added to fraternal conviviality, and many of the trippers went to a ball game at the New York Polo Grounds before reboarding the steamer to head upriver.

The Woodcliff amusement park north of the city drew many Poughkeepsians for picnics, games, and other Sunday or holiday pleasures. Eastman Park attracted skaters in the winter. Mixed crowds attended suppers, clambakes, and other "everybody invited" fund-raising events sponsored by churches, fraternal orders, and social clubs, as did Fourth of July and other parades. Patriotic occasions with flags and colorful uniforms may have added excitement to the sense that everyone present shared a common identity. Moments of sharing like these occasions leavened the usual pluralism of socializing with one's own kind in churches and other voluntary associations.

Whether these activities led to more and closer acquaintances between people of different backgrounds is a matter for speculation. Only scattered personal reminiscences survive and they do not suggest a simple answer. Everyday life, like work and shopping, brought exposure to the city's diversity, but did not require more than superficial acquaintance. Organizations generally pursued the interests of their members, though some like the Chamber of Commerce sought to stimulate economc growth for the city as a whole. Service clubs like Rotary and Kiwanis and fraternal orders like the Elks, Moose, Knights of Pythias, and Redmen did support many local good causes and charitable activities.

Both the Rotary and the Kiwanis clubs provided cars to drive people to the Salvation Army's annual outing in 1924. In the same year, Poughkeepsie Lodge of the B.P.O.E. (Elks) gave the largest amount of money to charity of any of the 1,300 lodges reporting that year, with donations of $25.32 per capita. The lodge spent it on "Americanization" and big brother programs, Boy and Girl Scouts, Thanksgiving and Christmas charities, hospital work, summer recreation camps, and outings for mothers and their children. The lodge also created its own summer camp for undernourished children, cooperating with Poughkeepsie's Tuberculosis Committee and the Dutchess County Health Association. Such programs undoubtedly involved some interaction between lodge members and their beneficiaries. Over time, assimilation and social mobility shifted the balance from a sense of separate identity toward a less differentiated sense of a common humanity among whites, but that progress was slow and did not include people of color until much later in the twentieth century.

# SIX

# Municipal Reform and Urban Planning

AS THE TWENTIETH CENTURY began, Poughkeepsie residents and businesspeople became more conscious of problems and deficiencies in their everyday environment. Like middle-class city dwellers in other parts of the nation, they wanted to make their city more livable and attractive, whether by removing ills and inconveniences or by creating new opportunities as in recreation for children. Calls for local improvements and reform would increasingly be augmented by a newly developing interest in urban planning.

## GARDENS AND VIOLETS

Ideas from the Village Improvement efforts that swept the nation in the period after the Civil War inspired citizens to beautify landscapes in towns as well as villages in both Yankee and Yorker regions of the northeast. Home owners planted trees and removed fences that had been built to keep out stray animals and the dust of the busy streets. As journalist and historian Edmund Platt remarked in 1905:

> Between 1889 and 1890 the movement for the removal of fences gathered headway and produced so great a change in the appearance of many residence streets that photographs taken before 1880 are almost unrecognizable now, even where the buildings remain almost as they were. Every house, not actually on the sidewalk line, formerly had its fence in front. Now very few fences remain except as dividing lines at the rear of lots.[1]

Gardening and landscaping domestic and public grounds in the Romantic aesthetics promoted by Downing, Vaux, and Olmsted were in vogue throughout the latter half of the nineteenth century and into the early decades of the twentieth. On the southern border of the city, private estates—like Vassar's Springside—exemplified the vogue, as did Locust Grove, an Italianate

Revival mansion remodeled by the architect A. J. Davis for Samuel F. B. Morse, artist and inventor of the telegraph. Nearby, the Poughkeepsie Rural Cemetery copied the designs of Downing and the rural cemetery movement. Within the city, homeowners on small and large lots also planted flowers, lawns, and exotic shrubs and trees to enhance the beauty of their properties.

Commercial ventures in landscaping and growing and selling plants and flowers also prospered. During the nineteenth century, a number of professional gardeners immigrated from England and Germany to the Hudson valley. They came to work on the large estates along the Hudson River in Dutchess and Columbia counties and at farms and country estates in Millbrook and other elite areas of the region.

Herbert Saltford, Poughkeepsie's superintendent of parks in the mid-twentieth century and later appointed the city's historian, recounted how Poughkeepsie became known as the "City of Cultivation." In 1872, Saltford's grandfather William emigrated from England to work as head gardener on the Rhinebeck estate of Levi Morton, vice president of the United States under Benjamin Harrison. A few years later, William moved to Poughkeepsie as head gardener for S. M. Buckingham. The 8-acre Buckingham estate was situated north of the railroad tracks, bounded by Washington, Bainbridge, and Talmadge streets. In 1886, William began growing violet plants there and soon had built five glass houses, each with 3,500 plants. Soon, other gardeners and florists began growing and selling violets, and by the end of the century the city and region became nationally known for its production of the flower.

Violets were grown by the hundreds of thousands in and around Poughkeepsie on South and Hooker avenues and northeast on renamed Violet Avenue, as well as to the south of the city in the hamlets and villages of Fishkill and New Hamburgh and north to Red Hook and Rhinebeck. William's brother George emigrated in the 1890s to Rhinebeck, which soon thereafter became the heart of violet production. By 1908, cultivation of more than a million plants represented a production of over fifty million blooms a year and an economic impact of over one million dollars. In 1912, 116 growers in the area managed over 455 greenhouses, shipping the bulk of the violets to distributors in New York City. By 1918, the "violet craze" had died down and most growers in the immediate vicinity of Poughkeepsie had stopped cultivation. Later, George moved from Rhinebeck to Poughkeepsie where the city chose him as its first superintendent of parks. Setting aside lands for public parks and their management became a civic enterprise.

## TRANSFORMING TREELESS STREETS

Meanwhile, the citizens of Poughkeepsie embraced Arbor Day as a national day to celebrate the role of trees in the human environment. Arbor Day had been established in 1872 by J. Sterling Morton as a community effort to plant trees in settlements on the treeless plains of Nebraska. Most states followed Nebraska Governor Morton's lead in 1874, and in 1888 New York State officially declared "the Friday following the first day of May" as Arbor Day so that "treeless streets and barren commons would be transformed and beautiful, that unattractive towns would be made attractive, and waste places would be redeemed."[2] Even more important for the observances in New York's public schools would be the educational benefits of building community spirit and patriotism, learning about nature, stimulating "the aesthetic sense," and learning "the lesson of economy and unselfish foresight" by providing for future generations.

Arbor Day celebrations began in the Poughkeepsie schools in the late nineteenth century, and continued throughout the twentieth century, earning the city of Poughkeepsie the national award of "Tree City U.S.A." for its efforts of continuing an annual observance. The Arbor Day Exercises of the Poughkeepsie Public Schools on May 6, 1898, took place at College Hill Park. Each elementary school offered either a recitation or a song, while two ministers gave a prayer and school administrators and city leaders addressed the gathering. Besides the national anthem, songs included: "Stars of the Union," "The Land that We Adore," and "America." Students recited William Cullen Bryant's poem "Forest Hymn," which remained an annual favorite for many years. Participants extolled trees, flowers, and birds, with Stanfordville even mounting a "Bird Day" celebration in 1930. Community events for tree-planting, speechmaking, and conservation education took place in city parks, along city streets, and in schoolyards.

Reformers throughout the United States, especially of the genteel and good government variety, took up the idea to encourage citizen participation and the celebration of community, as well as a way to improve the quality of life in growing cities. National celebrations such as the Fourth of July had become quite raucous, such reformers felt, while a day focused on improving the quality of their everyday environment could offer opportunities not only to beautify their environment but also build greater civic engagement.

## CLASS DIFFERENCES IN RECREATION

Needless to say, the "raucous" element in the city, most often working class, probably had quite different ideas of how best to celebrate the few respites from work that they had. In Worcester, Massachusetts, where the conflict over recreational opportunities between the "lower orders" and the "respectable" classes has been most fully documented, workers and immigrants sought open spaces where they could play baseball, football, and other competitive and sometimes rougher games. Generally they welcomed noisy spectatorship and consumption of various kinds of alcohol on such occasions where "respectability" would not.

Recreational activities and spaces in Poughkeepsie were often viewed along lines of social class. The river and riverfront afforded space for fishing and boating by all members of the community. Rowing races in the late nineteenth century tended to be quite rowdy affairs, with much gambling and drinking. The Apokeepsing Boat Club, chartered in 1879, organized its first regatta the following year. In 1895, the first intercollegiate regatta was held. Tens of thousands of visitors came to view the races over the first half of the twentieth century. Many rode flatbed cars on the rail lines on the west bank to follow the races from north of the city down to the finish line at the railroad bridge. The intercollegiate regatta left the Hudson for other venues in 1949.

Many local residents also swam in the river. Swimming could be enjoyed at a favorite amusement park, accessible by trolley for many Poughkeepsians of lesser means. Woodcliff Park occupied the former Winslow estate just north of the city line in 1892. The park not only created a swimming area in the river just off the shore, but also provided many sites for picnicking under trees, and had a Ferris wheel and other amusements.

At the other end of the social ladder, Poughkeepsie businessmen played golf at the turn of the century. The Dutchess County Golf Club, established in 1897 on the former Sloan farm just south of the city along the Albany Post Road, was one of the first two hundred golf clubs in the United States. As described in the *Poughkeepsie Eagle*: "Poughkeepsie is now in line with recent civilization. We have a golf club, with a good sized farm to range on, and a real Scotsman in command."[3] The "Scotsman" was John Foreman, who had previously been greenskeeper of the links at Leith, near St. Andrews. He was hired to be "greenskeeper, instructor in golf, and maker of clubs and balls." In 1901, the club joined with another to become the Dutchess County Golf and Country Club. In 1925, it expanded to eighteen holes.

College Hill Park, where the Arbor Day celebration took place in 1898 as well as many Fourth of July celebrations, provided an expansive area of open space within the municipal boundaries of the city. The 375-foot hill is the highest in the city and boasts views from its summit in all directions. A viewer can look toward the Catskills to the west, the Highlands to the south, and the Berkshires and Taconic to the east, as well as to the city at its foot. Formerly the site of the Poughkeepsie Collegiate School, later renamed the Riverview Academy, College Hill land was purchased by William W. Smith in 1892 and transferred to the city for use as a park. Downing Vaux, son of Calvert Vaux, developed a landscape design for the urban park; he presented his plan before the Architectural League of New York in 1900 and the American Society of Landscape Architects in 1903. Paths were laid out, trees and flowers planted, a rock garden constructed, and recreational facilities, such as tennis courts, picnic grounds, and a nine-hole golf course, developed. An open reservoir on the north slope, fed by water from the Hudson River, supplied water and pressure to the city's fire hydrants.

Across Lincoln Avenue from Eastman Park on the corner of Pine Street lay a small recreational park and settlement house named Lincoln Center. In 1917, Vassar College students began Lincoln Center to provide a playgroup for children in a house on Church Street. Riverview Academy for boys had moved from College Hill to these grounds in the late nineteenth century, but by 1915 had ceased operating. The city, which owned the abandoned academy building, offered it and the grounds to Lincoln Center in 1925 for use as a settlement house, health clinic, and public recreational space.

Progressive reformers of the early twentieth century believed it just as important to care for the physical environment of Poughkeepsie, including its parks, playgrounds, streets, tenement housing and sanitation, as to work for better labor conditions such as shorter work weeks, safer working conditions, and child labor laws. In their visions for a healthy and economically viable environment and their engagement in efforts to build and rebuild community, these reformers resembled in many ways the leadership class of Poughkeepsians who had built the city in the nineteenth century. But whereas the village's antebellum leadership consisted only of men, women would play a major role in shaping municipal reform during the Progressive era, in Poughkeepsie as in the nation.

## LUCY MAYNARD SALMON MEETS THE CITY

Some of the most frequent and well-informed calls for municipal reform in Poughkeepsie in the first decade of the twentieth century came from a new downtown resident. Lucy Maynard Salmon, head of Vassar's history department, was well known to Vassar students for her demanding seminars and her democratic insistence on equality between students and faculty in their manner of addressing each other. At the turn of the century, still fashionable Mill Street between Market and Hamilton streets attracted professional residents like Salmon. The teachers, doctors, attorneys, and judges residing there now included mid-century immigrants' descendants like Dr. Burns and Judge Morschauser. For Lucy Salmon, this thoroughly respectable neighborhood promised relief from the confinement and lack of privacy she felt living so near her students and colleagues in the college's Main Building. "I sigh for a quiet corner where I shall not have to get up by a bell, talk by priority of appointment and dress according to other people's standards of propriety."[4] Moving two miles away from campus typified Salmon's independence. She had upset Vassar's president in 1892 when, returning from a European trip, she bicycled around campus *sans-culotte*. He found that most undignified for a lady.

In 1901, Salmon and her friend, librarian Adelaide Underhill, occupied 263 Mill Street and set about changing it to suit their more modern tastes. Salmon's pioneering investigation in *Domestic Service* in the 1880s had shown her how much unnecessary labor inefficient arrangements in kitchens and laundries imposed on servants. Rearranging the kitchen into cooking, baking, and cleaning sides, the two women added new domestic technology like an instantaneous water heater, a gas range, and an electric fan for efficiency in doing household chores. Salmon valued rationality. Like other intellectuals, she also was attracted to the Arts and Crafts aesthetic design movement and ordered some Gustav Stickley furniture.

New for both Salmon and Underhill was the daily necessity of running errands, unlike living in Main Building where the college provided so much, including meals. As they walked to neighborhood shops, Salmon realized how much one could discover of a city's past in the objects of city streets, like the signs for various trades and professions harking back to the Middle Ages. In her brilliant little book, *Main Street* (1915), she also showed how much one could learn about contemporary culture from the window advertisements of local stores and favorite names and slogans generally. She noted of Pough-keepsie, "once known as the 'city of schools,' [that] its educational interests have been supplanted by its commercial interests as indicated by the names 'Bridge City' and 'Queen City' . . . names like Fairview Heights, Fairlawn Heights, and Oak Dale Park suggest the attractions held out by real estate development companies to induce suburban residence."[5]

Salmon was far ahead of her time as an historian in realizing how accu-mulations of physical evidence from all the environments people create, including her own *Backyard*, could create a richer, more revealing social his-tory. She saw national trends in local objects: "Monopoly lifts up its head in the wagons of the Standard Oil Company, the great packing houses of Armour, Morris, and Swift, and national express companies."[6]

But some of the sights, sounds, smells, and human behavior she encoun-tered in her errands and walks offended Salmon. Characteristically, she soon took action. When would-be advertisers littered her doorstep with circulars, she repeatedly carried them down to the local police station to report this vio-lation of municipal ordinance, to no avail except a good laugh for the cop on duty. Miss Salmon, like well-educated middle-class women across the United States, began to challenge local acceptance of conditions of uncleanliness, dis-order, and immorality that they would not tolerate in their own homes. Their efforts early in the twentieth century to clean up and otherwise improve their cities became known as "municipal housekeeping."[7]

An energetic member of that generation of college graduates who founded settlement houses, promoted children's playgrounds and parks, and urged drives to clean up cities, Lucy Salmon was very much a woman of and for her time as a would-be reformer. Probably she remained closer to a gen-teel middle-class outlook than Jane Addams did because Salmon never had the experience of living or working among the urban immigrant poor. An avid student of newspapers as the best means of learning about communi-ties, Salmon kept scrapbooks of clippings describing innovations in other cities, such as civic beautification campaigns, school gardens cultivated by the children, and playgrounds.

In her efforts to improve sanitation and health, Salmon turned to Lillian Wald at the Henry St. settlement house in New York for advice about getting a district nurse for Poughkeepsie and she assisted many causes, like special courts for children and campaigns against tuberculosis, by arranging lectures and public discussions. Looking back at past charitable institutions, Salmon saw them as largely "palliative . . . for the wreckage of life." She praised instead the growing sense of responsibility on the part of the community as a whole toward all of its citizens and their preference for "preventing social, civic, and industrial ills rather than curing them after they have arisen."[8]

## AROUSING THE PUBLIC

Salmon frequently sought in letters to local newspaper editors to inform her fellow citizens and urge them to take action, usually doing so under pseudonyms like "Concerned Citizen," "Housekeeper," or "Public Opinion."[9] In 1906, writing anonymously, she praised the organization of a new club in nearby Newburgh "to study municipal conditions in the most progressive cities here and in Europe."[10] She decried the complacency of another local newspaper, the *Eagle*, deriding its view that Poughkeepsie was "the most beautiful city in America."[11] Because of that kind of misplaced local patriotism, "we shall continue to have dirty, ill-paved streets, rear tenements, and the saloons running on Sundays." Salmon would be quick to dismiss the "puffs" promoting her city by businessmen eager to attract new customers and industries, like Mortimer Drake who described his fellow citizens in the *Poughkeepsie Illustrated* of 1906 as prosperous and contented, with poverty rare, labor conflict infrequent, and surroundings exceptionally picturesque.

In 1908, Salmon protested foodstuffs sitting outside food stores on Main Street, exposed to dirt from traffic. As "Housekeeper," she pleaded for more watering of streets to keep the dust down. In 1912, she complained about men puffing cigars under a "No smoking sign" and young men "sitting with their feet up on trolley seats."[12] Writing as "Poughkeepsian," she asked "why the great natural beauties of the city are allowed to become eyesores and plague spots." The Fall Kill had "become the dumping ground of those who live on its banks." She also wished "to know why a public meeting is called to consider the inducements to be offered a new manufacturing company to locate here while the smoke and dirt of those already established make the air vile and the buildings inside and outside grimy and unpleasing to the eye."[13]

Generally, Salmon believed in cooperation between the Chamber of Commerce, representing businessmen, and citizens seeking civic improvements, but she did not appreciate the Chamber's effort to raise $6,000 as part of an ultimately successful campaign to induce the Seneca Button Company to relocate its manufacturing in Poughkeepsie. The Chamber, for its part, valued Salmon's concern with the city's appearance by making it cleaner and otherwise more attractive to visitors and potential new customers and businesses. Salmon had no objection to growth per se, but wanted attention given to other civic purposes.

Measures to create civic consciousness that were being promoted in cities like Boston and New York appear early and late among her reform interests. In 1906, she had wondered in a letter to the editor of *The Enterprise* why Poughkeepsie was so far behind, compared to other American cities and towns, in forming organizations for civic improvement. Poughkeepsie talks about its fraternal societies, whist, social, and political clubs, she noted, but has not created the "municipal leagues, civic clubs, city improvement societies, art leagues, city music commissions, civic art guilds, playground associations, tree-planting societies . . . street cleaning leagues, societies for checking the abuse of public advertising, pleasant-Sunday-afternoon associations and scores of other organizations that make city improvements."[14] She did not refer back to the activities of Poughkeepsie's Improvement Party of the 1830s, so it is unclear whether she saw such earlier efforts as a precedent for contemporary organizations for civic improvements.

Pursuing the same concern in 1916, she wrote in support of a community services series being held Sunday afternoons in Poughkeepsie's Cohen Theatre. She claimed that the series had attracted three thousand people under one roof for consecutive Sundays. Arguing for the services' usefulness, Salmon said: "As a community we have very little unity of purpose, and no concerted action to accomplish a common end. Each man goes his own way, with little reference to his neighbor."[15]

## WISHING FOR THE CITY BEAUTIFUL

Salmon deplored the "excess individualism" in architectural choices that she believed blighted the visual appearance of Poughkeepsie. She admired the emphasis of the City Beautiful movement on the harmonies of neoclassicism that were most dramatically expressed at the world's fair Chicago Exposition of 1893, which she had attended. She complained in 1908 that the "finest location in the city [Poughkeepsie] is occupied by a crowded mass of buildings incongruous in style of architecture, in building material, in the purpose for which they are used." The courthouse square, almost entirely rebuilt for half a million dollars since 1900, "contains the court house, a bank building, a business block, the building of the express companies, an engine house and a saloon."[16]

Noting many new real estate developments under way, she asked whether Poughkeepsie might take steps toward "some united plan and harmonious action? A landscape architect could be secured who would make a careful study of all of our natural advantages, report on a general, harmonious scheme of improvement."[17] Like Matthew Vassar who had hired Downing, America's first landscape architect, to design a rural cemetery for Poughkeepsie, Salmon put her money where her mouth was. At her own considerable expense, Salmon brought one of the nation's most distinguished landscape architects, James Nolen, to Poughkeepsie to lecture and devise a plan for the city. To her great disappointment, that plan—like plans offered for another half-century—sat idle on archive shelves due to objections from real estate interests. The city continued its haphazard expansion according to developers' various interests and tastes.

She lamented the transformation from a residential to an industrial city: "Two-family houses and flats have sprung up by the hundred, while small cheap restaurants, furnished rooms, cheap amusements, and more than a score of public laundries record a population industrial in character and more or less floating in its domestic life." Congestion had increased to the point that rear houses were being built in the yards behind other houses, and a "large number of covered tenement-house outside stairways . . . have been attached to older residences."[18]

In the 1890s, still living at the college, Salmon had founded a Vassar chapter of the Daughters of the American Revolution, although she never seems to have shared the D.A.R.'s preoccupation with creating historical monuments and marking battle sites. But seeing the organization as a possible agency for addressing other social needs, she agreed to serve as regent of the D.A.R.'s Poughkeepsie chapter, where she soon named committees on streets, parks, and school playgrounds. In 1908, writing in the *Eagle* as DAR, she described at length Chicago's South Park System, the prize exhibit at the first annual convention of the National Playground Association. Replete with ball fields, tennis courts, swimming pools, lunch rooms, reading and assembly rooms, it had sharply reduced juvenile offenses in the stockyards district. Salmon argued, "the elements of their system are practicable for towns and smaller cities; and that this municipal equipment is less costly than jails . . . and as sound sense as good pavements and clean streets."[19] By 1911, Poughkeepsie created its first playground.

Shy and never one to seek publicity for herself, Salmon summoned up her courage to expose social evils in the belief that an aroused public would then attack them. Her favorite newspaper, the New York *Evening Post*, exemplified her faith when it observed in 1907 that "that great American institution, the revival meeting, is being ordered anew" to combat a variety of urban plagues. "After all, men need only 'get together' and be shown the light by earnest exhorters in order to strike down an evil, great or small."[20] Like earlier and contemporary American reformers, she assumed that the public, when properly informed, would demand reform.

### BATTLING POUGHKEEPSIE'S "EVILS"

That faith in the power of moral exhortation brought Lucy Salmon to public attention in 1906 and 1907. In two speeches, first at the YWCA, then the YMCA, she decried "city evils." She claimed: "there are 300 floating votes [to be bought] in Poughkeepsie. We know where the trading goes on, yet we say nothing. There's open gambling on the boat races. . . . Merchants say openly that they're afraid to vote against gambling because they're afraid to lose business."[21] Calling alcoholism a disease, she protested against the open saloons on Sunday, violating state law. She concluded by describing the reform of politics in Ithaca and in Galveston after its flood. Salmon asked, why can't Poughkeepsie get rid of money in politics and learn to vote a split ticket, removing national parties and issues from the municipal elections? In her letters to editors, she did not speak about the claims by some muckrakers that business, and their lobbyists, played a major role in political corruption.

But unlike Jane Addams at Hull House, who lived in an immigrant neighborhood and challenged the political boss controlling her district, Salmon watched corruption in local politics from the sidelines. She clipped the *Eagle*'s 1908 story of how "King William" McCabe's men beat a primary opponent in the Irish political stronghold in Ward 1. They admitted that "they had the Italian and Polack element solid, and they all turned out." The opponent claimed that the sheriff's bookkeeper had pockets wadded with "green," which he paid out to "floaters." Also the opponent "had no patronage to offer while McCabe has been getting people in the ward jobs right and left on the streets and in the department of public works."[22]

Good government reformers (referred to sarcastically as "GooGoos" by politicians) like Lucy Salmon saw a local ward leader like McCabe as the enemy. Their ideal of the good citizen assumed a detached, thoughtful consideration of issues and candidates followed by rational choices at the polls. Like native middle-class reformers in other American cities, they rarely appreciated the social usefulness of "bosses" who provided immigrant constituencies with urgently needed forms of assistance. On the other hand, by the 1900s, Poughkeepsie's second- and third-generation German- and Irish-Americans included "respectable" leaders like Judge Morschauser and Dr. Edward Burns with whom a Lucy Salmon could cooperate. She showed less interest in their immigrant origins. Although in *Main Street* she could enumerate Poughkeepsie's ethnic restaurants and count forty-seven nationalities in the city, immigrants and questions about assimilation and Americanization did not figure prominently in her writing about her city at the time of the second greatest wave of foreign immigration in its, and the nation's, history.

## THE LONELY PATH OF A WOMAN
## REFORMER IN A MALE WORLD '

Miss Salmon's public speaking and writing on local needs and issues did capture the attention of business and professional leaders hoping to promote local improvements. In 1907, she was the only woman member with fifteen leading men of Poughkeepsie on the organizing committee for a series of "public conferences on City Affairs" held at Vassar Brothers Institute in February and March.[23] That conference brought together the mayor and council, five representatives from the Chamber of Commerce, eleven from the Dutchess County Historical Society, ten from the Civic League, nine from the Knights of Columbus, seven each from the YMCA and the YWCA, six from Vassar Brothers Institute, four from the City Library, and others from the press, realty companies, and the Arts and Crafts movement.

The local Chamber of Commerce, founded in 1906, took an active role in promoting civic improvements. In 1910, it invited Miss Salmon to be a member of its Committee on Municipal Affairs and Legislation whose current topics included city planning, beautifying approaches to the city, clearing streets, and creating a truly patriotic Fourth of July. That may have meant taking the celebration away from rowdier and especially foreign groups. The Chamber then appointed Salmon as chair of its Committee on Cleanup. But New York City newspapers like the *Times* and the *Sun* got wind of her plans for that campaign, and the resulting "unpleasant notoriety" led her to resign, despite the efforts of the Chamber's president to persuade her to continue.[24] She was deeply distressed by caricatures of her plans and by spurious interviews attributed to her.

The cleanup campaign went on without her leadership in June 1911, although she was asked to choose the suburban Arlington contingent for its final inspection tour. In an article on "The Rejuvenation of Poughkeepsie" in the American Civic Association's magazine *The American City* in fall 1911, the Chamber of Commerce received credit for the campaign and for other improvements Salmon had been urging for some years. Whether this self-effacing reformer preferred that silence after her previous experience with unpleasant publicity is unknown. She seemed very happy with the local leadership of Mayor Horace Sague, a Democrat elected for three terms in this normally Republican city, who shared her interests in civic rejuvenation.

The acceptance of Miss Salmon as a partner in civic work did not extend to Chamber socializing. Although male members of her Cleanup Committee met regularly at her house, they would not include her in their company at Chamber dinners. Year after year she sent in her check for the cost of that event, only to have it returned with the note that having women at the banquet was impracticable. Generally, while a newspaper might refer to her as "one of the most progressive women in this part of New York State," Salmon's struggle to make women equal partners in civic improvement campaigns remained difficult. The Poughkeepsie *Evening Enterprise*, to her dismay, noted in 1914 that the very shy Professor Salmon is "the acknowledged leader of progressive thought and action at Vassar College. . . . Just a generation ahead of the times with visions of a purer democracy, she has naturally paid the penalty . . . of all great reformers . . . of being misunderstood."[25]

Salmon seems to have played a less active role in civic affairs after her Cleanup Committee resignation. But she continued to push for greater participation by women of all classes. Writing in 1912 as "Help Wanted," she protested the restriction of so many activities to men, or ladies, with no place for a working woman. In 1906, she had been urging formation of a Women's University Club; two years later she reminded Poughkeepsians in a sarcastic letter that city women were "rightly excluded" from all organizations but Vassar Brothers Institute.[26] She kept at it. In 1913, some members of Poughkeepsie's women's organizations tried to form a civic committee through which they could act to promote the general welfare. A Women's League for Civic Education paved the way for the League of Women Voters. By 1916, the president of the city's Common Council could say, in claiming Poughkeepsie was as progressive as any other city, that it "has the great mass of its women banded together in more than a dozen clubs."[27]

## LAYING FOUNDATIONS FOR REFORM

Civic improvement and a variety of related reforms received a powerful boost from the local women's suffrage drive during the 1910s. Leadership for that drive came from women faculty at Vassar College, especially those who had chosen to live in the city. The latter avoided the hindrance of the college's ban until 1916 of suffrage activity on campus. Lucy Salmon worked with the National American Woman Suffrage Association and she collaborated with her colleague, Professor of English Laura Johnson Wylie, in forming the local Equal Suffrage League. Wylie lived not far from Salmon at 116 Market Street, opposite Soldier's Fountain and just across Montgomery Street from Eastman Park. Known as Fite House after Dr. Emerson Fite, a professor at Vassar and city assemblyman who lived in the house after Wylie's death in 1932, the modest Carpenter's Gothic style dwelling became the home of the Hudson River Sloop Clearwater in the late twentieth century.

The league elected Wylie as its president in 1910. Years later, the *Poughkeepsie Courier* described her as a "woman of indomitable energy, she was the local leader of the woman suffrage movement from 1910 to 1928."[28] Of the seventy-four community members listed as supporters at a league event, twenty-eight were connected with Vassar. The league proved to be remarkably efficient and well informed in their ward canvassing. In the successful 1917 referendum on a state constitutional amendment enfranchising women,

Poughkeepsie was the only major population center along the Hudson River north of New York City that voted for the amendment.

Wylie believed that, having won the vote, women needed to demonstrate that they were responsible citizens. She led the way to a reorganization of suffragists, first as the Women's City Club and then as the Women's City and County Club, to promote "the cause of good government" and the "health, protection and welfare of all citizens."[29] No other area organization in the early twentieth century matched its range of civic and humanitarian efforts. Another offshoot of the Equal Suffrage League, the League of Women Voters, did not fare as well as the club during the interwar years but surpassed it in membership after World War II.

The Women's City and County Club began with a roster of highly educated and often socially prominent women. They included Mrs. Richard Aldrich of Barrytown, Mrs. Franklin D. Roosevelt of Hyde Park, Mrs. Henry Morgenthau, Jr. of Hopewell Junction, Mrs. Gordon Norrie, Mrs. Henry Noble MacCracken of Vassar College, and Miss Rhoda Hinkley, Mrs. Theodore DuBois, and Dr. Grace Kimball of Poughkeepsie. In their first year, this pioneering group felt that the community didn't take them very seriously until they established a Community Kitchen during the great flu epidemic. That helped many Poughkeepsians to realize "that there was a small group of women who were vitally interested in the advancement of public welfare and who wished to be of real service to the community."[30]

The club then brought Helen Thompson of New York City's Tenement House Department to conduct a survey of poor housing conditions in Poughkeepsie. With Thompson's report, the Women's City and County Club in its second year persuaded the City Council to pass an amendment to the city's building code that required more depth to lots, more air space between houses, and greater privacy in tenements. Prodded by individuals and organizations to do something "about the untidy condition of our streets," they also persuaded the Board of Health to create a "cleanup week."[31] The club emphasized members getting to know government officers through the visits and conferences that it sponsored. It also pursued group visits to local institutions like Hudson River State Hospital and other health agencies, the Community Theatre, Neighborhood House, and Lincoln Center, the Children's Home, public schools, and the City Home. As the club expanded its scope to the county, it turned to additional systematic surveys like one on health conditions in Dutchess County's rural schools.

When members discovered a major problem where their influence might be felt, they moved quickly to address it, as they did in hounding local officials to enforce the long-neglected rules on city garbage collection. That successful campaign brought them more public attention and encouraged further action. They mobilized local schools and other agencies to undertake or expand "Americanization" programs for immigrants. They cooperated with the Board of Education in urging foreign-born men to join night school classes, resulting in a doubling of attendance. Because home duties prevented women from attending, the club persuaded the board to start home classes in English and to pay for the teachers.

The club's Industrial Committee brought Florence Kelly of the National Consumers League to talk about pending legislation affecting women and children. It then held a meeting—one of the club's most successful—on the Industrial Crisis and How to Meet it, with discussion by the general manager of the Dutchess Manufacturing Co., the organizer for the International Garment Makers Union for Women, and the spokesman for the Operatives of the Garner Print Works of Wappingers Falls. The committee tried "to have employers represented equally with employees in the audience."[32] The 125 attending packed clubrooms to capacity.

The club created committees on juvenile court protection, child welfare, tuberculosis, city planning, Lincoln Center, law enforcement, civic education, and international relations, among other subjects. It sent representatives to Albany to lobby for reforms like abolition of child labor and to meetings sponsored by other local clubs and the Federation of Women's Clubs. In 1921, one national periodical cited Poughkeepsie's Women's City and County Club as one of the four most important clubs in the United States.

By the mid-1920s, however, the club's growth slowed and so did the activities of some of its committees. Yet, in its first years, the club had stirred officials at all levels of county government to address a number of neglected problems. It had brought together for discussion of shared issues representatives of diverse interest groups, notably leaders of women's unions and company officers or spokesmen. It had prodded and supported local voluntary associations in settlement house, Americanization, and other activities intended to help newcomers and the needy. It did not conduct those activities itself, however, nor did members interact closely or continuously with those being helped. While club members' attitudes were more inclusive and democratic than those of earlier charitable work, they still had overtones of philanthropy and of social distance between themselves and their beneficiaries. These qualifications should not obscure the fact, however, that these largely upper or upper-middle class women created the most important bridges—of concern and assistance, if not of direct social interaction—between the many diverse groups who made up the fragmented population of Poughkeepsie and Dutchess County.

A mosaic cannot serve as an adequate metaphor for a changing, fluid society, but it has the advantage of calling attention to the many fragments in that society at a given moment in time. Poughkeepsie was not then, or ever, a homogenous population, so it is a mistake to speak of Poughkeepsians as a whole as if they shared a common consciousness. That mistake imposes a unity that has never existed. But a lack of unity has not meant, as the Women's City and County Club story indicates, that important linkages cannot be made at times between the leaders of even quite diverse social groups, leading to shared purposes and action. Such linkages permit more broadly based civic actions that, to varying extent, benefit the many rather than just the few. That happened in the Progressive movement in the nation and also through the less powerful succession of largely women reformers in Poughkeepsie from Lucy Maynard Salmon to the Women's City and County Club.

## PROMOTING URBAN PLANNING FOR POUGHKEEPSIE

At Vassar College, Miss Salmon made an effort to incorporate her interest in city planning into the curriculum. She kept abreast of new developments through the American Civic Association. And she continued to speak out from time to time on local questions. After the Riverview military academy closed, she recommended that the academy be turned into a public trade or technical school because of its location close to large manufacturing firms on the river-front. Typically, she cited examples elsewhere of what she thought desirable: the University of Cincinnati had worked out cooperation between itself and manu-facturing whereby students could work part-time in the factory and in the uni-versity, getting both theory and application. Coming back to her long-standing concern with parks, she noted that Riverview's extensive grounds could be used for recreation and athletics in a congested part of Poughkeepsie that badly needed such opportunities. That use did come about; the trade school did not.

Salmon believed in working with business and professional leaders wher-ever her planning and reform interests converged with theirs, as they did in improving the city's appearance and its reputation as a healthy environment. But she did not share their preoccupation with spurring economic growth and their focus on attracting new businesses and industries. Significantly, the plan-ner she had brought at her own expense to Poughkeepsie in 1915 was noted for his expertise in landscaping, whereas the urban planners the city would turn to in the 1920s took for granted that their priority must be planning for population and economic growth.

Even before World War I, downtown traffic in Poughkeepsie had begun to be a problem. On Main and Market streets the increasingly frequent auto-mobile shared space with trolleys on twin tracks. Residents on nearby streets complained of parked cars blocking suppliers' access to their homes. The city's highly irregular street layout made car and truck progress through downtown particularly difficult. By the 1920s, the "Queen City" found its major thor-oughfares frequently brought to a standstill and confronted new requirements like parking lots and garages, wider streets, and improved street paving. Like many other cities and small towns, it began to consider citywide planning, including zoning, as a possible solution. Of the approximately one hundred plans completed in the United States between 1920 and 1926, municipalities of less than 100,000 population accounted for three-fourths of them.

## MYRON WEST'S PLAN FOR POUGHKEEPSIE

Interest in industrial expansion, city planning, and related reform of municipal government was evident immediately after World War I. Early in 1919,
the Chamber of Commerce reported that it had secured the greatest city planning exhibit in the United States with officials, engineers, and architects making suggestions for improvements that would beautify Poughkeepsie. The
Chamber also had raised an industrial expansion fund of $250,000. Noting
that it constantly distributed folders and circulars showing the industrial
advantages of Poughkeepsie and advertising the availability of vacant facilities,
the organization proudly announced some new industries it had helped attract
to the city. They included the Walsh brothers' hat factory, Knickerbocker
Motors (for whom the Chamber approved a loan of $25,000), the Pough-
keepsie Cutlery Works, expected to employ about one hundred men, and the
Century Steel Company. The Chamber arranged for purchase of 9 acres of
land just north of the city for Century and two members of the Chamber
joined Century's board.

But the headings under "Actual Accomplishments" in the Chamber's
report indicated the far more ambitious vision of its role in civic life exemplified by its sponsorship of the City Planning Exhibit. Rather than than simply
attracting and keeping new employers and investors, the Chamber saw itself as
making contributions to better "Community Loyalty, Housing and Employment, Mercantile, Municipal, Agricultural, Streets, Fraudulent Advertising,
City Plan, Educational, Transportation, Advertising, Legislation."[33]

To advance private education in the area, the Chamber made an agreement with the New York Yearly Meeting of Friends to raise $20,000 to help
build Oakwood School if the Meeting raised $175,000. As it had been doing
since 1910, the Chamber conducted a "cleanup" week in the city, taking away
much rubbish. It launched a variety of efforts to improve transportation
through suburban bus service and better train service. It also watched legislation at every level of government, opposing further regulation of Public Services corporations in 1918. Meanwhile, municipal government moved ahead
with its own projects to improve the urban region.

Journalist reformer Ray Stannard Baker spoke in Poughkeepsie about city
government reform. The city launched a health campaign, including construction of a new sewage disposal plant. Also, in 1919, the mayor began seeking funds for a bridge across the Hudson, though the state legislature did not
approve it until 1924. In 1920, the *Sunday Courier* presented a map showing
how the city might grow from its current 4 square miles to 9. Once again the
city imagined an expansive future, now supported by new planning ideas.

By 1923, the Common Council invited a well-known planner from
Chicago, Myron West, to come and make a presentation. West did so in 1924,
the same year that U.S. Secretary of Commerce Herbert Hoover published a

Standard Zoning Act intended as a model for cities everywhere. Common Council accepted West's offer to devise a plan for $5,000. West provided a comprehensive zoning and street plan, including street corrections, evaluation of the location of transit, rail, and water transportation, streets, schools, parks, and public buildings, and revitalization of its waterfront—a never-ending concern for Poughkeepsie. West also followed the usual urging by planners to plot streets beyond municipal boundaries in order to discourage haphazard provision by suburban developers and also, if possible, annex more territory for the city's future growth.

In 1920, the city of Poughkeepsie had a platted area of 4 square miles and a population of some 35,000, housed at an average density of sixteen persons per acre. Although West thought an additional 6 square miles could accommodate population growth during the next forty years, he added into his plan another 16 square miles to allow a decrease in population density and the normal dispersed urban fringe. The plan extended north beyond the State Hospital for the Insane, south to Spackenkill Road and east to Wappinger Creek. He assumed that future industries would follow the New York, New Haven and Hartford Railroad line eastward. That area would be at sufficient distance, given the prevailing winds, not to annoy what West expected to be the nicer residential area south and west of Vassar College.

West saw Poughkeepsie as ideally located for earning much more than the city did currently from serving tourists to the Hudson valley. West noted that the ferry company crossing the river to Highland made some 35,000 trips a month in summer compared to 4,600 in winter. He estimated that 150,000 tourists came through the city each summer and could be a bonanza for Poughkeepsie's economy if effectively cultivated.

West's plan provided a much more mixed evaluation of current provision and location of local business and services. "Factory location, bad—occupying river front on land ill adapted for industrial use. . . . Business, badly scattered. . . . Railroad locations, good, except use of riverfront. Parks, not adequate as to ratio of acreage to population, and not well distributed. Schools, fairly well distributed but of small units. Residence areas with a high average population density [reflecting the duplexes and triples Miss Salmon had noted]. Land values below normal considering population density." When he discussed the difficulty of devising a satisfactory street plan, he noted that the main thoroughfares had been laid out along trails winding through hills so platted subdivisions often had little relation to each other. "The city is consequently full of street misfits, difficult to remedy or to extend in a logical manner."[34]

West's ambitious plan, especially for dealing with traffic and city streets, received favorable public response in 1924. Although the Merchants' Association in 1919 had bitterly fought police department efforts to limit car parking on Main Street, by 1924 merchants had concluded that unrestricted parking prevented shoppers from getting into their stores. But it soon became apparent that Poughkeepsie's legislators and businessmen had narrower aims than West's plan. They primarily sought zoning, widening or extending streets, annexation of territory beyond municipal boundaries, and finding a suitable location for a new vehicular bridge across the Hudson. In 1926, the mayor appointed a committee of twenty-five representative businessmen and professionals to review West's plan, but did not set up a planning commission as West and urban planners generally preferred. Instead, the mayor assigned all responsibility for action to his Corporate Counsel and Board of Public Works, a clear sign that he was not committed to professional planning. Business goals and political concerns, usually in some tension with planning ideals then and now, prevailed.

## THE CITY TRIES TO ANNEX
## THE TOWN OF POUGHKEEPSIE

By 1926, local interest had shifted from zoning to annexation. The Chamber of Commerce submitted an act of annexation for about 15,000 acres of the town of Poughkeepsie to the Common Council. But the mayor vetoed it, arguing that so large an area would burden the city with responsibility for all state roads in it. A second bill presented in 1926 omitted the Fairview district, but Corporation Counsel declared it illegal. He and the mayor also declared that West's zoning ordinance was not appropriate for Poughkeepsie; they wanted a politically appointed Board of Appeals of five to six citizens. Opponents charged that that would open the door to corruption.

Meantime, a local businessman, James Sague, organized a new industrial league to attract industry to the city, arguing that any drive for annexation should be postponed. A local attorney replied that any new industries coming to Poughkeepsie would have to locate in the town since the congested city no longer had suitable sites. Already newcomers like Fiat and Schatz Federal Bearings had chosen town sites. Failure to extend the city's boundaries would make the new industrial league strictly a town affair.

But whether he intended it or not, Sague had defeated annexation for another year. In 1927, newly elected as mayor, he shifted course, calling for immediate annexation of one portion of the town only: Arlington. Later his chosen committee of businessmen proposed a plan in which a smaller area of the town than West had envisioned would be divided into three sections for referenda on annexation: Fairview, a central area (including Arlington), and the south side. In the meantime, two south side associations representing more than five hundred families—the Ferris Heights Association and the Southeast Avenue Association—had announced their desire to be annexed. Among areas within the town, interests and needs varied. This more prosperous south side area found the convenience of city services worth city taxes.

The Arlington and Fairview districts strongly opposed the proposal for divided referenda, arguing that without south side the remainder of the town could not afford the financial burden of independence from the city. Despite that opposition, the New York State legislature settled the issue by approving a separate referendum in south side for annexation of that area. South side voted in favor of annexation by a large majority. This story of twists and turns in the city's consideration of annexation and a comprehensive city plan had an ironic conclusion. After four years of paying no attention to West's plan, Common Council invited him "back to defend his plan and to consult with city engineers concerning a proper approach to the new Mid-Hudson Bridge."[35] The council's new enthusiasm for the plan led them to give unanimous approval in a 1928 meeting with West for creation of the planning commission they had once avoided. They may have been spurred partly by their embarrassment in learning at that meeting that the route now proposed for spanning the Hudson was identical to that which West had favored in his 1924 plan.

Incorporation of the town of Poughkeepsie's south side into the city did provide important space for growth in both the city's population and its tax

FIGURE 6.1. Aerial view of Poughkeepsie, 1935

base, given the relative attractiveness of that area for the residence of higher-income families. But, for the longer term, the failure to annex the remainder of the town meant that the city would not capture much of the new suburban growth in the region. The push outward from the city was clearly evident by the late 1920s in Fairview and Arlington, where local Roman Catholics formed their first suburban congregation, Holy Trinity, as a territorial rather than as a nationality-related parish.

The city increasingly suffered the fate of so many northeastern towns and cities with constricting boundaries. It did not benefit from the newer, more attractive housing being built in the region, except in the south side area that became the city's affluent Eighth Ward after annexation. An aging housing stock made workers who could afford to do so prefer newer housing with larger lots beyond the city; those who replaced them in the filter-down process often were poorer newcomers who could ill afford costly maintenance. Increasingly, reports characterized the city's oldest housing on the river slope as degraded and slum-like.

City businessmen lamented such housing conditions, but their preoccupation with keeping taxes low discouraged any major efforts at municipal housing reform. Ever since indebtedness—acquired in water, sanitation, and railroad improvements before 1873—came to haunt city leaders during the national depression of that decade, they had turned away from costly innovation of any kind. Pursuing a largely reactive politics of dealing with problems through small adjustments, they even starved their school system financially. By the 1890s, deterioration in many of the public school buildings and the city's reputation for paying its teachers poorly did produce, for a time, a faction willing to support a new school superintendent with more ambitious notions of reform.

The apex of city government remained largely in the hands of men from well-established local business, although there continued to be talented newer arrivals, like shoe manufacturer George Hine, chosen as mayor in 1900. Hine had come to Poughkeepsie in the late 1870s to work in the shoe factory of another newcomer, John Whitehouse from Brooklyn. Important but lesser positions increasingly went to the children or grandchildren of mid-nineteenth-century immigrants like Joseph Morschauser, chosen as recorder, then city judge. More troublesome, but a political fact to be accommodated, were immigrant-based organizations in the river wards.

The most significant change to the environment of the valley and its cities did not come from municipal government, however, or from the kinds of urban reform Miss Salmon and others envisioned. By the 1920s, the growing importance of the automobile for overland transportation spurred county and state governments to create a network of paved roads and bridges to facilitate traffic. In the process, they opened the rural countryside to city dwellers and led rural residents to travel further for better shopping and other opportunities. The new space economy would not only transform the relation between existing localities but facilitate a new, more spacious kind of urban development, the suburb, which in the longer run would sprawl over former farmland, dramatically changing the look of the valley.

SEVEN

# Changes to the Space Economy
# Between the Wars

POUGHKEEPSIE'S UPPER MIDDLE CLASS had its reform-minded minority like the members of the Women's City and County Club, carrying on progressive habits of serious social investigation in the Roaring Twenties. But at the opposite extreme in outlook the city also had its would-be "flappers" in affluent families, especially among the young who welcomed the new freedoms afforded by the automobile. Born in Poughkeepsie in 1907, Elizabeth "Lee" Miller enjoyed an affluent and relatively comfortable adolescence there. She moved on at age twenty-two into the bright lights and livelier social atmosphere of New York City, exemplifying those who found a small city too confining a sphere for their talents. But she shared with many Poughkeepsians the increased habit and love of traveling that the construction during the 1920s and 1930s of bridges and better roads made possible.

Miller quickly became one of New York's most famous flappers and, traveling to Paris in 1929, an internationally famous figure in the 1920s and 1930s. Part of a glamorous circle of photographers and artists in New York and Paris as a leading *Vogue* model, she posed for and was a muse and lover of the famous artist-photographer Man Ray, as well as close to Edward Steichen, Charlie Chaplin, Jean Cocteau, and Pablo Picasso. She would move through the artistic modes of Modernism and Surrealism of the decades between the wars to become one of World War II's first women war correspondents, and her photographs of a devastated Europe and Holocaust camps such as Dachau brought the horrors of the conflict to Americans at home.

Elizabeth's father Theodore was superintendent of De Laval Separator Company, then Poughkeepsie's largest employer. He was one of the city's elite businessmen and a member of the Amrita Club. Although his wife was denied membership in the D.A.R. because his Revolutionary roots were related to the

Hessians rather than the colonists and his wife was born in Canada, he took full advantage of his status in the business community. The family first lived in a "comfortable frame house" on South Clinton Street, "near the center of town," where Elizabeth's mother Florence could walk "to the local shops beneath the flowering cherry trees and Japanese maples that lined the street," and "an Italian organ-grinder played his spirited tunes outside their door, and the fife-and-drum band passed, waving banners, on the Fourth of July."[1] Later, the family moved to Cedar Hill south of the city across the Albany Post Road from Locust Grove, and eventually to Kingwood Park. Elizabeth enjoyed many of the cultural opportunities in the city, such as dance lessons at Miss Rutherford's, movies at the Collingwood Opera House, or being in productions of the Community Theater. The family also enjoyed touring the countryside in their "big Buick sedan," a leisure pursuit of growing interest in the Roaring Twenties among the better-off social classes. The automobile began to change the social behaviors and landscapes of America.

## BRIDGING THE HUDSON

The economic boom in the 1920s increased demands for more efficient means of crossing the Hudson River. The rapid growth in the use of automobiles and trucks formed bottlenecks at the ferry landings as they struggled to move people and goods across the river. Vehicles waiting for the next ferry trip began to fill up the lower blocks of Main Street as it approached the ferry slip. Traffic had increased since the late nineteenth century and the early twentieth century when it was not uncommon "for wagons to be backed up all the way to Bridge Street waiting for the ferry and in winter, the only way to get across the river was on foot or by horse-drawn sleighs, and then, only when the ice was thick enough to hold them."[2] Over the decades, Poughkeepsie businessmen and politicians developed various plans to bridge the river.

The construction of the Poughkeepsie Railroad Bridge in 1888 provided one option. Throughout the early twentieth century and well past World War I, it was the only bridge to span the river from Albany to the New York harbor. The original charter from the state legislature in 1871 for the railroad bridge provided "for the passage and transportation of passengers, railroad trains, teams, vehicles, cattle, horses, sheep, swine, and other merchandise and property."[3] However, built as a railroad structure, it was never used for other purposes.

Nonetheless, in 1913, John K. Sague, then mayor of Poughkeepsie, suggested that a passageway for pedestrians be added to the railroad bridge. The New Haven Railroad, owners of the bridge through its subsidiary the Central New England Railway, argued that changes to the original charter had removed them of any responsibility for another passageway, while also contending that the engineering of the structure would not allow the addition of a highway deck, either above or below the rail deck.

## THE MID-HUDSON BRIDGE

Over the next decade, pressure mounted to construct a passageway across the river for pedestrians and vehicles. The Right Reverend Monsignor Joseph F. Sheahan of St. Peter's Church brought many Poughkeepsians together to continue the effort. In 1919, they addressed a letter to New York Governor Al Smith urging that the state purchase the railroad bridge and convert it for automobile use, and the following year the Poughkeepsie Automobile Club invited engineer John F. O'Rourke to discuss the feasibility of such a purpose. He reported that a lower deck was possible with some structural strengthening, but noted that it would be quite expensive due to the cost of building highway approaches. A similar analysis in 1921 for the Poughkeepsie Chamber of Commerce by the engineer Gustav Lindenthal, who had constructed the Hell Gate Bridge over the East River in New York City, resulted in renewed support for an entirely new bridge to be constructed at Poughkeepsie.

In 1922, under the leadership of Monsignor Sheahan and the Reverend James H. Henry, the Kiwanis Club formed the Highway Vehicular Bridge Association to work for the construction of a new bridge. They invited the engineer George W. Goethals and his associates, who had designed the Panama Canal, to develop a design for a new bridge. The Kiwanis Club committee took this preliminary design with them to Albany to lobby the state legislature for funding. Although the resulting bill was defeated that year, a similar bill passed two years later that appropriated $4 million of the eventual $6 million cost of construction.

In 1923, the firm of Modjeski and Moran was engaged to design the bridge. Governor Al Smith laid the cornerstone on October 9, 1925, as the city celebrated with a parade and a reception at Nelson House. The final design for the suspension bridge consisted of three piers with a length of 3,000 feet from anchorage to anchorage, and a total length from Union Square in the city, where the eastern approach began, to the anchorage of the cables on the west bank of the river of 4,245 feet. The height of the main span above the navigation channel is 135 feet at mean high water. Over the five years of construction, four workers died in accidents; two plunged to their deaths just months before the completion of the bridge in 1930.

For the opening of the Mid-Hudson Bridge to traffic on August 25, 1930, the Poughkeepsie-Highland Bridge Opening Celebration Committee asked all the merchants along Main Street to "help make the visitors welcome by decorating" their buildings.[4] Opening day ceremonies included a "grand parade" and speeches by former Governor Alfred E. Smith, who had backed the project when he was in office, the equally enthusiastic supporter and current Governor Franklin D. Roosevelt, the former mayor of Poughkeepsie Daniel Wilbur, chairman of the event, and many others. At the conclusion of the ceremony, attended, it was reported, by fifteen thousand persons, an auto

FIGURE 7.1. Dedication of Mid-Hudson Bridge, 1930
Franklin D. Roosevelt and Eleanor Roosevelt with Al Smith

procession started from each side, with Eleanor Roosevelt cutting the ribbon on the west side and Mrs. Smith on the east side; the delegations met in the middle of the bridge with greetings expressed between the two groups, and then the bridge was opened to traffic, free of charge for the rest of the day.[5] Later that evening there was a baseball game "between two fast, snappy teams," a clambake, "gala ball," and fireworks at Woodcliff Park;[6] music and fireworks at Riverview Park; and a block dance on Church Street, from Market to Academy streets. The opening ceremony was considered of such interest well beyond the mid-Hudson region that a film crew from Paramount Studio took "talking pictures" of the event, "one of the first ever made," and a few days later "they were shown at the Bardavon on Market Street and created much interest."[7]

During the dedication ceremonies, Governor Roosevelt revealed his deep interest in local and regional history. He traced the history of transportation in the Hudson valley and noted his past concern for the need for a permanent river crossing in the area. "Let us take a look back 250 years," he began, and suggested, "the river itself became a barrier, instead of a highway." He added, "The span over the Hudson makes us neighbors and friends more than ever before."[8] He then proceeded to officially declare its name to be the Mid-Hudson Bridge.

The bridge's role in linking the counties and the communities of the region together was further elaborated on in the opening day editorial of the *Poughkeepsie Eagle-News*:

Highland and Poughkeepsie have become nextdoor neighbors; Ulster and Dutchess Counties have been joined. Trade will flow from side to side of the new structure; inevitably our business relations with the west shore will be closer than ever has been possible in the past. But even more important will be the effect of better understanding and greater solidarity. That effect will make itself felt throughout the entire Mid-Hudson Region, and will quicken the movement to make all of the Valley communities realize the essential fact that they hold their chief interests in common and that, by and large, they will prosper or decline together.[9]

The *Sunday Courier* editorial welcoming "The New Bridge" said that

in spite of the fact that it will give Poughkeepsie a new traffic problem, [it] is bound to be an asset of great value to the city. Motorists from every section of the land will know that the bridge is at Poughkeepsie. It will identify Poughkeepsie as the Bear Mountain bridge does not identify Peekskill. Because the Bear Mountain bridge is no part of Peekskill. The Mid-Hudson bridge is part of Poughkeepsie.[10]

## THE BEAR MOUNTAIN BRIDGE

The Mid-Hudson Bridge was not the first automobile bridge to span the Hudson River. In 1924, the Bear Mountain Bridge was constructed in the Highlands as a private venture by the Harriman family that catered primarily to auto tourists who traveled to the recently opened Bear Mountain State Park on the west bank or northward on the east bank, through Westchester County toward New England. Described as the longest suspended structure in the world when it was dedicated, the 1,632-foot suspension bridge was the first large bridge designed primarily for touring motorists, along with a walkway for hikers on the nascent Appalachian Trail. "Chains of pleasure grounds" were envisioned throughout Westchester County to parallel the picnic grounds in Bear Mountain State Park that would encourage recreational trips by urban New Yorkers to travel by auto into the rural hinterland. The bridge was also promoted as a link for "motorists as from as far away as Buffalo, Boston, Albany, New York City, and Philadelphia, allowing them to cross the Hudson 'anytime, day or night, regardless of weather conditions.'"[11]

Two other bridges spanning the Hudson River were built in the 1930s as auto and truck traffic increased. New York City's George Washington Bridge was opened one year after the Mid-Hudson in 1931, while the Rip Van Winkle Bridge connected the cities of Hudson and Catskill in 1935. The latter occasioned the establishment of the New York State Bridge Authority in 1932 as an independent entity to finance bridge construction during the Depression. It would be another two decades before other highway bridges would cross the Hudson, such as the Tappan Zee that opened in 1955, followed by the Kingston-Rhinecliff two years later, and the Newburgh-Beacon in 1963. Major additions were also constructed during this time with a lower deck added to the George Washington in 1962 and a second span for the Newburgh-Beacon in 1980.

## PARKWAYS

Auto touring in the rural countryside became quite fashionable during the Roaring Twenties as automobile ownership expanded. Mass production of the Ford Model T began in 1908 and only two years later the number of motor cars in America approached a half million. Two million cars were on the road in 1916, eight million in 1920, ten million three years later, and three years after that it had doubled to twenty million. Federal legislation in the early 1920s created a national network of roads, including a system of route numbers (odd numbers for north–south routes, even for east–west), indicative of the new spatial organization of the American landscape that resulted from the rise in automobile ownership and use.

Outside the densely packed cities a new American domesticated landscape was emerging throughout the late nineteenth and early twentieth centuries. The landscape design ideas of Andrew Jackson Downing and Calvert Vaux that led to the establishment of the suburb, and further developed in the urban parks projects of Vaux and Frederick Law Olmsted, were soon translated into scenic roads and parkways, such as Brookyn's Ocean Parkway, Boston's "Emerald Necklace," and parkways in Buffalo.

In the twentieth century, parkways for motorized vehicles were built specifically to bring urban dwellers into the bucolic countryside whose residents viewed their invasion with mixed feelings. Close to the city, parkways encouraged suburban development in the lands between the villages that had formed around stations of earlier commuter rail lines. In the metropolitan New York City region, as the parkways extended further out from the city into Long Island or northward into northern Westchester County and eventually Dutchess County, city dwellers could travel for day trips to parks, lakes, beaches, or mountain hideaways.

New York State was among the first to build limited-access motorways, starting with the Bronx River Parkway in 1913, which linked New York City with then-rural Westchester County. Others, such as the Saw Mill and Taconic parkways, soon followed. On the west bank of the Hudson River the Palisades Interstate Park had been established during the first decades of the twentieth century. Between 1921 and 1926, the Hudson River Drive running north–south along the top of the Palisades was opened, along with US Route 9W in the late 1920s that allowed access to Bear Mountain State Park, and the Bear Mountain Bridge.

In 1928, the Regional Plan Association published an influential, multi-volume survey and planning study, *Regional Plan for New York and Environs*. The study focused on developing regional road systems, including the creation of limited-access express "freeways" throughout the metropolitan area.[12] With the opening of the George Washington Bridge and the subsequent growth of population in suburban areas of northern New Jersey and southern New York, the Regional Plan Association recommended a new parkway to Bear Mountain State Park in 1931; portions of it were opened in the 1940s, while the entire route was not completely finished until 1961. As noted by Bob Binnewies of the Palisades Interstate Park Commission, "The artful link between city and park, envisioned for decades, was in place."[13]

Palisades Interstate Park linked the states of New Jersey and New York on the western border of the Hudson valley. Similarly, in the 1920s, an interstate park was established in the Taconic Hills, along the eastern border of the Hudson valley between New York and the New England states of Connecticut and Massachusetts. Begun in 1923, Taconic State Park would not become the terminus of the Taconic State Parkway, however; rather, after many decades of planning and construction that were interrupted by World War II, the parkway was extended to the Massachusetts Turnpike link to the New York State Thruway in northern Columbia County.

## TACONIC STATE PARKWAY

Originally designated as the "Bronx Parkway Extension," the route was designed in 1923 to link the already completed section of the Bronx River Parkway with the Bear Mountain Bridge; this section later became known as the Bear Mountain State Parkway. A second section continued north as the "Eastern State Parkway," which later became known as the Taconic State Parkway. The route in northern Westchester County to the Putnam County line was built between 1927 and 1932. Designed as a scenic road for auto touring, the parkway and the rural landscape through which it passed were described in artistic terms: "the parkway threads a region of wild, picturesque scenery. The Parkway will disclose the scenic charm of Westchester now unknown to the motoring public."[14]

In 1924, Governor Al Smith appointed Franklin Delano Roosevelt chairman of the Taconic State Park Commission. Roosevelt's plan for the parkway was to link a number of parks northward, through Putnam, Dutchess, Columbia, and Rensselaer counties to Albany. But funding for construction was held up by Robert Moses, who was head of the State Parks Council and who had also been appointed by Governor Smith as president of the Long Island State Park Commission. Roosevelt was elected governor in 1928 and he continued his interest in conservation and forestry, along with the development of parks and parkways in the Hudson valley. He convinced a number of New York's wealthiest families to donate land for parks to the State Park Commission, including 3,600 acres for Fahnestock State Park in Putnam County and 600 acres for the James Baird State Park in Dutchess County, and the parkway's winding route was chosen in part as a link between these parks.[15] Between 1932 and 1938, the Taconic State Parkway was extended north from the Westchester County line through Putnam County into southern Dutchess County as a single carriageway with stone-arch overpasses. The parkway's design was to complement the rural character of the landscape, insisted Roosevelt, so that it included rustic bridges made of large uncut stone and laid with thick mortar. This section, like the Palisades Interstate Parkway through Rockland County, would become a major commuter route in the latter half of the twentieth century; its peaceful, rustic character would be lost to the frenzy of high-speed commuter traffic.

Parkway construction further north was halted during World War II, but by 1955 the route traversed eastern Dutchess County, and was completed through Columbia County eight years later. Almost alone of all the parkways built from the 1920s and 1930s through the twentieth century, the northern section of the Taconic State Parkway retains its scenic landscape character of rolling farmlands and forests with extensive views of the Catskill and Berkshire mountains. It has been declared a U.S. Scenic Byway by the federal government.

## HIGHWAYS

With the advent of the automobile as the major form of transportation in the twentieth century, the road system throughout the United States became more firmly established. Technical advancements in construction and surfacing, and government financing, especially after the federal acts of 1916 and 1921 soon established a network of federal, state, and county highways throughout the region.

The Albany Post Road was designated as Route 9 in 1926. Essentially a northward extension of Broadway in New York City, the alignment of the Post Road, along whose route mail was carried for 150 years after the Revolution, generally followed a well-worn path laid out by local Native Americans who had maintained it as a major line of communication and trade between northern- and southern-based groups. The path often forded small tributaries to the Hudson where Native Americans might have encamped next to fresh springs or waterfalls. It is one such site at a spring just to the south of the city of Poughkeepsie on the east side of current Route 9 opposite the Rural Cemetery that the name for the city is said to have been used.

The Albany Post Road, as U.S. Route 9, has remained the main North–South arterial highway along the east bank of the Hudson, from New York City, through colonial settlements in Westchester County. It wound its way through the Highlands in Putnam County to emerge at Wiccopee Pass in southern Dutchess County, then passed through the villages of Fishkill, Wappingers Falls, Poughkeepsie, Hyde Park, Rhinebeck, and Upper Red Hook, on its way north toward Columbia and Rensselaer counties and the state capitol. In some sections, Route 9 bypasses the original Post Road alignment, such as through the village of Wappingers Falls, where it is now Route 9D, while from Fishkill to Poughkeepsie the former two-lane dirt road with trolley tracks alongside and overarching elm trees has been widened into four and six lanes with hard-surfaced parking lots, neon signs, and shopping centers mile after mile.

Road improvements throughout Dutchess County became increasingly significant public concerns during the 1920s and 1930s. From 1930 to 1934, the mileage of improved hard-surfaced roads increased from 158 to 212, yet there remained approximately 1,000 miles of unimproved, or dirt, roads.[16] During the late 1930s, the *Sunday Courier* listed "Deathproof Roads" as one of its half-dozen issues on a "Platform for City and County." In an editorial on the "side roads of Dutchess," the newspaper presaged the county's interest in developing a tourist economy a half century later when it opined: "the time has come for the more liberal development of the subsidiary highways, which act in a manner of branch lines to the trunk roads . . . the main highway soon loses its individuality and becomes a panorama of unsightly advertising signs, quick-lunch establishments, fuel stations and other accessories of the tourist business. . . . The trunk lines and speedways, the branch and subsidiary roads are 'journeys of experience.'"[17] Meanwhile, costs for acquisition of rights of way and construction of new highways, as well as maintenance and snow removal, became an increasing burden on the budgets of the towns and the county throughout these decades. The advent of school consolidation and the need for busing, as well as population increase and the construction of suburban and exurban housing, further expanded the road network through the rest of the twentieth century.

The widening, straightening, and hardening, either through the use of concrete or macadam, of existing roads to suit the demands of automobiles and trucks often resulted in the loss of scenic and historic features of the roadscape. Along the Albany Post Road, milestones had been erected after the Revolution that indicated distances between points that determined mail charges. As the highway was widened, many of these milestones were lost or damaged. However, some of the original red sandstone markers remain, such as one situated on the west side of Route 9 in the village of Hyde Park next to the stone wall at the Franklin Delano Roosevelt National Historic Site. It was encased in protective fieldstone as part of Roosevelt's Works Progress Administration (WPA) during the late 1930s.

Roosevelt's deep interest in local history and civic affairs led to many projects under the WPA. For example, a gymnasium was erected in Poughkeepsie at Lincoln Center "as a WPA gift to the city" with a basketball court, baths, dressing rooms, and club rooms for the boys' and girls' clubs.[18] Throughout Dutchess County, local sites of historical importance were inventoried in a county guide by the Federal Writer's Project and Historical Records Survey Project that employed out-of-work writers, teachers, historians, and artists. Roosevelt's interest in regional history, conservation, and the use of local materials was also evident in other WPA projects in the mid-Hudson area. The Civilian Conservation Corps (CCC) established a number of camps locally as it built structures at Mills-Norrie State Park in Staatsburg and stone walls along the course of the Fall Kill as a flood control measure as it flowed through Poughkeepsie.

## VAL-KILL

The Fall Kill originates north of the city in the springs and wetlands of the towns of Pleasant Valley, Clinton, and Hyde Park. As it flows through the town of Hyde Park, it is dammed as a small pond and marsh on the National Park Service property of Val-Kill. The stone cottage at Val-Kill, designed by Franklin in a rural Dutch Colonial style, was built for Eleanor Roosevelt in 1925 as a refuge from Springwood, her mother-in-law's home, a busy, formal house where she and Franklin raised their family and where Franklin often engaged in his political business. Along with her friends Nancy Cook and Marion Dickerman and their mutual friend Caroline O'Day, Eleanor established Val-Kill Industries on the site. They hired local craftsmen to produce furniture, textiles, and pewter ware over the following decade in hopes that they would inspire crafts industries in many poverty-stricken rural areas and slow the out-migration of farmers to urban areas in search of jobs.

Val-Kill was also used as an informal gathering place for important foreign visitors. For example, in April 1939, Franklin and Eleanor hosted the Crown Prince and Crown Princess of Norway for a festive event at Val-Kill and Franklin's other small nearby rustic dwelling named Top Cottage that he had built in 1937. Two years later in 1939, the President and First Lady had King George and Queen Elizabeth of England for a typical American summer picnic of hot dogs, pork and beans, salad, and cool drinks. That morning all had attended services at St. James Episcopal Church, a small 1844 edifice in the rural English Gothic Revival style located across the Albany Post Road from the Vanderbilt mansion. The royal visit was immensely popular in the region; 5,000 persons stood outside St. James on Sunday morning, June 11, for a glimpse of the king and queen, while 200,000 more had stood on sidewalks along the route that they traveled through the city the previous day. Obtaining good vantage points to view the royal entourage was of consuming interest for many local residents. Front rooms at the Nelson House were in heavy demand as were viewing sites from various public buildings; according to Sheriff Sedgwick, he handed out almost two hundred passes "to persons who will try to find space in windows of the courthouse."[19]

Eleanor continued to use Val-Kill as her home after Franklin died. She became known as the "First Lady of the World" and entertained many world leaders there, such as Nikita Khrushchev, Marshall Tito, Haile Selassie, and Jawaharal Nehru as well as American political and labor leaders such as Adlai Stevenson, Walter Reuther, and John F. Kennedy. Eight years after her death in 1962, the property was sold to developers, but a small group of concerned citizens, most of whom from the immediate area, created a national interest in preserving the property as a national historic site. In 1977, President Jimmy Carter signed the bill creating the Eleanor Roosevelt Historic Site; it joined FDR's home and presidential library under the aegis of the National Park Service.

Both Franklin and Eleanor cultivated their roots in the mid-Hudson valley; for both it was home. "The greatest thing I have learned is how good it is to come home again," the globe-trotting advocate for human rights declared, while the president remarked, "All that is in me cries out to go back to my home on the Hudson River," as he also declaimed, "I am pure Hudson Valley when you come down to it." Val-Kill and Top Cottage were early examples of FDR's interests in architectural design, historic reference, and the use of local materials. As president, he would integrate those considerations into national efforts to pull the country out of the Depression.

## DEPRESSION-ERA POST OFFICES

Roosevelt's most significant legacy in this regard is the design and construction of post offices in Poughkeepsie and the neighboring villages of Beacon, Wappingers Falls, Rhinebeck, and his own hometown of Hyde Park. As noted by the architectural historian William B. Rhoads: "Roosevelt believed in reproducing the old fieldstone structures of the county as a way of creating permanent memorials and reminders of the continuous thread of history linking the past, present, and future. He knew that his social programs might well disappear under a later administration, but he was confident that buildings like the [Poughkeepsie] post office would remain as bonds between the times of his Dutchess County ancestors, himself, and future generations."[20]

Federal construction projects were a significant aspect of the Roosevelt administration in digging America out of the depths of the Great Depression. Building eleven hundred post offices throughout the country was one small segment of the federal plans. Six that were built in the mid-Hudson valley are in a distinctive Dutch Colonial Revival style as a result of the influence of FDR, who traced his roots back to the early Dutch families in New York. He joined the Holland Society in 1910 as a "descendant in the direct male line of a Dutchman who was a native or resident of New York or of the American colonies prior to the year 1675," became a member of the Dutchess County

Historical Society upon its founding in 1914, and from 1926 to 1928 assisted the historian Helen Wilkinson Reynolds in her book *Dutch Houses in the Hudson Valley before 1776*. At the same time, FDR's interest in the use of local fieldstone and vernacular Hudson valley Dutch architecture was furthered by his involvement in the design of Val-Kill cottage, a refuge for his wife Eleanor. Roosevelt's personal interest in architecture and design as well as local history and regional cultural landscapes came together in the architectural designs for new post offices during the 1930s. As he remarked at the dedication of the Rhinebeck post office on May 1, 1939: "we are trying to adapt the design to the historical background of the locality and to use . . . the materials which are indigenous to the locality itself. Hence, the fieldstone for Dutchess County."[21]

The first of the six mid-Hudson post offices was begun in 1936 and opened the following year. Constructed out of local fieldstone in a vernacular Dutch Colonial style, an editorial in the *Beacon News* on its dedication declared it to be "in perfect sympathy with Beacon's outstanding Revolutionary history."[22] The second and only other city in Dutchess County, Beacon had been formed in 1913 out of two villages—Fishkill Landing and Matteawan—that had been settled along the Fishkill Creek. In the mid-1930s, Beacon remained a manufacturing community of many small industries and mills, including those for hats and bricks. The design of the Beacon post office was in a local vernacular style, whereas others in the group had specific buildings as historic models. For example, the model for the Rhinebeck post office begun in 1938 was one of the earliest Dutch stone houses in the area, the circa 1770 Kip House; the 1939 post office in Wappingers Falls was modeled after the still-standing wooden Brouwer-Mesier house of circa 1750 and 1777; while the Hyde Park post office one year later had as its design model the former 1772 wooden house of Dr. John Bard. The village of Hyde Park derived its name from the name for the Bard estate, which by the end of the nineteenth century had become the Vanderbilt estate.

All the post offices included murals depicting scenes of local historical events and social organization. The murals in the Hyde Park and Rhinebeck post offices by artist Olin Dows show life on the Hudson River with scenes of ice boating and sturgeon fishing, while the social landscape is drawn that includes blacks, both free and slave, that worked on the estates. Members of the local gentry are also shown, including FDR, whose interest in local history and architecture is depicted in Dows's mural in the Hyde Park post office of the president examining the architectural plans for Roosevelt High School.

## POUGHKEEPSIE POST OFFICE

The design for the Poughkeepsie post office was modeled after the former Dutchess County Court House built in 1809. This courthouse had stood on the same site where delegates to the New York State convention had met to ratify the federal Constitution in 1788, during which their debates eventually led to the enactment of amendments known as the Bill of Rights. As a former governor of the state as well as historian, Roosevelt was keenly aware of the role of the city of Poughkeepsie as the capitol of the state during the debates and the eventual ratification of the Constitution. The new post office, a federal project, would reflect that history.

The cornerstone of the Poughkeepsie post office was laid October 13, 1937. Completed in 1938, the building included a cast bronze bell in the copper-domed cupola and five large murals in the two-story lobby. The two on the first floor represent views of the city and waterfront from the west bank circa 1839 by artist Georgina Klitgaard and a similar view a century later by Charles Rosen. The three murals located on the walls of the second floor balcony depict earlier historical scenes by Gerald Foster. The first painting in the

FIGURE 7.2. Dedication of post office, 1937

series, *Poughkeepsie, c. 1692*, indicates a meeting between Dutch settlers and Wappinger Indians at a stream and waterfall, the legendary "reed covered lodge by the little watering place" that gave Poughkeepsie its name "Apo-keepsing." A second mural titled *Hamlet of Poughkeepsie, c. 1750* suggests the center of the settlement, with three important buildings: the Reformed Dutch Church, a farmhouse/tavern, and the second courthouse. All are composed of local fieldstone, as Roosevelt wished, and stand by the Kings Highway, which, after the Revolution, became known as the Albany Post Road. The third mural depicts the scene on July 26, 1788, when "New York Ratifies the United States Constitution in the Dutchess County Court House in Poughkeepsie."

FDR was particularly pleased to have his ancestor Isaac Roosevelt in the courthouse scene as one of the participants who ratified the Constitution, for even as FDR's New Deal programs were under attack, his ancestor's portrait in the mural symbolized the president's dedication to the Constitution. FDR alluded to his ancestry, and to the role of the city of Poughkeepsie, in an extemporaneous speech on election eve 1936 to a crowd of "more than 5,000" given from the balcony of the Nelson House hotel in the center of the city: "About a block from where I stand . . . there was a little old stone building and in the year 1788 there was held there the constitutional convention of the State of New York. . . . My great, great-grandfather was a member of the convention. . . . And so you will see that not only in my own person but also by inheritance I know something not only about the Constitution . . . but also about the Bill of Rights."[23] According to Secretary of the Treasury Henry Morgenthau, Jr., who spoke at the ceremony laying the cornerstone of the Poughkeepsie post office, "the president never tired of telling audiences of his kinship with Isaac the ratifier," so that the mural was clearly meant to certify forever the great, great-grandson's deep-rooted allegiance to the American Constitution.[24]

Across New Market Street from the new post office, Merrit C. Speidel, owner and publisher of a newspaper chain that included the *Poughkeepsie New Yorker* and *Eagle-News* asked for Roosevelt's advice on plans for a new building to house his city papers. The "News Cathedral" was built between 1941 and 1943 in a colonial design with a "modified Independence Hall tower" and constructed, through Roosevelt's influence, of fieldstone "acquired from the meadows, stone fences, and quarries of the county."[25]

The two imposing buildings were sited at the north end of New Market Street, which had been opened between 1916 and 1928 by the Sague Realty Company headed by James E. Sague. As Speidel's news building was situated on the southeast corner of Mansion and New Market, FDR suggested that a third civic structure be built opposite it on the southwest corner to complete the effect of a plaza. His call for a new city hall on that corner in 1941 would not be heeded for two decades, and then it would be built in a contrasting modernist style. Roosevelt's plan for historical and civic coherence would be broken, yet the symbolic power of the structures built under his influence remains.

## FDR AND CONSERVATION

Dutch Colonial fieldstone architecture was not the only cultural landscape legacy of Franklin Roosevelt in the Hudson valley. FDR was a farmer and conservationist as well as a political figure. In his first term in Albany in 1911–1912, as a state senator representing Dutchess County, he was selected as chairman of the Forest, Fish and Game Committee, and in his second term he chaired the Agriculture Committee. He was an ardent supporter of open-space management and forestry on his estate in Hyde Park. In 1911, he had his farm crew clear overgrown farmland at Springwood and the following year planted thousands of white pine, red pine, Scotch pine, and Norway spruce seedlings that he got from the New York State Conservation Commission. He ordered and planted close to one-half million trees on his property throughout his life. Roosevelt worked with professional foresters from the College of Forestry at Syracuse to plan his tree-planting efforts. After the chestnut blight moved up the Hudson valley, Roosevelt attempted experiments to reintroduce the chestnut with Asiatic species in 1937. As president, FDR's interest in forestry became an important part of the work of the Civilian Conservation Corps in the national park system.

Even while busy as president of the United States, he continued to support ecological surveys and historical research in the Hudson valley. In a letter to historian and friend Helen Wilkinson Reynolds in 1937, he wrote of his support for the survey work of Vassar College Professor Edith Adelaide Roberts on the botanical resources of Dutchess County, and added some historical landscape comments of his own:

> I am glad Miss Roberts is doing the ecological survey. Does she know the story about the two fields in front of our house? There are still three or four very old white oaks and when I was a boy there were about eight of them. From the rings we counted when they fell down we figured that they dated to about the year 1650. In other words, they attained large sizes before the white man bought the land. They grew up as field trees because they spread out from the bottom without hindrance from other trees. This is definite proof that these fields between the house and road were not forestland between 1650 and 1725. The final deduction is that they must have been fields cultivated by the Indians—otherwise there would have been a forest growth all over them.
>
> To prove the conclusion, we have found on several occasions Indian bone needles and arrowheads in these fields. As you know, the field at the foot of the hill at Ellie's place—Vly—was also an Indian site. I hope Miss Roberts knows the reference in "de Chastellux Travels." He speaks of the ridges between the Connecticut line and Fishkill and mentions one ridge completely covered by "tulipiers"—in other words, tulip poplars. Another ridge was white pine, another ridge oak.

It might be worthwhile to try to dig into early Beekman and Livingston letters. They may show the location of the white pine forest the Palatines were brought over to cut down.[26]

During the 1930s, many local efforts in soil, water, and forest conservation were undertaken by both public agencies and private property owners. Trees from the county were planted on the grounds of the New York World's Fair in 1939, and many remained to landscape the 1,200-acre park that followed the exposition. Mostly these conservation efforts did not provoke controversy, nor did the facilitation of auto transportation through road and bridge improvements, except for questions of siting and priority in funding. FDR's contributions to both remain important and appreciated parts of his legacy, but they did not change the lack of support for his leadership and his New Deal among a majority of county voters.

Resentment against New Deal encroachments on what leading businessmen regarded as their prerogatives and freedoms could be especially sharp. After Roosevelt's death in 1945, Hyde Park was proposed as a permanent site for the United Nations. However, Republican opposition to memorializing FDR, even though it might have strongly influenced economic development in the region, was both national and local "on account of the Roosevelt association."[27] Even a decade later, when a young teacher, new to Poughkeepsie in the 1950s, mentioned to a prominent local guest that he and his wife had visited the Roosevelt home in Hyde Park, the guest retorted that he would never set foot in that man's house.

# EIGHT

# Business and Labor in the 1920s and 1930s

ADJUSTING TO THE changing numbers and influence of successive immigrant groups and to the recent increase in local activity by the federal government under FDR were ongoing challenges for the city's largely native-born white Protestant business leaders. So was their continuous preoccupation with economic growth.

## MAIN STREET RETAIL

The "Queen City" had long been a major retailing center for the region, and that importance grew after 1900 as the city outpaced Kingston and Newburgh. The city's leading department store, Luckey, Platt & Company, grew steadily, adding new departments, floor space, and staff and becoming ever more ambitious in its advertising outreach. Milestones implanted throughout the county marked the distance to the store that by 1903 exhibited at the county fair. Annual harvest and anniversary sales followed, preceded by a wide distribution of circulars. Expanding through multiple buildings near the corner of Academy and Main, the store increased its workforce from 46 men in 1886 to 125 men and women in 1906, and 250 in 1919. By that date, women composed fifteen, or nearly half, of the thirty-two department managers. But the presumption that male judgment and camaraderie mattered most for the store's overall success no doubt accounts for the creation in 1917 of an all-male advisory board to discuss problems and challenges.

By that date, the Wallace department store—started in 1916 by outside investors—had become a well-established competitor on the opposite side of Main Street. The two shopping giants served as a magnet, drawing customers to the heart of the central business district where they could also find a host of smaller merchants and some medium-sized shops; in the 1920s, an increasing number of these were owned by immigrant Jews, often former peddlers,

or their children. One of the earliest success stories was clothing merchant
Mark Shwartz. A Prussian Jew who came to Poughkeepsie in the 1860s, he
preceded the great East European influx at the turn of the century and already
employed a workforce of sixty immigrant tailors by 1880.

Among the many smaller businesses, the larger among them, such as wholesalers, tended to have longer lives. Overall, however, a majority of firms in
Poughkeepsie would fold within three years, a precariousness that did not change
between the nineteenth and the early twentieth centuries. The poor prospects for
survival frequently reflected a lack of acquaintance with the line of business being
undertaken. Tracing Poughkeepsie businessmen through city directories from
1936 to 1956 showed that the previous occupations of 62 percent of all proprietors were unrelated to their enterprises.[1] Two exceptions to this lack of continuity were owners of meat markets, one-third of whom had previously been butchers, and tobacconists, one-fourth of whom had been cigar makers.

The most common forms of small retailing not only required little capital to start but also could be opened in the same bulding that housed the shop
owner's family. The percentages of shops and homes under one roof were 42
percent of all cigar stores, 54 percent of groceries, 58 percent of confectionar-
ies, and 86 percent of saloons. One could easily get a drink close by in many
of the city's residential neighborhoods. Meat markets, with their problems of
spoilage and less attractive waste and odors, were the great exception among
small businesses in Poughkeepsie—the vast majority were located in buildings
other than their owners' residences.

## A FAMILY FIRM GROWS

Some small retailing ventures survived for decades, growing gradually over
time to become middle-sized enterprises, sometimes turning to wholesaling,
and extending beyond local customers to regional markets. Where a Luckey,
Platt drew shoppers from the surrounding region to downtown Poughkeepsie,
a Fitchett's Dairy began by taking their milk directly to the homes of their
customers in a few neighborhoods. The Fitchett family had been engaged in
farming locally since the 1740s. Before long, so many families with that name
lived along Cream Street that that lane became known as Fitchetts' Alley.
When the farmland ran out, family members moved into a variety of jobs in
plumbing, upholstery, fancy goods, and cabinetmaking, with some becoming
railroad workers, telegraph operators, and livery stablemen.

In 1904, Edwin B. Fitchett and his brother, John, bought a milk route
that served the area around Mount Carmel church, a good place to start, given
the physical proximity and the loyalty of the immigrant customers there.
Horse and wagon delivery limited the region one could cover because the
horse could only go so far and the wagon only carry so much. The route purchased required delivering 250 quarts a day to 150 customers. Edwin's work-

day the first winter began with getting up half an hour after midnight, having breakfast, loading his sleigh, and starting the route about 1:30 A.M., usually finishing it around 1:30 P.M. Like other milkmen, he carried 40-quart cans, using large dippers to transfer milk to the 10-quart cans he carried to customers' doors, then using a pint dipper to pour the desired amount into the customer's pitcher or pail.

Milk had sold for 6 cents a quart in 1904 with no licenses, inspection, or pasteurization; customers knew they couldn't count on the milk remaining unspoiled overnight. To prevent spoilage in the summer, ice was put between the cans. To prevent freezing on winter mornings, a lantern was put between the big cans and covered with a blanket. When city snowplows piled so much snow that only the city trolley tracks remained cleared, the milk wagon often got stuck in the tracks, leading motormen to clang their bells furiously at this obstacle to their progress. Kids throwing snowballs at the horses sometimes upset them enough to make them bolt; on a downhill slope that could result in a shattered wagon and milk cans rolling every which way. This was a far cry from the orderliness of a department store.

In the 1920s, the Fitchetts expanded by purchasing two farms on either side of Bedell Road, keeping 350 head of cattle by the 1940s. In the 1930s, now with eight routes, they began adding some trucks, but the last horse was not retired from delivery until 1946. By then, a new plant, with stainless steel equipment, pasteurized and bottled the raw milk so that "it is never touched or exposed to air."[2] The family atmosphere remained; Edwin, Jr. and his wife Bernice continued to live in a house adjacent to the new processing plant and the parking area, chatting with the drivers when they came in from their local routes. But that kind of intimacy would become limited by Fitchett's success; by the 1960s, two decades before its demise, the company had acquired sixty-five routes in the Hudson valley as far down as Westchester county. Fitchett's had shown how one small family retail business could grow to regional importance as producer, retailer, and wholesaler in less than three-quarters of a century. Trucking made the expansion of local into regional businesses easier, increasing connections throughout the Hudson valley.

## ATTRACTING NEW INDUSTRIES
## AND ECONOMIC GROWTH

By the early twentieth century, retailers and wholesalers arose or settled in Poughkeepsie without inducements. But in a diversified local manufacturing economy where important employers disappeared from time to time, hope sprang eternal that new industries could be induced to relocate in the city. The glass factory and cream separator maker had done that at the end of the nineteenth century when the city lost longtime employers like the dyewood mill, iron furnaces, and the Vassar brewery.

Since the 1870s, a Board of Trade composed of local businessmen sought to encourage new startups or relocation of businesses to their city. However, the only major permanent addition to industry in the 1890s was the attraction of Sweden's De Laval Separator Company through a subsidy for site purchase from the Board of Trade. By the early 1900s, an aging board remained ready to provide information on possible sites, transportation, and taxes for potential newcomers. But, lacking even a paid secretary despite its 150 members, the board was not aggressively seeking them. To overcome this passivity, six young businessmen in 1906 organized an alternative, the Chamber of Commerce, merging it with the Retail Merchants' Association. The Chamber moved quickly to create a $50,000 guaranty fund to provide up to $10,000 in a given year for efforts to attract new industries and persuade others to relocate to Poughkeepsie. The Chamber emphasized the new jobs added and the increased consumer purchasing power benefiting local retailers. Before that fund reached its intended level, they solicited money directly for their campaign to induce the Seneca Button Company to relocate from upstate New York. With that campaign's success, according to a 1911 article in *The American City*, "people began to see that it was worth while putting up money for industrial development."[3]

By that year, the Chamber had reached a membership of 450 and had fully subscribed the guaranty fund. The Chamber's paid secretary proudly noted that its "board members take time off from their companies to go investigate new prospects. A dozen or more [firms] with a payroll of more than $1 million have been attracted,"[4] including an American branch of the Fiat Automobile Co. from Turin, Italy, Schatz Manufacturing Co. making hardware specialties from Chappaqua, New York, the Delapenha canning factory from Jersey City, and the American Mineral Wood Co. from Switzerland. Four New York City firms set up Poughkeepsie plants manufacturing cigars, shirtwaists, ledgers, and portable bungalows. Fiat, Schatz, and Delapenha chose locations in the *town* of Poughkeepse rather than in the city, showing that the tendency for manufacturing to migrate to suburban locations preceded by at least three decades IBM's choice of the town in 1941. Indeed, IBM began by purchasing the Delapenha's site and factory buildings.

While diversification continued to characterize the city's industries, the largest employers in the second decade of the twentieth century concentrated in the manufacture of agricultural machinery, garments, and glass. Five of these firms accounted for 2,200 workers, well over a third of them women continuing the growth of female factory employment since the 1870s. That growth, especially in the expanding local garment industry, had become an important concern of the Women's City and County Club. Local manufacture of garments would decline, but the increase of women in the labor force would continue.

The two largest factories in the early twentieth century, Adriance Platt Mower and Reaper Works and De Laval Separator Company, each employed five hundred men. The sixth largest factory was a local success story. A confectionery founded by a Scottish immigrant in the 1850s had spawned Smith Brothers Cough Drops that employed two hundred workers in 1911, many of them women. The brothers gained national celebrity by appearing as Trade and Mark on the cough drop boxes.

Poughkeepsie continued to have a wide variety of manufacturers employing fewer than one hundred workers, making everything from cigars and ball bearings to chairs. Chair manufacturing once had employed a good many women, especially in caning seats. The industry persisted on a small scale, but the Kaal Rock chair factory hired skilled men. A few of the once numerous small artisan shops doing custom work remained, but in trades like shoemaking they disappeared or turned to repairing, just as the carriage and wagon shops turned to repairing bicycles and automobiles. Small firms dominated residential and commercial construction that was the city's second largest industry after agricultural machinery. In short, the Poughkeepsie area never came close to the specialization in one or a few industries like upstate Troy in iron foundries and stoves and Cohoes in collar making.

## WORKPLACE CONDITIONS

Segregation of the sexes remained the rule in local workplaces, all male in machine-making, all female in garments, except for male foremen and supervisors. By the 1880s, in Poughkeepsie as in other northeastern cities, new ready-made clothing factories began to hire hundreds of women. As early as 1910, the federal census showed 15 percent of all locally employed women working as sewing machine operators in factories. By that date, second- or third-generation native women of Irish or German descent generally preferred factory employment to domestic service. Since 43 percent of the city's 27,936 inhabitants then were classified as foreign stock (foreign-born or foreign parentage), these relative newcomers constituted a large part of the labor force.

Contemporary accounts stress the respectability and wholesome conditions provided by the largest employers for women. Dutchess Manufacturing, which produced trousers guaranteed to last—or else reimbursement at "Ten Cents a Button, a Dollar a Rip"—offered not only light and airy workrooms but also a circulating library and a piano on the factory floor where they "sometimes have dances and receptions."[5] By contrast, a 1911 account of Adriance Platt's Buckeye mower and reaper works emphasized plant noise: the pounding of trip hammers, swish of blacksmiths' forges, hum of machines, and whistling of compressed air released by lifting devices.

What most contemporary accounts of local manufacturing did not note were the low pay, long hours, and little time off in many workplaces. In 1904, 59 percent of Poughkeepsie's employees worked ten-hour days, six days a week, a common workweek in industrial America then. By 1913, the workday had been reduced to nine hours, but workers still had only Sunday free. One report by Florence Brewer in 1911 on the kinds of work open to women in Poughkeepsie mentioned some of the problems they should expect. Brewer described sales jobs as hard and poorly paid, work in steam laundries as too difficult and hot for women under twenty-five, and stenography as a crowded field. Factory sewing machine operation frequently created troubles with eyes, and packing in a biscuit factory required constant standing with no prospect of advancement. Brewer found waitresses poorly paid in smaller restaurants, but treated much better at the Hudson River state psychiatric center.

## LABOR CONFLICT AND ORGANIZATION

The limited and fluctuating growth of labor organization in the Poughkeepsie area before 1900 handicapped attempts at winning concessions from employers. The Knights of Labor had organized four local assemblies in the 1880s, all of them small, one composed of bottle blowers at the glass factory and another with mixed membership. But reports from these locals ended by 1891. Unionization was most continuous in the building trades among carpenters, bricklayers, and plasterers, although a protective association for mutual insurance among glassblowers appears in the mid-1890s.

The end of the national economic depression after 1897 put workers in a better bargaining position with employers. More aggressive national leadership for unionization in the crafts by the American Federation of Labor favored an upsurge in unionism. The *Poughkeepsie Eagle* reported in 1903 that the city's teamsters "are perfecting an organization and are planning on demanding higher wages and shorter hours."[6] In March of that year, the newspaper noted a big victory for unionization in its own industry. By contrast, only five of the city's bakers complied with the demands of the Journeymen Bakers' Union, leading the union to consider a boycott. And local cigar makers worried about [John] Schwartz and Sons' cigar stores that were selling cigars made by the American Tobacco Company, an employer of nonunion workers.

By 1910, however, Poughkeepsie had a Trade and Labor Council representing unions of bakers, barbers, bartenders, brewery workers, cigar makers, electrical workers, glassblowers, iron and steel workers, machinists, molders, stone cutters, tailors, tin and sheet metal workers, and typographers. Other labor organizations included a structural trades' alliance, steam engineers and team owners' associations, and the Women's Label League. In this changed environment, conflict with even the largest employers became more likely, although sustained collective action across trades was rare given Poughkeepsie's highly diversified manufacturing. The speaker at a Labor Day program in 1903 recalled the history of the ongoing "troubles" that began when De Laval Separator locked out its workers in May. The company claimed it had closed to make improvements, but then conducted no repairs. In partial resumption on July 10, "membership in a union barred men from employment."[7]

Joint committees of the Machinists, Metal Mechanics and Machinery Painters endeavored unsuccessfully to adjust the "trouble." The national officers of the unions likewise failed, as did "Hon. John I. Platt and M. Shwartz, one of Poughkeepsie's heaviest taxpayers and most prominent business men. [Shwartz] was instrumental in raising the last of the $10,000 which was donated by our citizens to bring [De Laval] here. . . . Possessed of naught but the $10,000 donated for the land which [the company] afterwards mortgaged for $7,000, against the protests of the contributors, the company started with about 40 men and no credit." Yet when local merchants petitioned the company for arbitration of the dispute, De Laval refused. Describing the company's response as "snarling," the Labor Day program speaker commented: "To-day Bradstreet rates them as a millionaire concern, unlimited credit, and at the time of the lockout employing between five and six hundred men. . . . The immense profits from the labor of their men, apparently instilled a desire for greater returns by reducing wages."[8]

On July 10, 1903, the day that De Laval ended the lockout, the company announced abolition of time-and-a-half for overtime and reduction of prices on piecework. One job that had paid thirteen and one-half cents a piece now paid seven and one-quarter cents. The employees then went out on strike not for union recognition but "simply to preserve existing conditions." De Laval replaced them with strikebreakers, many of them from places other than Poughkeepsie. The company also was "blacklisting those whose committee work forced prominence upon them. Former employees have been trailed to Walden, Waterbury, Matteawan, and Schenectady, and attempts made to deprive them of a livelihood even outside of Poughkeepsie."[9]

Blacklisting dramatically resurfaced as an issue in January 1927 when former Mayor John K. Sague went before Judge Morschauser to make a formal complaint charging a conspiracy to blacklist by the local Manufacturers' Association, then composed of seventeen firms. A grand jury was convened to investigate the charge. Sague gave names of witnesses to the district attorney and went before the jury himself. Among the witnesses called were a representative of De Laval and the employment agent for the Schatz Manufacturing Co. As the *Eagle* noted, the "history of the blacklist goes back many years."[10]

One newspaper, *The Truth*, claimed that the employers' association's "list" of workers was used extensively by a few manufacturers to prevent a discharged worker "from securing employment in another factory hence must move from the city. It is particularly severe in the cases of workers who desire to obtain better wages or who talk of joining a trade union. It is effective in maintaining the 'open shop' policy of certain hard-boiled manufacturers here."[11] The grand jury concluded that there was insufficient evidence of conspiracy in the preceding two years, necessary for an indictment given the

statute of limitations. But the jury criticized the past actions of the Manufacturers' Association, noting that its secretary had made some notations on the
character, disposition, and affiliations on its list of local employees.

During the same year, Sague organized a Poughkeepsie Industrial League
to recruit new companies to fill the city's vacant factories, then numbering ten,
including the giant works of Moline Plow (formerly Buckeye). Sague evi-
dently felt the need for an alternative to the Chamber of Commerce for this
purpose. He claimed that the league's "negotiations had reached an advanced
stage in regard to at least two large companies. . . . Applications have been
made for the Fiat plant"[12] by an unnamed factory making a nationally advertised product and employing more than five hundred skilled mechanics on a
high wage scale. Sague's claims attracted small financial contributions to the
league from local merchants and some unions.

## A LOW-WAGE TOWN

The Poughkeepsie business community's preoccupation with attracting
investors and customers largely shaped public views of labor and struggles for
higher wages. Local advocates of municipal reform and cleanups like Professor Salmon turned generally to business organizations like the Chamber
rather than to unions for support. The *Eagle* worried editorially about their
impact on "the high cost of living."[13] Yet Poughkeepsie's wage standards
remained low in both retailing and manufacturing during the 1920s and
1930s. The city's success in luring new businesses did not improve the level of
wages. Indeed, there is reason to believe that some companies may have relocated in Poughkeepsie because it afforded cheaper labor costs. In 1919, a year
of widespread labor organizing and strikes elsewhere, the *Sunday Courier*
described it as an open shop city. Tension between employers and workers
might be high at times in the "Queen City," but it less often erupted in public struggles.

In the late 1920s, unions deemed the city a "scab town" where some clothing manufacturers relocated, as they did to other small cities, "to avoid the ever
growing strength of the unions in New York City."[14] The contrast with the
metropolis can be seen in the annual report of the New York State Bureau of
Labor Statistics in which the Board of Mediation and Arbitration reported its
interventions in strikes and their relative success. In 1909–1911, when the board
intervened in seventy-five or more strikes each year, Poughkeepsie did not
appear at all in two years but had three interventions in 1909 in strikes involving 20 painters, 35 plumbers, and 25 sheet metal workers. Some larger turnouts
appear in subsequent years, such as 200 unsuccessful cigar workers in 1920, 50
plumbers who won a wage increase, and 110 painters currently working elsewhere. Workers in the older and generally stronger building trades unions figure more often in strikes than employees of the city's largest manufacturers.

Mrs. Bessie Harden Payne, a prominent African American, recalled, regretfully, that the Ford Motor Company might have opened a facility in Poughkeepsie, "but the Chamber of Commerce thought Ford's wage standards so high as to make it difficult for other local businesses, so they didn't encourage Ford."[15] A little later this mid-Hudson urban region's combination of low wages and many skilled workers in metal trades was advantageous in World War II for hiring by the most important manufacturing newcomer in the area's history: IBM.

## JOBS FOR YOUNG WOMEN

Women continued to face the handicap of earning lower wages than men received for the same work. But change in the kinds of jobs available made labor outside the home more appealing, especially for young unmarried white women in cities. Since the turn of the century, white-collar work, primarily as office clerks and sales persons, had expanded dramatically and a high school education had become a prerequisite for hiring.

That change benefited from the continuing growth of the high school population with related revision in curriculum and the increasing frequency of female graduation during the same period of time. As late as 1901, Poughkeepsie High School had only three programs for its diploma: English, Latin and Science, and Classical. In 1908, Commercial and Teacher's sequences had been added. In 1922, the Superintendent reported that, just a few years before, everyone thought the function of a high school education was preparation for college, but now they realized that that group of students formed only "a small fraction of our high school population."[16]

By 1933, the first suburban high school, Arlington, included General Bookkeeping, Secretarial, and General Business among its programs. In 1939, a survey of employers for the Board of Education found that only one-fifth of their office and store employees had not graduated from high school. Overall, the dropout rate from high school remained high, with a loss of 56 percent of the class of 1937 that had entered in 1933. But boys dropped out more often than girls.

While a steadily increasing number of young women with high school educations found white-collar jobs, for young women without that educational advantage manufacturing continued to offer better wages and mostly better working conditions than domestic service. Factory work for women, most often as sewing machine operators, had grown faster than the population. The mostly unmarried women who filled these jobs often found the supervision, regulations, work conditions, and the long hours onerous. But the wages they earned gave them a new importance and degree of freedom within many working-class families, not least in reducing parental control over their social lives. Also they did not as frequently face on the job the kinds of personal humiliations experienced by household servants, especially the majority who served families of different ethnic or racial origin than their own. Growing up more accustomed than their parents to American freedoms, the native-born children of immigrant parents found being at a mistress's or master's beck and call demeaning.

The increasing unattractiveness of domestic service coupled with restriction of immigration in the early 1920s meant fewer servants available for many middle- and upper-class homes. Noting that "women of the business class" in Muncie, Indiana in the 1920s had half as much hired help as their mothers had in the 1890s, Robert and Helen Lynd concluded that a major factor "in this diminution of full-time servants [was] the increased opportunities for women to get a living in other kinds of work."[17] The labor force in the nation as in Dutchess County experienced this change in the job opportunities for women with mixed feelings.

## WHAT DID WAGE EARNERS THINK?

Recorded memories of servants or wage earners of any kind in the Poughkeepsie urban region are rare, especially before 1940. We do not know how Poughkeepsie's workers saw their lives during the 1930s or what their perspective on the Depression and on the New Deal programs they encountered was. Bayne, in her *County at Large*, commented, "little is known about working conditions prevalent in local factories." She reported that "the commonly held opinion that workers in this region are not often 'union conscious,'" although by 1937 the Communist Party had recruited effectively "from certain groups of workers."[18]

Bayne added that local unions had not found the National Labor Relations Board helpful. The board did hold a hearing on complaint "that the Federal Bearings Company and the Schatz Manufacturing Company [which employed 700 or more men and women] discharged workers because they joined a national union, and that the owners dominated a local association of employees." Those attending the hearing, she said, "were impressed by the absence of strong allegiance to either organization on the part of the workers questioned."[19]

New employment opportunities in the private sector were limited during the 1930s. A few major new firms did start up in the years of depression. In the greater Beacon area, the Texas Company (Texaco) purchased thirty buildings and houses in 1931 for their research on an old manufacturing site in Glenham. During the Civil War, with the assistance of capital from John Jacob Astor, a factory with six hundred employees made the Union army's blue uniforms, "the Dutchess indigo blue thus becoming a national heritage."[20] Subsequently, a carpet and then a woolen factory occupied the site that beginning in the 1930s would house chemical and physical researchers, with new buildings added for jet-fuel, high pressure, and super-pressure research. By

1956, the Glenham campus, renamed the Texaco Research Center, had 1,150 employees, including 330 graduates of 154 colleges.

In Poughkeepsie, Western Printing Company, began a fifty-year publishing history there in 1934. But, according to economist Mabel Newcomer, "whereas the industrial activity index [nationally] started upward in 1933, the number of Poughkepie enterprises was still declining in 1936."[21] Newcomer believed that the city's relatively stable population during the 1930s discouraged the start-up of new businesses. In contrast, she thought that the rapid increase in population during the 1920s had stimulated too rapid a growth of new firms. Their owners often had insufficient capital and experience in their line of business to survive a major downturn in the economy.

For the native-born children of the turn-of-the-century immigration from southern, central, and eastern Europe who came of age during the 1930s, the Depression meant more limited and often deferred opportunities for upward occupational and economic mobility. This frustration of their hopes for advancement would not begin to diminish until World War II brought about a full-employment economy. As late as 1940, larger cities in New York State reported between 12 percent and 18 percent of male residents seeking work. The proportion of foreign-born males unemployed was slightly higher than the proportion of native-born whites.

For another group of Poughkeepsians, however, the Depression years did not seem much different from the 1920s. African Americans, many of them area residents for generations, had long found employment precarious. Attorney Gaius Bolin, Dr. Robert Morgan, and other leaders of the black community formed a local chapter of the NAACP in 1931. But they did not make much headway in opening up new jobs until the late 1930s and early 1940s. Their appeals to and negotiations with major employers like Hudson River State Hospital finally yielded some openings for African Americans; wartime labor shortage would bring more.

The Depression years did have individual success stories. A young Italian immigrant like Tony di Rosa had struggled for several years with a variety of low-paying jobs like water boy, but had no sense of obstacles to his advancement comparable to the viewpoint of local African Americans. By the end of the Depression, di Rosa had his own coal business. His optimism as a newcomer may have been atypical of young adult males in the early 1930s. But his story reminds us that for those who had not known valley towns during the prosperity of the 1920s as well as for those who did not participate in the prosperity, the Depression might not be seen as much of a loss.

## ORGANIZED LABOR DURING WORLD WAR II

World War II military orders produced the full economic recovery that had eluded New Deal efforts. The home front in Poughkeepsie shared in the national improvement in opportunities for employment and, despite rationing, the improved standard of living. But manufacturers in the valley, like their counterparts elsewhere, worried about the expanded influence of labor unions in the wake of the Wagner Act of 1935 and of CIO organizing drives thereafter, distressing manufacturers. Poughkeepsie and Dutchess County did not see much change until resurgence in employment in 1939. Local organizing and collective bargaining increased in wartime, although the War Labor Board might hold up wage increases trying to avoid inflation.

In 1939, a union calling itself the Bearing Workers of Poughkeepsie distributed handouts urging "Why Should a Worker Belong to a Union" to employees of the Schatz and Federal Bearing companies.[22] By not joining, the handout argued, you harm your fellow workers and help the boss lengthen hours and lower wages and working conditions. But not until April 1942 did these employees, now members of a CIO United Automobile Workers Union, win collective bargaining rights through plant elections. The union proved more cautious in subsequent disputes with Schatz management than the 175 workers who in September 1942 walked out without notice to the company or authorization by the union. They returned to work, but, in a sign of changed times under FDR's New Deal, a labor conciliator from the federal Department of Labor planned a visit.

Another "wildcat" strike followed in 1943, this time initially by women workers insisting they could not live on 43 cents an hour but with 75–90 percent of the workforce joining them the next day. Slow to act, the War Labor Board granted an increase of nearly 9 cents an hour, having shortly before ordered a wage increase for six hundred workers, largely women, in mid-Hudson area dress factories affiliated with the AFL's International Ladies Garment Workers' Union. Employment of women at Schatz received a further stimulus from a visit by General William Knudsen, chairman of production for the War Department, who urged stepped-up production by building up the night shift. The company would be "permitted" to extend the hours for women, as needed.[23] Anticipating loss of female employment in previously male-dominated industries at war's end, Cecile Weiss, of the Cigar Maker's Union, urged that many women wanted to keep their jobs in peacetime.

Meanwhile, the Schatz companies took out full-page newspaper advertisements disputing union claims and lauding their own and other local manufacturers' contributions to the war effort, especially earning Army/Navy E awards for Excellence. Boeing and Ford Motors, big purchasers of Schatz bearings, claimed that the ads had "increased employment, reduced labor turnover, and raised morale" in the plant.[24] Schatz also installed further inducements for workers, including its own "modern" First Aid hospital complete with operating room and also a new athletic field. The company already had baseball, basketball, bowling, and golf teams.

Local labor-management relations changed in other ways. By war's end, Schatz employees voted for a union shop and a big wage increase that President Bennett decried as "outrageous."[25] The union denied that the vote intended an immediate strike, but believed that the vote strengthened the union's bargaining hand. Two Vassar College professors offered to mediate; one of them, Professor of Economics Emily Clark Brown had just mediated between striking members of the CIO Electrical, Radio, and Machine Workers union and Poughkeepsie's Standard Gage Company.

Yet, overall, Poughkeepsie did not have strong unions even in this period of union expansion, although the UAW had organized Schatz since Schatz worked for Ford Motor Company. Jesse Effron recalled some kind of fragile labor organization in the city in the 1940s, but mostly of workmen in the building trades. He thought nobody locally paid much attention to what the National Labor Relations Board decided until the Reverend James Pike, later Bishop of California but then rector of Christ Church, developed a reference book with the board's administrative rulings. Jesse had voted for Henry Wallace and the Progressive Party in 1948 and previously, as an employee of Marshall Field, had tried to organize a union in Chicago. The liberal and the political left community met at the Three Arts, the store Jesse and his wife Leah first opened at 7 Cannon Street, around the corner from Academy, and later moved to Arlington.

The book, music, and art store offered a congenial atmosphere for conversation among political dissenters. Disagreements were out in the open, sometimes startlingly so. Interested in music, young David Aldeborgh, son of the president of Standard Gage that made precision instruments, happened to be in the Three Arts when a union organizer was talking about organizing at Standard Gage. When David mentioned that his father was ailing, the organizer responded, "Nothing trivial I hope."[26]

Nationally, the war years saw unionization advance to its strongest position yet, aided by both ongoing CIO efforts to organize industrial workers outside the AFL's traditional craft orientation and by the Roosevelt administration's concern to do whatever it could to avoid strikes that would interfere with wartime production. That meant an improvement in wages and benefits for those workers who achieved collective bargaining rights that enabled many working-class families for the first time to enjoy benefits more often associated with the middle class like home ownership. But, in the mid-Hudson valley, the greatest stimulus to expansion of the middle and upper middle class would come from the higher wages and salaries paid by a recently arrived nonunion corporation just beginning the expansion that would at its peak make the valley seem like a company town of the benevolent sort.

# NINE

# Depression in FDR's Home County

THE 1930s CAN BE VIEWED as part of the transition nationally and locally to the era of automobile and truck transportation. That transition entailed the development of a network of paved roads, as chapter 7 shows for Dutchess County, giving farmers easier access to towns and markets, integrating the countryside through consolidation of schools, and overcoming the geographic isolation of rural Americans. This view emphasizes the process of modernization that ultimately would transform regions, blurring the differences between urban and rural Americans and creating a common culture of consumption.

A different and more frequent view of the 1930s, concerned with that decade's current troubles rather than with developments leading to a different future, looks at the 1930s as a time of national catastrophe and of only partially successful attempts to end it through Roosevelt's New Deal before World War II. That view focuses on the bitter consequences for so many families of the Great Depression that at its lowest point found one-fourth of the American labor force unemployed. Poughkeepsie, with its diversified economy, seems to have suffered less, but in the city and the valley, as elsewhere in the nation, the needy overwhelmed local provisions for public and private relief. A few of the city's jobless sold apples on street corners rather than resort to begging, but the popular song that seemed to say it all was "Brother, Can You Spare a Dime?"

## THE SPIRAL DOWNWARD

The Depression began with a jolt in the stock market early in September 1929. Then, after an October panic, the economy began its spiral downward in the Hudson valley as in the nation, despite continuing reassurances from those prominent in public life that all would soon be well. That optimism turned out to be whistling in the dark, but many pundits and newspapers kept on whistling.

Like the mostly conservative press throughout the country, Dutchess County's press supplied a steady stream of optimism about an early recovery. It echoed President Hoover's belief that the best cure was for all Americans to "Buy Now." It also shared Hoover's opposition to government efforts to "fix" the economy and saw Franklin D. Roosevelt, New York State's governor after 1928, as a dangerous experimenter. The devoutly Republican *Eagle-News*— still published by the Platt family, including local historian Edmund Platt— caricatured the Democratic donkey walking from his convertible coupe into a ditch labeled Radical Wilderness Trail. The donkey kicked at a road sign pointing toward Recovery that advised "safe leadership, government economy, protected national credit, honest dollar, and employer-worker cooperation."[1]

The Poughkeepsie Chamber of Commerce in its industrial survey of the city in 1930 reported that the city had had comparatively few labor difficulties in recent years. It claimed that the low cost-of-living in Poughkeepsie "enables the workers to maintain higher living standards than large industrial centers where wages are higher."[2] The Chamber estimated the average weekly wage for all classes of labor at $22.50 for a forty-eight-hour week, or a little less than 50 cents an hour. The organization listed ten vacant factories, including those of formerly large employers like Moline Plow (previously the Buckeye Mower and Reaper Works) and the Fiat plant.

Poughkeepsie's Board of Charities had an early foretaste of the hard times ahead, a few weeks after previously surging stock prices on Wall Street began their decline. At its meeting with the Common Council on September 20, 1929, the board's president reported that "the prevalence of unemployment in Poughkeepsie" had exhausted the appropriation for outdoor relief for the needy early in the month.[3] The board would have to ask for an increase in its annual budget of $39,000. The board could not have imagined then that the budget would soar during the deepening Depression to $212,210 by 1932. Nor did the city's leadership, especially its newspapers, anticipate the depth of the unfolding economic crisis.

As winter arrived in 1929, however, county residents focused on immediate problems of survival rather than thoughts of the future. Two days before Christmas, the privately funded Associated Charities reported adding ninety-eight needy families to their list of those eligible for relief. Early in January 1930, bitterly cold weather brought a record number of applicants for overnight lodging at police headquarters. Meanwhile, local merchants called "upon the police for better protection, reflecting an increase of crimes against business as desperation among the poor increased."[4]

When Associated Charities investigators visited homes in the winter of 1930, they found children "without warm clothing, huddled about the stoves [and reported that] babies pinched faces show lack of nourishment, and aged persons, not yet eligible for Old Age Allowances, are discovered trying to eke out an existence."[5] The year 1931 would bring a sharp increase in hospital care paid for by the city's Board of Public Welfare. Then the years 1932 and 1933 would see the highest proportion yet of the city of Poughkeepsie's budget devoted to relief.

## DESPERATE FOR RELIEF

In the winter of 1930–1931, the city discovered how severe the Depression could be. By the end of November 1930, a sudden swing from Indian summer to bitter cold had "precipitated one of the greatest floods of economic distress the city has ever known. . . . Families left destitute by unemployment, their troubles increased by the cold, stormed the Board of Public Welfare, the Associated Charities and the Salvation Army for clothing, food and fuel."[6] The Army gave out fifty-two overcoats and provided meals for hundreds, so many that an officer said, "We're swamped. . . . If it keeps up I don't know what we'll do."[7] The Army also embarked on a luncheon program for schoolchildren that in one month served 3,685 meals.

But most private and public concern focused on creating full-time or part-time jobs for the unemployed, like cutting wood for the Salvation Army's woodpile or working on street repairs for the city. Within a few months, a Citizens' Committee on the Relief of Unemployment fund, raised by local merchants and other citizens, had been largely used up. Repeated calls for further donations yielded nothing, the Eagle-News noted in a story headed "Appeal Falls on Deaf Ears." A separate appeal for Jewish charities evoked letters lamenting the writers' inability to give anything due to their own lack of employment or destitution.

By the day before Christmas 1931, the local American Legion tried a different approach to relief, securing small donations to purchase a box of apples for each of ten needy, jobless legionnaires. The ten men would try to sell their apples at various points around the city. With what they earned, they were expected to buy subsequent boxes of apples themselves. We do not know how helpful these small start-ups to vending were, but Poughkeepsie was only one of many cities where jobless men tried selling apples on street corners. The legion also arranged hiring for an additional forty-eight men; it claimed that another private fundraiser, the Emergency Work Bureau, was too slow in providing jobs, being required by the state to investigate all applicants. The bureau had managed to find work for 153 men so far, but reported that it had 1,736 applicants. Donations and pledges combined had yielded only $19,000 of a projected $40,000.

## THE PUNDITS' OPTIMISM

Throughout the increase in local hardships, the Eagle-News claimed that Poughkeepsie had not suffered as much as other localities. While it did publish some horror stories on Depression-induced suffering and tragedy, these stories mostly took place elsewhere in the nation, suggesting that the editors wished to avoid depressing their readership. The newspaper preferred to publish upbeat forecasts like that of a General Electric Company speaker at a local Rotary Club luncheon in December 1930. He "characterized the present economic situation as merely a dip in the upward surge of prosperity."[8]

The *Eagle-News* agreed with the Episcopalian economist, speaking at Christ Church's annual Service of Lights in December 1931, "that recovery would occur only if [we] restrict government control of the individual." Opposed to government pensions, he contended that Americans need not fear economic difficulty if they "will only emphasize individualism and accept simplicity."[9] On the same day, the newspaper published an unflattering cartoon of "Another Hunger March" on Washington, D.C., just one of many sarcastic cartoons about protesters and would-be reformers. The *Eagle-News* offered its own simple solution to local and national Depression late in 1930: "If everyone would buy normally, the greater part of the present problem would be solved."[10]

The problem was not solved by local efforts, private or public. At the end of 1931, the city of Poughkeepsie had reached its borrowing limit and had to announce a delay in paying old-age pension claims. But by that time New York State, led by then Governor Roosevelt, had stepped in by enacting in 1930 Old Age Security. In 1931, the governor authorized $6 million for work relief under the Temporary Emergency Relief Administration (TERA).

Such initiatives prompted the Dutchess County Taxpayers Association to demand that the county supervisors seek relief from the increasing tax burden. The association's preferred solution, shared by local newspapers and other conservatives, called for cutting government spending, and thus services and jobs, even in this time of deflation. Yet simultaneously they were urging consumers, many of them jobless and without income, to spend more. As an economy measure, the county supervisors rejected needed renovation of the County Court House and municipal employees were asked to give up 10 percent of their pay. While the Chamber of Commerce did not encourage economy measures in the private sector generally, it did propose that local labor unions should accept reduction in workers' wages. In an already notoriously low-wage town, that suggestion had no takers.

Then, late in 1932, the national political landscape changed. An *Eagle-News* headline a week before the presidential vote had President Hoover warning that the "Coming Election Will Decide if Radical Thought Is to Supplant American System."[11] An accompanying cartoon showed FDR steering a car with the help of Louisiana's "Kingfisher" Huey Long and journalist William Randolph Hearst and running head-on into a brick wall. But the gentleman from Hyde Park beat Hoover nationally, if not in his home county of Dutchess.

Dutchess County would never vote for FDR for president. Yet New Deal agencies created by the gentleman from Hyde Park, like the Civilian Conservation Corps (CCC), the Civil Works, Public Works, and Works Projects administrations, would bring numerous improvements in public infrastructure to city, county, and the valley. Sometimes FDR himself or Eleanor Roosevelt were directly involved in the planning. Ironically, given the rejection of "that man" at the polls by a majority of county voters, the Roosevelts' Springwood residence and Eleanor's Val-Kill would be of great benefit in increasing tourism in the region down to the present.

By 1933, with banks closing and local governments and private charities unable to cope with mounting unemployment, a man from Dutchess County—never its favorite son—was about to move from the governor's mansion in Albany to the White House, taking the nation in uncharted directions. New Deal policies and the continuing personal involvement of Franklin and Eleanor Roosevelt with their homes in Hyde Park and the valley they loved would be a long-term boon to the mid-Hudson region. But, in 1933, the pain of economic hardship preoccupied its population.

## FDR'S CIVIL WORKS ADMINISTRATION

Relief programs loomed large among the remarkable array of Roosevelt's legislative initiatives during 1933. By the fall of 1933, FDR launched the Civil

FIGURE 9.1. Franklin D. Roosevelt at Nelson House, 1932

Works Administration (CWA) as a temporary emergency job-creation project to put four million people to work for two and a half months that winter. The CWA's director in Dutchess County estimated that the unemployed there had reached 10,000 persons, a staggering number for a county with a total population, including children, of 105,452. Some 5,000 would receive wages in Dutchess that winter on projects that included the long-hoped-for renovation of the County Court House, improvement of the sewerage system at Bowne hospital, grading of major thoroughfares, building walls along the Fall Kill, and other construction projects for male workers. As a young boy, John Wolf recalled when CCC workers repaired the sidewalks in front of his house, and when his uncle earned $20 a week on a crew that built the walls along the creek. CWA renovated Lincoln Center, the city-owned clubhouse for poor children, and installed a new gymnasium floor. College Hill Park received new storm sewers, improving drainage at the Municipal Golf Course, and 115 laborers made grounds improvements at Hudson River State Psychiatric Hospital.

A variety of service projects employed women as clerks, stenographers, nurses, cooks, teachers, and sewers. The CWA tried to balance jobs fairly among unskilled, skilled, and white-collar and professional workers. But since most of the unemployed were unskilled, most of those hired had to be unskilled. Two handicaps had to be overcome early on: lack of readiness for hard physical labor among men long unemployed and insufficient clothing for winter weather. In the bitterly cold early weeks, men appeared for work on construction gangs in shoes without soles and gloves with fingers missing. Some even showed up just dressed in overalls, without shirts or underwear. Foremen often turned to local welfare committees to help out with clothing.

The CWA's local organizing committee got space rent-free from the Board of Education, office furniture and equipment from local industries, and running expenses from the county supervisors. Vassar College students prepared news releases and other publicity under the direction of Professor Helen Lockwood who taught a course on the American press. Political scientist Dorothy Schaffter organized a public-speaking unit to address business and women's clubs, church organizations, and granges throughout the county. Speakers explained the CWA's functions, emphasizing its temporary character and its anticipated absorption in Public Works Administration (PWA) projects. The politically conservative leadership of the county worried out loud about the possible adverse consequences of this intervention by the federal government for liberty and local independence.

Nationally, the peak of unemployment came in the winter of 1934. Relief rolls in Dutchess lagged behind metropolitan areas because much of the county's rural area suffered less from the layoffs in manufacturing and commerce. New Deal relief programs eased the crisis of unemployment for many urban workers. But for young women and men first entering the labor force in the 1930s, including whites of native parentage, the continuing limitation in job opportunities handicapped their prospects until World War II restored the nation to full employment. More than one-third of the class of 1936 graduates from Beacon High School were unemployed or had left town within the next year.

## "MODERNIZE MAIN STREET"

In an attempt to increase domestic spending and thereby bring the economy out of the Depression, a national project was undertaken through the joint efforts of the building industry, American Institute of Architects, and the federal government to increase sales of merchandise in the shops of the nation's downtowns. A major effort in the 1930s was to update the "image" of the two million businesses on the Main Streets of America. Store facades and interiors were remodeled in modern styles, using new materials to inspire customer interest in the products and designs of the machine age, especially in Art Deco. "Modernize Main Street" became a slogan of business during the 1930s as a way to attract customers. In 1935, the FHA offered loans to local business owners for remodeling, while the building industry instituted a nationwide competition sponsored by the Libbey-Owens-Ford Glass Company and a traveling exhibition of modern storefronts sponsored by the Pittsburgh Plate Glass Company in 1936.[12]

Downtown's commercial architecture throughout the Hudson valley began to modernize. Many of the storefronts along Poughkeepsie's Main Street were remodeled with large plate glass windows over marble bases, with terra cotta and aluminum friezes above. Some added color and excitement with neon signs. The Church Building on the corner of Market and Main was designed in 1931 in the modernist architectural style of Art Deco. The building's mustard-colored stone facade is glazed, with terra cotta moldings around the doorways, and metal trim in a floral motif around the windows that are above a black marble base with bronze trim. Surrounding the doorways are classic Art Deco style multicolored Aztec and Mayan Indian and geometric designs. The building houses a number of small shops at the street level and professional offices on the second floor.

Up along Main Street, the stores and restaurants promoted a diversity of architectural styles and storefronts. Intermingled with the many local businesses were a growing number of chain stores, such as variety and drugstores. Their facades and signage were determined by their companies at the national or district level, but all were eager to attract customers by remodeling and modernizing their stores. As the "Modernize Main Street" program promoted, stores should "attract the public, display goods to the best advantage, and provide space, convenience, and light so that purchasing is a pleasure," especially for the woman as buyer whose "resistance is lowered when she is surrounded by an atmosphere which subtly whets that craving for the beautiful."[13]

FIGURE 9.2. Main Street, 1944

In Poughkeepsie, the diversity of downtown retail included locally owned shops such as Saltford's flower shop and Arax photo, as well as jewelry, footwear, and hardware stores. Apparel and large department stores, such as Luckey, Platt, Up-to-Date, Shwartz & Co., and Wallace's were clustered in the 2–300 block along Main Street, and brought crowds of customers from throughout Dutchess County to Poughkeepsie. National chain stores added to the retail mix. IGA supermarkets was founded in 1926 and opened its first store in Poughkeepsie. One of the first of the chain variety stores in Pough-keepsie was Woolworth's Five and Ten, opened in 1888; the manager was Mary Ann Creighton, sister-in-law of Woolworth, who had the distinction of becoming the first woman store manager in the corporation. The store remained an important destination for shoppers in Poughkeepsie for close to a century.

The Poughkeepsie Woolworth store included a soda fountain and lunch counter, as did many others throughout the country. By 1960, the 1,750 Woolworth stores served over 700,000 food customers daily, and the chain was reputed to be the largest commercial dispenser of food prepared and served on the premises. Sit-in demonstrations during the 1960s at Woolworth lunch counters were significant moments in the civil rights movement. But most important for Main Street, the variety store was a magnet for young and old of all social and economic classes, especially during the hard days of the Depression, and gave life and a bit of fun to the downtown. As recalled by architectural critic Ada Louise Huxtable:

> For millions of young Americans, the climax and greatest joy of every down-town outing had been the trip to the five-and-ten. For the boys it was the lure of unlimited gadgets and hardware counters that displayed every size and shape of shining hooks, nails and screws. For girls it was the clandestinely pur-chased Tangee lipstick and the dazzling array of forbidden costume jewelry.
>
> In the fall, the back-to-school counter supplied the marbleized card-board notebooks and cedar-scented pencils, the snap-ringed loose-leaf binders, and fresh sheaves of paper that signaled the season's start. There were after-school banana splits and tricolored ice cream sandwiches enclosed in square cookie covers with the flavor of pasteboard—a taste that became addictive. The stores smelled of sweet candles and cosmetics and burned toast from the luncheonette counters along the wall; they echoed to the sound of feet on hardwood floors, the ringing of old-fashioned cash regis-ters; and the clanging of bells for change.

FIGURE 9.3. Main Street, 1956

And there was the absolute saturation of the eye with every conceivable knickknack, arranged with a geometric precision based on the sales and aesthetic theory that more is more.[14]

The decline of the five and ten store as a Main Street magnet would symbolize the decline of the economic and social function of downtown. Some chain stores left to reinvent themselves in shopping centers on the edge of town, such as the Kress store in Poughkeepsie, moving from Main Street to become K-Mart at 44-Plaza. Others simply died or morphed into other commercial enterprises such as the Grants building on Main Street to house Pronto Printers, renamed Spectrum Graphics at the end of the century. The Woolworth Syndicate eliminated its five-and-ten variety department completely in the 1990s. As one commentator lamented:

> Customers who had frequented the Woolworth stores, many of them senior citizens who gathered at the lunch counters at noon or later for afternoon coffee, were depressed by the closing announcement. Where else could they go to chat and linger over coffee and doughnuts? Where else could they go to buy bobby pins, clear plastic rain bonnets, cap guns and slingshots for grandchildren. . . . Where else were yards of red-and-white checked plastic (unrolled from large spools) so accessible for table-coverings at a church bazaar or ice-cream social; crepe paper and trimmings for a child's bike in a Fourth of July parade. . . . And all under one roof on Main Street, without walking the long corridors at a mall. To the loyal customers of Main Street's 'Dime Stores,' the final closing announcement sounded like a dirge.[15]

The loss of the Woolworth store and the economic decline of the city would become a familiar story in Poughkeepsie in the latter half of the twentieth century. But, for Poughkeepsians in the decades before and after World War II, shopping on Main Street in a vibrant downtown was a favorite pastime.

## MARKET AND MAIN STREETS

The intersection of Main and Market streets had long served as the center of the city. In 1917, Market Street had been extended north as New Market Street from Main Street to Mansion Street. The Poughkeepsie Hotel, which had stood at the Main and Market intersection since 1886 was razed to make way for this north–south extension of Market Street. For many years, the hotel was an annex to the Nelson House on Market Street, and had had many distinguished guests during its time, such as Lafayette, Henry Clay, Aaron Burr, and Martin Van Buren.

The Nelson House, where Franklin Roosevelt often began his campaigns for political office, stood a half-block south from the Poughkeepsie Hotel on 28 Market Street next to the County Court House. Occupying the site of a hostelry since 1777, the Nelson House was built in 1875 with an annex added around 1930. The hotel hosted many famous guests, including musicians George M. Cohan and Cab Calloway, and served as the summer executive office building for key staff members in FDR's White House when the president was in residence at his home in Hyde Park. For close to a century, the hotel was a major civic center for community events until the main structure was torn down in the early 1960s to make way for the new Dutchess County office building. Part of the hotel, including the annex, remained and was used as a Family Court building until 1996. Vacant since then, it would be slated for demolition for a parking lot for the county office building, although local preservationists questioned the plan.

On the east side of Market Street across from the courthouse and the Nelson House was the Smith Brothers Restaurant. Described in the 1930s as "a landmark in epicurean circles," the restaurant was known for its role in fostering the nationally famous candy and cough drop business of Smith Brothers, Incorporated. Post cards of the era showed the interior of the restaurant, whose "spacious dining room, with its great mirrors and portraits of the Smith brothers, 'Trade' and 'Mark,' preserves an atmosphere of substantial dignity."[16]

Nearby the Smith Brothers Restaurant was the Bardavon Theater. Originally constructed as the Collingwood Opera House in 1869, the theater had become outdated and in 1923 reopened as a "palace" for silent movies and vaudeville. In the 1930s, with the advent of talking pictures, the Bardavon became purely a movie house. Movies were one source of cheap entertainment during the Great Depression. As a survey in 1935–1936 pointed out: "Poughkeepsie and Beacon have their share of commercial entertainment. They have moving picture theaters, bowling alleys, and innumerable road houses and restaurants where one is urged to 'dine and dance, dinner—$1.'"[17] According to long-time theater manager Pete Bergamo, Poughkeepsie had six movie houses that competed with one another: they included the Bardavon, Stratford, State, Rialto, Liberty, and Playhouse in the city and the Juliet in Arlington, in the town.[18]

The Juliet opened as the first movie theater in the area to be built for sound pictures in the midst of the Depression on January 6, 1938. According to the *Poughkeepsie Eagle-News*, "The opening had something of the impressiveness of a metropolitan opening night, as a good share of the 500 guests arrived in formal dress."[19] Planned as a "deluxe neighborhood theatre" to show only first-rate films, and located next to Vassar College, it was constructed with a Gothic Revival facade to emulate the collegiate architectural style. The theater had Art Modern furnishings, and included a "club room" on the second floor for Vassar students. Vassar's president Henry Noble MacCracken gave the name to the theater and was the featured speaker at the opening. However, as the Depression continued, attendance declined and the theater struggled to survive with lower prices and second-rate as well as first-run films. The Juliet remained a movie theater into the 1980s as it became the first twinned theater and the first multiplex in the Poughkeepsie area. Nevertheless, under pressure from the numerous movie theaters that had been built in the more suburban areas, it finally closed in 1990, only to reopen as a café and billiard parlor the next year. It would later be purchased by Vassar College planning to relocate its bookstore off campus.

## PLEASURES IN THE MIDST OF DEPRESSION

As a young boy in the city of Hudson, historian Bernard Weisberger recalled:

> AND thrill of thrills, on week-ends there was vaudeville at one of the local theaters [and sometimes] real actors talking to my Grandpa before my very eyes!!! I've been stage-struck ever since. Saturday night was the busiest night, when the town jumped. . . . Grandma would take me along from brightly lit and crowded store to store, stopping for what I found interminable social conversations with friends out on similar errands.[20]

Movies loomed large for both kids and families. Hudson had five film houses in the 1930s for a population of 12,000, with eighteen films running during a week. Three of the houses charged a dime for admission to a small auditorium, probably a converted ground-floor store, with uncushioned wood seats. Late in the Depression, the most expensive theater, charging a quarter, competed for families by offering giveaways "like free dishes, one piece per attendance, so that you could build place settings gradually by being a frequent moviegoer." The great attraction for kids was the adventure films: "cowboys, darkest Africa, World War I flying aces. . . ."

But mostly the kids spent leisure time

> playing tag, hide-and-seek, and other unorganized games in the park or in any open space we could find. . . . We really did a lot of making up of our own games. We acted out movies we had seen, and once, I recall, there were trenches dug in courthouse park to lay some pipes. Ah, ha! We could do trench warfare just like the movies. . . . You're rarely out of sight of someone who knows you. Of course that can be a pain in the butt, too, but not really when you're nine to thirteen years old. We also peeked into the shadows of a local pool hall (off limits) and sometimes sat around in one of the local barber shops, reading the free magazines. . . .
>
> Odd as it sounds, one of our favorite things was to wander down to the DEE-POE and watch trains come in and leave; several a day. . . . Once you were down in that locale you could play in the park on Promenade Hill, which overlooked the river. You could spend a lot of time just watching traffic on the river AND, best of all, at 4:30 every day you could see the Hudson River Day Line steamer en route to Albany pull in to discharge

and take on passengers. . . . We weren't exactly like Mark Twain's boyhood pals who yearned to be steamboat pilots, but it was exciting to watch those big side wheelers.

Sailing and boating on the Hudson River have been important recreational activities since the beginning of settlement of the river towns. Both the Poughkeepsie Yacht Club and the Pirate Canoe Club had their clubhouses on the city waterfront at Kaal Rock from the 1890s, only to be forced to move during urban renewal efforts along the waterfront in the 1960s. Poughkeepsie became famous for hosting the national intercollegiate regatta. Beginning in the late nineteenth century and continuing throughout the 1920s and 1930s, the races became so popular that tens of thousands of visitors crowded along the Poughkeepsie and Highland shorelines to watch, and gamble, at the annual events.

Poughkeepsie businessmen encouraged recreational activities like the regatta that would draw attention to the city. For example, the Board of Trade, the Retail Merchants' Association, the Apokeepsing Boat Club, and the Poughkeepsie Yacht Club made up a finance committee to seek funding for races that attracted a crowd estimated at thirty thousand in 1895 with lots of spending for accommodations, food, and entertainment. The ground around Highland Station looked like a country fair with popcorn, fruits, programs of the race, flags, canes, chewing gum, and "all the little delicacies that country folk invest in at these fairs."[21] Besides vendors, you could count on shell game operators, swindlers, and pickpockets. At the opposite social extreme, some of the estate owners along the river gladly entertained the Ivy League scullers and other appropriate visitors.

Bets could be placed with bookmakers at betting centers in Poughkeepsie, with the Nelson House even providing safe storage for the money bet. College-aged spectators "jammed the Nelson House, the Morgan House, and every available boarding house."[22] The 1896 Regatta Ball at the Collingwood Opera House featured an eighteen-piece orchestra and M. Shwartz's clothing store won the contest for the best decorations and display. For the races themselves, farm wagons mingled with carriages along the shores, and private vessels, excursion steamers, and barges with fitted grandstands filled the river near the stretch.

The regatta continued to draw visitors to Poughkeepsie throughout the early twentieth century. Even during the Depression, in June 1939, more than 75,000 spectators saw the University of California Golden Bears varsity beat the University of Washington Huskies in a record time over the 4-mile course from Krum Elbow on the Hyde Park and town of Poughkeepsie shoreline south to finish under the railroad bridge at Poughkeepsie. The Navy crew, winners the previous year, was third, followed by boats from Cornell, Syracuse, Wisconsin, and Columbia. Many of the spectators followed the boats by riding on railroad flatcars along the west bank, while others crowded onto boats and ships, including a U.S. destroyer in the river. After the races, many in the crowd attended parties and banquets throughout the city, and filled the hundreds of rooms in local hotels. During and after World War II, interest in the regatta declined and as the river became more polluted, the national races ended in 1949.

## RECREATION, SOCIAL CLASS, AND RACE

Other recreational activities in the 1930s included baseball and football games at public parks and social activities at local clubs, such as the Elks, Knights of Columbus, Germania Singing Society, and the Progressive Lodge of the Sons of Italy. Programs at the YMCA for approximately 1,500 young men and boys and at the YWCA for about 2,000 girls and young women included swimming, skating, tennis, and games in each of the gymnasia. Most of the Y's members came from the southeastern, or middle-class, parts of Poughkeepsie, while the youth of the southwestern section of the city, especially in the tenement houses along the riverfront, attended programs at the Lincoln Center settlement house. Mixing of socioeconomic classes, however, continued in a number of venues, especially at ball games and at Woodcliff Park.

Woodcliff Amusement Park was opened in the late 1920s and became a favorite venue for recreational activities throughout the Depression years. The park was built on the former grounds of John F. Winslow's estate just north of the city border on the Hudson River. Winslow had amassed his fortune with an iron manufacturing company in the nineteenth century that, among other items, had made the iron sides for the Union's *Monitor* naval vessel during the Civil War.

The park contained an Olympic-sized swimming pool, picnic tables, and food stands, among other facilities. The most remarkable structure was the "Blue Streak" coaster. The park's roller coaster was noteworthy as the highest ever built in America. Variously described as 120 feet or 138 feet high and 3,200 feet long, it was designed by Vernon Keenen who also had created the "Cyclone" at Coney Island. Poughkeepsie residents took a trolley to the park, while other visitors came from as far as New York City on steamboats up the Hudson River for summer outings.

Social mixing did not occur, however, without occasional incidents. In August 1941, three thousand African American excursionists disembarked from the steamer *State of Delaware* at the Woodcliff dock for an outing. Although they had thought that they had reserved a picnic area prior to their trip, unfortunately, more than one thousand local Polish parishioners from the St. Joseph's church club had already taken most of the tables and claimed that they had already rented the inn for the day. The ensuing dispute resulted in chaos and violence.

The *Poughkeepsie Eagle-News* headlined the incident as a "riot." "Hurling rocks and bottles and brandishing knives and a hatchet, rioting New York Negroes yesterday afternoon caused extensive damage to buildings at Wood-cliff Amusement Park, smashed windows and windshields of police cars and menaced scores of picnickers at the amusement place," ran the first sentence of the front-page story.[23] The report continued: "State police in Dutchess county, attaches of the sheriff's office and 22 city policemen rushed to the park in response to riot calls sent out over the teletype and radio systems. For more than half an hour they battled enraged crowds." The news reports detailed many incidents of individual policemen or sheriff's deputies involved in the melee. In one, Deputy Sheriff Quinlan had his nightstick "yanked from his hands by a group of colored women." Two decades later, Quinlan would become county sheriff and authorize a raid on Timothy Leary's retreat in Millbrook that brought national attention to the county.

Racial incidents were not uncommon during the Depression, even in the North, and even at recreational sites. The 1941 incident was not the first to occur at Woodcliff Amusement Park. Commenting on the August 1941 "riot," Sheriff Close "recalled that a minor outbreak of trouble resulted about a month ago," according to the newspaper, "when about 3,000 New York Negroes arrived at the park and hurled stones after they claimed they were refused admission to the swimming pool."[24] Segregation remained in other venues in the city as well, as actors and musicians toured but were refused entrance to some restaurants or hotels. By 1944, the park had closed and the city debated adding it as a public park, but funds were later used to upgrade Pulaski Park's swimming pool.

The population of Poughkeepsie and Dutchess County was not unusual in its attempts to live through the Depression. Times were difficult for most, yet the ownership of automobiles by the more well-off increased social and spatial separation. New urban neighborhoods with more spacious lots and housing, in areas such as the south side, and the development of suburban districts in Arlington and Red Oaks Mills, presaged increasing suburbanization during the war years of the 1940s and the postwar 1950s.

## CHANGE IN THE RIVER ESTATES

Even before the New Deal inheritance tax of 1935 made it costly for owners of the great Hudson River estates to pass them along to their heirs, staffing such extensive houses and grounds had become less easy. At one time, the superintendent of the Frederick W. Vanderbilt estate in Hyde Park directed more than sixty full-time employees. Seventeen worked in the house, two in the pavilion, and forty-four on the grounds and the farm. Maintaining the lawns and gardens occupied thirteen of them. The staff had to be expanded when guests stayed at the pavilion, bringing in more maids and cooks from Hyde Park village.

Mrs. Vanderbilt's niece inherited the estate in 1938 and chose, with urging from FDR, to donate the property to the federal government. By that time, a number of the riverside estates had passed into religious, charitable, or government hands. The Children's Aid Society had received the Bowdoin estate south of Poughkeepsie as a bequest in the 1920s; in the 1960s it would become a park for the general public.

In 1937, Gladys Mills Phipps donated Staatsburgh in Hyde Park (more often referred to as the Mills Mansion) to New York State to be used as a museum. The then powerful planner Robert Moses, learning of her uncertainty about what to do with this large and largely staffed property, had suggested this donation. Gladys had received the estate from her mother, Ruth Livingston Mills, but Gladys already had three houses at Newport, Palm Beach, and Long Island and did not want a fourth. So, in the mid-1930s, she asked each of her children whether they wished to inherit Staatsburgh. All said no, with her daughter Sonia explaining "that they no longer lived like that."[25] In the mansion's heyday early in the century, emulating English aristocracy, the butler reigned over a large staff. The housekeeper had more than ten parlor and chambermaids. The chef had an assistant cook, pastry chef, and several scullery maids. Six footmen also served as waiters. Coachmen, grooms, maintenance men, and grounds crew staffed the working farm.

As some of the self-styled landed gentry of the valley passed from the scene, they left behind individuals and families who had worked for them. These former servitors could be found along the Hudson south of Poughkeepsie and in Hyde Park, Staatsburg, Rhinebeck, Tivoli, and Barrytown. Whatever their memories of life in the great houses, they often faced diminished prospects for their immediate futures. At least one Vanderbilt servant, employed as a guide for the new national monument, relished detailing his former employers' paternalism toward the villagers of Hyde Park. He observed that Mrs. Vanderbilt occasionally made gifts of her own clothing to village women who had admired it.

In 1937, Martha Bayne wrote that estate "owners have been generous in these villages, and have given libraries, schools, and community centers, and contributed to churches. They now feel responsible for the welfare of their employees, and even continue some farming on their land, in order to provide for their old retainers." But Bayne saw this local aristocracy as largely cut off from life in the county, with "little social unity with their farmer neighbors."[26]

Those rural neighbors often did not share even the household conveniences available to many urban working-class families. While eight of every ten farms had radios, fifteen of every one hundred farm families in a large Dutchess County sample still depended on an outdoor pump for water, kerosene for lighting, a cold cellar for refrigeration, and an outhouse for sanitation. Most now owned automobiles and those near enough did their Saturday shopping in Poughkeepsie. However, Bayne reported, "they mourn the passing of neighborhood gatherings and resent losing their small local schools and stores."[27] The lesser availability of urban employment during the Depression also meant that many farm children did not move to larger towns and cities as so many had previously. Even high school graduates remained at home.

The Depression exaggerated hardships that had long been the lot of many rural residents in the valley, especially those who still pursued farming or had farmed previously. Agricultural expansion in Dutchess had reached its peak in 1880 with 95 percent of county land in farms. By then, dairying had long since displaced the earlier dominance of wheat and cattle as exports. And whereas most farms had been self-sufficient as late as the 1830s, that capacity had largely disappeared by 1880, evident in the sharp reduction in numbers of sheep and hogs. Farm acreage and prices declined steadily over the next half-century. By the 1930s, 30 percent of former farmland had been put to other uses, and Dutchess dairy farmers suffered from competition from upstate dairy farmers able to pay their farm labor 20 percent less. The refrigerated truck revolution had begun disrupting dairying just as western competition unleashed by the Erie Canal had disrupted wheat farming one hundred years earlier. Bulk tanks for milk would be introduced in southeastern Columbia County in 1949, followed by more specialized agricultural production for urban markets.

The agricultural labor force changed accordingly. In 1880, farm boys eagerly seeking apprenticeship in their family's profession readily accepted work for their room and board plus a few dollars a week. By 1900, industrial labor in valley cities as well as in New York helped raise farm wages, but prosperous farmers still could afford to have four hired men. In the 1930s, with wages at $3 a day plus board, a farmer might need to cut down his help to one or two men, reducing his livestock and his cultivated acreage. By that decade, the turnover in tenant farm families also posed a greater problem for farm proprietors employing them. Living in small houses with little equipment or privacy, near the main house, they no longer looked forward to becoming farm owners themselves.

A generation later, the situation of Dutchess farmers had taken another turn, this time for the better. Acreage of farms increased, tenancy decreased, and greater demand for land by nonfarmers improved the prices farmers could get when selling their properties. Farm work remained hard, with long hours, but to an outside observer like former president of Vassar College Henry Noble MacCracken, improved transportation and other forms of modernization had made the life of farmers more enjoyable by 1958.

> One must attend, as I have done, the annual dinner of the 4-II Club, for example, to see the farm family in a moment of relaxation. The public exercises of the grange, the couples club of the rural church, the fishermen and hunters from the farms, the new public health clinics and regional hospitals,

tell the same story, as do . . . the visiting from farm to farm and inspecting a new tractor. Telephone and television have brought the farm family right into town, and mail orders have made the consumers' market nationwide. In no part of the nation has the family life been more fully transformed.[28]

## "SUBURBAN" NEWCOMERS

A different group of newcomers to the valley received less attention from local observers initially than foreign immigrants and their children. A prescient exception, Martha Collins Bayne, projected the new "suburbanites" as a transforming influence for the area's future. In particular, she observed that the "sudden popularity of a suburban residence for New York people has had a profound effect upon its farm dwellers."[29] When they had trouble "making ends meet" in some form of commercial agriculture, they now mostly sold their farms to city people rather than, as previously, returning to a poor self-sufficiency or simply giving up their farms to move in with relatives or seek public relief.

Bayne divided the "suburban" newcomers into three groups. Gentlemen farmers predominated in the attractive hills of Pawling and Millbrook. Campers stopped wherever their automobiles would take them. But the majority of nonfarm newcomers simply wanted a few acres in the country with an old house for their getaways. At the bottom end they included the "scores of cheaply constructed summer cabins which form small independent summer communities that take over the recreational facilities of [county lakes like Sylvan and Whaley] to the exclusion of people the campers call 'natives.'"[30] But Bayne also noted that a miniature suburban trend, inspired partly by the New York newcomers, had emerged in Poughkeepsie and Beacon where some residents bought summer places in towns like Pleasant Valley and Fishkill. The demand of newcomers for better roads meant increasing taxes for farmers as did the rise in land values. That increased the likelihood of failure for marginal farmers at a time when one alternative, jobs as managers and tenants of estate owners, was diminishing. The years of the Great Depression posed severe challenges to the rural population as well as to urban industrial workers.

What Bayne did not consider in her examination of the suburban trend was the extent to which Poughkeepsians had begun to move beyond the city's boundaries. In 1939, a speaker at a Chamber of Commerce meeting noted the lack of adequate housing in the city and the boom in surrounding areas, notably the towns of Poughkeepsie, Hyde Park, and LaGrange. "Why? It's cheaper to buy land, build, and live outside the city" escaping the high taxes for services there.[31] The movement outward would increase dramatically in postwar years.

## PART III

# IBM Remakes the Region as Its Largest Employer

# TEN

# Technological Revolution
# Transforms the Region: IBM

IBM'S ENORMOUS IMPACT on the Poughkeepsie urban region and Kingston during the second half of the twentieth century is hard to overstate. This corporate newcomer would increase both population and prosperity and also greatly improve the educational level of the region's labor force. It was a wartime novelty for the area to start with, but its subsequent peacetime development proved revolutionary for the company and for the valley.

In 1941, the Munitions Manufacturing Company, a newly created subsidiary of the International Business Machines corporation, acquired 215 acres in the *town* of Poughkeepsie, just south of the *city*. The start-up began operations in a factory and house near the river, but soon expanded. By 1943, the parent company absorbed its subsidiary and IBM Poughkeepsie won an Army-Navy award for excellence in manufacturing for the war. Continuing growth after the war made IBM Dutchess County's largest employer by far, on which a majority of families depended directly or indirectly for their livelihood. The company also added major operations in Kingston, across the river in Ulster County. Its generous benefits and paternalism made IBM the envy of other businesses and their employees and lifted the economic status of the valley.

## IBM'S PATRIARCH: THOMAS WATSON, SENIOR

What did the outlook of IBM's founder and the policies at his main plant in Endicott, New York, portend for Poughkeepsie? Thomas J. Watson, Sr., had begun as a traveling salesman for the National Cash Register Company. It provided its employees with a variety of benefits to improve their motivation on the job, foster corporate solidarity, and stave off unionization. Watson would fashion similar labor policies when he acquired the Computing-Tabulating-Recording

Corporation in 1924, renaming it International Business Machines. Besides emulating the welfare capitalism pioneered by National Cash Register, Watson shared its preoccupation with salesmanship and service to the customer. IBM would pioneer in introducing computation to government, business, and academia through its punch card and tabulation machines. It also manufactured a wide array of other kinds of business machines from scales and time clocks to typewriters.

The benefits that Watson provided his workers at his central operation in Endicott, New York, began with programs to train them and upgrade their skills. Other benefits included day care for their children and a country club. The club served dinner three nights a week to free IBM wives from cooking. Watson constantly emphasized company spirit and the idea of an IBM family. His One Hundred Percent Club honored salesmen who had made their sales quotas for the year at a huge banquet. Watson would bring similar policies to his new operations in the Hudson valley. At the end of the war, IBM Poughkeepsie inaugurated family dinners. New plans for health and accident benefits, hospitalization, and retirement made employment at the company even more attractive.

## CHOOSING POUGHKEEPSIE
## FOR WARTIME MANUFACTURE

Why did Watson choose Poughkeepsie for his wartime subsidiary? His son, Thomas, Jr., recalled the War Department pressing IBM in the fall of 1940 to contract to manufacture machine guns. But his father had opposed setting up an arms plant at Endicott. In 1941, however, the elder Watson did offer President Roosevelt IBM facilities for manufacturing munitions. By that time, IBM had prepared for the possibility. Following his policy of avoiding firing workers whenever he could, Watson had them cleaning machines and painting floors to provide them with work until completion of the new arrangements with the government. Like other practitioners of welfare capitalism, Watson preferred to maintain security in employment by moving employees around within the company to other jobs rather than laying them off during elimination of their current jobs. Unions, in contrast, sought security through contracts that emphasized protection of workers in their current jobs, making firing or transferring workers difficult. Group layoffs, followed by strikes to restore contract conditions, often resulted. Both sides insisted their approach was fairer to workers.

General Gillespie and Colonel Connors at the Watervliet Arsenal in the Albany area had urged Watson to pick a site nearby, taking advantage of the Hudson River region. The town of Poughkeepsie, 70-odd miles away, had some potential advantages. IBM already had subcontracted there with Frederick Hart's machine works on Main Street in Arlington for parts for keypunches. When Watson asked about a factory site, Hart mentioned the plant of R. U. Delapenha "where in the First World War the Vassar girls had canned tomatoes."[1] If Watson hoped for his new plant to become the most important employer in the area, as it was not in its Endicott or Rochester locations, then the town of Poughkeepsie could serve that aim. The lack of any strong unions or labor consciousness in the area also must have appealed since that was a major consideration whenever IBM considered a new site.

IBM began modestly in the town of Poughkeepsie. The R. U. Delapenha Co. land that IBM purchased had a history of wartime endeavor. A blacksmith shop, long since gone, had forged some of the iron chain intended to block British ships from traveling up the Hudson River during the Revolutionary War. The Delapenha's canning factory had produced and preserved staple foods during World War I. Its land had been used for "Victory Gardens" worked by groups of Vassar College students.

The factory IBM acquired had 35,000 square feet of floor space. A cellar storage area held two vats from which the Delapenhas pumped olive oil from Italy for canning. Francis Ritz, later IBM's assistant general manager in Poughkeepsie, recalls setting up shop above the vats while other employees made cylinders for gun barrels in the main factory building. IBM soon built a new cement block Plant #1 that manufactured the big Browning automatic rifle. For test firing of carbines near the banks of the Hudson, the company required testers to shoot into a sand curtain to prevent shells from reaching the river.

As early as the spring of 1942, increased employment led the company to construct a new cafeteria building seating five hundred people. It served its first meal that June. Also early on, the elder Watson moved to implement his long-standing concern with proper instruction for his labor force. By January 1943, 41 percent of the entire plant personnel in Poughkeepsie had enrolled in a General Education Program. As he had in Endicott, Watson created a country club for his employees. In 1944, he personally arranged to acquire a site off South Road near his still small manufacturing campus in the town of Poughkeepsie. Before long, the club would provide a golf course, tennis courts, swimming pool, and clubhouse for his Hudson Valley employees.

## IBM'S WARTIME WORKFORCE

Who were IBM Poughkeepsie's wartime workers? Watson described them proudly as a gathering of farmers, clerks, artists, and teachers. They grew in number from 250 in 1942 to 1,400 by 1945. Even before the end of the war, their success in meeting production goals made Watson favor further growth in Poughkeepsie. But this workforce was not quite as random as Watson's description might suggest.

IBM attracted some of its wartime workers from local factories, notorious for lower wages than IBM paid. De Laval Separator and Daystrom Electric's machine and assembly workers proved susceptible to recruiting. And IBM's Endicott plant sent some "seed workers," a usual transplanting strategy whenever IBM opened a new facility. The company prided itself on always having talented machine-educated workers ready to move where they were needed.

Yet, local and initially less-skilled workers must have provided the large majority of IBM's wartime workforce. Nationally, IBM doubled its manufacturing operatives during the war and one-third of its 15,000 new operatives were women. One local estimate thought women composed as much as 70 percent of the Poughkeepsie plant, adapting with remarkable agility and enthusiasm to wartime demand for manufacturing workers as women did elsewhere in the nation.

At all its locations, IBM emphasized training for its employees, drawing upon local schools to provide instruction in certain subjects. In the 1930s at Endicott, manufacturing workers generally had received one month's training, paid for by the company, initiating them in metallurgy, plating, grinding, drill press, and punch cards. Two nights a week, workers went to a local high school

FIGURE 10.1. IBM Building #002, South Road, 1948

for a program that included custom engineering. Francis Ritz, who joined IBM in 1937, had taken a toolmaking engineering course for four years.

IBM had little visible impact on the town of Poughkeepsie during the war years apart from the few buildings on South Road and the beginning development of sports facilities at the country club. But with 1,400 employees by 1945 and future expansion anticipated, this sparsely settled area of the town would need to facilitate traffic and expect construction of new housing. Like other cities at war's end, Poughkeepsie had a housing shortage and its older housing, especially on the river slope (referred to by local businessmen as the Lower Section), was in bad condition. It was so bad, as IBM manager Dause Bibby told a meeting of the Poughkeepsie Civic Conference in 1943, that seeing the area might appall visitors. "During our E award ceremony some of the boys asked us not to drive our people, coming in from New York, through certain parts of the city."[2]

FIGURE 10.2. IBM Building #002, 1948 dedication with Dwight D. Eisenhower, Eleanor Roosevelt, and Thomas Watson, Sr.

## IBM BEGINS TO RESHAPE THE LANDSCAPE

The most dramatic change in the landscape, coinciding with IBM's coming to the town of Poughkeepsie, was the widening of Route 9. Two lanes became four lanes from Poughkeepsie south to Fishkill in the late 1940s, coinciding with IBM's construction of its mammoth South Road Plant #2. Less dramatic were new housing developments that anticipated the rapid transformation of former fields and woods into residential neighborhoods. They populated a wide belt of land from the South Road IBM campus to Red Oaks Mill and beyond.

The elder Watson himself in 1946–1947 bought more than 400 acres to create the Spackenkill Heights subdivision. Watson offered individual building lots to IBM employees at $450 each. Purchasers then had a choice of three grades of homes. The basic house with carport cost $8,500, an upgrade required $10,500, and, largest of all, a four-bedroom house with garage went for $12,500. Watson advertised the new housing within the IBM world, meeting demand from his employees first, then selling to non-IBMers. The result: 93 percent of the residents of Spackenkill Heights worked for the company. Many privately developed streets in the belt between IBM's South Road and Boardman Road campuses came close to that high level of residential concentration of IBM employees.

## CORPORATE PATERNALISM

Watson's paternalism in the Hudson valley went far beyond housing as it did in Endicott. Natives of Poughkeepsie very quickly sensed and began gossiping about certain policies of its new employer. The dress code of white shirt and tie for engineers as well as for salesmen and clerical workers visibly reminded everyone of company regulations. So did the taboo against any publicly visible consumption of alcohol. Joking was frequent about IBMers having to pull the shades in their homes to enjoy a cocktail.

So was joking about the contents of the IBM songbook, with its many verses praising the founder and boosting the company. To the tune of "Pack Up Your Troubles," a song for IBM's president concluded, "He's a real father and a friend so true, Say all we boys. Ever he thinks of things to say and do, to increase our joys. He's a builder real and true. His work will never die. That's why we love T. J. Watson all the while—He's God's best style." "The I. B. M. Family," sung to the tune of "Yip-I-Addy-I-Aye," exulted: "We're co-workers in I. B. M.—all one big family. We save materials, time, and men; increasing profits to all business when Accurate figures and weights and time—our machines guarantee. Oh, joy! Oh, what bliss! We are members of this I. B. M. Company." And "Ever Onward IBM" proclaimed, "There's a feeling everywhere of bigger things in store. Of new horizons coming into view. . . . Our products now are known in every zone. Our reputation sparkles like a gem."[3]

The 1931 edition of the songbook also provided paeans to a host of company officials and work groups. Salesmen whose records admitted them to the One Hundred Percent Club sang, to the tune of "I've Been Working on the Railroad," "We're the I. B. M. Go-getters, All the live-long-day. We are all Hundred Percenters and will strive to be alway. We have learned from Mr. Watson, Loyally we'll serve him all the time. And we'll help all of our salesmen To sell our whole big line." Servicemen could join in, to the tune of "Over There," with "Our machines benefit business men. Yes, the world now knows us; all men adore us, Because our products profit them."

The IBM Welcome Wagon visited incoming employees to help them feel more at home in their new, and often temporary, world. That seemed a more congenial form of paternalism. So did the country club with its enviable array of sports facilities and activities that astonished employees of other local industries accustomed to low wages and few perquisites. The elder Watson loved family day at the club. The local management organized the day like a carnival, complete with stage acts, horse rides for the children, and abundant food. The founder enjoyed sitting in the shade and receiving the people who kept coming up to him to pay homage. Tom Watson, Jr., didn't share his father's enthusiasm for such occasions. After he became head of IBM in 1956, family days would be transferred to the Dutchess County fairgrounds in Rhinebeck. The Poughkeepsie plant held its last big barbecue in 1954. The crowd of nearly 3,000 consumed 2 1/2 tons of steak, 3,400 baked potatoes, and nearly 25,000 clams.

## "MR. IBM" IN POUGHKEEPSIE IS BILL MAIR

Leadership of the new Poughkeepsie plant had been given to former toolmaker William J. Mair, brought from Endicott in 1942 to be plant superintendent. However, Dause Bibby from sales became the overall IBM Poughkeepsie general manager the following summer; IBM's top executives normally came from marketing. Not until 1952 would the company elevate superintendent Mair to be Poughkeepsie resident manager and IBM vice-president, providing a major inspiration for rank-and-file manufacturing workers in the valley. By that time, Mair had become, in reputation, a much-admired "Mr. IBM" for the Hudson valley.

As the Poughkeepsie plant grew in the late 1940s and early 1950s, Bill Mair maintained a remarkably personal style of leadership. When he heard that one employee was enlisting in 1944, he phoned him, "You goddamned fool; come back and make the guns; let others fire them."[4] Mair and IBM welcomed this veteran back after the war. When another worker lost an eye, hit by a drill bit, Mair, in a less litigious age, went to the man's home to assure him that he would be fully taken care of. William Cole went on to complete forty-one years of employment at IBM before retiring in the 1970s.

Mair took the helm at a time when college graduates were still unusual at the plant, but about to become much more frequent. He seemed surprised by the request of a new graduate from MIT. Charles Lawson asked to begin his IBM employment as an ordinary operative on the manufacturing floor, looking toward a career in industrial management. Bemused, Mair let him start in the machine shop with punch presses and then moved him to the apprentice toolmaker's shop near the river. Later, the young man asked to take on the lowest level supervising of an unloading section. There he managed to reduce the needed workforce substantially. After that Lawson won successively greater opportunities to move upward, including managing the creation of a new IBM site in Rochester, Minnesota. Mair proved to be a helpful counselor on his way up.

Mair oversaw the South Road plant's shift from wartime production back to IBM's usual manufacture of electromechanical computing and business machines, such as keypunchers, punch card sorters, and typewriters. Typewriters had been made at IBM's Rochester plant since 1933; their manufacture was moved in 1945 to Plant #1 in Poughkeepsie after the machinery for making carbines and other war equipment had been cleared out. Always looking for ways to upgrade, IBM soon had development groups working on a new rotary-wheel typewriter. This model would be given a more elegant exterior look by fashion designer Norman Bel Geddes.

## MISS KENYON'S MANSION BECOMES "THE LAB"

The new project was moved to another local site that had been purchased by IBM in 1944, again in the *town* of Poughkeepsie, not the *city*. Some 2 miles from the growing IBM campus at South Road, Cliffdale had been the 217-acre estate of Helen Kenyon. Daughter of a rich Brooklyn clothing manufacturer, Miss Kenyon had lived at Cliffdale for thirty-one years. A Vassar alumna, she served as chairman of the college's Board of Trustees for ten years after 1929. Kenyon Hall, Vassar's old athletic building, would bear her name. Her hospitality and lawn parties at Cliffdale and her involvement in local community affairs as a fighter for the underprivileged became legendary.

IBM had purchased Cliffdale to house a development laboratory, following its practice of connecting laboratories to its manufacturing plants. For ten years, until the corporation could construct its own buildings for that purpose, the Kenyon family's large yellow-brick mansion served as the lab. It was an odd transformation. The house's twenty-three rooms had included four master bedrooms, six baths, three guest rooms, six servants' bedrooms, as well as several secret hiding places for the family silver and business documents. The mansion crowned a hilltop with a sweeping view westward to the hills across the Hudson River.

Some lab engineers would work more on developing new technology while others worked more closely with manufacturing teams at South Road.

The Kenyon mansion soon housed such a mix. One group worked on the second floor on a new typewriter, still in its engineering phase, while groups worked on a printer downstairs. The superintendent's house and the manor's garage and carriage house served initially as the engineering and electrical workshops for the IBM laboratory. Later they became part of the laboratory's educational complex.

The mansion enjoyed similar changes in use over time after serving temporarily as the lab. Restored and redecorated as the Homestead, it provided living accommodations for distinguished guests and for IBM's customer representatives. Later it would house the Corporate Headquarters Management School-Northeast. After downsizing at the end of the twentieth century, IBM sold the Boardman Road properties; the Poughkeepsie Day School purchased the mansion.

## IBM ENTERS THE WORLD OF ELECTRONICS

After 1944, Cliffdale became the scene of major technological breakthroughs, like the invention of the tape drive. Under the leadership of Ralph Palmer, a

FIGURE 10.3. IBM Building #701 research lab, Boardman Road, c. 1954

small team of electronic engineers in the late 1940s pursued innovations like the 604 Electronic Calculator that used vacuum tubes. Some of these engineers had had wartime experience with the emerging field of electronics such as participation in code-breaking projects.

Before long, Palmer's lab overflowed the Kenyon mansion and spilled into the Delapenha house near the river. In both locations, a new breed of development engineers pursued new ideas in the collaborative atmosphere frequently found in rapidly developing new fields. Increasingly, they came with advanced degrees like freshly recruited Werner Buchholz with a PhD from Caltech. Their excitement and sense of a limitless future impressed Tom Watson, Jr., soon to become president of the company. By contrast with the buzz he found in Poughkeepsie, Watson saw IBM's main laboratory at Endicott as less dynamic and stuffy, with everybody guarding his own turf.

After the 604, IBM's most complex machine so far but not yet a computer, a team that included Buchholz developed the 701, a computer for scientific purposes that could do 2,200 multiplications a second. The team worked at Kenyon and in the new 701 building dedicated in 1953 on Boardman Road where a second campus of lab buildings would be constructed. By 1956, buildings 702 and 703 had been added to the laboratory complex. Poughkeepsie became recognized as a major center for creation of the company's computer products. IBM's revenues still derived largely from its traditional electromechanical machines, but new electronic projects burgeoned. Tom Watson would be very proud of IBM's success in developing assembly-line manufacture for these complex innovations.

Responding to the Korean War in the 1950s, IBM once again offered its services for defense work. It took on projects for bombing navigational systems and for high-speed electronic calculators for air defense. The company often leased space for these projects to avoid a physical expansion that would be difficult to maintain in peacetime. In 1952–1953, a group of engineers from the Poughkeepsie lab raced to carry out their part in designing an Early Warning System for the U.S. Defense Department. IBM rented two floors for them in a High Street building in the city, which would later house the Dutchess County Department of Planning. This group designed the system on blackboards, running back and forth working out the necessary equations. Together with planners and cost estimators, they scrambled to meet the deadline of making a proposal to the government in three weeks.

## IBM'S NEW FACILITY IN KINGSTON

Manufacturing the resulting SAGE system for protection against foreign missiles was a huge project, too big for the Poughkeepsie plant. So IBM built a new facility in Kingston, close enough for easier coordination of operations and for shipping workers back and forth between Kingston and Poughkeepsie as needed. Thus began a major regional linkage, connecting the largest urban areas in Dutchess and Ulster counties. The Kingston plant started with 2,500 employees in the mid-1950s, ultimately reaching 10,000. By 1959, IBM had opened an engineering laboratory there. Short of room for manufacturing packages for the SAGE project, the company rented a local bowling alley for that purpose.

In 1962, IBM's Data Systems Division established its systems test mission at Kingston that by 1991 had the largest test area in the world. In the late 1960s, one employee, Huyler Van Buren, received a $75,000 IBM Suggestion Award for salvaging defective core planes. Corporate amenities developed apace; the plant held its own family days and built a new swim center. Local managers encouraged civic participation and contributions, just as their counterparts did at other IBM sites. For the year 1990, IBM Kingston's financial contributions to the community through the Employees Charitable Contribution Campaign, Fund for Community Service, Local Discretionary Grants, Corporate Contributions and Matching Grants totaled about $1,195,000. IBM largesse in the valley spread well beyond Poughkeepsie.

The plant and laboratory had a much wider reach through its educational activities. In the 1950s, IBM Kingston had to train hundreds of engineers to relate radar inputs to known flight patterns in order to make the display for air force generals. IBM Kingston also graduated more than 1,850 field engineers from its course on SAGE computer maintenance.

For the next three decades, IBM's expanding production in the valley would require additional facilities and more workers. Already by the end of 1957, the accumulating leased areas totaled 461,820 square feet. Beyond the benefit to owners of these properties rented for IBM's overflow lay the stimulus of their earnings to the regional economy. Occasionally, the company purchased a previously leased area, as it did with the South Road laboratory.

After World War II, returning servicemen, rural migrants and local boys found employment at the company. One new hire, fresh out of high school in 1953, recalled a surprise one night while he was working the second shift as a machine operator. Thomas Watson, Sr., came through on a tour of the plant. John DuBois's wrench slipped while he tightened a gear, and he cut his finger badly. Watson stopped to make sure he would be all right. Then to DuBois's surprise, on another tour a few months later, the founder stopped by his workstation to ask about his finger.

## UPGRADING IBM'S WORKFORCE

High school hires still fed IBM's traditional business machine manufacture. However, increasingly during the 1940s and 1950s the company recruited recently minted engineers, often "city boys raised in the Depression and educated on the GI Bill."[5] One Rensselaer Polytechnic graduate, class of 1951, recalled that he had no interest in IBM employment "because they just made machines that put holes in cards—and I wanted to work on computers." When he learned otherwise, he accepted an offer from the Poughkeepsie lab, as did several classmates.

Already in the mid-1950s, IBM had nearly ten thousand employees, making it the largest employer in the valley. The number increased steadily, with no downward fluctuations. By 1984, IBMers constituted one-fifth of Dutchess County's workforce and they were much better educated than the employees of the 1940s. By 1962, the company's revenues from electronics exceeded those from its electromechanical machines. Electronics required more recruitment of college graduates and specialists with advanced degrees like physicists and mathematicians. So complex an organization in turn required an increasing number of managers and white-collar workers.

Because IBM brought more and better-paying jobs to the region, most local residents had welcomed the corporation gladly. One important local group did not, however. Richard Mitchell, the city of Poughkeepsie's mayor from 1966 to 1969, recalled a certain animosity in the first reactions from local companies in the 1940s. Why? Because IBM came with a higher wage scale, more benefits, and eventually things "like the IBM country club which nobody else had or could afford."[6]

The end result would be improvement of the wage scale in the entire region. But the short-run impact hurt manufacturers like De Laval, Schatz Federal Bearings, and Western Printing who had benefited from Poughkeepsie's well-known reputation for lower wages. Regarding themselves as the established business community, local manufacturers found themselves losing workers to IBM. One well-placed IBMer in the company's early years in Poughkeepsie believed that these older local firms, together with some bankers and lawyers, had long compared information on wages. In his view, they formed a tightly knit group within the Amrita Club, collaborating to keep labor costs down and also maintaining a blacklist of workers they saw as problematical.

Aware of this kind of resentment among local businessmen, the elder Watson went out of his way to allay it at the dedication ceremony for the huge Plant #2 in 1948. He assured the gathering that IBM's benefits for employees beyond the payroll did not represent philanthropy. He insisted these benefits represented just reward for service rendered. Appealing to Poughkeepsians' hopes for their economic future, Watson said the new Plant #2 would house three thousand workers. More workers would be added when IBM could train them and sufficient housing became available.

The dedication was a grand event organized by Poughkeepsie's Chamber of Commerce. It began with Gladys Swarthout and Lawrence Tibbett of the Metropolitan Opera House leading the invited crowd in singing "The Star-Spangled Banner." Distinguished guests included Eleanor Roosevelt and the day's main speaker on "The American Faith in Free Enterprise," General Dwight Eisenhower. Luncheon followed at the Nelson House hotel.

Poughkeepsie's elite did not rush to invite IBM's management into their select gathering places. The elder Watson did get resident manager Dause Bibby into the Tennis Club. Bill Mair would follow with membership in the Dutchess County Golf Club. However, others waited until the right kinds of local friends made a proper introduction possible. As in the city's past, over time, successful newcomers were accepted socially by their local peers.

A good golfer, Mair got to know Poughkeepsie's business leaders playing at the club. Recognizing the animus against IBM, he succeeded in softening it, especially by getting IBM executives to become civic participants. He would tell his men to go on to the boards of United Way, the Civic Center, or one of the hospitals. Mair himself agreed to become a director of St. Francis Hospital. IBM would loan executives to local charities, a practice that continued until the 1980s. The company paid their salaries during the loans.

When members of Poughkeepsie's Chamber of Commerce and Development Council visited Kalamazoo, Michigan, to examine its widely praised downtown mall, Mair provided corporate aircraft to fly them there. A major indirect contribution by IBM wives took the form of active participation in local civic groups, especially the League of Women Voters. Such direct and indirect contribution to the city's and the town's welfare created goodwill.

## IBM'S IMPACT ON LOCAL RETAILING

Some indirect results of IBM's presence hurt the city by the 1960s, however. As late as 1950, anyone living in the town to the south of the city still shopped on Main Street in the central business district. Going in the other direction down Route 9 from Poughkeepsie to Fishkill, town residents would pass one motel but no retailer, recalled local realtor Steve Iko. But IBM employees' desire for newer housing with an easy commute to the manufacturing plant or lab spurred residential growth in the town. That, in turn, attracted retailers to locate there. In 1958, the urban region's first shopping mall, Poughkeepsie Plaza, opened. That mall would be followed in the next three years by Bradlees and Hudson Plaza malls, all of them close to the South Road plant.

The new shopping malls and strip development, trends throughout the United States in that decade, gained momentum from IBM's decision to locate outside the city. They would take business away from the downtown, ultimately crippling its retailing. That destructive impact did not become immediately evident, however. When one young IBM programmer moved to Poughkeepsie in 1963, Main Street still thrived, with two big department stores serving the whole mid-Hudson valley. Thursday night was still a time for area residents to converge on city shops.

The new shape of the Poughkeepsie urban region was signaled by other developments. The year 1958 saw construction of the overpass spanning South Road to facilitate traffic in and out of IBM's plant buildings. Who could not be impressed by the huge parking lots filled with thousands of cars surrounding the plant? New construction altered the landscape in every direction as suburban housing spread steadily over an area that had been largely countryside before the war.

## CORPORATE CULTURE CHANGES UNDER TOM, JR.

IBM itself changed in that decade. Thomas Watson, Sr., retired in 1956, dying shortly thereafter. Tom, Jr., took the helm. The shift toward electronics as the company's primary business could now push forward more rapidly. Corporate culture at IBM gradually moved away from the more enthusiastic, less sophisticated style of the founder. That happened partly because the son disliked it, but also because it was alien to the computer-oriented workers then becoming increasingly important within IBM. The corporation changed with the times and its increasingly highly educated workforce. In 1958, young Watson announced that all workers previously paid on an hourly basis now would receive salaries.

The songbook appeared at company occasions less often and finally disappeared. The taboo on alcohol lessened. At one gathering of senior engineers at Boca Raton just before the founder died, Ralph Palmer, director of the lab, audaciously ordered a bottle of wine for his table. The old policy did not die altogether, however. Questions about its scope led the founder's son to remind his managers in 1965 that liquor remained taboo on company premises, at IBM business meetings, and at company social affairs. The taboo did not apply, however, to purely social IBM club activities when held off company premises and paid for personally by the participants. Lou Gerstner in the 1990s complained that IBM airplanes still were not prepared to provide him with a drink.

The dress code remained after 1956, but was no longer rigidly enforced throughout the company. Nothing but white shirt and tie were permissible in sales and marketing, the core of IBM and the road to top management. But engineers and scientists could wear a blue shirt at Kenyon House, now turned into a conference center for the lab. A programmer at the lab recalled not wearing a tie sometimes, asserting his independence.

Manufacturing workers had more leeway in dress, but managers still worried about whether their workers fit the corporate image. In 1960, the manager of an accounting machine operator then growing a beard told him to shave it off. The manager fired the operator when he refused. Complaint led to his rehiring. Reporting the episode, Tom Watson commented, "Let's not confuse propriety with uniformity."[7]

## ONGOING CHANGE IN IBM'S WORKFORCE

By 1956, the presence of numerous IBM electronic engineers in Polk's Pough-keepsie directory signaled alteration in IBM's workforce as the company focused increasingly on computers. Not so prominent yet were the mathe-maticians, physicists, and chemists whom the company would recruit in larger numbers and the programmers it would train as it undertook ever more ambi-tious projects for computer manufacture, leaping into the technology of the future. In 1956, the large complement of customer, mechanical, electrical, and production engineers reflected the continued predominance in IBM sales rev-enues of electromechanical products from typewriters to card sorters. This also meant that IBM Poughkeepsie's almost entirely male manufacturing force in the 1950s relied heavily on machinists, machine operators, and a vari-ety of specialized metal workers such as tool and die makers, drill press oper-ators, grinders, and finishers.

Second- and third-generation male descendants of Poughkeepsie's immi-grants from southern and central Europe filled many of these jobs. The city directory shows many IBM blue-collar workers among Italian-Americans—the city's largest recent immigrant group—who still resided in the city's largely working- and lower-middle-class north side. The frequency of several employees with the same surname suggests the continuing importance of informal employment recruiting within family networks. However, by the 1950s, the earlier prejudice among Italian-Americans against women working outside the home had abated, as several of them appeared as assemblers on IBM production lines.

With the large wartime employment of women in manufacturing jobs a dimming memory by 1956, women became a small minority of assemblers and inspectors. Poughkeepsie and IBM had had their equivalents of Rosie the Riveter in the early 1940s, but now women occupied the jobs deemed more appropriate for their sex. They comprised the telephone operators, secretaries, typists, and stenographers, most cafeteria workers, and a small minority of the clerks. Otherwise men monopolized not only manufacturing jobs but also the company's white-collar employment. Men were the clerks, office workers, accountants, and educational instructors as well as the draftsmen, expediters, buyers, and dispatchers.

In the 1950s, most Americans still accepted gender stereotyping of occupa-tions and assumed that married women normally should be at home taking care of their families. The resurgence of feminism and demands for affirmative action for women and racial minorities in the 1960s and after would coincide in time with the triumph of the mainframe at IBM. Women would find more opportu-nities later on when the age of electronics turned increasingly to miniaturization.

The initial shift to electronics had entailed a host of difficult challenges. Tom Watson, Jr., recalled the complicated problems in the 1950s in moving away from punch cards to so fast a new technology, "trying to develop logic and memory circuits, tape-handling devices, recording heads, card-to-tape data transfer, and the vacuum tubes and tapes themselves."[8] Change was unending. In 1957, the young Watson ordered an end to the use of vacuum tubes in future products. The transistor, first discrete and then integrated, became the computer building block of the future.

In less than a decade, IBM had moved from tool technology to solid-state physics. In 1956, with the word "transistor" just coming into vogue, Building 705 on Boardman Road had eight or nine lab employees assembling transistors. The factory made ferrite cores for memory. In the ensuing scramble to increase production, Francis Ritz doubled that workforce in less than a year. Next he set up a transferred workforce in Plant #1, adding thirty or more new workers together with four or five engineers. Then they needed more space, so the company built Plant #3 on the South Road campus.

## THE STRETCH COMPUTER PROJECT

Meanwhile, the lab campus on Boardman Road kept growing, as did the desire for greater coherence in IBM's computer products. By 1960, the company sold eight different solid-state computers. Six of them were incompatible and could not communicate with each other. To resolve its quandary, IBM turned in the late 1950s to the man whom a company historian deemed its greatest product engineer, Steven "Red" Dunwell. Dunwell, who had joined IBM in the 1930s, participated in code-breaking during World War II. In 1954, he came, at Ralph Palmer's request, from the Future Demands Department at IBM's New York offices to the Poughkeepsie lab. Dunwell aimed to create a machine powerful enough to provide a common architecture for an entire line of computers. He projected a speed for his Stretch computer one hundred times faster than the 701, IBM's first product computer. The finished Stretch could perform tens of billions of computations a day.

The problems in implementing so ambitious a project led to subsequent scaling down of the targets for its speed. But the stress of meeting the variety of deadlines remained high. Bernard ("Bob") Slade remembered many days, even weeks, when he didn't get home until midnight. Meetings ran late in the evening. After one midnight return, he learned from Ralph Palmer that a cost analysis of the transistor used in the Stretch program must be completed by the next morning. So Slade drove across town and city to do the cost analysis at Church Street, one of the innumerable locations that IBM leased when more space was needed. Slade got home at 4 A.M.

IBM delivered Stretch to Los Alamos in 1961. Ultimately, the company sold eighteen systems, but at half-price. Watson cancelled further production as too costly. Dunwell was reassigned to IBM's research center at Yorktown Heights. In the longer run, the technological benefits derived from the

Stretch project proved so great that Watson would admit, "A better 50 million we never spent, but it took us 7 or 8 years to find that out." In the meantime, "Poor Dunwell had to crawl into a cocoon for three or four years, but I apologized to him publicly later."[9]

That apology came at the dinner in 1966 when Watson announced the naming of "Red" Dunwell as an IBM Fellow, IBM's highest honor for its top engineers. The fellowship freed a fellow for five to ten years to pursue projects of his own choosing. Dunwell would apply his creativity to the development of Computer Assisted Instruction and to his proposal for a universal software.

Despite his persistence in urging acceptance of his software proposal that he had supported with an extensive monograph, the company showed no interest—to Dunwell's great frustration. Such a universal software would be in competition with what IBM already was doing proprietarily. More satisfying to Dunwell, because the helpfulness to others occurred immediately, were the major computer upgrades he made for important Hudson Valley nonprofits like Scenic Hudson. After his retirement from IBM in 1975, he and his wife, Julia Dunwell, would play crucial roles in saving and renovating Poughkeepsie's historic Bardavon theater as a civic treasure and venue for music and drama.

## WORK WORLDS AT IBM POUGHKEEPSIE AFTER 1956

The workaday world of senior engineers like Dunwell and Werner Buchholz, who assisted Dunwell on Stretch, included some interplay with production. Since Development and Manufacturing had to collaborate closely in bringing new designs to market readiness, mixing of these divisions had to be frequent. But normally lab employees didn't work at the manufacturing plant except temporarily. And some of them looked down a little on factory operatives, like grinders and drill press workers, as the "white socks and dirty fingernails" guys.[10]

Gathering workers of different skill and status together did characterize company cafeterias. The range in education was less at Boardman Road than at South Road, however. At the main campus, managers, engineers, technicians, and manufacturing operatives shared the same space. In choosing tables, they tended to cluster with their workmates in a democratic kind of separatism. Top management generally ate elsewhere.

Manufacturing operatives and technicians encountered marketing and sales employees when these outsiders to the factory floor brought their customers to see how the machines they leased were made. But otherwise the work worlds of these white- and blue-collar workers within IBM were far apart. Sales had always been the chief way to top management in IBM, attracting the more ambitious. Not all white-collar workers shared that ambition, however.

As the company continued to grow in size and complexity, a fundamental difference appeared between those who aspired to run the company and those in the middle ranks who settled for a less pressured and comfortable way of life with limited upward mobility. In an increasingly bureaucratized and paternalistic corporation, many seemed content with interesting, well-paid work, job security, and numerous benefits. They enjoyed considerable freedom to choose the projects they wished to work on and to take time off to pursue interests unrelated to the company.

Eric Lindbloom came to IBM in 1963 from graduate work in philosophy at Stanford. His knowledge of symbolic logic, set theory, and Boolean algebra appealed to the company mathematician hiring him who had an analytical method for testing logic chips. The ever-increasing sophistication of chips meant that Lindbloom as an engineering programmer worked on a very practical, unsettled problem. What tests should be generated for the next chip to be produced? Yes, Lindbloom's concern was with the consumer and service rather than with innovation. But he never had to sit in a room with a customer, had no relation to sales, and did not need to meet top management.

Lindbloom came to believe early on in his IBM career that he could always have a job at the company. If it closed out any group he'd been working with, he could job shop. He could trade on personal friendships to join a new project before management moved him. His drive was his own, not based on pressure from managers. So he found his twenty-two years with a forty-hour week not unduly stressful. He never punched a time clock and normally got to work around 9:30.

Lindbloom didn't mind working in different locations. He had started with a development group working in an abandoned tire factory on the Fall Kill. He served as a first-level manager in manufacturing for a time. He also worked in Kingston and Fishkill, commuting from Poughkeepsie. Overall, Lindbloom enjoyed his career at IBM. He discovered early on that the company would be flexible about his schedule when he had outside commitments that mattered to him. In 1966, he ran for public office in Dutchess County on a peace ticket, writing long speeches that his wife—poet and novelist Nancy Willard—typed out. He was able to leave work for radio interviews and did not suffer from criticism at IBM. Instead his colleagues seemed to regard his campaigning as useful civic participation.

Lindbloom's freedom may have been more than was usual even in the upper middle and middle ranks of the company. In a briefing to his managers in 1967, Tom Watson reported that a survey questioning ex-IBMers about why they left the company revealed that they hadn't been aware of opportunities in other IBM divisions, foundations, and locations. Lindbloom was far from alone, however, in finding comfortable niches. As one ex-IBMer said, "You can talk all you like about paternalism; it's the first company that ever treated people like human beings."[11]

The downside for the company, especially in its higher echelons, could be a greater feathering of individual nests and unwillingness to take risks. Tom Watson complained in briefings to his managers about a tendency to "play it safe" and "creeping paralysis" in decision-making, governing by committee and consensus, with excessive copying to everybody.[12] Projects could be hamstrung by individuals failing to "concur" in choices. Bureaucratization had progressed so far by the 1990s, when IBM's previous prosperity collapsed dramatically, that Lou Gerstner would see it as one of the chief obstacles to his campaign to turn the company around.

The work world of men at or near the top of the organization mixed tension and teamwork. Their life at IBM could range from friendly competition to periods of great stress trying to meet tough demands. At the more enjoyable end of that range, a group of fifteen or sixteen officers used to meet somewhere internationally for a show-and-tell to see who could achieve the best yield in chip size or costs. At the other extreme, the pressures became enormous when Tom, Jr., "bet the company" in the early 1960s on the risky gamble of creating a new line of computers with a common architecture.

# ELEVEN

# IBM Triumphs with the
# 360 Mainframe Computer

IBM'S GREAT GAMBLE began with the Spread report of 1961 that led to new engineering in Germany, England, and France with cross-pollination between sites. A common technology allowed designing part of a system in one location and then transmitting it electronically to plants all over the world. IBM in the Hudson valley had become part of an international network. The unprecedented success of the result, the fabled 360 line of computers, would make IBM the world's foremost computer manufacturer.

## THE LABORIOUS BIRTH OF A
## GREAT SUCCESS: THE 360

The crucial component for 360, the transistor, had been announced in 1947, but mass production of transistors did not become operational until 1963. After an intense argument over whether IBM should manufacture its own transistors or subcontract for them with Texas Instruments, the company chose to undertake production itself at a new site in nearby East Fishkill, to the southwest in Dutchess County where there still was a fair amount of land in farms. The South Road plant in Poughkeepsie could not provide enough space, so another Hudson valley location, Kingston, had been considered before East Fishkill. Space had become available in Kingston through the winding down of the SAGE project. But that city would be a long commute from the Poughkeepsie urban region. Why disrupt the lives of prospective staff who had purchased homes in Dutchess County?

For some time, IBMers had fueled the spread of suburbanization south and west from the town of Poughkeepsie. East Fishkill would be much closer for these workers and IBM could obtain some 500 acres of farmland for a building site near Lime Kiln Road in the hamlet of Wicopee. The corporation built factories, hired many local residents, and, according to one official, "became a sugar daddy to local causes, from money for charities to radios for the town police." IBM's plants became the local growth engine creating other jobs. IBMers would "go out to buy sandwiches, buy their newspaper, go over to the local hardware store during the week."[1] The map of new housing developments spurred by the plants was characterized by some residents as the IBM football, with one tip of the football at the Main South Road plant and the other at the East Fishkill facility. IBM continued to be the county's main engine of growth through the 1980s.

To manufacture transistors, the new plant needed to upgrade and retrain workers. The new technology required the equivalent of a technician's skills under the previous electromechanical technology. East Fishkill also needed to hire a lot of highly trained newcomers, often with PhDs in metallurgy or chemistry and with a lot of experience in industry. The new facility also recruited a lot of engineers with BS, MS, and PhD degrees. Overall, East Fishkill's workforce had a high percentage of men with postgraduate degrees. They covered the gamut of skills needed for electronics manufacturing.

Bob Slade, who first ran the plant, recalled an egalitarian atmosphere prevailing there. As at Poughkeepsie, work groups tended to eat together, but shared the same cafeteria with others. More important, a lot of mixing occurred on the job. Engineers constantly worked with assembly-line workers who might help them solve problems. Slade himself moved around the plant constantly. He would talk to those on the factory floor to increase their motivation, go into the lab with questions, give advice to anyone, and attend meetings on financial issues. He called this Management by Walking Around, being a great believer in what teamwork can accomplish.

East Fishkill manufactured the transistor for the 360. In 1965, the announced delivery dates for the 360 provoked a management crisis at that plant. Slade had already accepted an ambitious production commitment, but the quantity he agreed to deliver did not satisfy top management. They demanded that the number be doubled to 56 million transistors. Slade said that couldn't be done, warning of the probability of many flawed components. He proposed a compromise. He would install equipment capable of producing 38 million transistors, but would agree only to an initial plant commitment to produce 27 million.

IBM top management rejected Slade's proposal and replaced him as head of the plant. But his warning became painful reality for IBM. Slade's successor only reached the target of 38 million with the aid of a new chip factory in Burlington, Vermont. Worse by far, many flawed parts resulted. The need to disassemble and then reassemble systems in replacing those parts caused a delay of three to six months in system delivery.

The company reassigned Slade to convert two IBM plants in France and Germany from production of electromechanical business machines to the modern technology now dominant at Poughkeepsie and Endicott. The project turned out to be very satisfying, and Slade quickly began sending French and German staff to Poughkeepsie for retraining. But, at the moment of his reassignment to another location, Slade found himself in the same position as Steve Dunwell and so many other IBMers had been at some point in their company careers. Since salary and perquisites often remained the same or even improved a little, those being replaced and reassigned had to wonder at least briefly whether they had been promoted, demoted, or just pushed sideways. Did the acronym IBM really mean, as employees joked, "I've Been Moved"?

The human costs of bringing the 360 to market included, as Tom Watson told his managers, "severe strain on many of our people [with a] large number of manufacturing people on continuing planned overtime basis working every Saturday."[2] But the costs went beyond intense pressures on the job to more painful individual failures and demotions. As Watson wrote in a draft memo in October 1965, "We somehow have an organization that destroys more men than it produces at the upper end of the scale."[3]

Beyond the costs to current employees, expansion of plants in the drive to complete the 360 required a huge recruitment effort to achieve a more highly educated workforce. IBM looked for new scientists and engineers at thirty-seven colleges. Programming slippages complicated the work of systems engineers in the field. Salesmen found themselves insufficiently knowledgeable about the new line's features. Costs on the job spilled over into home life for those in positions of responsibility. Michael Joyce recalled that young managers involved themselves so fully in bringing forth a system that they forgot not only recreation, but also their families. By the late 1960s, some began to think of less stressful jobs.

## A SHORT-LIVED LOCAL
## START-UP COMPETITOR: COGAR

In the midst of this time of difficult, rapid development, two technically talented IBMers left the company but remained nearby in Wappingers. One of them previously had been sent to Harvard Business School by IBM. Joining a well-reputed former UNIVAC computer designer, George Cogar, they planned to create a competing start-up producing and selling complete memory systems in the very shadow of their former employer. But rather than adopting production techniques off the shelf and subcontracting for some components, they chose IBM's costlier and time-consuming practice of developing their own technology. Cogar sought to create its own distinctive product and method of production from scratch. They did so, however, without IBM's resources.

Cogar did not heed the example of the highly competitive start-ups in Silicon Valley that operated on a shoestring. It failed to adapt to its situation as a beginning entity. Instead, Cogar imitated "IBM managers' offices, with wood desks, matching water pitchers and coffee sets,"[4] in-house library, and patent lawyer. Their cafeteria sometimes served filet mignon. They recruited sixty-six former IBM engineers by 1969, attracted capital easily, and spent $27 million before failing spectacularly in 1972. Since IBM would not consider rehiring any of them, Cogar's engineers fled the valley, scattering to jobs across the country.

In the same years, IBM had been reaping the rewards of the 360's huge success. Before the 360 line's use of a precursor of the integrated chip, computers had been giant room-sized machines, energy inefficient, and costly to manufacture. Now that dramatically improved line, for which Tom Watson had "bet the company," provided the profits that enabled IBM to manufacture components for internal use. IBM did not have to worry constantly, as an Intel had, about how well its products could meet competition from other firms in the same lines. The 360 would shape the computer industry for the next decade. By 1970, IBM had triumphed in mainframes. Its components manufacturing division had become more productive than anyone else in the semiconductor industry.

## IBM'S GROWTH AFTER THE 360

The consequences for the growth of IBM worldwide showed up immediately in the need to build five new factories and increase the company's workforce by 50 percent. By 1984, the peak year for IBM employment in the Hudson valley, Poughkeepsie had 12,000 to 14,000 workers, East Fishkill 10,000, and Kingston 8,000 to 9,000. No other manufacturer in Dutchess County came close to IBM's size. In 1972, Western Printing, the utility Central Hudson, and Texaco Research had between 1,000 and 1,999 employees each, De Laval Separator and Schatz Federal Bearings had between 500 and 999, and Fargo less than 500.

Describing how IBM had changed by 1970, the Regional Plan Association's 1972 report, *The Future of Dutchess County*, said that most employees at the South Road plant previously had worked at machines. But now the report claimed that only four hundred out of the ten thousand plant employees operated machines. The impact of this upgrading could be seen in the county as a whole. By 1970, blue-collar workers composed only one-fourth of the Dutchess labor force. Two years later, IBM phased out the machining operations in Building 001, replacing them with light manufacturing. Changes in both systems and subproducts technology transformed what the Poughkeepsie plant did and needed for its activities. Meanwhile, supervision, sharing of personnel, and shifting of operations among its three mid-Hudson valley locations increased commuting and regional awareness among IBMers. The announcement of a System Products Division realignment included the for-

FIGURE 11.1. IBM South Road campus, 1970s

mation of a mid-Hudson manufacturing organization by the integration of the Kingston and Poughkeepsie organizations and closer links with major East Fishkill component production activities.

IBM had long been a corporate welfare state. But the profitability of the 360 line made easier the paternalism for which the company was famous. The last major expansion of the country club came in 1978 with annual dues still at $1. Employees ran the club through an elected Board of Directors, on which supervisors, managers, and executives could not serve.

The clubhouse and field house provided a snack bar and soda fountain, eight regulation bowling alleys, a darkroom for photographers, and a room for dance instruction with full-length mirrors and kick bars. The club also had billiards, an indoor shooting range, gymnastic equipment, basketball courts, and a theater-type projection room in the gym for showing free adult movies on Sunday nights and movies for kids on Friday.

The club sponsored a host of other nonwork activities like choruses, speaking groups, an amateur theatrical group, hardball and softball teams, rifle shooting, and instruction in fencing and sewing. The IBM Study Club brought in guest speakers, including Werner von Braun in 1958. A plant brochure claimed that many plant women took the club's course in physical fitness and slenderizing. No wonder that Poughkeepsians employed by other companies with nothing like these perquisites marveled at all the country club offered and saw IBM as a world apart.

To help maintain camaraderie, the club opened for breakfast. Many IBM mothers brought their kids to the swimming pool in the summer. IBM sponsored a children's club, provided tennis lessons, a summer camp for kids, and a professionally run nursery for preschoolers. Fathers varied in their use of the club. One remembered playing basketball at noon or later at night. Or he would work out with a friend, treating the club mainly as a gym. But he and his wife took their son to family day at the county fairgrounds. They appreciated the Christmas parties, the award dinners at Dutchess Manor, and especially a company-sponsored trip to an Orlando celebration that included guest stars like Richard Attenborough.

Corporate awards for high technical achievement and division awards added to IBMers sense of a company that rewarded performance. But, by the late 1950s, under Tom, Jr., that came with a more relaxed social atmosphere at company occasions. While salesmen honored at One Hundred Percent Club dinners continued to sing company songs, senior engineers and increasingly other workers rarely did.

## BENEFITS IN JOB SECURITY, HOUSING, AND EDUCATION

What mattered more to most IBMers were the benefits they received, the most important being job security. As a *Poughkeepsie Journal* story noted in 1985, IBM had proved remarkably creative in finding ways to employ displaced workers elsewhere. "People who once assembled typewriters turn up as secretaries, computer programmers and operators, robot controllers, and even students going to classes to learn other new jobs."[5]

By the 1950s, IBM's housing guarantee plan pleased upper-level employees being moved to new locations. The company would buy the employee's house, then take the responsibility for selling it through a local real estate broker. The housing boom in the Poughkeepsie urban region from 1950s onward brought large increases in appraised valuation for the Cape Cod with two bathrooms that originally had gone for $13,000 to 15,000. Expectations of profit, especially in popular neighborhoods, sometimes led an IBM manager who was being moved to complain that the appraisal had undervalued his house. He could point to relocating friends who had done much better.

Some benefits had little visibility, like the subsidized cafeterias where meals cost an employee half to two-thirds of a comparable meal in town. Another benefit, dental insurance, made many Poughkeepsians without it envious. But the benefit that helped many IBMers more was the continuous retraining of workers that often improved their career prospects. Dutchess

Community College helped by teaching a company-developed course for technicians in electromechanical engineering. All programming education at IBM was internal, and potential programmers were selected by aptitude tests. The company trained its own instructors.

IBM also would finance graduate education for some employees, turning both to Syracuse University (which rented space for its instruction from Marist College) and to Union College (which rented space locally from Vassar). One senior engineer recalled that IBM sent three of his close friends away to get their PhDs without any obligation to return, though such employees often did. IBM also went out of its way to create schools in their own languages for the children of foreign IBMers temporarily in Poughkeepsie for retraining. Spackenkill, for example, had a French school.

The temporary presence in the valley of so many domestic and foreign IBMers provided an additional stimulus to the regional economy as a whole. Sometimes it offered unexpected boosts to individual businesses. Jonah Sherman had dreamed up a profitable furniture rental business during the Korean War, whereby potential draftees could rent furniture for two years before owning it. But most purchasers under his plan turned out to be young IBMers fresh out of college or foreign IBMers in Poughkeepsie for a limited time.

IBM contributed to cultural and ethnic diversity in the Hudson valley through its recruitment of permanent workers, especially Asians, from the top engineering schools. In their wake, other Asian professionals, such as doctors, came to the Poughkeepsie area. Together they proved numerous enough to support Hindu and Buddhist congregations and voluntary associations based on national origin.

In domestic recruiting in the early years in the valley, IBM seems not to have hired local African Americans. Mrs. Bessie Payne complained, "as they came, they brought people from other factories that they had. But they still hired in Poughkeepsie, but they didn't hire Negroes."[6] She and some other black leaders apparently did persuade the company to hire a young black woman. Affirmative action as corporate policy was initiated by Tom Watson, Jr., in the 1960s and reiterated in required annual meetings thereafter.

Reception of racial minorities, immigrants, and women within the company is difficult to estimate. Most people in the lab seem to have been supportive of immigrants, although racial and ethnic diversity could create problems in interpersonal communication. One former IBMer who left the company for a successful career in Silicon Valley recalled how co-workers often reacted to seeing a photograph of his racially mixed family, staring at it, and then remarking, "nice frame." The company was a male-dominated environment. IBM's senior ranks, as in most corporations, remained white and male in the 1960s and 1970s. In the late 1960s, the number of women in professional and management positions in IBM grew more than twice as fast as total employment growth in the company. By 1970, the corporation employed

25,000 women nationally, 15 percent of its workforce. Toward the other end of IBM's employment ladder for women, a "proud IBM secretary" wrote Tom Watson the previous year that secretaries should have more status in the company. Responding to changing social aims at home and abroad, IBM, an international company, embraced a new inclusiveness.

IBM did bring in African American and Jamaican professional and white-collar workers for whom access to suburban housing became an immediate issue. Some of these newcomers worked to involve leaders of the local black community in a campaign against the racially restrictive habits of realtors and white home owners. Some of those local African American leaders later complained that the newcomers lost interest in working with them once the housing market opened up a bit.

Resistance of white IBMers to black co-workers moving into their neighborhoods created one memorable occasion. An African American IBM family purchased a house in one of the new residential developments in the Southgate area below the main plant. That provoked residents to call a neighborhood meeting to discuss how to keep this family out. Into the tense atmosphere before the meeting began walked Resident Manager Bill Mair, who proceeded to circulate quietly but visibly around the room before taking a seat in the rear. Conscious of his silent presence, an uneasy discussion followed in which, before long, the participants began outdoing themselves with talk about how to make the new family feel welcome.

## OCCUPATIONAL AND GEOGRAPHIC
## MOBILITY AMONG IBMERS

Perceptions of the frequency of upward mobility within IBM vary by division and by period of time, with some striking stories of rise from toolmaker to management in the company's early years. Less spectacular but widespread improvement in status and reward within career impressed many during those same early years. Jack Economou, mayor of the city of Poughkeepsie from 1971 to 1973, recalled that most of his graduating class of 1947 at Poughkeepsie High School found work at IBM. Usually they started a step above the opportunities their parents had had and continued to benefit from the company's higher wages and salaries. Most IBM employees probably looked forward to limited mobility. While a senior engineer might aspire to become an IBM Fellow, others might hope at best to progress through the management chain.

Upward occupational mobility between generations must have been quite common since so many of IBM's recruits had benefited from the GI Bill, acquiring degrees or technical education unavailable to their parents. The ethnic diversity in employees' surnames at every level of occupational status in Polk's directories for Poughkeepsie is impressive. So is the frequency of multiple workers with the same distinctive surnames among city residents, especially Italian-Americans.

Geographic mobility among IBMers was ubiquitous. Continually starting new projects and opening new sites, IBM needed to seed them with experienced workers. As some employees recalled when the company told you they wanted you to move elsewhere, management normally would say you had a choice. But, should you refuse, they showed their disappointment. So most IBMers moved when asked, sometimes often. In a 1968 briefing, Tom Watson complained that the "attitude persists in many parts of IBM that the only way to get ahead is to move. So relocation is used too often and the human costs are high." Four years earlier, he had urged managers to better prepare workers for the fact that in "our growing company, organizational changes— or individual and group transfers—may be a way of life to many of us."[7]

One Poughkeepsie realtor who for twenty-eight years appraised houses for relocating IBMers saw high rates of turnover among IBM families in many neighborhoods. He recalled a conversation with one woman who had just moved into a brand new house. When he asked why her family was moving so soon, she responded by telling him that she had five children, each born in a different part of the country. Another IBM wife said "she didn't want to make another friend who was just going to move away." The IBM husband of a Vassar professor thought himself to be "in a distinct minority for having worked so long in one place, and even I should logically have moved."[8] Those IBMers who did spend most of their working lives in the valley often worked for varying periods of time in Poughkeepsie, Kingston, East Fishkill, Yorktown Heights, or Armonk. They did a lot of commuting. IBM took intraregional mobility of this kind for granted and generally expected considerable transience of its workers, unlike most other local businesses.

Together the growth and the mobility of IBM's workforce reshaped the Poughkeepsie urban region. The postwar national trend of suburbanization was already apparent in Dutchess County before the war. That trend received a huge boost from IBM's decision to locate both its manufacturing plant and its laboratory in the *town* of Poughkeepsie, not in the *city*. Supporters of annexation of the town by the city had warned as early as the 1920s that the city no longer had attractive sites available. They argued that major manufacturers attracted to the Poughkeepsie area would decide on the town. And, like IBM, they did.

## IBM FACILITIES SITING FURTHERS
## SUBURBANIZATION IN DUTCHESS

While most of IBM's philanthropy focused on the city, generally the company did not locate its work sites there. That choice meant a corresponding loss of tax revenues for the municipal government. Additional facilities built after the South

Road and Boardman Road campuses located even further away from the city. East Fishkill strongly reinforced the previous suburban settlement of IBMers in southern Dutchess and in a few townships to the east and north of the city.

The timing and direction of that suburban thrust appear clearly in township population change by decade after 1950. Hyde Park, LaGrange, Fishkill, and East Fishkill doubled in population between 1950 and 1960 while most townships in Dutchess showed little change or some decrease. Between 1960 and 1970, when IBM located its new plant there, East Fishkill more than doubled from 4,778 to 11,092 inhabitants. Fishkill increased from 6,050 to 11,022, LaGrange from 6,079 to 20,902, and Hyde Park from 12,681 to 16,910.

Parallel patterns of new growth show up in the age of housing in different parts of the town of Poughkeepsie. In older Fairview just north of the city boundary, 44 percent of the houses in 1970 had been built before 1940. In the already well-established villages of Hyde Park and Pleasant Valley 35 percent of the housing predated IBM. In suburban Arlington, where Vassar College had located as early as the 1860s, 31 percent of the housing had been built before the coming of IBM to the region.

By contrast, in both Red Oaks Mill and Spackenkill, near IBM's manufacturing and laboratory campuses, 62 percent and 59 percent, respectively, of the housing in 1970 had been constructed between 1949 and 1959. The continuing push eastward and southward into what had been rural Dutchess shows up in LaGrange where 40 percent of the homes had been built before 1959 and another 40 percent between 1960 and 1970. Most dramatically, the suburban thrust southward to Myers Corners saw 85 percent of the houses in that area constructed during the 1960s.

## POUGHKEEPSIE CITY LOSES WHILE TOWNSHIPS GAIN

The loss for the city can be seen in both population and manufacturing workforce change over the same two decades. Poughkeepsie had reached its population peak in 1950 with 41,023 residents. By 1960, the city had dropped to 38,330 residents. In that same decade, the town of Poughkeepsie grew from 18,169 to 31,129 inhabitants. A parallel shift in manufacturing employment (not including professional workers) saw job loss in the city from 5,165 in 1960 to 3,483 in 1970. That loss contrasted with gain in the town from 3,926 up to 5,639 manufacturing jobs during the 1960s. In that decade, managers, engineers, and other professional workers decreased slightly in the city from 2,194 to 2,019. In sharp contrast, that category of white-collar workers in the town soared from 2,194 to 4,728, clearly reflecting the upgrading within IBM's workforce.

By the early 1970s, the higher proportion of professional and managerial workers in parts of the town of Poughkeepsie and in other townships where IBMers concentrated resulted in lower income and educational levels in the city and other surrounding areas with few middle- and upper-level IBMers. In short, the character and relative prosperity of suburbanization within this urban region varied substantially by area. Frequency of new suburban housing and proximity to IBM's two campuses seem to explain the difference. In three areas, Spackenkill, LaGrange, and Red Oaks Mill, 10 percent or more of the families reported incomes of $25,000 or more in 1970. That contrasted with 5 percent in the town of Amenia and the city of Beacon and less than 3 percent in the city of Poughkeepsie. The average for the town of Poughkeepsie was 7 percent.

Home ownership varied correspondingly, with the most striking contrast between the older valley cities and the newer suburban areas where IBMers settled. Owners occupied only 42 percent of the houses in the cities of Poughkeepsie and Hudson and the village of Wappingers Falls. Rentals accounted for a majority of units in all three. Newburgh and Kingston had higher frequencies of 57 percent and 59 percent home owners. But East Fishkill, Hyde Park, and LaGrange had 80 percent or more, and in high-income Spackenkill, Red Oaks Mill, and Myers Corner 93 percent or more of all houses had resident owners.

Of employed workers in Spackenkill and Red Oaks Mill, 40 percent were professional and technical workers. LaGrange, Arlington, East Fishkill, and Hyde Park had between 29 and 31 percent. By contrast, Beacon and the city of Poughkeepsie had only 15 percent, and older Fairview with its older housing within the town had 18 percent in that category. A similar difference between these areas appears in the frequencies of workers with undergraduate and postgraduate degrees.

In sum, IBM had an uneven impact on suburbanization in the Poughkeepsie urban region. Areas where more highly paid IBMers clustered residentially, as in parts of Spackenkill, had amenities lacking in Fairview, even though single-family dwellings characterized both. Suburban areas differed in size of lots, age and value of housing, family income, and occupational status and education of heads of household. Poughkeepsie's outward sprawl was anything but a uniform tide.

The benefits of the company's spatial needs also were unevenly spread between areas in the region. To avoid the costs of building new plants, IBM leased buildings scattered across Dutchess County to meet its constantly changing, but mostly expanding, requirements for space. The city benefited much less from IBM's leasing than surrounding townships. For varying periods, the company occupied the Daystrom and the Page buildings to the east on Route 55, the Merritt department store building in Hudson Plaza on Route 9, the big plant built for IBM on Myers Corner Road, and many smaller sites like the Asciotto building in Arlington.

Developers with foresight could be optimistic about leasing or renting whatever office and shop space they erected within easy driving distance of the lab and the main plant. For many years, Misak Arslanian had envisioned a cluster of new businesses at Red Oaks Mill, long since bereft of its revolutionary-era gristmill. In the 1930s, part of the current shopping area there had held the recreational aerodrome that would later move to its current location in Rhinebeck. Arslanian gradually purchased properties along Vassar and New Hackensack Roads near the intersection with Spackenkill Road. By persistence and persuasion after the war, he attracted a bank and other businesses. But his biggest success came when some IBM officers walked in wanting to rent all four of the new buildings he had just constructed. To the initial horror of his wife, Arslanian agreed to this rental without a lease.

## WHERE IBMers CONCENTRATED IN RESIDENCE

The area prospered, with businesses lining both sides of Vassar Road; IBMers occupied more than one-third of the adjacent housing facing that well-traveled road in 1965. They also clustered residentially two miles north of Red Oaks Mill. At Greenvale Farms, not far from the Poughkeepsie Day School and Vassar College, IBMers composed two-thirds of the heads of household in a new housing development. Almost all of them were engineers.

Red Oaks Mill became the convenience shopping and service center for the recently built suburban homes on many streets winding out from Spackenkill Road near the IBM lab. On some of these streets, 80 percent or more of the heads of household in 1965 worked for IBM, mostly engineers with some managers and technicians. At the other end of Spackenkill Road, the hills rising up from Route 9 had attracted executives, senior engineers, and PhD scientists.

Some of these developments had begun before the IBM influx. In Kingwood Park, known to residents as "pill hill" for its doctors and dentists, officers of a nearby Quaker school, Oakwood, and local professionals outnumbered IBMers. Long-time area residents also predominated on Cottam Hill in Wappingers. Newcomers IBMer Werner and Ann Buchholz built a house there in the spirit of Marcel Breuer; its architectural difference from conventional ranch styles discomfited some of their neighbors.

On the lowland directly south of the plant and west of Route 9, IBM engineers and technicians predominated. But their houses and lots were smaller than in the more affluent hilltop developments. Higher concentration of IBMers on a street coupled with closer physical proximity increased the likelihood of interaction with fellow employees and their families off as well as on the job. That created a world of shared experience with comforting familiarity for transient families. It seems likely that many IBM children shared the tendency reported by one IBM son of liking to hang out with others who had IBM fathers more than with his peer group.

IBM's impact on the towns of Fishkill and East Fishkill during the 1960s was profound. For example, the population of Hopewell Junction, an unincorporated hamlet in the town of East Fishkill, more than doubled from 4,778 in 1960 to 11,092 in 1970. Almost all of this increase could be attributed to IBM employees and their families; as newcomers, they did not identify with the local place or interact with the existing local community, but rather with their social and occupational group. When queried about where they *lived*, many of the newcomers responded "IBM."

For African American IBMers and other professionals, however, the push into suburban Poughkeepsie could not have been easy, despite Bill Mair's quelling in one episode of resistance from white IBMers. Highly educated black couples like architect Jeh Johnson and his wife Norma found a mixed reception from their new neighbors, some welcoming, some not. A family next door waited ten years to extend an invitation—refused at that late date—to swim in their pool.

Spackenkill residents in the late 1960s organized a campaign to create their own school district so that their teenagers would not have to attend Poughkeepsie High School. The organizers complained that the city facility had become too crowded, with a corresponding lowering of academic standards. The complaint may have had some merit, and separation from the *city* certainly would mean that the new district would be well funded by IBM taxes paid to the *town*, accounting for 40 percent of Spackenkill's assessment. But the preceding two decades had seen a large influx into the city of new black residents from the American South. So it was hard for citizens not to wonder about the racial dimension of this campaign, and although the state education department initially questioned the rationale for the split, they eventually went along. Constructed in 1970, the high school hired many of Poughkeepsie's most experienced teachers and graduated its first class in 1974.

Race riots and urban crime preoccupied the national media, and the proportion of African Americans in the city of Poughkeepsie had increased by 1970 to 20 percent. For black IBMers, sharing the same employer with white IBMers may not have led to a comforting feeling of shared experience.

The fact of a common employer for so many residents in parts of the town in the 1960s and 1970s contrasts sharply with the neighborhoods of the pre–World War II city of Poughkeepsie with its highly diversified economy. Then, most streets housed workers employed in a variety of different businesses. That occupational diversity persisted into IBM's early years in the town of Poughkeepsie when the company recruited local workers already dispersed residentially across the city.

Some of that earlier dispersion would remain in the transformed IBM of the mainframe heyday, but now often more sharply divided by status. Secretaries and clerical workers of all kinds, manufacturing operatives without higher education or technical training, and service workers continue to appear scattered through city streets where older, cheaper housing predominated. Also, the frequency with which IBMers changed location undoubtedly made temporary accommodation in city apartments, rather than purchase of homes, more desirable for some employees, especially those just arrived or less well-paid.

Affectionately known as Birdland, a subdivision of relatively affordable homes located south of IBM's main plant with all of its streets named after birds attracted many young IBM families. Further south along Route 9D, the Chelsea Ridge apartments and town houses became home to many new IBM employees. A complex of apartments on Flannery Avenue in the city, when new, had attracted some of the lab's "brains." But, by 1965, when IBMers numbered one out of four occupants in the complex, they mostly reported themselves as "employees." The complex did include one engineer, designer, staff assistant, and physicist. In the newer Town Gardens apartments north on Innis Avenue, engineers, technicians, and programmers were more numerous, but the IBMers there included a manager, maintenance man, and stenographer. No doubt some of these apartment dwellers hoped soon to join the suburban trend by buying their own new homes to the south or east of the city or maybe farther to the north in Hyde Park.

## IBM'S IMPACT ON LOCAL
## ECONOMY AND GOVERNMENT

Postwar suburbanization would have brought shopping malls and strip development to the Poughkeepsie area as it did everywhere else in urban America. But the construction of three malls near IBM's South Road campus in the town, with strip development and later malls southward on Route 9, testified to the company's impact on the local economy. It also suggested the preference of many employees for a short commute to work and shopping when they could afford housing available close to the plant or lab.

The impact of IBM on local government, especially on tax revenues, could be great. As late as 2003, the company still paid 45 percent of Spackenkill school district taxes. When IBM sold its Boardman Road lab campus to nonprofit institutions in the 1990s, the town of Poughkeepsie tax roll lost heavily. To be sure, the tax benefits from IBM facilities had had a downside. Surrounding townships had huge construction costs to create more school space during the influx of IBM newcomers in the 1960s. Since none of IBM's facilities were located in the city, neither the city of Poughkeepsie nor the city school district ever received much from taxes paid by the company. City capital expenditures increased to provide sufficient secured water and electricity delivery for IBM, however, although Richard Mitchell thought both improvements benefited the city as well. Nevertheless, after Bill Mair, "the only man in IBM who was interested in the City of Poughkeepsie," according to one long-time resident, for IBM's senior managers the city was "off their compass."[9]

The company did not involve itself in local politics nor did it contribute money to either party. But IBM did encourage its employees to be visible in the community. During Lucille Pattison's time as county executive, as many as one-third of the county legislature were IBMers. She believed that on the garbage issue that dominated ten of her years in office the IBM members had a profound influence. Their habits of engineering thinking, interest in technical issues, and long-range planning helped bring about the county's choice of a resource recovery policy.

IBM always had been conscious of the need for regional planning where it located major sites, not wanting to overload an area. Influenced also by the Great Society mood of the 1960s, the company became a founding member of the valley's Pattern for Progress, a planning organization concerned with overall regional development. The corporation carried its own regional planning to a new level when it announced in 1973 formation of its mid-Hudson valley organization that entailed integrating IBM's Poughkeepsie and Kingston manufacturing organizations and linking them more closely with East Fishkill component production. In the late 1960s, when Vassar College's administration and trustees envisioned ambitious new educational programs, the college discussed with IBM the possibility of creating a Vassar Institute of Technology. However, faculty and student protest at Vassar in that highly politicized time led the college to back off that project.

What many nonprofit organizations in the valley remember about IBM's heyday is the many forms of help they received. IBM maintained a Community Service Fund to which IBM retirees as well as regular employees could apply for funds to aid community organizations where they participated as volunteers. Initial applications for up to $2,000 to assist with equipment could be followed later by grants of $5,000.

Under Bill Mair and Tom Watson, Jr., the company had matching programs with hospitals, educational, and cultural institutions, giving them dollar for dollar. The company also made gifts of equipment to some institutions, providing Marist College with computers, for example. The country club allowed a community-wide project like United Way to hold its annual meeting there, but generally tried to avoid seeming to favor particular groups.

At least one IBMer concerned with culture and the arts thought that lack of interest in them among the company's many engineers meant less support for organizations like the Hudson Valley Philharmonic. But individual IBMers made major contributions, as the Dunwells did in reviving the Bardavon as musical and theatrical venue. More generally, the influx of so many highly educated IBMers created a much larger clientele with sophisticated tastes in the Poughkeepsie urban region. Improvement in consumer options followed, including the finer foods at the Adams' farm-stand-turned-emporium, meals at the Culinary Institute of America and Institute graduates opening their own restaurants, and better wines at liquor stores. The continuing infusion of foreign IBMers for varying periods of time also helped make the region more cosmopolitan. That unintended and less noticed result may be one of IBM's more important contributions to longer-term change in the Hudson valley.

TWELVE

# The Quest for Inner-City
# Revitalization: Urban Renewal

IBM'S DECISION TO LOCATE outside of the city of Poughkeepsie exemplified a national trend. In the second half of the twentieth century, metropolitan landscapes had changed as urban Americans moved into the countryside,
making Main Street seem obsolete or irrelevant. The population of central
cities declined as suburbs exploded. Federal funds for new housing and highways encouraged growth outside urban cores, while employment and shopping similarly fled the nation's downtowns. Poughkeepsie reached its peak in
1950 at 41,000 and did not recover through the end of the century.

## URBAN DECENTRALIZATION

Most of the land area within the city's boundaries had been developed, and
the decision not to expand the boundaries beyond the annexation of the
Eighth Ward in 1928 meant that any new major development would have
to take place in the town rather than in the city. For example, from 1940 to
1950, the town's population grew by 37.9 percent, while the city's only
increased by 1.3 percent, and between 1950 and 1960 the city actually
declined by −6.6 percent while the town increased by 61 percent. These
trends continued: between 1960 and 1970, the town grew b y 27.7 percent
to the city's former level of 41,000, while the city declined further by −16,4
percent to 32,000. Meanwhile, Dutchess County, especially the southern
half, similarly felt the impact of IBM and suburbanization as the county
population increased from 136,781 in 1950, to 176,008 in 1960, 222,295 in
1970, and 245,055 in 1980. In the three decades from 1950 to 1980, the
population of the city had declined by 11,206, while the county had
increased by 108,274.

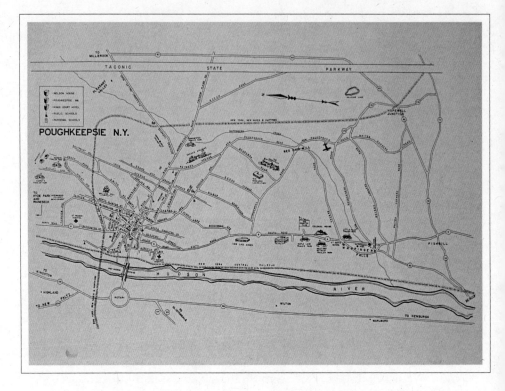

FIGURE 12.1. Sketch map of city and town of Poughkeepsie, c. 1955

The development of the surrounding area resulted from a number of factors. The availability of land meant that new industries and housing were built outside the city. IBM accounted for many of the new jobs, while others in retail sales and service left Main Street for the new shopping centers that sprang up along the Route 9 corridor and other highways. Meanwhile, many middle- and upper-class residents began to move out of the city in search of newer housing, perhaps with more modern utilities or larger acreage, and often with lower taxes, "better schools," and racial homogeneity. Aspects of "white flight" along with social class contributed to the changing social geography. For example, whereas the city's population was 96 percent white and only 4 percent nonwhite in 1950, its demographic composition in 1980 had changed to 74 percent white and 26 percent nonwhite over those three decades; this constituted a loss of 17,304 white residents and a corresponding increase of 6,038 nonwhite residents. In terms of social class, the city had 3,150 middle-class families in 1950, whereas there were only 2,892 in the rest of the county; three decades later, the socioeconomic situation had changed: there were 20 percent more middle-class families in the county than in the urban center.

Suburbanization, as experienced in the Poughkeepsie metropolitan area, was a national phenomenon, fueled by federal policies that encouraged massive home building and the construction of highways. The landscape outside the city boundaries was auto-centered and relatively homogeneous in terms of social class and race. For example, in 1980, Dutchess County was 91 percent white and 9 percent nonwhite, with most of the nonwhite population living in the two cities of Beacon and Poughkeepsie, although the small but growing Asian population generally located outside the cities. New single-family homes, often in housing developments with multiple units, sprawled across the land. "Traversing space now mattered more than creating space. Subsidized home owners had taken their subsidized cars from their subsidized homes on their subsidized roads to their malls."[1] Like other older northeastern industrialized cities, Poughkeepsie's growth stalled as suburbs grew.

The location of employment began to shift. As indicated in previous chapters, most of the city's labor force in 1950 worked in manufacturing; the largest employers were the machinery, textile and apparel, and printing and publishing firms. However, of the four major companies based in the Poughkeepsie area, which included IBM, Schatz Federal Bearing, Western Printing, and De Laval Separator, only De Laval located within the city's boundaries, and it moved out to the town in the 1960s. The relocation of industry outside the city boundaries had a severe impact on the city's tax base. Although manufacturing employment continued to rise in the immediate vicinity, its economic benefits spread outward from the city core to the surrounding towns. City residents employed in manufacturing declined from 11,000 in 1965 to 3,700 (or 28 percent) in 1970, whereas in the county the number employed in manufacturing continued to rise, reaching 26,000 by 1960, or 31 percent of the total workforce.

The crucial change, of course, was the growth of IBM. As indicated in the previous chapter, IBM grew from a workforce of 1,800 in 1945 to 15,500 in 1965. By the 1980s IBM accounted for 70 percent of all manufacturing employment in the county, but only 11 percent of the city's labor force worked for IBM. IBM's major facilities were in the towns of Poughkeepsie and East Fishkill, constructed in 1963 less than 20 miles south of the city. During that time, most of IBM's employees chose to live outside the city in suburban developments closer to those facilities as the company's workforce became more technically trained and therefore more highly paid. Unfortunately for many less educated city residents, IBM phased out their lower skilled assembly-line employment. Although the county's population and economy grew as a result of IBM's expansion, the city of Poughkeepsie did not benefit greatly and its development languished. An article in the *New York Times* in 1964 put it rather bluntly in its headline: "IBM Expansion Strains Dutchess—Growth of Corporation Has Contributed to Problems of Cities and Suburbs."[2] The city was particularly impacted, the article noted: "[B]acked up against the Hudson with no place or way to grow, [the city] has been almost garroted by the expanding towns. . . . A walk down the main street of Poughkeepsie can be a depressing experience." The article continued with a regional view, as it suggested, "those who try to look at the county as a unit see its salvation in the revival of Poughkeepsie."[3] Nonetheless, although efforts by some IBM employees to assist in the revitalization of the city helped, the force of IBM in employment, housing, and shopping separated the city from growth in the rest of the county.

IBM was not the only employer to affect the economic relationship between city and suburb. During the 1960s, the number of manufacturing establishments within the city declined; while there were eighty-one in the city in 1958, by 1973, there were only fifty-five, of which more than half employed less than twenty people. Industrial movement outside the city's borders in this period typified what was happening to the nation's nineteenth-century cities. Also consistent with national economic trends, the service economy began to grow. In Poughkeepsie, over five thousand were employed in business and personal services, health, education, government, finance, and real estate by 1970. However, due to the decline in manufacturing employment, the city's unemployment rate rose from 5.6 percent in 1950 to 9.6 percent in 1980.

The shift of industries outside the borders of Poughkeepsie resulted in major land use changes. The Hudson River shorefront, along with the land alongside the railroads, began to be abandoned. By the mid-1950s, Poughkeepsie no longer had an active industrial riverfront, and much of the land became available for different uses.

## TRAFFIC AND PARKING

Industrial land use spread on the city's north side in a sector closely related to the rail lines. By the 1920s, however, road transportation became more significant as trucks could service industries and businesses on cheaper land at distances from the rail lines. Also, the number of automobiles increased dramatically as housing spread out from the central core. Gas stations and other roadside features such as billboards and automobile salesrooms and used car lots changed the landscape of Main Street as well as streets leading into and out of cities. By mid-century, three out of four Americans owned cars. Traffic congestion had become a problem; indeed, the colloquialism "traffic jam" was already in common use in national magazines and newspapers.[4] Cities tried to cope by placing traffic signals at intersections; initially they were designed with red and green lenses in the 'teens and then with an additional yellow for caution in the twenties. Cities also attempted to limit the time for parking, even developing parking meters, but most efforts failed. Off-street parking in lots emerged as a category of urban land use. Main Street, itself, became a parking lot.

Municipalities attempted to deal with the increasing congestion in their business districts, and the accompanying noise, fumes, and accidents, by drawing up plans to accommodate motor vehicles. City governments widened and straightened streets in the manner of the "City Beautiful" that emerged from the "White City" or as "efficient" streetscapes that reflected the approach of city engineers. Corporations that promoted "automobility" argued for major changes to the streetscape to enhance traffic flow. As the president of the automobile maker Studebaker stated: "We must dream of gashing our way ruthlessly through built up sections of overcrowded cities, in order to create traffic ways."[5] Many cities responded by tearing down abandoned buildings to use the land for parking lots or by constructing arterial highways around and through the downtown.

In Poughkeepsie, the increasing number of vehicles, plus limited parking spaces, created traffic jams on Main Street and at the intersection of Market and Main in the heart of downtown. North–south traffic on Route 9, along South Avenue and Market Street, became constricted by having to go through the center of the downtown, while east–west traffic was similarly congested along Main Street. At the beginning of the decade in January 1950, a member of the Chamber of Commerce declared that traffic congestion harmed business: "If the city is to grow and prosper, something must be done to relieve traffic conditions. . . . Our merchants must depend on patronage from residents within a twenty-five mile radius of the city. If traffic conditions leading into the city are favorable and good, merchants will get more business."[6]

## ARTERIALS

In 1953, the city, along with the state, began plans for a North–South arterial to bypass the center of downtown. It would become one of the first major physical changes wrought by external forces that would come to dominate the changing face of the city over the following two decades.

The North–South arterial highway got under way in 1959, although construction did not actually begin until 1963 due to delays in rights-of-way arrangements. Completed in 1966 at a total cost of $14 million, the high-speed highway had bulldozed its way through historic neighborhoods and had created a real and a perceptual barrier between the river slope area and the central core along the ridge paralleling Market and Bridge streets. Lost open space included a "section some still know as 'Livingston Woods,'" and the triangular area between South Avenue and the end of Academy Street, where the Lynch family had their violet greenhouses at the turn of the century. The construction imposed a heavy cost on neighborhoods, families, and the built environment: it cut into 228 parcels, including 178 dwellings housing 200 families, as well as entailing a loss of $600,000 in tax revenue, at the then-current rate.

Many Poughkeepsians opposed the alignment of the North–South arterial. Residents in the vicinity of St. John the Baptist Church on Grand Street fought the demolition of their neighborhood unsuccessfully, whereas two churches successfully halted the bulldozer: Church of the Holy Comforter, a magnificent English neo-Gothic church designed by nineteenth-century architect Richard M. Upjohn in 1859 on Davies Place; and St. Peter's Roman Catholic church, circa 1853, located in the Mount Carmel district. In both cases, the highway was moved slightly to the west, closer to the railroad right-of-way, rather than through their properties. By the end of the twentieth century, the structures of all three churches remained, although only the latter two had parishioners. The arterial essentially obliterated the historically ethnic German neighborhood surrounding St. John's, while Holy Comforter's congregation became minuscule. With the closing of the primarily ethnic Italian Mount Carmel Roman Catholic Church in the mid-century and the out-migration of many Irish-Americans from the neighborhood, St. Peter's, renamed Mount Carmel, remained a vital spiritual and social space for the ethnic Italian community in the city and suburbs.

FIGURE 12.2. East–West arterial construction, 1977

Meanwhile, east–west traffic through the city continued to be a problem. In 1960, Candeub & Fleissig, consultants to the city's master plan, reported that "Main Street shows the most severe congestion: peak hour traffic volumes exceed the street capacity by about 42 percent. . . . With the exception of Market Street all the capacity deficiencies are observed on the east–west roads."[7] Further studies also showed that east–west traffic on the Mid-Hudson Bridge exceeded capacity, while traffic east of the city on routes 44 and 55 generated twice as many vehicles as they were designed to carry. In 1966, the same year as completion of the North–South arterial, the city planning board presented a proposal for an East–West arterial to run from routes US44 and NY55, on the eastern border of the city, to the Mid-Hudson Bridge. In phrases that echo urban planning rhetoric of the time, the proposal posited that an arterial roadway, sliced through the built-up area of the city core, would relieve congestion for through traffic and act as "a convenient and efficient way to bring City and area residents from their homes to Downtown."[8] Although the arterial achieved the former objective, the latter would rather act in reverse, as many businesses on Main Street moved out of the city to shopping centers that had been established on Route 9 and other highways in the surrounding towns.

In 1973, the New York State Department of Transportation (DOT) presented a complete draft of the plans, which the federal highway administration approved in 1974. Both the eastbound and westbound arterials undermined the livability of neighborhoods that the high-traffic highway dissected. House lots that fronted onto city streets widened to make room for the arterial, such as along Church Street, were cut so that sidewalks abutted front steps and porches. According to one observer of urban arterial landscaping during this period, "Transition spaces vanished, along with the street as public space. Wide streets, treacherous intersections, and fast cars blurred our view and corrupted our built environment." Street lighting and traffic poles were built higher than many rooftops and lighting was bright and harsh. "Urban light, once the artful form-giver illuminating evening . . . succumbed to lighting shaped for speed . . . the traffic engineers' goosenecked forms and elevated poles create a tunnel down the road to nowhere. Light . . . the agent of comfort, security, and sense of place, was altered." Street lamps, "whose glow signified human warmth," were replaced by tall, look-alike, widely spaced highway lighting fixtures.[9]

Arterial highways are hardscapes, engineered for speed and clear sightlines. The roadbed is often made of concrete that reflects sunlight and powerful lights from grey metal lighting fixtures, with hard-packed shoulders and concrete sidewalks or metal guardrails. The North–South arterial lacks vegetation to soften or shade the surroundings as it swings south from the sewage treatment plant that borders Marist College, past the rail lines to the southern border of the city with the town at the rural cemetery. Landscaping is also limited along the entire length of the East–West arterial from the Mid-Hudson

Bridge through the center of the downtown area north and south of Main Street toward the eastern border with the town. Not until a decade after its construction did the newly appointed Shade Tree Commission take up the question of planting "in yards of people on Church Street and plantings in center of East–West arterial."[10] Housing values of structures along the arterials declined and many became rental properties.

Sporadic citizen protest against the alignment and landscaping plans of the East–West arterial, particularly with respect to the routing of the highway so close to three schools in the city and the town, echoed public criticism of the probable economic and social effects of the North–South arterial a decade earlier.[11] In 1956, opponents of the North–South arterial had predicted that easing traffic flow past the city "will drain business from the city and will provide a flow of customer traffic to out-lying shopping districts."[12] The East–West arterial had an even greater impact on the city's social and economic landscape: in housing it displaced forty-eight owners and fifty-nine tenants, as well as twenty-six businesses, led to further loss of the city's tax base, and became a primary factor in the demise of Main Street as the major retail area in the county.

## MAIN STREET HUB

Poughkeepsie's Main Street served as the commercial center of Dutchess County from the nineteenth and into the first half of the twentieth century. Even as late as 1964, planning consultants could declare: "The City of Poughkeepsie's role as a retail trade center is very significant, and it is the Hudson Valley's principal shopping center. Its Central Business District is the strongest downtown area between Albany and White Plains."[13] In the years prior to and after the two world wars, over 150 individual shops, together with six department stores, created an urban magnet that drew customers from throughout the region. From the intersection with Market Street, commercial enterprises fronted on both sides of Main Street, in city blocks numbered from the high 200s to the high 400s.

Although there were a great variety of shops, similar retail enterprises tended to locate near one another. For example, five of the department stores sat close together in the 300 block between Academy and Catherine streets to the east and Market Street on the west. The grandest of them, the home-grown Luckey, Platt, anchored the block on the corner of Academy Street, with Up-to-Date a few doors down and Wallace's and M. Shwartz & Co. across the street. Others, including franchise department stores such as Kresge, W. T. Grant, and Woolworth, occupied spaces within a block. On these blocks and west toward Market Street many other shops selling women's and men's wear, a beauty shop, and stores selling shoes and jewelry as well as restaurants suggest a streetscape that was familiar and comfortable for women. Fredrica Goodman grew up in Poughkeepsie in the

1940s and 1950s when going downtown was "considered an outing" and ladies would "dress up."

East from Catherine–Academy streets toward Crannel Street shoppers visited the Mohican Market, well known for its fresh fruits and vegetables. William N. Smith, recently retired as president of Luckey, Platt in 1971, recalled the Mohican Market and its importance as a gathering place for shoppers across Main Street from his department store: "It was a darn good food market and attracted people right to this area, to the department stores and the banks. It was a core. The women would meet there and they didn't have to go to the outskirts for their marketing. There weren't any markets on the outskirts."[14]

Other domestic shops sold men's and women's apparel, boots, shoes and hats, drugs and cosmetics, Singer sewing machines and luggage. Furniture could be purchased at Luckey, Platt or in specialty stores like Perlmutter's, while further east along Main Street into the upper 300s and 400 blocks, stores catered more to men, with hardware, auto supply, and barber shops, although Effron's children's store at the corner of Clinton, and food stores,

FIGURE 12.3. Main Street, 1970

such as Karl Ehmer's meat market, bakers and dry goods also located toward the east. Two Arax photo labs and retail stores could be found a few blocks apart. Meanwhile, three cigar stores and a number of lawyers' offices located very close to the courthouse at the Market and Main intersection.

Retail sales on Main Street increased in the years following World War II as the consumer economy gained strength. From 1948 to 1954, citywide sales rose from $72 million to $89 million. The greatest growth occurred in eating and drinking places (over 50 percent), automobile sales (over 40 percent), and service stations (over 60 percent). However, by the end of the decade, even long-established local stores began to close. Van Kleeck's men's furnishing store at 259 Main Street closed in 1960. Opened in 1799, it was Poughkeepsie's oldest firm, and possibly, according to Peter Van Kleeck, "the nation's oldest retail business carried on under the same family."[15]

Meanwhile, the number of restaurants declined from 102 in 1950 to 56 in 1980, while the gas stations and car dealerships would move out of the city to cheaper land on the periphery, along with supermarkets, drive-in eateries, dry cleaners, pharmacies, floral shops, and stores selling sporting goods and hardware. As automobile sales rose, businesses outside the crowded streets of the city increased dramatically. Initially, some of the shops on Main Street opened branches in the new shopping centers; eventually, most would close down their urban shop and concentrate their business in their former branch store. Franchise businesses, such as drive-in eateries including the golden arches of McDonald's or self-service shoe retailers, located almost exclusively along the highways that radiated out from downtown or in the new shopping centers on the edge of town.

The decline of Poughkeepsie's central business district (CBD) typified the trend in the nation's cities in the mid-1950s. Three main forces were involved: the population of the city had reached its peak and actually began to decline, while the population of the surrounding towns increased rapidly; the growth of IBM and associated businesses in the town, and the loss of manufacturing jobs and other businesses in the city; and "the almost universal preference of the shopper to use the automobile," combined with the development of shopping plazas and supermarkets on highways outside the city boundaries. Parking spaces were available, and free, at the new shopping plazas. Poughkeepsie Plaza opened in 1958 and advertised itself as the "largest parking area between Westchester County and Albany" with 1,450 parking spaces. Its anchor stores of W.T. Grant, Woolworth's, and Grand Union were among the first major franchise stores to move their primary sales off Main Street and into the suburbs.

From the late 1950s to the late 1960s, six shopping centers, built outside the city in Arlington and along Route 9 in the town and as far south as Wappingers Falls and Fishkill, began to draw a greater volume of retail trade, first in food and increasingly in soft and hard goods. These six shopping centers, or plazas, including Hudson, Poughkeepsie, and 44 Plaza, contained nearly double the floor space of Poughkeepsie's downtown area. In 1954, the city, with over 70 percent of the commercial space of the county, accounted for 58 percent of all sales volume; by 1961, sales volume had slipped to 47 percent and rapidly decreased to 38 percent by 1966 to only 28 percent in 1980; an overall decrease from 1950 to 1980 of more than 40 percent.

In an attempt to answer the rise in competition, the city responded in three ways: by building up its employment base by creating a coherent plan for the downtown as the center for financial and governmental activity; by increasing available parking; and by constructing a downtown pedestrian shopping area. The continued presence in the city of two hospitals, banks, and the county courthouse and office building underlay the first strategy. Downtown Poughkeepsie, according to the director of urban planning and development at the dedication of the new County Office Building on Market Street in 1965, would "become the city of the white-collar worker, sitting high in his air-conditioned splendor, and looking down upon a city revitalized with new life, important construction, and the beginnings of fulfillment of the promise of the future."[16] Law offices and financial service offices remained close to the courthouse and the banks at the center of the central business district, while numerous physicians' offices and medical services located near the hospitals. But, increasingly, the professionals themselves, including doctors, lawyers, and bankers, lived outside the city; for example, whereas 76 percent of the county's attorneys lived in the city in 1950, thirty years later only 40 percent did, and during the same three decade span from 1950 to 1980, the percentage of CPAs who lived in the city fell from 77 percent to 25 percent.

## THE PARKING DILEMMA

In an effort to respond to the increasing demands on space caused by the use of the automobile, the Poughkeepsie Area Development Association (PADA) presented a plan in 1950 for increased downtown parking. The PADA had been instituted two years earlier in response to a report from the Regional Plan Association and described itself as a "non-profit, nonpartisan, fact-finding organization devoted to the development of the Poughkeepsie area." Although Mayor Graham declared in his annual address to the Common Council in January 1950 that the two most important physical problems to be solved by the city were to fix drainage in the Eighth Ward and to provide a new sewage treatment plant, the merchants on Main Street and other businessmen in the PADA were equally concerned with traffic flow along and parking on Main Street.

Like most American urban areas as the decade began, Poughkeepsie was being devoured by the explosion of automobiles and their use in the postwar era. Viewing the situation across America, the historian Daniel J. Boorstein lamented: "If we are an automobile-riding, we are also an automobile-ridden people. Despite the daily offerings that Americans insert in parking meters, and the grand new parking temples rising in the centers of our cities, we seem unable to appease the motor goddess."[17] Between 1950 and 1960, Poughkeepsie managed to increase available parking spaces by almost 50 percent. However, in their study of the CBD for a master plan, the planning firm Candeub & Fleissig noted that "while there is an overall adequacy of spaces, the high utilization rates in many sectors indicate that *the critical problem is in the distribution of these spaces.*"[18] Attempts to accommodate the automobile would be on the Common Council's agenda throughout the latter half of the twentieth century.

In 1955, the city undertook plans to create off-street parking. The Mill–Catherine Street Project was begun as the "first urban renewal project," and led to a fundamentally different approach to changing the face of the cityscape: instead of private funds from individual "boosters" such as members of the Improvement Party in the nineteenth century, the city, as a corporation, would now use federal monies to adjust land uses.[19] As Leon Bloom, chairman of the Poughkeepsie Urban Renewal Agency (PURA) in 1966, commented, "the Project has achieved its goals. From this Project, the city gathered the necessary experience to proceed with additional activities."[20] Among other changes, clearance for the project displaced twenty families. It was a harbinger of changes to come.

The city established the General Neighborhood Renewal Plan in 1961 as a direct outgrowth of the Catherine–Mill Street Project. The area of the city in the plan encompassed 500 acres from the Hudson River east into the CBD. Out of this overall plan came specific projects, all of which included some federal funding, such as the 14-acre City Hall Project that was designed to provide space for new public office buildings. The core of this revitalized and modern city, in the futuristic vision of the mid-1960s, would be centered around the new county office building on Market Street, which "will have been joined by many such modern, high-rise buildings, making liberal use of prestressed concrete, and vast expanses of glass."[21] The new county office building rose on the site of the former post office, which had ceased its service in 1938 after the opening of the present one at the end of New Market Street; it then became civil defense headquarters for the county from 1942 to 1944, when other county offices, such as the motor vehicle bureau and the welfare department, worked out of the space.

The federal secretary of HUD Robert C. Weaver dedicated the county's modern high-rise in 1965; in his speech, he posited that rational planning for urban growth was a serious issue for the nation. Central cities, he noted, were deteriorating and being torn apart by suburban development. "And, as most of this growth shows no coherent pattern, we have come to refer to it as urban sprawl. Coupled with central city blight, this constitutes the core of our urban problem today."[22] According to the secretary, the containment of urban sprawl through "comprehensive area-wide planning" and the rebuilding of central cities through urban renewal projects needed to work together to advance President Johnson's thrust to enhance "quality of life" for Americans.

Plans to create a central core of public and private civic structures at the intersection of Market and Main streets continued over the following decade. Designs for a new city hall were first proposed in 1967, and five years later in June 1972 the new municipal building was dedicated. Mayor Economou planned a day-long celebration of the arts, which the *Poughkeepsie Journal* asserted in an editorial as "the first attempt by city leaders in recent years to fire-up some community spirit which, in the long run, is the really key ingredient in any lasting urban renewal."[23] The West Point military band performed at the ceremony, while Frivolous Sal's Volunteer banjo band, the IBM mixed chorus, and Pete Seeger performed at a candlelight songfest later at Riverfront Park.

At the dedication, however, the keynote speaker John V. Lindsay, mayor of New York City, struck a more somber note. Urban America was in crisis, he pointed out: "There is no urban need that is not a national need. . . . There is no urban crisis that is not a national crisis. . . . The future of America will be determined by what becomes of its cities, for in our urban areas are the symptoms of what all Americans suffer." He argued that the war in Vietnam was one of the most important reasons why America's cities were in such dire straits: "That war is hell on cities, not only Hanoi or Haiphong, Hue or An Loc. . . . We've got war-torn cities all over America. All the cities and towns from Poughkeepsie to Pasadena that have ancient schools, crowded hospitals, abandoned buildings and inadequate transportation." The war, he asserted was taking resources away from America's urban populations. "Isn't it time Americans said, 'Enough'? Isn't it ever going to be our turn in urban America?" he wondered.[24] "The decline and fall of cities," he stated, "was a precursor to a nation's disintegration. City Hall itself would later emulate Lindsay's comments. Built in the modernist design of a progressive future, it would have to be evacuated in the 1980s due to severe engineering problems, to be re-inhabited at great cost in 2000.

Meanwhile, three other major buildings were planned to concentrate commercial and cultural activity downtown at the intersection of Main and Market streets. Between the county office building and the new City Hall, the city erected a civic center complex, including a large exhibition hall and an ice rink, attached to a five-story hotel. Across New Market Street would be built a three-story parking garage connected to an office building, planned as a financial center, on the northeast corner of Main and Market. The latter building, initially called the Barney building after its developer, faced the Art Deco facade of the Church building across Main Street with a complementary scale, although it posed a sharp contrast to the bulk and height of the civic center and hotel across New Market Street. All these buildings, built during the 1970s and 1980s for governmental, service, and cultural functions rather than retail commercial uses, established the symbolic core of the CBD for the latter half of the twentieth century.

## MAIN MALL

The most controversial construction program to improve the CBD and maintain its retail sales function called for the development of a pedestrian shopping area along three blocks of Main Street, to be known as Main Mall. The idea of a central city pedestrian mall received favorable attention in medium-sized cities that were in the process of revitalizing their CBDs in the late 1950s. The first two pedestrian malls in the United States, in Toledo, Ohio, and Kalamazoo, Michigan, opened in 1959, and newspapers reported on the innovative schemes. George Spitz, the mayor of Poughkeepsie in 1959, liked the idea "as a means of adding to the midtown business district attractions."[25] As a "hustling, bustling center of activity," it would be a lively competitor to the suburban malls.

In April 1960, Candeub & Fleissig, consultants to the city on the development of an overall master plan, presented the idea of a Main Street mall that would include the closing of Main Street between Market and Hamilton streets. They concluded that Main Street had "become increasingly important for pedestrians and less important for motorists," and that a mall "exclusively devoted to pedestrian movement" would "establish a pleasant environment for carrying on commercial and leisure activities."[26] However, although the *Poughkeepsie New Yorker* continued to cover the growing prosperity of Kalamazoo, known as "mall city," the concept appeared to lose momentum after Spitz's term. The buildup of other aspects of urban redevelopment, particularly transportation and housing, also distracted attention from it.

The idea of a pedestrian mall received serious consideration once again in 1967 after a visit to Kalamazoo by Poughkeepsie resident Stephen Dunwell, who was so impressed with the Kalamazoo mall that he rented a camera and extensively photographed it. He saw similarities between the two cities in terms of both size and distance from the metropolises and became convinced that such a mall was exactly what Poughkeepsie needed. When he returned to Poughkeepsie, he made a slide presentation of the Kalamazoo mall to the Poughkeepsie Downtown Council.

City business executives responded by organizing "Operation Speed-Up." Along with the Poughkeepsie Urban Renewal Agency (PURA), they commissioned two studies. A study by Larry Smith & Co. of economic and marketing aspects led to a capital improvement program. More significant in terms of the emerging cityscape, the Poughkeepsie Area Chamber of Commerce, with Jonah Sherman as president, commissioned a study from Victor Gruen Associates, the same urban design consultants who had done a study for the Kalamazoo mall. Completed in 1969, the Gruen plan contained many of the ideas first suggested by Candeub & Fleissig ten years earlier.

On November 6, 1969, forty-two of Poughkeepsie's civic leaders visited Kalamazoo, and many came back believing, according to the *Poughkeepsie Journal*, that "what has proven results 620 miles west of Main and Market Streets would be given a green light here too."[27] Mayor Richard Mitchell, an active supporter of the East–West arterial, increased parking, and other efforts to stimulate business in the CBD, was a prime proponent. Some had their doubts, however. Louis Fiore, an alderman at the time, had also gone on the trip and he noted that Kalamazoo "was not surrounded by shopping centers," as Poughkeepsie already was.[28] Kalamazoo also "had two existing four-lane streets on either side of the mall able to accommodate traffic diverted from Main Street," whereas traffic jams continued in downtown Poughkeepsie.

The Downtown Council announced plans that fall for a $400,000 pedestrian mall, to be financed by Main Street property owners and businessmen through the establishment of a twelve-year public improvement tax district. However, Fiore became mayor in 1970: he combined his initial misgivings about the success of a mall with dislike of the tax assessment district funding mechanism, which seemed, to him, to be detrimental to the small merchants. Without the mayor's support, the concept could not pass through the Common Council. Meanwhile, in 1971, the Chamber of Commerce proposed a semi-mall, similar to the Gruen plan, that widened sidewalks, removed on-street parking, and allowed some traffic flow.

FIGURE 12.4. Main Mall construction, 1973

Two years later, Mayor Jack Economou revived the concept of a fully closed-off pedestrian mall. Some opposition among Main Street merchants continued. In April 1972, Arthur Bressman, president of Luckey, Platt, wrote a letter to the Common Council and published it in the *Poughkeepsie Journal*. He was in favor of "either a semi-mall or a complete mall. However," he warned, "the planning and execution must encompass much more than the completed final product which we will see on Main Street. . . . Unless we provide satisfactory traffic flow around and into the city, the building of a mall will choke off all city bound traffic. . . . We are firmly convinced that the solution of traffic flow, parking and public transportation must be fully completed before any part of Main Street is closed to traffic."[29] Planning for the East–West arterial had long been advanced; however, it was not in place by this time.

Mayor Economou appointed a task force to study the idea and report back quickly. In October, the task force presented their report. Citing a need for the "City of Poughkeepsie to act as the one center for the entire county," the report supported the idea of a fully closed-off pedestrian mall. In citing the benefits of such a mall, the report stated, "A full mall will draw people once more into the heart of the city, and it will revitalize the whole CBD."[30] On January 22, 1973, the Common Council authorized construction that began in April and lasted for almost a year. The design consultant was William Gindele of Gindele & Johnson in Poughkeepsie.

Two years later, the mall was judged to be a partial success, according to the city's planning consultants Llewelyn-Davies Associates of Binghamton, New York. They added, however: "It has not made a major change in the economic environment of the city."[31] Although the city and the local business community staged various events to encourage shoppers to congregate in the public space of the mall, and thereby stimulate a safe and welcome shopping environment, by the summer of 1975 there were three vacant stores and two of the major department stores were in severe financial condition and about to close. As one observer reflected, "The five-year delay between the opening of the Mall and completion of the East/West arterial—which had been intended to absorb the diverted traffic-created difficulties, and the national economic downturn in the late seventies made matters much worse. But the fundamental problem was that the attraction of shopping in downtown Poughkeepsie was not strong enough to offset the scale, convenience and variety of the suburban malls."[32]

In 1975, Main Mall had replaced Main Street, but the CBD had only just begun to adjust to the latter half of the twentieth century. Originally conceived as a moderately expensive renovation to be funded by local merchants themselves, the mall, when dedicated on September 6, 1974, cost ten times more than anticipated and was completely federally financed. Its cost of approximately $4,000,000, however, was only one-tenth of the total of federal

FIGURE 12.5. Main Mall, 1980

funds allocated to the city of Poughkeepsie during this period. Poughkeepsie became "famous" as one of the highest federally funded cities per capita in the nation. Most of this money went into the demolition and rehabilitation of the housing stock in the city.

## HOUSING

As noted in earlier chapters, residential housing occupied most of the land area within the borders of the city of Poughkeepsie. Most of the housing had been built by mid-century. In 1958, about 45 percent of the city's total of approximately 13,000 units had been constructed prior to the twentieth century. According to one consultant, "Although the charm and character of these older homes is an important aesthetic asset to the City, they represent problems both in terms of maintenance and in compliance with today's plumbing, electrical and fire regulatory standards."[33]

Many of the older cities of the nation were undergoing similar review of their housing stock, especially for low-income families, and it became a political issue. A national housing goal was stated in the Housing Act of 1949 when Congress declared that every American, regardless of income or origin, was entitled to "a decent home and a suitable living environment"; this goal was further promoted in the 1956 Housing Act. In 1958, Poughkeepsie hired

Candeub & Fleissig as consultants to create a master plan. In their 1960 *General Development Plan*, they noted that the city's housing stock was aging rapidly and much of it had deteriorated. "In terms of land area," they reported, "roughly 260 acres, or 14 per cent of the total built-up area of the city, excluding streets, are taken up by blocks in which over 60 per cent of the units were rated as deteriorated."[34]

The city administration particularly focused on lower Main Street between the CBD and the river where they judged that most of the city's "serious land and human problems" had been located since before World War II. Fresh from graduating with a planning degree in 1964, Kenneth Toole began work with the Dutchess County Planning Department. One of his first assignments was to join city planner Ian Stewart on a study of the Lower Main Street neighborhood. It was, he recalled, his first experience with "real poverty." They surveyed many apartments that were described as "hovels," yet, Toole added, "They were wonderful buildings, Greek Revival and so on; they were terrific buildings."[35] He lamented the loss of many of the streets and structures during urban renewal. "It was," he declared, "physical planning without much social context." Homes were eliminated and the people moved. However, the promised new housing never materialized. Toole commented further that the "people were never really taken care of like they should have been."

Toole and Stewart were young and idealistic planners. They were both intensely interested in the social as well as the physical fabric of Lower Main Street and both later fought to save some of the neighborhoods from complete destruction. By 1971, however, the city administration had begun urban renewal efforts in the city and viewed the situation more darkly. Lower Main Street was characterized by Leon Bloom, the city's director of urban renewal, as a "critical area of derelict alcoholism." Bloom reported that the Lower Main Street area was where most of the city's low-income families lived, as well as almost 30 percent of the city's senior citizens. And, he added, "The lower part of Main Street has become a Negro ghetto."[36]

The studies undertaken by the city's consultants and their own staff in the early 1960s led to specific plans by the middle of the decade and the city applied for federal funds for projects in this downtown area. One project proposed a new county office building that included the acquisition and demolition of the Nelson House property. This 77-acre project relocated 725 families and 291 nonresidential occupants. The original part of the Nelson House was demolished; the new county office building was dedicated in September 1965. Also in 1965 the city created the Poughkeepsie Urban Renewal Agency (PURA) in response to the federal government's creation of the Housing and Urban Development agency (HUD).

PURA designated five major project areas, about one-fifth of the total area of the city and one-third of the population, for redevelopment, rehabilitation, or demolition. The completion of clearance in much of these areas, the preservation of some of the neighborhoods that fought against the original plans of urban renewal, and the construction of new buildings on many, but not all, of the cleared acres substantially changed the face of Poughkeepsie over the next decade.

Entering the city from the west and crossing the Mid-Hudson Bridge, a driver's first impression of Poughkeepsie had dramatically changed. Arterial roadways had eliminated whole neighborhoods, such as along Gate Street not far from the bridge. One no longer encountered a bustling urban center; rather the multilane highway channeled the passage through the city, past vacant lots and buildings, and east or south to vast parking lots and strip shopping centers. For all practical purposes, the city as vital core for the larger community had ceased to exist, except for judicial hearings at the county courthouse or the purchase of automobile driving licenses at the county office building.

## WATERFRONT

The greatest overall land use impact came from the Riverview Project along the riverslope. This project, described by PURA as being a "well planned and physically integrated" residential plan that would "eliminate blight," encompassed all the area bounded by Main Street on the north, Pine Street on the south, the railroad and North–South arterial on the east and the Hudson River on the west. The plan stipulated ten "Development and Design Objectives" that included the improvement of vehicular and pedestrian circulation, parking, compatible development, the construction of "moderate"-income housing, landscaping, the elimination of overhead wires and signs, the provision of lighting and paving, and economic benefits. The auto-centered landscape overtook Main Street, as the plans became as concerned with accommodating the automobile as they were with housing the people.

On July 19, 1966, PURA demolished the first building in the project area. By the end of the demolition period, 120 residential and thirty business and industrial sites, including the Poughkeepsie Yacht Club and the Pirate Canoe Club, were cleared. Some of the residents had lived in the area for fifty years or more and were extremely upset with being in the way of "progress," but urban renewal through eminent domain trumped private property concerns. By October 1967, residential relocation had been completed, followed by commercial relocation and demolition. Poughkeepsie's waterfront and river slope up lower Main Street was now cleared for a modernist vision of an urban-suburban metropolis.

Planners and developers wished to transform the nineteenth-century, pedestrian-oriented city into a twentieth-century, auto-related and amenity-filled metropolis. Indeed, the preferred developer, Roger H. Corbetta, drew up a dramatic plan that would include more than a thousand dwellings of "moderate" housing, five hundred units of "middle-income" housing, and one hundred town houses for "upper-middle" housing, with "the kind of home environment that modern families want, but usually can't find." The prospectus promoted its suburban rather than urban qualities: "It will combine features characteristic of suburban living, with an in-town location and many community services. It will offer more recreational facilities than many resorts or private clubs." For the future resident, "a choice will be offered between high-rise apartments, garden apartments with balconies and town houses with private gardens, both for rent and for sale. Spacious house and apartment designs will appeal to families used to country living. Residents of Riverview will enjoy country living advantages with city conveniences."[37]

The vision, entitled "Poughkeepsie Is Awake," was boldly described in the brochure distributed at the groundbreaking in the summer of 1968: "It is planned to phase out poverty and unwarranted misery." Four religious leaders blessed the site while a dozen members of PURA and the Common Council looked on. Leon R. Bloom, chairman of PURA, Victor C. Waryas, mayor in 1963, and Richard W. Mitchell, mayor in 1968, gave speeches. However, Corbetta built only the eighteen-story Rip Van Winkle apartment house in the next two years, and a row of low-rise units over the next several years. As sub-

FIGURE 12.6. Lower Main Street, view west, 1980
Rip Van Winkle apartments (left)

sidized housing, isolated from the rest of the city by the railroad tracks and the North–South Arterial, the Riverview section developed only very slowly as a residential area. Corbetta's vision of 1968 would never be fulfilled.

Land use change produced a far different riverfront in the twentieth century from that at the turn of the century. It was no longer filled with industrial structures, and, other than sporadic redevelopment for housing, became established as open space. Urban renewal funds were used to fix up Riverfront Park at the foot of Main Street in 1968, although it was not until 1974–1975 that major redevelopment took place. The park was later named Waryas Park in recognition of the efforts of former Mayor Waryas to redevelop the area. The city constructed two boat docks, one at the southern end of the park abutting Kaal Rock for use by the Hudson River Sloop Clearwater, and a boat ramp for free public access to the river. The park contained a small children's playground with swings and climbing sculptures. The sculptures were built out of steel rebar and cement and covered by ceramic tile mosaics. Local schoolchildren made the mosaics as a city arts project; they referred to persons and events in Poughkeepsie's history and remained unmarked by graffiti for decades, reflecting the pride that city residents held for them.

Also in the early 1970s, the city created Kaal Rock Park from a former industrial site. Located under the span of the Mid-Hudson Bridge, and with only one means of access, it soon earned a reputation for drug dealing and fell into neglect. Its waterfront walkway and boat dock were lost to winter ice and river erosion, and thirty years would pass before it was once again scheduled by city planners for rehabilitation. Waterfront revitalization plans at the end of the century would include an agreement, after much public debate, to design a small park on the summit of Kaal Rock on the site of a former restaurant. At century's end, the Bonura family who owned and operated the Grand Hotel next to the Civic Center in the city center leased the former sewage treatment plant and the former De Laval property to the south of Kaal Rock for a restaurant and catering facility. To the north of Waryas Park, at the mouth of the Fall Kill on property of the former Innis Dye Works, a restaurant was established, which would become the Children's Museum at the beginning of the twenty-first century. Other amenity features in Waryas Park would include a skate park and boat launch.

During the same period as the redevelopment of Riverview, other urban renewal projects began. By the end of 1968, demolition for construction of the East–West arterial highway was under way, city parks and open space improvements were undertaken, and a new middle school had been built. In a review of developments at this time, Mayor Richard Mitchell stated that Poughkeepsie's plans closely followed the fourteen points outlined in President Lyndon Johnson's "Demonstration Cities" message, indicating that the city of Poughkeepsie was an excellent example of the national idea of urban renewal.

# THIRTEEN

# Social Planning:
# The Model Cities Experiment

URBAN RENEWAL PROJECTS focused on the physical infrastructure: housing, streets, lighting, water, and sewer, while President Johnson's Great Society agencies directed federal funds towards antipoverty and community development programs. In Poughkeepsie, as in hundreds of other American cities, city administrations, neighborhoods, and community activists vied with one another for access to those funds. As certain critics observed, "At issue are those who seek to commodify place versus those who try to protect suitable qualities of life"[1]

## MODEL CITIES

In November 1967, Poughkeepsie had learned that it was one of sixty-three communities in the nation to be selected as a Model City under the federal administration's "War on Poverty." This designation made Poughkeepsie eligible for funding innovative social, educational, and health programs; its goal was to do for the city residents' human service needs what urban renewal was intended to do for their physical surroundings. In an additional, if symbolic, note, President Johnson appointed Jeh V. Johnson, an African American Poughkeepsie architect active nationally in the American Institute of Architects as well as an instructor at Vassar College, as one of sixteen members of the National Commission on Urban Problems for the two-year life of the commission.

Located primarily north of Main Street, the designated Model City neighborhood covered nearly half the city. All of the programs under Model Cities, including public housing and neighborhood improvements that worked alongside urban renewal, required citizen participation. Poughkeepsie's newly created Model Cities Agency quickly distributed federal funds to local service agencies and created a variety of new programs.

The "Poughkeepsie Plan" involved nine citizen-planning task forces that established goals to improve both the physical and social environment of the urban area. In an introduction to the city's proposal for Model City designation in April 1967, Mayor Richard Mitchell promoted the local community's efforts in designing the project:

> The effort is completely 'home grown'; no outside consultants were used. It is the result of hundreds of persons, and dozens of organizations in our City who gave unstintingly of their time out of their conviction that this was a duty and without additional or special remuneration. . . . This then is a self-analysis of our city. We have delineated the problems and I believe we have developed solutions that are sound and workable. If these solutions are implemented, Poughkeepsie will truly become a Model City for cities of its size in the United States. [2]

Poughkeepsie presented its case with a stark view of the social, economic, and physical problems that faced the urban area. In its introduction, it described the city's population of 37,000 as "diminishing steadily for the past fifteen years. At the same time the adjacent areas have been growing at a spectacular rate." Along with the population shift, the economy was suffering: "Commensurate with the exodus of industries and the city's middle income families has been an influx of lower income wage earners as well as some of the County's hard-core poverty families."[3] The north side of the city was designated as the "target area" and described in even more desperate terms: "Poughkeepsie's model neighborhood is the Old City. Its 14,298 people have a disproportionate share of our social problems and substandard housing. . . . It includes 98 percent of the City's welfare cases, 95.6 percent of the City's families earning less than $2,000, 92 percent of the City's unemployed, as well as 78 percent of the City's deteriorated housing units." Deteriorated and abandoned housing in specific neighborhoods and streets was documented. For example, on Pershing Avenue "about half of the dwelling units" were without indoor plumbing.

Housing and infrastructure needed repair, according to the proposal, as well as human resources. "The neighborhood was developed in an era which preceded the use of automobiles and has many vestiges of the relatively self-sufficient pedestrian scale amenities which served another era. Nevertheless, the general obsolescence of the streets and structures and the dispair [sic] of the people make restoration and revitalization imperative."[4]

The authors of the "Poughkeepsie Plan" added a litany of social, economic, and physical infrastructure problems to the extensive introduction: lack of education, high levels of alcoholism and tuberculosis, and juvenile delinquency. They noted the need for increased employment opportunities and the lack of educational attainment necessary for available jobs. "The eighth grade education requirement for participation in employment training programs is an insurmountable obstacle for many of Poughkeepsie's unemployed." The authors pointed out discrepancies between the urban and rural realms, noting, for example, that the vast majority of welfare cases were in the city rather than the county and that many of the urban cases were a result of unemployed rural migrant workers who found housing in the city. "Perennially the [Model neighborhood] area is the repository of numbers of migrant laborers who remain in the City after the season is over. This results in a predictable impact on the welfare facilities of the community. These migrant workers constitute approximately half of the welfare case load in the City."[5]

Although Poughkeepsie's draft Model Cities proposal focused on the problems of one area of the city, the economic issues were argued in a larger spatial context. "The City's poverty problems are made more severe," the proposal stated, "because taxable industrial property to support welfare programs lies mostly outside the City." They also pointed out that many of the poor who live in rural areas outside the city, such as in the Harlem valley in eastern Dutchess County, moved into the city in order to take advantage of services provided by the county department of social services, thus putting an extra burden on city resources such as housing. Meanwhile, they lamented, "Middle class leadership people live outside the City and are thus less effective in dealing with urban problems."[6] The "Poughkeepsie Plan" early on recognized the dynamic relationship between the economic and social health of the city and its hinterland.

Two years later, Poughkeepsie submitted its proposal for major Model Cities funding. In its introduction, it continued a litany of social and economic problems associated with the residents in the model neighborhood, yet also wrote optimistically of "The Climate for Change." "The Model Neighborhood," the proposal suggested, " hums with activities of civil rights, antipoverty, social, civic, fraternal, and religious organizations." Specifically noted were black organizations, "some of them stable and/or enjoying respected positions of many years, others new, springing from an immediate need, then floundering after the need is met." The authors of the report described the white community as containing "a few closely-knit social and ethnic organizations and several protest groups," but added, "generally it is even more loosely organized than the black community." Summing up the race question optimistically, the report declared, "Oftentimes the question is not race but economics [that] unite communities for a common cause."[7]

The report continued to enumerate "various attitudes toward the social and economic conditions" of the Model Neighborhood:

Among the blacks of very little means, the attitudes range from resignation to intense resentment; some strive to improve as evidenced by moves to "better" areas within the Model Neighborhood as soon as they have amassed enough funds to do so. Most blacks with incomes that would permit them to move to other areas of the city express a dedication to remain within the Model Neighborhood to help improve it; the few who do move from the Model Neighborhood move completely out of the city. Some whites prefer not to accept the fact that they live in the Model Neighborhood and strive to eradicate evidence of the Model Neighborhood, at least for their own satisfaction.

Other citizens, black and white, feel, as expressed by a dissenting faction, that the needs of the Model Neighborhood can only be met by assumption of complete control by Model Neighborhood residents.

Basically, the attitude of the Model Neighborhood is one for a multiracial community with education, justice and opportunity for all.

Taken together, these represent a healthy climate for change. Effecting that change will depend greatly upon the speed with which new radical approaches will be utilized and departures from the status quo will be made and the determination with which the following program is funded and pursued.[8]

The proposal's introductory remarks on the problems within the target area and the possibilities for change focused, in part, on a racial divide in the city and between the city and the county populations. In the mid-1960s, according to the proposal, although the black population constituted less than 10 percent of the city's population, 99 percent lived in the Model Neighborhood, compared to 37 percent of the city's white population. As the black population doubled during the decade, friction arose between the city's whites and blacks, as well as within the black population itself, between those who had lived in Poughkeepsie for many years and newer immigrants. As one long-time African American resident observed: "The only trouble started when the people began coming from the South. For a long time a lot of northern colored people didn't accept them because their ways were different, you know, than our ways."[9] The influx of poor newcomers in the 1950s and 1960s overwhelmed the county Department of Social Services. In 1965, the department's allocation of $1,500,000 constituted 21 percent of the county budget; by 1970, the allocation of $4,000,000 accounted for 34 percent of the total budget.

Many of the newcomers were families with young children, resulting in racial separation among the elementary schools; for example, in 1967, Columbus and Warring schools, both within the Model Neighborhood, were 68 and 73 percent black, respectively, while Krieger and Smith, both on the south side, were 2 percent and 18 percent nonwhite. Overall in the elementary grades, there were 41 percent black pupils to 59 percent white, while in the upper grades the percentage of black students decreased; for example, of the 1,525 students in high school, only14 percent were black while 86 percent were white. This suggested, according to the 1968 analysis, "a dropout problem which must be solved."[10] In the summer of 1967, simmering unrest among young blacks led to a minor outburst of 150 youths who ran through downtown streets shouting against white political and economic dominance. Although some windows were damaged, no looting occurred; yet a state of emergency was declared, "anxieties in the community" were raised, "and it reinforced the impression that Poughkeepsie was no place for the middle class."[11]

The city's lack of readiness to deal with the social and economic problems resulting from an influx of mainly African American newcomers, and the flight of many whites from various sections of the city, coincided with growing unhappiness among many citizens with the demolition of older housing by Poughkeepsie's urban renewal agency (PURA). The resentment of longer-term white residents burst forth in municipal politics in 1970. Where businessmen and professionals acceptable to the economic leadership of the city usually occupied the mayor's office, white blue-collar workers chose a populist politician Louis Fiore. As Joan Sherman wrote at that time, "With the dramatic population loss in the city of the last twenty years, with the shift from an industrial to a service community, and with the rising expectations of the black community, the working class perceives a threat to its very existence."[12] Fiore politicized that perception, decrying an urban renewal that "threatens our homes" and characterizing Model Cities as a "give-away program to those who refuse to work as hard as we have all our lives."

Anger over issues of class and race became outspoken to an extent not seen under recent mayors, drawn from the business and professional community as they had been throughout the city's history. Similar anger surfaced in many American cities in the late 1960s and 1970s, sparked by urban renewal, the assassinations of President Kennedy and Martin Luther King, Jr., race riots, and the push for maximum participation by the poor in the national "War on Poverty" launched by President Johnson. The city's economic leaders had initiated the local poverty program and the successful application for designation as a Model City, but their priority was revitalization of the central business district, not the needs of the poor. Their primary aim was to make downtown more attractive to potential taxpayers, raising property values. They had embraced urban renewal, wanting to remove older, deteriorating, and so cheaper housing to make way for new and generally more costly commercial and residential development.

Like businessmen and political leaders elsewhere in the nation, they disliked challenges to their authority. Correspondingly, they preferred working with the Model City Program, which was directly responsible to local public officials, rather than with the Office of Economic Opportunity (OEO), which tried to welcome everyone in the neighborhood, regardless of income, skill, or literacy. Throughout the 1970s and 1980s, disagreements arose between those, especially citizen-participation advocates, who placed an emphasis on the social programs of Model Cities and the city administration and business community who focused on physical planning. As participation and lengthy discussion of local concerns increased at OEO, the city's economic and political leaders withdrew from it. In contrast, by 1974, the Model Cities Board consisted of thirty-two members, chaired by Mayor Arthur Weinberg and directed by Marie Tarver.

## PHDC

The emphasis under urban renewal to eliminate blight by demolishing deteriorated tenements, abandoned housing units, and various industrial structures, dislocated hundreds of individuals and families. To address the burgeoning housing needs, especially of low-income households and senior citizens, Poughkeepsie undertook a major effort to construct multiple-unit public housing facilities. By the mid-1970s, state and federal funds had assisted in the construction or management of the 185-unit Smith Street, 100-unit Charles Street, 44-unit Delafield, 70-unit Martin Luther King, 25-unit Boulevard Knolls, 63-unit King's Court, 33-unit Schwartz, and 140-unit Eastman Terrace low-income apartments, while subsidy programs initially assisted the 99-unit St. Simeon Senior Citizen complex of moderate-income units, the 204-unit Harriet Tubman housing complex for low-to-moderate income, the 118-unit Admiral Halsey, and the 135-unit Interfaith Towers. All of these units were in the city; public housing was considered an urban issue. Poughkeepsie architects Gindele & Johnson designed the Towers apartments that had originated as a cooperative effort by local churches and synagogues. Burt Gold, a Poughkeepsie developer, built Interfaith Towers, along with Admiral Halsey and other units. Many local churches were involved in addressing the housing issues of the era; for example, the Smith Street A.M.E. Zion and Trinity Methodist churches sponsored Tubman Terrace in the Jefferson Urban Renewal Area and Zion Episcopal, located in Wappingers Falls, sponsored St. Simeon on Beechwood Avenue on the south side.

To address many of the social issues as so many of the city's housing units were eliminated or the physical framework of neighborhoods changed, the People's Housing Development Corporation (PHDC) became the housing component of the Model Cities Agency. A "diverse group" of local citizens formed in 1971 by PHDC to aid home owners with rehabilitation grants, to assist eligible applicants in obtaining home ownership, and to help in the relocation of families displaced as a result of urban renewal activities. According to Kenneth Toole, president of the board in the 1970s, PHDC's "function was to acquire multiple family houses, two and three story houses, to rehabilitate them, and then sell them to people of modest means who used the income from the apartment or apartments to finance [the mortgage] and allow them to live in those houses."[13] He recalled it as a successful program and a "very rewarding experience because you get to see the project from beginning to the end." From 1971 to 1975, PHDC gave thirty-three home ownership grants totaling $43,412.00; thirty-eight rehabilitation grants totaling $74,751.00; twenty-three moving expenses grants and forty-four household necessities grants; as well as a grant to the A.M.E. Zion-Trinity Housing Development Corporation to pay for the costs of constructing a community room in the Harriet Tubman Terrace Housing Development. They also managed a rehabilitation revolving fund that was used to create $300,000 worth of rehabilitated modular housing in the city. PHDC's focus on private home ownership rather than on rental apartments in public "projects" nevertheless became undermined as a result of political and racial tensions.

As the housing arm of Poughkeepsie's Model Cities Agency, PHDC was required to renew its contract with the city on an annual basis. In December 1975, Toole met with Arthur Weinberg, then the mayor, to discuss PHDC's contract with the city for use of first-year community development funds. According to documents submitted to the U.S. District Court, Southern District of New York as part of a lawsuit filed by PHDC against the city of Poughkeepsie for withholding federal funds, "Mayor Weinberg indicated he would like PHDC to meet four conditions prior to the Common Council passing a resolution authorizing a contract with PHDC."[14]

One of the conditions presented by Mayor Weinberg was the removal of Mrs. Desti Jackson as PHDC's executive director. Toole recalled that the mayor's reason for firing her was "that he felt that Desti Jackson's 'kind of people' were making too much money from PHDC." Weinberg, like Fiore before him, was unhappy with federal funds being administered by the Model Cities Agency. Neighborhood changes were also in question as PHDC created home ownership opportunities for African Americans throughout the city. Toole added that Weinberg suggested that Jackson "lived in a neighborhood where she does not belong." She owned a house on the corner of Academy and Barclay streets, across from Christ Episcopal Church, on the south side.

After "protracted discussions," the Common Council authorized a community development contract in the spring of 1976. However, they soon cancelled it "for the convenience of the City."[15] The reason was that PHDC planned to rehabilitate "Apple Hill," also known as Corlies Manor, a brick, garden-type apartment development of 22 acres, containing 292 units, located on Corlies Avenue, in a neighborhood of modest single-family dwellings. Soon after the filing of the public notice by PHDC, a group of residents of the Seventh Ward held a meeting to oppose PHDC's application for federal loan subsidies "on the grounds that low-income persons, including blacks, were potential occupants of the Apple Hill apartments."[16]

Although the majority of the apartments were vacant, badly in need of repairs, and vandalized, Mayor Weinberg and Councilman John Green were adamantly opposed to PHDC's efforts. They acted to terminate the contract with PHDC. In response to a staff writer for the *Poughkeepsie Journal* in May, Green replied, "I have several reasons why I want to do this, but it's just something I really can't discuss now."[17] Toole, however, explained, "Frankly, the reaction from everyone is 'we don't want those people in that neighborhood.'"

The vote in the Common Council to cancel PHDC's contract was 8–2. Voting in favor were the then-current mayor Robert E. Ahmed; Stephen Babiarz representing the First Ward; John T. Kennedy, representing the Second Ward and a former mayor; Colette Lafuente, representing the Fourth Ward and a future mayor; Pasquale Letterii representing the Sixth Ward; John Green, whose Seventh Ward contained Corlies Manor; and Arthur Weinberg, representing the Eighth Ward and mayor during the initiation of PHDC's proposal. Two councilmen voted against the termination of the contract: Columbus Stanley, representing the Fifth Ward on the north side with the highest concentration of black families in the city in 1970 and the only African American on the council; and Alfred Weil, representing the Third Ward, with the blocks with the highest concentration of "multiple" and "acute" deficiencies in the city's survey of substandard residential housing.[18] Racial tensions rose throughout Poughkeepsie's business and political elite and the community.

PHDC sued in federal court to reinstate the contract since the funds were from federal community development grants rather than municipal coffers. U.S. District Court Judge Charles S. Haight, Jr. dismissed the suit in November on procedural grounds. However, he pointed to a pattern of racial discrimination that underlay the Common Council's action against PHDC. In a footnote to his twenty-eight page decision, the *Poughkeepsie Journal* reported, Judge Haight said, "While I make no finding on the issue, the papers submitted by (PHDC), in particular the minutes of meetings attended by members of the Common Council, leave the court with the clear impression that the City of Poughkeepsie terminated (PHDC's) contract for reasons deplorably rooted in prejudice and bigotry."[19]

## BATTLING THE BULLDOZER

Congressional passage of the federal Housing and Community Development Act of 1974 meant that Poughkeepsie would continue to receive federal funding to reshape its cityscape throughout the 1970s. However, by that time, wholesale acquisition and demolition of properties as a strategy for urban renewal had come under severe criticism nationally by numerous urban sociologists and geographers. Slums had been mapped by planners and subsequently cleared; yet many of these blocks had been vital communities prior to their destruction. Some of these neighborhoods opposed the "federal bulldozer" with mixed success. In 1970, six hundred homes were included in a neighborhood improvement program designed to bring existing structures up to code standards, improve street lighting, street resurfacing, and sidewalks. But in those areas slated for clearance under PURA, it was only under the "citizen participation" rubric of Model Cities that local residents could affect a change of demolition plans in an attempt to maintain their neighborhood community. In many cases, the social structures of entire neighborhoods were dismantled, often leading to economic problems and mental duress among former residents. For example, during 1971 and 1972, the Vietnam War was winding down and many veterans returned to Beacon and Poughkeepsie to find their former neighborhoods completely vanished, further complicating their sociopsychological reentry process.

The residents of Poughkeepsie's Gate Street neighborhood attempted to preserve their close-knit community when it came under pressure by PURA in 1970–1971. The *Poughkeepsie Journal* reported on a "stormy session" at a public hearing: "The plight of those to be displaced was explained by Joseph Molinaro, 85 Gate Street, who drew applause when he said he wants to live in a home and not in a Rip Van Winkle apartment. 'I don't want no part of any apartment. I lived in my home since 1921. . . . It is nice inside. You give me $12,000 for my home. I can't buy one for $20,000.'"[20] However, over the next three years, PURA overcame local opposition and demolished seven of the houses and sold the remaining thirteen to a developer who rehabilitated and resold them, but the neighborhood community structure was destroyed and the cleared land remained unused for a decade.

The situation in the Union Street area was somewhat similar, but the opposition there was stronger. Local residents, such as Carolyn Merte and Eleanor Massa, joined forces with local preservationists, including Stephanie Mauri and Jeanne Opdycke of Landmarks, to halt total demolition and begin rehabilitation through a facade easement program. The designation of the Union Street Historic District in 1971 resulted in the preservation of a pedestrian-oriented, low-rise, brick town house neighborhood in a nineteenth-century urban fabric.

## UNION STREET

The Union Street area was part of the Queen City Project Area known as the Lower Queen area. Initial survey of the area in 1969 argued that the vast majority of the structures in the area needed to be demolished. It called for "total clearance," and made plans for the relocation of its residents. At the same time, the possibility of historical and architectural resources were acknowledged in the immediate vicinity; the neighborhood included relatively small Victorian brick residences that had a district level of integrity and were reasonably well-maintained. However, the area's proximity to the CBD suggested that it would be better suited for offices and professional use than for continued residential use. As described by PURA in their housing analysis of Union Street the next year:

"The notion of returning this key section of the city to a tree-lined neighbor-hood is romantic at best. . . . It is beyond the understanding of Urban Renewal how potentially prime city land can be retained with no greater density than 10–15 dwelling units per acre, at tremendous costs and individual effort. . . . Currently, the area is a physical slum."[21]

In 1970, the same year that PURA's consultants described the Union Street neighborhood as a "slum," the New York State Historic Trust submit-ted a preliminary survey with a list of buildings of "historic, architectural or urbanistic significance" to PURA that identified some resources in the Union Street area.[22] However, the city's consultants on their master plan reported early the next year that 57 percent of the 140 residential structures in the area of Union Street were owned by absentee landlords, and 64 percent were found to be "substandard." They were therefore selected for demolition; only seven-teen houses on Grand Street were to be spared from the bulldozer.

Strong opposition to the findings was presented in letters to the editor of the *Poughkeepsie Journal* and at public meetings throughout the spring of 1971. For example, in an unpublished letter to the newspaper Carolyn Merte, whose family had lived at 23 Delano Street for ninety-seven years, wrote: "We who have lived here . . . wish . . . a tree-lined vital area of the future . . . we do not wish to emulate Williamsburg and become a museum. We do wish, however, to have the opportunity to become a clean . . . healthy and viable part of the City of Poughkeepsie."[23] Pro- and anti-demolition petitions were signed by property owners and residents, while Dutchess County Landmarks presented an appli-cation to the state and federal governments for listing on the National Register as one of the nation's first historic districts of "working men's houses" rather than those of the elite. Landmarks' application argued the case for designation with great urgency: "The area stands like an oasis in the midst of land which has been cleared for arterials or housing projects: all sides have been razed."[24] The appli-cation was processed quickly; the area was designated by the state, and by the end of the year was entered into the National Register of Historic Places.

The establishment of Union Street as an Historic District removed the threat of immediate demolition, although its future could not be certain. Land-marks purchased and began restoration of a house at 190 Union Street and pressed for federal rehabilitation funds for the area. Meanwhile, PURA con-tracted with another consultant for a second study of the area. That study did not recommend the wholesale demolition of the area, so that, in the spring of 1972, PURA formally announced its decision not to go ahead with clearance.

PURA, however, was not terribly interested in a major rehabilitation effort, and awaited yet another consultant's report by Walter Thabit, the individual who had recommended the demolition of Gate Street. Residents of the Union Street area continued to organize for assistance to rehabilitate their properties, and through the Queen City Model Cities Agency (QCMC) protested the lack of movement on the part of PURA. In early 1972, QCMC wrote PURA's board of directors, "Another year in limbo . . . will drive people who are now interested away, and it will make rehabilitation harder and more expensive." Landmarks established a rehabilitation revolving fund; PHDC had some funds for rehabilitation and attempted to use some supplementary funds to address emergency repairs. However, little could be done effectively while PURA focused on other areas of demolition, and housing conditions worsened. Some buildings owned by absentee landlords were condemned and the tenants evicted.

In 1973, a facade easement program was instituted by PURA, using federal money and guidelines, which considerably changed the situation. The program was designed to enable owner occupancy of buildings, with low-cost loans to rehabilitate the outside of the structure to meet federal historic guidelines set by the Department of the Interior. However, many of the tenants were older and did not want to burden themselves with loan payments, while many of the absentee landlords took advantage of the program. Interior renovation was not included, and many developers and landlords took the option to completely "gut" the inside and create a modern environment packaged inside a Victorian facade.

Rents began to increase and many of the former low- and moderate-income tenants left. In 1976, the Tax Reform Act increased the interest of investors in rehabilitating commercial properties in historic districts. Residential rental properties are considered commercial properties under this act and became a new reason for private investment in the housing market. Burt Gold, an active developer throughout the urban renewal period, developed many rental units in the area at this time. Gold grew up in the city of Poughkeepsie; his family arrived in 1910 and his father opened a cleaning business five years later. As a developer, Burt Gold worked on many projects for IBM as well as single-family houses throughout the south side, including Wilmot Terrace and Tamidan Road. He bought over two dozen abandoned structures in the Union Street district and restored them as affordable dwelling units.

According to the city manager William Theyson, the facade easement program served as a "catalyst" for comprehensive "renewal," and entailed "the creation of wholly new units within structural shells and, ultimately, the complete reconstruction of the streetscape and infrastructure: water and sewer services, streets, curbs, walks, landscaping and street lighting."[25] However, the social cost was great. The area became "primarily inhabited by professional people—many of them single—who can afford to pay $425, plus utilities, for a one-bedroom apartment."[26] The rehabilitation of vacant buildings, along with some displacement, resulted in the "gentrification" of one of Poughkeepsie's older working-class and middle-class neighborhoods.

## BARDAVON THEATER

The year of the bicentennial also spurred interest in other areas of historic preservation. Revolutionary period historic sites in the mid-Hudson cities of

Kingston and Newburgh were given new life and even small towns and villages celebrated their own stories. Some, in fact, allowed a critical perspective, such as the decisions regarding the evolution of the suburban landscape in Hyde Park as told in a National Trust for Historic Preservation award-winning documentary film by Ralph Arlyck, an independent filmmaker from the town of Poughkeepsie. In the city of Poughkeepsie, elements of the nineteenth-century landscape began to be more appreciated by the general public.

The Collingwood Opera House on Market Street had opened on February 1, 1869, and remained in continuous use as an operating theater for over a century. In 1923, it reopened as a movie theater and was renamed the Bardavon. By the 1970s, the Boston-based owners had allowed it to fall into disrepair. In 1975, a local partnership purchased the theater with the intention of tearing it down in order to provide the Poughkeepsie Savings Bank, located next door, with a parking lot. A citizen's committee, including the director of the Dutchess County Arts Council John Berg, chaired by former mayor Economou, recommended an alternative to PURA that removed the immediate threat of demolition. The theater was listed on the National Register of Historic Places and activities continued under the supervision of Stephen and Julia Dunwell. Negotiations between the nonprofit Bardavon 1869 Opera House, Inc. and the local partnership continued for four years during which time great public concern was shown about the continued threat of demolition. As one of the partners stressed, "The only way we can make office rentals attractive to local businesses is to provide parking. . . . We didn't buy that theatre to run it as a theatre."[27] Eventually, funds were raised and ownership was transferred on March 3, 1979.

Julia and Stephen Dunwell served as executive director and managers of the Bardavon from 1976 to 1979. Julia coordinated the early drama, dance, and musical programs along with local organizations. The theater became the main cultural foundation in the city and region. In 1987, the couple received the Dutchess County Executive's Arts Award for their work and the stage was named after the family in 1993. Julia involved herself in a number of community and arts organizations and remained an active volunteer at the theater until her death in 2006. At that time, her son Stephen Dunwell, Jr., recounted her love of the arts and added, "I think for her everything about the Bardavon was her greatest accomplishment."[28]

## URBAN DISLOCATION

The 1970s saw a shift from one kind of urban renewal to another set of urban redevelopment strategies. Federal monies for demolition and reconstruction declined, while new approaches and techniques for maintaining and rehabilitating the existing social and physical fabric came to the forefront.

The period of broad-brush clearance had left its mark. Between 1960 and 1974, about 1,300 dwelling-units were destroyed, either for urban renewal or the two arterial highways. In the same period, three thousand new units were created, nearly half of them subsidized in some way. After demolition, Lower Main Street's streetscape was pockmarked with vacant lots strewn with broken bricks and other demolition debris. Vacant buildings were interspersed with drug-infested "parking lots" along Mill and Cannon streets. Ethnic and multiracial neighborhoods had been decimated, while much of the Model Neighborhood became even more densely crowded with low-income residents. "The dislocation involved in moving so many families necessarily carried some social cost which cannot be measured, but the falling population figures suggested many families—in particular, probably, those with higher incomes and more options—chose to leave the city rather than resettle in Poughkeepsie."[29] The city of 41,000 in 1950 had lost 9,000 people by 1970 and close to another 3,000 by 1980, while the county had gained 95,000 between 1950 and 1970 and another 23,000 by 1980. By the end of the 1970s, with only 12 percent of the county's population, Poughkeepsie still accounted for 57 percent of the individuals on public assistance, as well as 30 percent of the families in poverty, 47 percent of the county's Medicaid recipients, 37 percent of its child-abuse cases, and 79 percent of its black families in poverty. Poughkeepsie's population had not only declined, its socioeconomic makeup had also been reshaped.

The dramatic demographic, social, cultural, and economic shifts during the three decades after World War II were reflected in community perceptions of the city. The process of decline in Poughkeepsie and other Hudson valley cities mirrored much of urban America in the 1980s where "the older cities were not the center of American life that they had once been. . . . In the postwar automobile-oriented world of decentralized residence and business, they were inevitably relegated to a lesser role. With an increasingly poor black population, they also grew increasingly out of sight and out of mind for many middle-class whites. . . . The outer belts were to become the main streets of the late-twentieth-century metropolis."[30]

Poughkeepsie's Main Street was deserted; it was no longer the center of gravity for the community. The extraordinary physical changes to the city's transportation network and the quality and quantity of housing undermined Poughkeepsie as a "hometown." The growth of suburban Dutchess County— its quiet, middle-class homogeneous neighborhoods, shopping centers, and gas stations—constituted the new American landscape. For the city of Poughkeepsie, internal social forces would be challenged throughout the latter half of the twentieth century by external crises peaking in the 1960s, such as the civil rights revolution, the Vietnam War, spiraling drug use and crime, as well as massive economic shifts related to deindustrialization, downsizing, suburban retail expansion, and the growth of the health and social service industry. Revitalization of Main Street would have to wait until the end of the century.

FOURTEEN

# Issues and Causes of the 1960s

THE 1960s IN THE VALLEY, as in the nation, saw a variety of new initiatives
not only in civil rights, but also in environmental concerns, politics, popular
culture, and higher education that would, collectively, lay foundations for its
emerging postindustrial economy and culture. During these years, the new
initiatives sometimes seemed disparate and unrelated. Later liberal analysts
came to see them as complementary contributions to a healthier democracy,
but with longer hindsight their contributions to an emerging service economy
loom larger. Obvious at the time was the beginning, as in other American
communities, of attempts to address the demands of African Americans for
the equality so long denied them. Efforts to widen opportunities for all Americans through access to higher education increased. So did the search for ways
to decrease human damage to the natural environment at a time when cities,
with federal help, experimented with programs to improve environments in
which many of their poorest residents lived. At the same time, proponents of
more controversial values and behavior such as recreational drug use contributed both to immediate conflict with traditionalists and, for the future,
wider toleration of previously unacceptable opinions, tastes, and behavior.

## VIETNAM AND CIVIL RIGHTS

A newly challenging urban world was in the making. The many causes that
came to prominence in the 1960s, defined broadly as spanning the late 1950s
through the early 1970s, sparked national debate about culture and values. That
debate would reshape notions of what kind of society Poughkeepsie and valley
residents could expect, or desire to bring about, in the spreading urban regions
where they lived. The valley participated in mostly quieter ways in the ferment
of this nationally turbulent time. Marches and teach-ins against the war in
Vietnam engaged many in the Hudson valley, while national and international

politics were energetically discussed in regional congressional races. Students at local colleges staged campus demonstrations and sit-ins about Cambodia, Kent State, and black studies programs, but did not carry them to the extremes of the radical students' assault on Columbia University in 1968. Local civil rights protests did not produce race riots, despite a teenage outburst downtown in 1967.

A campaign to save Storm King Mountain from alteration by a power plant was led by affluent residents with country homes concerned about preserving the beauty of the Highlands landscape; they later coalesced as Scenic Hudson, one of the nation's most influential and effective environmental organizations. By contrast, in the same years, local businessmen promoted urban renewal as a means to modernize the built cityscape by demolishing and replacing older buildings believed to be deteriorated. Scenic Hudson's campaign won national attention, stimulating the environmental movement that gathered steam in the wake of Rachel Carson's *Silent Spring* of 1962. That campaign made previously unimaginable bedfellows of politically radical folksinger Pete Seeger and wealthy conservatives who prized the natural beauty of the Highlands. Then Seeger's sloop *Clearwater* won wide support as

FIGURE 14.1. Vassar College student demonstration, Main Street, 1968

an attractive and innovative means of environmental education that had a spirit similar to Students for a Democratic Society's emphasis on participatory democracy. A similar vision of widening opportunities for ordinary citizens inspired James Hall's leadership of Dutchess County's new community college. And a surprising willingness to change with the times helped a very young president Brother Linus Foy to persuade the Marist Brothers to accept coeducation and then the transfer of their college to lay leadership. A similarly youthful, innovative, and musically gifted Leon Botstein took the helm at the previously culturally conservative Bard College.

But the 1960s in the valley did not consist only of fragmentation and new directions in what some historians call the "liberal project" in which civil rights, environmentalism, and feminism became separate if often overlapping movements. Conservative Republicanism maintained its political grip on the region, despite the moderate political views of then congressman Hamilton Fish, Jr. Sheriff Lawrence Quinlan and his new hire, G. Gordon Liddy, were ready to pounce on violators of traditional moral standards like Timothy Leary's drug-promoting entourage temporarily ensconced on a Millbrook estate.

Nationally, Barry Goldwater's defeat of Nelson Rockefeller for the 1964 Republican nomination and the subsequent successful wooing of white blue-collar workers by southern segregationist George Wallace encouraged local hopes of future political movement toward the right. So did the shocked reaction locally to the valley becoming a prime example of the new drug culture at the Woodstock concert in nearby Sullivan county. In short, the 1960s in the Poughkeepsie urban region and the valley spanned the gamut of causes and points of view in the decade that most now see as a pivotal time in post–World War II America. Whether defined narrowly from 1964 to the assassinations and Democratic convention of 1968 or more broadly, say from the late 1950s to the early 1970s, the valley, like the nation, knew their society and culture had changed in important ways. Some of the more important local changes have become foundations for the region's present and future attractiveness to resident newcomers and to tourists and other visitors.

## AFRICAN AMERICAN ACTIVISM

On March 15, 1960, a news brief on the front page of the *Poughkeepsie New Yorker* reported that "400 Negroes" staged a protest at the Woolworth's lunch counter in Orangeburg, South Carolina. The protest in Orangeburg was one of many that followed the first sit-in at a Woolworth's lunch counter in Greensboro, North Carolina, the previous month. On March 16, the *Poughkeepsie New Yorker* continued to report on numerous lunch counter "sit-downs" that were spreading throughout the South. On March 17, one hundred Vassar students picketed the Woolworth's on Main Street.

The picketing by Vassar students followed a campus civil rights rally two days earlier. Speakers at the rally included Herbert Hill, labor secretary of the NAACP, and Paul DuBrul, from the U.S. National Student Association (USNSA). Both speakers and the student organizers of the rally urged participation in the picket. "Although the picket did not significantly deter shoppers from entering Woolworth's," according to the student newspaper report on the protest, "it did accomplish our primary purpose of bringing this issue of segregation in the South to the attention of the citizens of Poughkeepsie."[1] Several small civil rights actions continued through the spring. Vassar students held a fund-raising event for a scholarship and defense fund that the USNSA had established for students who had been arrested, and the local NAACP picketed Woolworth's on a number of Saturdays.

Local civil rights protests did not produce race riots, despite three days of "unrest" downtown by two hundred youths in the summer of 1967. Local black clergy hastened to quell the disturbance and reduce its racial implications. As Harold Anderson, director of the Poughkeepsie Opportunity Center of the Dutchess County Committee for Economic Opportunity, suggested: "I don't believe the incident was racial per se, but that certainly played a part in it. The seed has been planted for quite a while. There is unrest in the community."[2] Unemployment continued to plague black youth throughout the period, yet Poughkeepsie and Dutchess County remained relatively quiet during the decade, even while many other cities in the Hudson valley and across the nation erupted. In Newburgh, also in July 1967, a rally by the neo-Nazi National Renaissance Party in the Orange County Courthouse turned violent, resulting in the arrests of thirty young blacks.

America's cities were sites of major disturbances throughout the decade, and most were fueled by racial animosity. Malcolm X was assassinated in 1965 in New York City. The assassination of Martin Luther King, Jr. on April 4, 1968, sparked upheavals in many cities. Not, however, in Poughkeepsie. The community came together to honor King's nonviolent activism in churches and synagogues and public gatherings. At a large rally held in Riverview Field on April 6, hundreds of people heard speakers reflect on King's life. As reported in the local newspaper:

> They came pouring into Riverview Field yesterday, black and white together. . . . Young families came, parents carrying babies or pushing them in carriages; elderly people, some wearing black arm bands, shuffled along with the crowd; young flower people with incense; wealthy looking people in fine clothes; Boy Scouts hurrying along with their flags; a man wearing his Legion cap; a great cross section of the community; black and white together. . . . And while they sat or stood at a field in Poughkeepsie, other cities were covered by clouds of smoke from burning buildings and armed troops stood on the street corners.[3]

But, the view from the African American community was not so rosy. As the Reverend Belvie Jackson, pastor of the A.M.E. Zion Church remarked at a silent march along Main Street the next day:

> If Dr. King were here . . . he would be calling on Poughkeepsie to settle its labor and employment problems, challenging the education system to search for better ways to improve racial imbalance and calling for a Negro on the school administration staff. . . .
>
> Dr. King would be calling for a 'good neighbor policy' in housing, instead of the flight to suburbs which is perpetuating segregation.
>
> He would be urging increased support of the local self-help Negro groups as the Hudson Valley Opportunities Industrialization Center. He would call for increased backing of the Dutchess County Committee for Economic Opportunity; improvement in the welfare department, progress in rebuilding a Catherine St. Community Center, and for increased recruiting of black people on the police forces.[4]

The call for new programs to redress the problems of inequality and discrimination in Poughkeepsie would continue through the rest of the twentieth century. Black school teachers and administrators would be hired, as would members of the police force. Acting on a petition drive organized by the Afro-American Youth Movement, chaired by Edward L. Pittman, the Board of Education would rename Morse School Park on Mansion Street between Beulah Baptist Church and Morse Elementary School as Malcolm X Park in 1978. Catherine Street Community Center would host an annual M. L. King Breakfast as a fund-raising event, attended by close to a thousand individuals from Poughkeepsie and Dutchess County. But the flight to the suburbs increased, draining the city of a large percentage of its white middle class, and perpetuating a view among those outside the city's boundaries of a dangerous, chaotic urban "wilderness." Two problems that severely impacted cities were drugs and crime; safety became a major concern on Main Street and in other public spaces in Poughkeepsie.

The outward migration of people and businesses from the city in the 1960s together with local black activism accelerated an ongoing process in the Poughkeepsie urban region. Newcomers to the valley like IBMers as well as long-term Poughkeepsie residents, including second- and third-generation whites from the turn-of-the-century immigration, sought new suburban housing. African Americans had not participated in that process prior to the 1960s; their aspirations were frustrated by racial discrimination in the housing market.

Black leaders in Poughkeepsie and in the valley had pushed for the aims of the civil rights movement over a long period of time. In the early decades of the twentieth century, Joel Spingarn, literary critic and the first Jewish professor at Columbia University, invited many of the nation's intellectual and political elite to Troutbeck, his estate in Amenia, a bit less than 30 miles east of Poughkeep-sie. At one such gathering he brought the Negro activist W. E. B. DuBois together with followers of Booker T. Washington that emerged as the National Association for the Advancement of Colored People (NAACP) in 1910. How-ever, the quest for reform in the valley proved to be frustratingly slow.

The city's NAACP chapter was not founded until 1931 when it struggled to persuade local businesses to employ black residents. Hiring did not even begin, and then only sparsely, until the late 1930s and early 1940s when world war increased overall employment. The guest of honor at the city's annual American Brotherhood dinner in 1944 called attention to the lack of progress. Jane Bolin Mizelle, the first black woman judge in the United States and daughter of local attorney Gaius Bolin, Sr., noted the absence of "Negroes on the staffs of the District Attorney's Office, on the City Council, in the Fire and Police Departments, or in the local hospitals as doctors and nurses." She asked, "Can America stand the human waste?"[5]

Born in Poughkeepsie in 1909, Jane Bolin graduated from Poughkeepsie High School at the age of fifteen. She would soon learn, as a young woman, how hard it was to cross the color line. One of two black freshmen at Welles-ley College in 1924, the two "were assigned to the same room in a family's apartment off campus, the first instance of many episodes of discrimination she said she encountered there. . . . When she broached the subject of a law career to a Wellesley guidance counselor, she was told that black women had little chance."[6] Nevertheless, she persevered to become the first black woman to earn a degree from Yale Law School in 1931. In 1939, she was appointed by then-New York City Mayor Fiorello LaGuardia to a judgeship in Domes-tic Relations Court, the precursor of Family Court in New York State, where she served for forty years. It would not be until after her death on January 7, 2007, that her accomplishment as the first black woman judge in the nation would be celebrated by the County Bar Association.

The firsts-to-be-hired in various occupations came slowly: the first African American county public health nurse was hired in 1940, but the first black nurse at Vassar Brothers Hospital, not until 1946. When Mrs. Bessie Payne, a native Poughkeepsian, came back to the city in the 1950s, the NAACP "was having meetings on getting people to work in the stores on Main Street . . . didn't have any Negro clerks." IBM "hired [white residents] in Poughkeepsie, but they didn't hire Negroes."[7]

## THE QUEST FOR FAIRNESS IN HOUSING

Discrimination was rampant in the housing market, too. Mrs. Earline Patrice remembered calling an advertised rental on Winnikee Street, now an area where many blacks live, asking, "Do you rent to blacks as well as whites?" The lady answered, "Oh no, I don't rent to those." Those?[8]

Outsiders arriving in the county helped to open up some opportunities previously unavailable. In the 1950s, an infusion of highly educated, better-paid black employees at IBM, situated in the town of Poughkeepsie, not the city, focused attention on the problem of access to suburban housing. The corporation's housing office could not assist the newcomers beyond giving them lists of houses that would not rent or sell to blacks. Housing became the first focus for civil rights mobilization in Poughkeepsie. In 1957, IBM electrical engineer Victor Morris began publishing a newspaper, *Antlers Digest*, aimed at black residents. Some old-timers joined in the campaign against discrimination in suburban realty. Mrs. Payne later would complain that "as soon as the IBMers got homes, we didn't have any more housing problem . . . the majority of them don't have anything to do with Poughkeepsie."[9]

Some black IBMers had succeeded in buying houses by 1962, but progress was painfully slow. Calvin Waite, who had purchased a house in Southgate near IBM's main plant, tried to help a non-IBM newcomer, architect Jeh Johnson and his wife Norma, when they began searching for a place to live. Although the Johnsons had better personal connections than most African American newcomers, their search took three months. The best they could do initially was to rent a farmhouse that a black IBM family had rented before them. As late as 1963, middle-class blacks focused on one house at a time, with no clustering.

But change was on its way. An accumulation of small advances locally and nationally culminated in the optimistic mood of 1963–1964. A biracial committee of local religious groups pushed for a state ban on discrimination in housing, achieving a Fair Housing Bill in 1961. That bill opened about 15 percent of the housing market and a 1963 act opened the remainder. Locally, the Dutchess County Council of Churches sponsored the Good Neighbor Pledge campaign. Each signer of the pledge agreed "to take an active part in helping achieve . . . freedom of opportunity in housing" and to "welcome into my neighborhood any responsible person of whatever race, religion or national origin."[10] The campaign sought to combat the standard argument of opponents that letting black Americans buy houses in a neighborhood would hurt property values.

A group of about ten women pursued the campaign aggressively for several years. Lou Glasse and Lonnie Gindele went to the churches first to canvass for pledges, then widened visitation, recording progress with pins on a huge map of the area. In 1965, they also organized a local march in support of the huge march of blacks and whites on Selma, Alabama, led by Martin Luther King, Jr. Cal Waite urged them to get the *New York Times* to report the event, and they did. The local NAACP in the early 1960s still had a half-white membership, including the son of painter Norman Rockwell.

The formation of the Dutchess County Community Council under New York State's new Commission for Human Rights brought a wider representation of local leaders together for discussion of how to advance civil rights.

State auspices provided much-needed subpoena power; a state representative established the agenda and set the parameters of what the council could do. African Americans composed about one-third of the thirty-two-member council that encompassed business and nonprofit-organization executives, college presidents, ministers, lawyers, doctors, journalists, and activists.

Because the state had now banned discrimination in the housing market, the question of enforcement received special attention from the council's chairman, Victor Morris. He repeatedly pressed charges against developers, government departments, and other major players who violated the 1963 law. In council discussions, he never seemed quite satisfied with local progress, insisting that more needed to be done. By the late 1960s, the council became less active as other players took center-stage.

On the national scene, in the wake of President Kennedy's assassination, President Johnson pushed ahead fundamental reforms like the Civil Rights Act of 1964 and the Voting Rights Act of 1965. His War on Poverty, including the Office of Economic Opportunity, temporarily created a mood of optimism about further improvement in the situation of African Americans. Locally, by the mid-1960s, the focus of black and white activists shifted to the continuing problem of discrimination in employment. The picketing at Woolworth's on Main Street saw Mrs. Earline Patrice worrying about, and warning against, the tendency of old-timers in the black community—who didn't like the idea of demonstrations of any kind—crossing the picket line. She welcomed the presence of a few black Vassar students on the line and would later praise their boldness in pulling off a sit-in at the college's Main Building to press their demands for curricular and other changes.

The bigger news locally was the appearance of local African American leaders in major elected or appointed positions. In 1965, Helen Vaughan joined the governing board of the Poughkeepsie Urban Renewal Agency (PURA). Marie Tarver won election to the Board of Education, becoming in the early 1970s the chief executive of the Model Cities Program.

Other cultural and political movements of the 1960s seemed to have less extended preparation. Following the widely publicized new bohemianism of the beatniks, a "drug culture" burst upon the national scene through a succession of dramatic events, two of which took place in the mid-Hudson valley in very different locales. The first occurred on an estate in fashionable Millbrook; the second, Woodstock, a nationally televised spectacle, on a farm across the river in Sullivan County.

## TIMOTHY LEARY BRINGS "DRUG CULTURE" TO THE VALLEY

In the fall of 1963, Timothy Leary and his entourage from Boston inaugurated a bizarre and controversial, if short-lived, transformation of Millbrook's

Hitchcock estate. To the distress of many local residents, they temporarily made the estate a center for experimentation with mind-altering drugs like LSD. Thanks to three younger Mellon heirs, they now occupied a four-story mansion with sixty-four rooms, "surrounded by elegant lawns, stables, and an ornate two-story chalet, which held a bowling alley. A mile across rolling fields stood a more modern mansion called 'the bungalow.'"[11]

Delighted with contemporary phenomena like the Beatles, Marshall McLuhan, and the Beach Boys who "sent mellow California vibrations eastward," Leary believed traditional culture was "exploding" in 1963 and the psychedelic revolution, well under way. By 1965, Leary felt the revolution had been won because a "sufficient number of Americans had learned the secret of brain-change." Officials from the Food and Drug Administration (FDA) visited Millbrook "to learn what we were up to." Expressing their dismay, one FDAer reported that law enforcement people "can't wait for these drugs to be illegal so they can bust your ass."[12]

As it turned out, another newcomer to Dutchess County would undertake that mission. For G. Gordon Liddy, the "conflict over the Vietnam war and especially the tactics used by the antiwar movement were eroding the national will and respect for authority. The young were sinking into the netherworld of the drug culture." The district attorney's office in Republican Dutchess County, "somewhere to the right of Barry Goldwater," seemed perfect for Liddy's purpose.

Harassment of the Leary crowd had begun two years before when unmarked cars began driving through the property and strangers dressed in the borrowed "uniforms of telephone repairmen made unannounced visits, claiming to check the wires." Leary recalled that they "put up 'No Admittance' signs and locked the gates."[13] And he noted that an "ambitious assistant district attorney [Liddy] with a poetic flair told the local Kiwanis that 'the panties were dropping faster than the acid in Leary's lair.'"[14]

Liddy's big moment came on a wintry midnight at Millbrook in 1966. The raid, by Liddy's admission, produced scientific journals of Leary's experimentation with psychedelic drugs but fell "short on the drugs themselves."[15] In subsequent court action, American Civil Liberties Union attorney and Poughkeepsie resident Noel Tepper, representing Leary, drove Judge Baratta to distraction by calling a succession of Hindu witnesses to testify to the religious significance of drugs like marijuana. So Baratta approved a compromise in which "nobody lost." Both Leary and Liddy left the county. Liddy returned to Washington where he would achieve celebrity as one of the thieves ("plumbers") in the Watergate break-in. He had not "saved civilization" in Dutchess. Remaining an outsider, looking ahead to bigger opportunities elsewhere, Liddy had never viewed the valley as his future home. Nor had Leary or his entourage. Always alien nomads, they had moved in and out frequently during their four-year stay. Their "movement" had no valley roots.

Nor, obviously, did the even more widely publicized gathering of some 400,000 people at the Woodstock concert. One journalist wrote: "Everyone swam nude in the lake. Balling was easier than getting breakfast, and the 'pigs' just smiled and passed out the oats."[16] Whatever "community" those attending felt, in the freedom provided by anonymity among strangers, was as transient as their coming and going at Bethel. By contrast, the emerging concern with protecting the environment—in which local activism in the Hudson valley would become a national inspiration—came initially from long-term residents for whom the new bohemianism had little appeal. A small group of them began a long but ultimately successful struggle to save a beloved river and landscape from degradation. Their struggle became a celebrated cause, helping spur a new national movement for environmental protection.

## THE CAMPAIGN TO SAVE STORM KING MOUNTAIN

While civil rights had been to the forefront of national issues ever since the *Brown v. Board of Education* decision, environmental concerns had not gained the same prominence during the 1950s. But, in 1962, Rachel Carson's *Silent Spring* brought the dangers of pesticides to the fore. The following year, Storm King Mountain at the north end of the Highlands near Newburgh became the scene of a widely publicized battle over the possibly destructive impact on river ecology and landscape aesthetics of a new hydroelectric power plant. The initiator, Consolidated Edison (Con Ed), had presumed no obstacle to obtaining approval by the Federal Power Commission (FPC) of its application for permission to build, given the commission's preference for "efficiency" in increasing power supplies. When the corporation announced the project in 1962, reaction came mostly from politicians and labor leaders in localities in the Storm King's immediate vicinity who stood to benefit from taxes paid by Con Ed and from construction employment.

The Highlands area did have wealthy residents, known locally as "the mountain people." Their scenic views would be marred by a power plant on Storm King, but some of them debated whether they should sacrifice that interest to a presumed public good, security of power production. The enthusiastic support of Cornwall and Newburgh for the project made it difficult for others to oppose it, but Mrs. Stephen Duggan of Garrison, across the river, did. Others soon joined her, founding the Scenic Hudson Preservation Conference. Cornwall's mayor characterized sarcastically the "weekend crowd" as preferring their lovely "views" to local needs for school, police, and fire services that could be improved with Con Ed taxes.[17]

Disorganized and lacking preparation, the opponents practically stumbled through their first intervention in an FPC hearing on the project. By the second hearing, however, their lawyer put together a case against using the Storm King for a power project, combining "technical, economic, aesthetic, and spiritual considerations. It was a clever combination, but it demonstrated above all how difficult it is for a group of outsiders to challenge a large technological bureaucracy, particularly when a specialized administrative agency such as the FPC is sitting in judgment."[18] Scenic Hudson understood the difficulty, agreeing that their purpose for the time being was to delay action by the FPC. As Alexander Saunders wisely noted, "there's quite an area to fight on."[19]

## THE SCENIC HUDSON PRESERVATION
## CONFERENCE INTERVENTION

Scenic Hudson's intervention resulted in a complicated succession of hearings on fish welfare and the location of power lines, and numerous appeals to legislative and judicial bodies. When the FPC in March 1965 granted Con Ed a license, opponents appealed to the U.S. Court of Appeals. On December 29, 1965, the Court of Appeals ruled against Con Ed and the FPC; the court set aside the licensing order and remanded the case for further proceedings. In the unexpected and historic verdict, the judges quoted "the great German traveler, Baedeker" who had called the Hudson "finer than the Rhine."[20] The judges thus emphasized the aesthetic concerns central to Scenic Hudson's argument rather than the efficiency in power production sought by Con Ed. The court ordered further FPC hearings on alternatives for sites and power lines.

The judgment had national implications as it became the basis for federal environmental policy. The federal government passed the National Environmental Policy Act in 1969 (NEPA); further policy acts would emerge over the next few years to protect air, water, and endangered species. NEPA also created procedures to study potential impacts of a proposal on an area's aesthetics, ecology, and social services; these were to be examined as important as economic issues. And, most important for Scenic Hudson and other environmental organizations, the right to question development proposals was broadened beyond appurtenant landowners to other concerned citizens.

The fight over Storm King and the future of the river had exposed an ongoing disagreement between those whose priority was economic growth and those more concerned with environmental protection. Pete Seeger conceded that one segment of the coalition of opponents was more concerned with "a high-tension line marring their view than with the desperate living conditions of several million fellow citizens a few miles south." But Seeger called the claim that "continual 'economic growth' is essential for America" a lie, arguing that "we want to pass a cleaner earth on to all future generations" and "devise a better economic system."[21] Frances Reese and others sought to bridge the gap by contending that Con Ed had been "prone to thinking 'big is better' in all aspects of power generation"[22] and that Scenic Hudson had proposed more efficient and economical alternatives.

The Storm King battle did not end until 1980 when all eleven parties (including four power companies, the EPA, and the Natural Resources Defense Council) agreed to mediation. As the *New York Times* noted, "Every side gave up something." [23] Before then, in the 1970s, Mrs. Reese and others felt the need for a coordinating office as environmental groups with various aims multiplied. The Scenic Hudson Preservation Conference was a one-issue organization. Franny, as she was known to all her many friends and co-workers, put up part of the funding to create a new organization, the Center for the Hudson Valley, with Franny as president, Laurance Rockefeller as vice-president, and Fran Dunwell as executive director. At the beginning, the center worked with existing programs, both doing lobbying and education on such issues as water quality, planning for open space, fisheries, and the successes and failures of a predecessor: Nelson Rockefeller's Hudson River Valley Commission. By the late 1970s, the center became more activist, pursuing a legislative agenda including the Hudson River Study Act, concerned with land acquisition and open space, and legislative authorization for a Heritage Task Force, the precursor to greenway.

Soon after the signing of the 1980 "peace treaty," the center merged with the Preservation Conference, taking its name, Scenic Hudson, and its donor base, but keeping the center's agenda. Klara Sauer became the new executive director, beginning twenty years of expanding the organization, its scope, and its influence on preservation in the valley. Franny by herself continued to assist numerous local preservation and other good causes; tragically, she died in July 2003 as a result of a car accident while returning from one of her many meetings. As John Adams, president of the Natural Resources Defense Council (NRDC), recalled, "Franny was a champion of the environment before the word environmentalist came into fashion. Her years of leadership and hard work set a high standard and spurred others—including myself—to lives defending the natural world." Pete and Toshi Seeger added, "We know that thousands will carry on greening our Hudson Valley in Franny's spirit."[24]

## UNUSUAL BEACON RESIDENTS:
## PETE AND TOSHI SEEGER

Pete and Toshi Seeger had rejoiced in Scenic Hudson's 1980 victory, too, in their cabin in the woods on the Beacon side near Dutchess Junction, whose brickyard had been worked over the years by different ethnic and racial groups. Seeger had spent much of his young adulthood as a singer on the political left, often with groups like the Almanac Singers and the Weavers, traversing the country supporting radical causes and union battles against corporations. But, well before the 1960s, Seeger had tired of cities. Remembering his growing up in the rural Hudson valley town of Patterson, New York, he wanted a quiet place to come home to, close to nature. His favorite book as a child had been Ernest Thompson Seton's *Two Little Savages* and Seeger had envisioned hooking the pioneer spirit in that book to a socialist ideal in New York City during the 1930s.

Now he was glad to find a quiet place south of the city of Beacon in 1947, although he already had a sense of the political conservatism of many valley residents. The Seegers endured a brutal attack on those who had attended a concert by Paul Robeson, African American and Communist, downriver at Peekskill in 1946 for the benefit of the Harlem chapter of the Civil Rights Congress. As they drove out of the protected area of the concert, women and men along the roadside jeered at them and youths regularly threw stones the size of baseballs at the windows of the cars, smashing them to smithereens. Toshi's father put the Seegers' children on the car floor, then laid on top them. "Seeger drove to a campground that had showers—there was no running water at his place—and he and Toshi and her father washed the glass from the children's hair. They all had to move carefully in order not to be cut by shards that were hidden in their clothes."[25]

The Seegers' neighbors in Beacon nearly ran them out of town in September 1965 in an unexpected local conflict. After repeated requests from students and teachers at Beacon High School, Seeger had agreed to give a benefit to endow a scholarship at the high school. Prompted by a local Catholic pastor who handed out to his parishioners leaflets based on information from the U.S. House Unamerican Activities Committee (HUAC) and the right-wing John Birch Society, a Stop Pete Seeger committee launched a boycott, sponsored by the Veterans of Foreign Wars, the Knights of Columbus, and the Catholic Daughters of America. Composed more of working-class residents than of rich conservatives, this opposition depicted the Seegers as an alien presence in Beacon. Even the Seegers' near neighbors signed a petition against the concert. Discovering so painfully that his itinerant way of life had given him few local ties, Seeger later observed that "I may have friends all around the world, but in my own neighborhood, I am in a very weak position, and can be knocked down by anyone who wants to tell a few lies about me."[26] The year 1965 saw Seeger at a temporary, depressing hiatus in his extraordinary and controversial singing career.

## PETE SEEGER, THE RIVER, AND SCENIC HUDSON

This bad time made Seeger do some rethinking that took him in a new direction. As early as 1958, Seeger had told an interviewer, "Look at the waste we make of our rivers, beautiful clear streams like the Hudson which flows past my door—an open sewer! . . . Nobody swims in it; you go on a boating trip, you just don't look down."[27] In 1963, Pete had begun writing songs about the river like "Sailing Down My Dirty Stream." Friends in 1963 had given him a book about sloops on the Hudson that inspired him. He began to envision putting a boat on the Hudson that would capture the public's imagination and bring about a cleanup of the river.

During the same time, Seeger joined Scenic Hudson in the Storm King fight, but his celebrity provoked dissension in the fledgling organization. Some conservatives in the movement questioned Seeger's participation. They detested his use of his musical skills to ask in so many ways "Which Side Are You On?" Seeger, in turn, faced criticism from friends for joining up with local "millionaires" concerned, whatever their environmental principles, about protecting their scenic vistas.

When Seeger, in 1966, proposed giving a concert whose proceeds would go to Scenic Hudson, its Executive Committee had a long discussion of the possible dangers of linking Seeger with their organization, given his connection "in the past with left-wing elements." Some argued that his participation "might alienate some of our large contributors; it might make future hearings more difficult if we are questioned by the F. P. C. or Con Edison at future hearings."[28] The committee deferred any decision. The contrast in political views had proved too unsettling.

A month after Scenic Hudson deferred action on Seeger's proposal, the sympathetic member who had brought it to the committee took action by himself. Alexander Saunders hosted a gathering of 166 people on his family's field where they saw a mockup of a Hudson River sloop there, and then Seeger himself arrived. The gathering organized a new committee, which Saunders chaired, with conservatives, an IBMer, artists, and others willing to consider a pioneering innovation. Their purpose was to discuss Seeger's dream of building a sloop to be used for educating folk along the river about their environment and how to protect it.

## THE SLOOP *CLEARWATER*

A shipyard in South Bristol, Maine, built the *Clearwater* in 1969, with some deliberate deviations from known sloop practice. An auxiliary engine could supply electricity to keep the ship on schedule during tours and to facilitate handling in crowded river docks and marinas. But "the overall design of the rig was clearly patterned after the practices of the 1850s." The ship "has carried thousands of children, and adults, too, on educational cruises on the Hudson, New York Bay, and Long Island Sound, promoting an awareness of the state of the river and its estuary, what has been accomplished in cleaning it up, and what remains still to be completed. In addition, those who have sailed on board have learned much of the operating conditions on these sloops, and anyone who has participated in the labor of hoisting the mainsail will well understand the rationale behind the switch to a schooner rig."[29]

Over the years since 1969, Seeger's singing and talking at *Clearwater* festivals and other local events have made him at last a much beloved neighbor in a region that once mostly turned its back on him. When he sang some songs for an assembly of schoolchildren in Beacon in March 2006, the principal, in introducing him, said that "he's probably the person who's done more for the country than anyone else," prompting Toshi to comment that that couldn't have been said fifty years ago.[30] Even more improbable, given former Dutchess County Sheriff Quinlan's detestation of Seeger, was the presentation by the sheriff's department at another occasion of a certificate honoring Pete.

Seeger's populist vision, like his singing, sought to include everyone in a shared quest to improve their world. Post–World War II America saw other efforts and programs that cut across class, ethnic, and racial lines, notably the GI Bill of Rights. For so many working-class veterans, the GI Bill helped pay for educational opportunities that allowed them to move into more highly paid skilled or white-collar work. The community college movement expanded those opportunities by offering both liberal arts and occupational studies. In the mid-Hudson valley, the establishment of Dutchess Community College was one of several important changes in its institutions of higher learning.

FIFTEEN

# Change in Higher Education in the Valley

EVER SINCE THE early nineteenth century, Poughkeepsie had prided itself on being a city of schools and colleges, with Matthew Vassar's college for women a nationally recognized pioneer. The 1960s witnessed growth, innovation, and turbulence in American higher education generally and locally in the mid-Hudson valley. Established institutions changed, sometimes in dramatic ways, and new ones broadened the kinds of opportunities available. When IBM, still the largest single employer, drastically reduced its workforce in the 1990s, higher education, like other service industries, increased in importance among local employers.

## MOBILIZING FOR A COMMUNITY COLLEGE IN DUTCHESS

Reading about the community college movement elsewhere in New York State, Martha Reifler Myers, a county resident long concerned with expanding educational opportunities for more people, began mobilizing support in the 1950s for a community college in Dutchess. However, the chairman of the county board of supervisors, Robert Blinn, initially did not respond favorably, arguing that mostly rural Dutchess County did not need a community college. The low tax mentality of Dutchess made a major new budgetary commitment unlikely. Blinn would not back a proposal unless supporters could prove a need and win the backing of the citizenry. He did not anticipate the campaign that followed. In a decade presumed to favor female domesticity, activist women, many of them married, came together in a coalition from the American Association of University Women (AAUW), PTA, and League of Women Voters to promote the college idea. In September 1955, "The coalition made the brilliant decision to sponsor a county-wide survey to gauge (and in the process build) public support for a community college."[1]

Myers found the strongest opposition not in rural townships, but in the city of Poughkeepsie. At one social extreme, higher-income parents sent their children to private colleges. In less affluent, especially ethnic neighborhoods, many families opposed career education for girls, fearing loss of control over their daughters. (Ironically, the heaviest enrollment would ultimately come from these neighborhoods because a community college turned out to be the best compromise choice for parents, letting their daughters have the education they desired while keeping them close to home.)

Responding to requests from county organizations, Blinn did appoint a committee to conduct a feasibility study. Its positive report led to creation of a Board of Trustees chosen by New York State's governor and the Dutchess supervisors and to the acquisition for a campus of 76 acres of overgrown grounds and dilapidated buildings of the former Bowne Hospital. In looking for the first president of the new college, trustee Edna Macmahon remembered that the search committee had consulted with the head of Columbia University Teachers College's new program on community colleges. He singled out Jim Hall, a wartime captain who had attended Columbia on the GI Bill, as a leader, especially in analyzing problems, with a reputation for making quick decisions and fighting for them. The committee decided they needed a strong man, liking his courage if not his temper. Responding to the committee's desire for someone who would stay at Dutchess, Hall said, "If I create the kind of college I believe in, I know I will ruffle feathers and will need to leave in ten years."[2]

## JAMES HALL, LEADER WITH A VISION

Hall's commitment to the community college ideal was profound, nurtured by his own sense of indebtedness to the GI Bill for giving him the opportunity to move beyond his working-class background. Among the major inspirations for his vision of a truly democratic education were the 1864 act providing for land-grant public universities and the report of Harry Truman's 1948 Presidential Commission on Higher Education.

In choosing the first members of his faculty, Hall knew they represented varied philosophies of education. He realized it would not be easy to overcome this diversity to make Dutchess a truly "comprehensive" college, balancing liberal arts and vocational education. The struggle would continue into the twenty-first century, with the long-term head of the English Department Howard Winn concerned about a "saleable skills" emphasis. What Hall did get, immediately, from his faculty was intense, enthusiastic discussion and argument. The development of a new college, like any new frontier, unleashed fresh energies.

They were not applied only to ideas. When the parts for five hundred classroom chairs arrived late, the professional staff scrambled to assemble them. Staff joined in painting the new student center and formed a book brigade to transfer books to the new library, passing them hand-to-hand. Hall was in the thick of it, characteristically checking on every detail. On the first day of classes, he put on his Navy cap to direct traffic, trying to ensure safe parking. The college opened with eleven faculty members and 650 full- and part-time students; when Hall left in 1972, Dutchess had 4,300 students.

Hall wanted, and mostly achieved, autonomy for the college that kept the county's political arm at a distance. Having a county legislator as trustee like Ken Utter and later David Schoentag helped when Hall defended the college against what he saw as inappropriate interventions, whether on equipment purchased or infringement on academic freedom. He consistently showed just as much concern with students, especially with providing scholarships for those too poor to continue their education. Once, he asked black militant Bill Duke how he was doing financially and what he planned to do. Proud, Duke could only admit to "struggling a little bit" and said that maybe he'd get a job as a Pullman porter. After a moment of silence, Hall "took a check book out of his pocket and wrote me a personal check in the amount of all my expenses for the following year. That is something that changed my life, my way of thinking about myself, about other people."[3]

Hall stayed longer than the ten years he had predicted. But, by the mid-1960s, the strains of office, especially the repeated building delays that increased construction costs, took their toll. The college began without a governing document to establish ground rules for relations between trustees, administration, and faculty; while his faculty generally conceded the good intentions of Hall's paternalism, they moved toward organizing a union to represent their interests. That became a source of conflict. Hall, distressed, responded by finally providing a governing document, but he imposed it. After Richard (Dick) Reitano, whom Hall had hired, became chair of the union, Hall recalled numerous occasions when he expostulated about that "damn Reitano," although they remained good friends.[4]

By the time Hall left in 1972, however, the college had grown to a size in which the early camaraderie of the first faculty had been lost. Helen Baldwin, Professor of Music, recalled seeing her colleagues more often in the old cafeteria and feeling more isolated on campus by the 1970s. For her, as for others, the excitement and pulling together of the early years were never to be forgotten, even as the college they built became an ongoing major contributor to the opportunities of its citizens. By 2008, the college had over 8,000 full- and part-time students. The majority of its 33,000 alumni have stayed in the county, and a study of local economic benefit found that "Dutchess County's economy is more than $800 million stronger annually thanks to Dutchess Community College."[5]

## THE MARIST BROTHERS COME TO THE VALLEY

Another local college also became a major contributor to the community after undergoing quite an extraordinary transformation from the late 1950s to the early 1970s. Marist College began as a training school for future members of a Roman Catholic teaching order, founded in France during the nineteenth century. In 1905, the Marist brothers, having established apostolates in Canada and the United States, chose parcels of the Beck and MacPherson estates overlooking the Hudson River at the north end of Poughkeepsie that they named St. Anne's Hermitage.

By 1929, the Marist Normal Training School let men study in the community for two years, then transfer to Fordham to complete their bachelors' degrees. By 1946, New York State authorized a newly named Marian College to grant four-year degrees. Under the leadership of Brother Paul Fontaine, the brothers and their students built the college's chapel, gym, and academic, administrative, and dormitory halls. President Fontaine helped in the construction, and in growing fruits and vegetables and raising animals. The brothers traded farm goods for services from others, selling eggs and milk from the campus farm through the 1950s.

A new and very different era began in 1958 when Brother Linus Foy at age twenty-eight became America's youngest college president, beginning a twenty-one-year presidency. An exuberant "democrat" who emphasized both community and freedom, Foy wanted the college to have an entrepreneurial spirit. A liberal as well as a multiculturalist before the term existed, he hired a Jewish rabbi and faculty members in the 1960s, created the Martin Luther King, Jr. scholarships, and invited Timothy Leary and Daniel Berrigan to speak on campus. Impressed by the national social ferment, including student activism, in the 1960s, Foy believed in bold innovation by the church to show it still could serve. The ecumenicism and conciliar reform of John XXIII's papacy from 1958 to 1963 reinforced the progressive inclinations of the Hudson valley Marist brothers, already more liberal than other American branches of the brotherhood.

In 1960, the college changed its name from Marian to Marist; three years later came the first big spurt of hiring lay faculty, followed by a second and even larger spurt in 1966–1967. Until 1967, if a brother left the order, he also had to leave the college. Bill Murphy, an innovator in teacher education working with Upward Bound, resigned in that year. After that, however, some brothers left the order but remained on the faculty.

## MARIST BECOMES COEDUCATIONAL
## AND RUN BY LAITY

In 1966, Marist took another new step that would change the college fundamentally by admitting women to its evening division. Full coeducation came in 1968 when women entered day classes. By that date, Linus Foy and the local Marist brothers had become convinced that the religious life was drying up and therefore the order could no longer support the college economically. They persuaded the order's leadership, despite differences in their general outlook, to take the extraordinary step of transferring control of Marist College to an independent, lay board of trustees that would receive all the college property as a gift. At the time, this transition to a lay-run, coeducational college seemed natural, given certain religious continuities. Classes still began with prayers and the brothers still wore their cassocks. The curriculum continued to be classical liberal arts with a core of required courses until 1972, when the college briefly tried a plan that let students concentrate more heavily in a single field. Faculty believers in the liberal arts objected to the resulting specialization. Under the leadership of Louis Zuccarello, who became dean in 1975, they created a new value-centered core.

The college's student body changed, too. While 60 to 65 percent still came from Catholic homes, suburbanization meant that an increasing proportion of students had attended public rather than Catholic high schools. Only 20 percent or less have had a parochial education. In the 1960s and 1970s, Marist students came mostly from blue-collar families, but that, too, has changed. Like other successful colleges in an increasingly service-oriented economy, Marist began to attract students disproportionately from white-collar families, who often brought a consumer orientation to their college experience.

In its transition to a lay-run coeducational college, Marist faculty felt uneasy about reaching out to other regional institutions of higher education. Vassar College, for example, seemed a distant, unfriendly place that would not take them seriously. Dean Zuccarello remembered a discouraging response from area colleges to his proposal for periodic get-togethers between their political scientists. But he and his predecessor did make efforts throughout the 1970s to share a special education program with Vassar, criminal justice with Dutchess Community College, and a joint nursing program with Mount St. Mary.

In 1979, Linus Foy retired as president, having previously left the Marist order. His successor, Dennis Murray, doubled Marist's enrollment, introduced sixteen new academic programs, and expanded the campus to 150 acres. During the 1980s, Marist would undertake a partnership with IBM and, by 1995, win, together with Cornell, Stanford, and Duquesne universities, a CAUSE award for use of technology in teaching. Renowned for its political polling under Lee Miringoff and for recent distinction in other activities, Marist has achieved a national reputation as one of the better liberal arts colleges in the northeast.

During the decade when Marist transformed itself under Foy's leadership, another Catholic training school responded very differently to a similar perception that decrease in religious callings could no longer support it economically. The Jesuit novitiate of St. Andrew on Hudson, a few miles north of Marist, had a magnificent home in a French chateaux style building on 704 acres overlooking the river. The order's local membership included the distinguished philosopher-scientist Teilhard de Chardin, who is buried on the former novitiate grounds.

After three years of investigation, the Jesuits in 1969 announced their plan to leave Hyde Park for Syracuse where their students could benefit from the academic program at LeMoyne College. In May 1969, they held their last classes in the valley, with their property already listed for sale. Two years earlier, the soon-to-be new occupier, the Culinary Institute of America, who would move from New Haven, Connecticut, would, in a curiously ironic twist, have its home in New Haven included in the thinking of another valley institution that, for a time, considered the possibility of leaving Poughkeepsie for New Haven.

## VASSAR COLLEGE PONDERS ITS FUTURE, INCLUDING A MOVE TO NEW HAVEN

For very different reasons, geographical location had become an issue for Vassar College by the mid-1960s. As early as the mid-1950s, a major study by professional psychologists of the undergraduate experience at Vassar, financed by a gift from Paul Mellon, noted frequent student unhappiness with the need to travel 75 miles or more to date men at Yale, Princeton, and other schools they habitually visited. They also disliked meeting men there in the "meat market" atmosphere of freshman mixers, hoping instead for opportunities to get to know men informally, over coffee or in the library, before deciding to date them. In 1966, a college questionnaire asked students whom Vassar had accepted who chose to go elsewhere what factors influenced their choice. A majority indicated that they preferred coeducation or a Seven Sisters college in a metropolitan setting with comparable men's colleges nearby.

These findings came at a time when small colleges worried about their future viability in an educational world in which public and private universities increasingly attracted government funds and faculty interested in research. As early as 1961, President Sarah Blanding presciently told an alumnae luncheon that of the more than one hundred women's colleges currently, no more than ten would survive the next century. She predicted that in twenty-five years many would have become coeducational, public, or joined a university as a coordinate college. Indeed, she herself had made a secret visit to Yale at President Griswold's invitation, walking Prospect Street that then housed the Divinity School and the Culinary Institute of America.

Nothing came of that visit, but, in 1966, Yale dropped an "academic bombshell" by inviting Vassar to join in a study of the feasibility and desirability of Vassar's moving to New Haven and affiliating with Yale University as a coordinate college. Vassar's new president, Alan Simpson, described the possibility to his board as a "royal marriage";[6] his trustees accepted the invitation to a study without presuming its outcome. Poughkeepsie's business and political leadership openly expressed their shocked dismay at the potential loss of a major employer and consumer. State leaders, like Governor Nelson Rockefeller, privately did what they could to discourage a relocation happening on their watch.

But the most important opposition increasingly came from alumnae who feared loss of Vassar's separate identity over time. For many, the idea of selling the beautiful, tranquil 950-acre campus they loved to remember and revisit in order to move to a necessarily postage-stamp-size campus in Yale's vicinity was intolerable. The spaces most often discussed as potential sites in New Haven were on the Prospect Street ridge that then housed the Divinity School and the seriously overcrowded Culinary Institute, with nine buildings mostly consisting of adaptations of nineteenth-century houses on 7 acres. In 1966, the Institute was known to be looking for another campus, focusing then on the New Haven area.

The opponents demanded and got the appointment of a smaller staff, led by Dean Elizabeth Daniels, to study alternatives to relocation, should Vassar choose to remain in Poughkeepsie. The result would be an ambitious report that called for coeducation in some form, the creation of graduate institutes at Vassar, a hoped-for-development of a graduate center for the State of New York on the Vassar farm, and innovations in curriculum, independent study, and fieldwork.

The Vassar trustees welcomed that ambitiousness as a means of justifying their decision to say no to affiliation with Yale, moving "Full Steam Ahead in Poughkeepsie." But no state center materialized, despite some promising planning, and the one graduate institute that began would never reach launching for students. Cooperation with the Mid-Hudson Association of Colleges did encourage more regional outreach by some faculty at Vassar, but they remained, as before, a minority. Responding to the demands of black students, who took over the college's Main building in a nationally publicized sit-in, Vassar created an urban studies center on Winikee Avenue in a heavily black residential area. But that experiment was abandoned in the 1980s.

## VASSAR CHOOSES COEDUCATION

Coeducation did move ahead, but not in the form of a coordinate college for men at Vassar that many had expected. When the faculty realized that a coordinate institution would mean that they would not shape or control that college, they voted instead for admission of men directly to Vassar, a fundamental transformation. And so, in a time made turbulent by antiwar protests and black student militancy, the college turned first to attracting male exchange students in 1969, giving them the option of transfer, and then to admitting its own first male freshmen in the fall of 1970.

The transition to educating men at Vassar, to nobody's surprise, had many bumps, not only in frequent shocks to Vassar sensibilities by free-wheeling male behavior, but in some national publicity that worried the Admissions department. Men coming to Vassar on exchange or as freshmen had reputations to defend; men from other schools just coming on weekends to visit their girl friends did not. They could take advantage of the new freedom from regulation since Vassar had just abandoned parietals to avoid any double standard between the sexes. So there were some awkward and embarrassing moments in adapting to increasingly coeducational use of bathrooms, but mostly men and women learned to brush their teeth side by side, occupying the other facilities separately.

The national publicity in *Esquire* magazine for the first coeducational senior class election in 1974—as a lark—of flamboyant Jackie St. James (a.k.a. Sheldon Weiss) as their class president made some members of the Vassar community worry about a "gay" image for the college. The college generally seems to have been a relatively friendly environment for gay students—though some gay alumnae/i dispute that—because of its liberal, mostly secular atmosphere. That issue abated, while another emerged strongly for a time in the 1970s. A resurgent feminism made some students question whether Vassar should have become coeducational. Faculty and administration wrestled with the problem of defining a truly coequal coeducation in a college whose historic mission had been improving opportunities for women.

The need for one change in direction was glaringly evident to feminists. By 1970, the effects of years of increased recruitment of younger male faculty—more often than not educated in public and coeducational institutions—became all too evident. Women had composed three-fifths of the faculty in 1945; by 1970, men had become a majority overall and also of tenured members. By the end of the century, that trend had been reversed and by 2004 women constituted nearly one-half of both all and tenured faculty.

What did remain the same for Vassar in Poughkeepsie was the landscape beloved of alumnae. Had the college relocated, that would have been up for sale. Would the campus have become a "white elephant," vacant and deteriorating? If it were sold, would the new owner have provided comparable employment and purchasing power for the Poughkeepsie urban region? Would New York State have been willing to purchase the campus as a site for a new graduate center? Those questions are a distant memory now, since by the early twenty-first century a coeducational Vassar had flourished, many new buildings were constructed, including the Frances Lehman Loeb Art Center costing $17,000,000, and the landscape had never been more beautiful, thanks to former President Frances Fergusson. Catherine Bond Hill succeeded Fergusson in 2006 with a focus on a greater involvement of the college with the local and regional community.

## SUNY NEW PALTZ AND
## BARD COLLEGE IN THE 1960s

The trend toward more vocational education in the valley's institutions of higher learning would loom large in the expansion of the State University

College of New York at New Paltz across the river in Ulster County. Under President Alice Chandler in the 1980s, New Paltz would host the valley's first program in electrical engineering as well as a nursing school and other professional programs. But, in the 1960s, the campus experienced the turbulence that so many Americans identify with that decade. Having begun as a normal school in the 1880s, New Paltz had recently made the transition from being a college for the education of teachers to a liberal arts college.

As a new president in 1968, John J. Neumeier wished to reach out more both to the students and the wider world. His arrival coincided with the upsurge of student mobilization for antiwar protest, cresting with their angry reaction to the bombing of Cambodia and the murder of students by state militia at Kent State. He sympathized with their participation in demonstrations in Washington and elsewhere. Some faculty recalled that Neumeier made the symbolically supportive gesture of coming in person late at night at the exit from the New York Thruway to greet their returning buses.

He also gave students the option of not attending classes and faculty the option of not holding them during the height of protests. Faculty who continued to hold their classes remembered academic buildings as becoming like the tower of Babel where they not only heard noisy demonstrators but also occasionally encountered strange surprises. On her way to her classroom, one teacher unexpectedly came upon what seemed a bloody body on the hallway floor; it turned out to be a dummy sprayed with ketchup.

During these turbulent years, local opinion described New Paltz as a haven for the new drug culture. Meanwhile, Neumeier led the way in establishing multiple off-campus learning centers. One result of so much change so fast was a severe budgetary crunch that led to retrenchment in faculty and programs under his successor after 1972, although Neumeier did lead the campus successfully through a difficult period of social unrest.

In contrast, Bard College at Annandale in rural northern Dutchess did not become strongly politicized during the last decade, 1965–1975, of the presidency of the Reverend Reamer Kline. Bard long had emphasized the performing arts, attracting some bohemian spirits. It also had the distinction among valley colleges of hosting distinguished artists and writers-in-residence like Saul Bellow and Ralph Ellison who did not have the usual faculty responsibilities. Because of Bard's small size—some eight hundred students—its regular faculty often needed to be versatile. A language instructor might teach Spanish and German at times as well as French. Equally demanding for faculty was Bard's distinctive curriculum, a variation like Sarah Lawrence's and Bennington's, on Oxford and Cambridge models that required tutorials and a rite of passage to advanced study called the "moderation."

Bard's time of expansion in student body, faculty, and innovative institutes would come gradually after 1975 when Leon Botstein, then age twenty-eight, became one of the youngest college presidents in the United States, paralleling the previous elevation of Linus Foy at Marist College. But Botstein remained at the helm of Bard into the twenty-first century even as he devoted more time to his second career as director of the American Symphony Orchestra. Upon the completion of the 110,000-square-foot, Frank Gehry-designed Richard B. Fisher Center for the Performing Arts in the 1990s, Bard's annual festivals devoted to particular composers drew music lovers far and wide as well as coverage in major national newspapers like the *New York Times*, thus adding to the growing sense that the mid-Hudson valley fosters the arts and attracts tourists interested in them, a fascinating development for a school that began in the Civil War era as a preparatory institution for candidates for clergy of the Episcopal church.

## THE CULINARY INSTITUTE OF AMERICA LEAVES NEW HAVEN FOR HYDE PARK

The celebrity of the arts at Bard and elsewhere in the valley was one of several postwar developments encouraging residents to see their region as becoming more cosmopolitan. That self-perception received a huge boost from the decision of another institution of higher education devoted to advancing the culinary arts to move from New Haven to Hyde Park. The Culinary Institute of America (CIA) had begun in 1946 as a vocational training school for World War II veterans under the name New Haven Restaurant Institute, offering a sixteen-week program with a faculty composed of a chef, baker, and dietitian. It grew in size and reputation, earning Craig Claiborne's praise as the school where chefs are made. By the 1960s, the CIA wanted to escape the congestion of its 7-acre property on Prospect Street, a property that Vassar College might well have tried to purchase had it chosen to move to New Haven. In 1969, the CIA inaugurated double-class sessions to accommodate one thousand students in badly strained facilities. The previous year an article headline in the city's *Journal-Courier* cried: "The CIA Faces Problems, Weighs Transfer."[7]

By choosing to buy the campus of St. Andrew's Jesuit novitiate it saved that beautiful riverside place from subdivision. The Jesuit property had been purchased for $2,500,000 in 1969 by a New York City real estate investor, Irving Maidman, after six months of negotiation with the order. Maidman planned to divide up the estate. He projected a 250-acre industrial park to be developed by someone expecting to spend at least $25,000,000. He wanted a rezoning by Hyde Park to include not only uses like the industrial park, but also a shopping center and high-rise residential development. He envisioned the Jesuits' beautiful main building being used for executive and sales training for a large company.

Instead the CIA purchased the main building and 80 acres, initially, for $1 million and began planning to move most of its current faculty of fifty-seven to its new site. By then, it had become the only institution in the United States offering two-year, post-high school courses solely for training high-level chefs. A food industry journal predicted that the CIA would have a considerable impact on Dutchess County's economy. Welcoming this new stimulus, chief executives of local businesses like IBM and De Laval endorsed CIA aims.

The renovation of the main building cost $4,000,000 and provided twenty modern, full-sized, fully equipped restaurant kitchens where students would take turns at being chefs, sous-chefs, and all assistant roles, in producing full-course meals. The former Jesuit chapel became the Great Hall, used to serve meals prepared during morning and afternoon classes. Distress at the possibility that religious art on the chapel walls might be painted over led to the alternative of covering boards. One inspired innovation outside the main building came from Milton Chazen of Poughkeepsie, supervising engineer for the renovation. Spotting an abandoned chrome roadside diner in New Jersey, he had it shipped to the new CIA campus to serve as a feeding oasis for students and a testing ground for short-order chefs. A tally in 1973 of where CIA graduates worked found 37 percent in restaurants, cafeterias, and diners, 18 percent in hotel restaurants, 9 percent in colleges, and 6 percent each in clubs, schools, and nursing homes. Only 50 of the 1,135 students in 1971 were women, but their proportion increased to 30 percent by the end of the century.

In 1971, New York State gave the CIA authority to grant a two-year Associate Degree in Occupational Studies. A decade later, the American Culinary Federation designated the CIA as the only location to administer its master chef certification exam. Success brought rewards like a 4-Star designation from Mobil for CIA's Escoffier restaurant and Julia Child addressing the graduates in 1976. It also brought the complaint in 1978 by the executive chef of Manhattan's La Caravelle restaurant, himself a CIA corporation member, "that too many graduates come away with the feeling that they've learned all they need to know."[8] Since then, the campus has grown with new buildings, tastefully designed and sited. The school has offered an increasing variety of dining experiences, including preliminary wine tastings conducted by major vineyards. For the valley, the coming of the Culinary Institute has seemed almost pure gain, adding to its attractiveness to visitors as well as to its residents. The sophistication about food and wine it encouraged was reinforced for valley residents by the experience of shopping at another regional success story, this time in retailing.

## ADAMS FAIRACRE FARMS BRINGS
## SOPHISTICATION TO FOOD RETAILING

Adams Fairacre Farms, which established emporia in Kingston and Newburgh as well as in the town of Poughkeepsie, began in 1932 as a roadside fruit and vegetable stand. The family put the stand in front of their home on

Dutchess Turnpike, then a dirt road, but later a heavily trafficked Route 44. Ralph Adams, Sr., and his family sold to passers-by fresh produce and plants from their 60-acre farm, which had a labor force of about twenty-five workers.

During the Depression and subsequent wartime, roadside customers bought in large quantities in order to can their own produce for the winter. They also purchased plants for their home gardens. For Poughkeepsie's Italian population, both the plants for their backyards and the fresh vegetables, especially tomatoes and peppers, were great attractions. A half-bushel of tomatoes sold for 25 cents. Ralph Sr.'s father, Jimmy, had emigrated from Italy near the turn of the century, farming land on Cedar Avenue, peddling, and also selling his vegetables to merchants in Poughkeepsie.

After World War II, with steadily growing customers at the stand, the Adams family added a greenhouse and expanded their original farm structure. Situated just east of Arlington on Route 44, their market attracted many IBMers as well as other professionals and businesspeople purchasing new single-family homes in the expanding suburban subdivisions in Spackenkill, Red Oaks Mill, and LaGrange. The addition of landscaping to the family business came with the IBMers. Overall, the tastes of this relatively affluent and well-educated clientele encouraged the Adamses to expand their buildings to make room for deli meats, gourmet foods, and groceries. Increasingly, Fairacre Farms became a shopping mecca for specialty foods in the Poughkeepsie urban region. Area supermarkets, also expanding their product lines, provided the additional pressure of "keeping up with the competition." According to Ralph and his wife Doris, their success in growing beyond selling vegetables and fruits and expanding their market came after hiring Mark Griffin to manage sales of groceries and high-value items.

Despite the Adamses greater sophistication in purchasing, the store ambience remained friendly and informal. At more than eighty years old, Ralph Adams, Jr., circulated through the store frequently, picking up small tasks he found undone, including wielding a broom to sweep the sidewalk. Fairacre employed many high school and college students for work after the daytime cashiers went home. Even part-timers at Fairacre received benefits, unusual anywhere. Unlike most big stores in the region, Fairacre Farms let charities collect donations just outside their front doors. The pastor of the nearby Catholic parish often asked for and received from the Adamses gifts of food for the hungry.

The business outgrew its origin in the farm. The Adamses no longer raised their own fruits and vegetables, with sweet corn the last to go. In the twenty-first century, produce came from wholesalers in Pennsylvania and Connecticut while cut flowers often came from South America. The cut-flower production that once supported Dutchess County's greenhouse industry faded with high fuel and labor costs. Mark Adams observed, "Competition from warm weather areas like Florida and Colombia has forced local growers to concentrate on heavier garden plants with high shipping costs."[9]

The scale of the operation changed, with the parking area alone enlarged to accommodate 350 cars. The technology employed also changed dramatically. In the early roadside stand days without even a cash register, Doris Adams remembered toting up customers' purchases in her head while transferring plants from boxes to paper. But, in the twenty-first century, she noted, Adams moved into a new business world altogether with its bar codes and instant communication. Her son Mark, who ran one of the largest greenhouse operations in the valley, said "we use computers in many phases of our business. Not only are our plants' feeding and watering computer controlled, but we can determine which plants are profitable by use of computer graphs."[10] The *Wall Street Journal* and the *Economist* allowed him "to follow the worldwide trends that affect growers."

The willingness to try new things remained a constant at Fairacre Farms; it sometimes made Ralph, Jr., nervous, but provided a natural outlet for brother Donald's entrepreneurial zest. For a time, Fairacre became an Agway store, but they didn't sell enough refrigerators so they quit the franchise. In 1981, Donald took the initiative in opening a second store in Kingston, across the river, where household incomes benefited from another large IBM installation. Five years later, they spent $4 million to expand floor space in the Poughkeepsie store from 35,000 to 55,000 square feet. Completing their outreach to the mid-Hudson valley's major towns, Donald opened a Newburgh branch in 1998 with 65,000 square feet and two years later expanded the Poughkeepsie store to 70,000 square feet.

The Adamses employed 650 workers in their three locations by 2004. Once all white, the workforce, like the clientele, by then included African Americans. Ralph also hired Mexicans, mostly in produce. Brothers Ralph and Donald and their sons still ran the company, with three of them starting each day at the Poughkeepsie store. To their surprise, having feared the worst, IBM's downsizing did not have much effect on their business either in Poughkeepsie or in Kingston where a large new mall brought in customers from a wider region, including northern Dutchess County. Like other regional businesses, Fairacre Farms added to the sense of connections and connectedness across the valley that have grown steadily since the 1960s. While not an institution of higher education, it also contributed enormously to the sense of middle-class valley residents that their region had become more sophisticated and cosmopolitan in its way of life, making it more attractive to tourists and metropolitan seekers of second homes.

## HIGHER EDUCATION AND THE VALLEY'S FUTURE

The creations and transformations of Dutchess Community College, Marist, Vassar, the new programs and developments at New Paltz and at Bard, and the transplantation of the CIA increased educational opportunities in the

Poughkeepsie urban region. They also complemented the new attention to environmental beauty along the river as the Storm King battle led to the ambitious programs of an expanded Scenic Hudson and the *Clearwater* campaign encouraged firsthand environmental education.

These complementary changes mostly had their origin in individual institutional needs or initially localized controversies. They had not begun with a shared vision of future development in the Hudson valley, nor did they see their respective ventures as laying foundations for a reoriented regional economy. Modest planning ventures, such as Pattern for Progress, seemed sufficient in the 1960s and 1970s with a prosperous, paternalistic IBM as by far the valley's dominant employer. Tourism and higher education had augmented the advantage IBM gave mid-Hudson counties. But who foresaw that, in the 1990s, colleges, universities, and tourism, along with the arts, hospitals, and other services, would assume such a large role in the regional economy in the wake of IBM's drastic downsizing? Well-laid and much needed foundations they proved to be.

# SIXTEEN

# IBM Downsizes, but the Valley Recovers

THE EARLY 1980s looked promising for the economies of Dutchess and Ulster counties, given the apparent health and huge prosperity of its major employer, IBM. In 1979, the corporation announced a four-for-one stock split, the largest in IBM's history. Two years later, it brought out its personal computer, and the IBM PC quickly became the industry standard. The next year, 1982, saw the government withdraw its antitrust case against IBM, ending thirteen years of litigation.

## IBM'S PROSPERITY IN THE EARLY 1980s

The corporation seemed "home free" and locally the continuing growth in IBM employment and in its workers' incomes made Dutchess and Ulster economic success stories in New York, compared to the rest of the state and most of the metropolitan region. Both counties became ever more dependent on their major employer. As late as 1975, IBM's 22,734 employees in Poughkeepsie, Kingston, and East Fishkill composed 53.3 percent of all manufacturing workers in Dutchess and Ulster. By 1985, 31,042 employees accounted for 62.9 percent. No wonder the area could be seen as a modern, but much happier, version of a company town, given IBM's generous paternalism and philanthropy.

In contrast, salaries among non-IBM manufacturing employees in the valley averaged significantly less than those received by IBM workers. In the valley's chemical and scientific equipment industries in 1990, salaries for their more than 16,000 workers ran $35,000–$40,000. In the computer industry which IBM dominated, some 16,000 semiconductor makers earned an average of $40,000, some 5,000 software makers averaged about $48,000 and the more than 25,000 making computers averaged $55,000. Within Dutchess County, the difference in median household income was dramatic between its two large cities, Beacon and Poughkeepsie, and townships with big concentrations of

IBM workers like the towns of Fishkill, Hyde Park, Poughkeepsie, Wap-pingers, LaGrange, and East Fishkill. The last two reported the highest median household incomes in the county in 1990, with $53,859 and $54,510, respectively, double the median for the lowest area: the city of Poughkeepsie.

IBM's continued growth in revenues during the early 1980s made the region's increasing dependence on the corporation for employment less wor-risome. But that dependence partly reflected shrinkage in other kinds of manufacturing in the valley and in the nation as a whole. In 1964, De Laval Separator Corporation had left its city of Poughkeepsie riverfront site where it had been located since 1892 and moved inland to a newly built sprawling complex on the former Frank farm property on Route 44 in the town of LaGrange. Just before that move, De Laval sold the separator company that had been its origin. It continued to manufacture machines—in World War II, it had made ball turrets for bombers—but now it also "marketed processes, a new ball game."[1] Where previously the company had few engi-neers, Poughkeepsie's five-member engineering department and the inde-pendence generally of the American De Laval aroused the jealousy of Euro-pean branches of the company. After the retirement of an American

FIGURE 16.1. De Laval factory, aerial view, 1954

president in 1974, the parent company in Sweden picked as his successor a foreigner who did not know American practice.

Only thirteen years later, in 1979, the company signaled a major change in its relation to the region. Long headquartered in Poughkeepsie and advertising itself as "Home Industry" during World War II, De Laval announced that it would move its main office to Fort Lewis, New Jersey, in order to be nearer to international airports. The company, which had employed as many as 2,300 workers in the 1940s, now had less than 1,000, and had been struggling in the late 1970s. In the early 1980s, it cut back operations and its use of space radically, leasing space to the nonprofit Rehabilitation Programs and to J and J Manufacturing, a machine shop begun by former De Laval employees. In 1986, De Laval, now renamed Alfa-Laval, announced that it would sell its 450,000 square feet of manufacturing and office space on 80 acres. In 1989, the company left the valley.

## THE STRUGGLE FOR SURVIVAL OF
## SCHATZ FEDERAL BEARING COMPANY

More immediately ominous was the unsuccessful struggle for survival between 1979 and 1981 of one of Dutchess' highest wage manufacturers apart from IBM. The Schatz Federal Bearing Company, with its big plant in Fairview in the town of Poughkeepsie, failed to remain competitive. Schatz was a family firm that had begun in New Haven in 1896, but moved to the town of Poughkeepsie in 1910. Seeing a much larger potential market in the developing automobile industry, Schatz organized the Federal Bearings Co. to manufacture bearings for autos. Unlike many firms, Schatz grew during the Depression and by the mid-1940s employed as many as 1,400 workers.

In the 1960s, Schatz began to worry about foreign competition, primarily from Japan, that by 1963 exported 58 percent of all ball bearings received in the United States. Seeing harm to their business and workers, however, Schatz and Federal refused to join some American bearing companies in arranging joint ventures with Japanese firms. The Poughkeepsie firm negotiated its labor contracts with a local of the United Automobile Workers of America (UAW).

In January 1967, in a dispute over whether the company would adopt the UAW's standard pension plan, Schatz workers walked out for what turned out to be one of the longest strikes in UAW history. The union won its demand, but at an unexpected and terrible cost. Schatz lost its big-volume jobs, which were the least expensive to process. During the strike, the Ford Motor Co. built its own plant to manufacture bearings in Puerto Rico. Schatz's other major customer, auto parts supplier NAPA, turned to a domestic competitor. With that, Schatz became more of a short-run job shop, producing small volumes of bearings in a large number of different sizes. The company also chose to concentrate more on the service market rather than the new equipment market. Both changes made Schatz a high-cost operation. In addition, the company lost some of its most skilled workers, who took jobs elsewhere during the strike and did not come back.

The strike had proved so painful to both sides that they bent over backwards to create a new mood of cooperation. In 1977, the union got such a good contract so easily—surprising union officials—that some said management just didn't want to fight anymore. In the wake of Schatz's ultimate failure, some employees, including John Bahret, Jr., once the company's executive vice president, argued that mismanagement was a key factor, that its older rambling buildings made it harder to operate efficiently, and that Schatz should have downsized as soon as it lost its major customers.

Family leadership of the firm continued with James Neighbors, a grandson of the founder, serving as president. Only when Schatz filed for reorganization under federal bankruptcy laws was Neighbors replaced as CEO by Herbert Kishbaugh, a former executive of the De Laval Separator Co. Kishbaugh attributed the company's failure to overconcentration on automotive products—a highly competitive sector with low profit margins—and "failure to react quickly enough to obvious trouble signs by getting into new product lines earlier."[2] Skyrocketing interest rates in the late 1970s also hurt; at the beginning of 1980, Schatz, forced to pay a premium of 4 percent, paid a total of 21 percent interest on their secured loan with their New York banker.

Kishbaugh struggled for a year after the filing in March 1980 to find a way to keep Schatz in business, hoping to retain as many as 500 employees after laying off 260. He moved to terminate the company's pension plan. He also claimed to have held discussions with some seventy-five potential purchasers or sources of new capital, but he found no financial angel. Kishbaugh did have the support of a conscientious judge in White Plains who agreed to several reprieves; the judge worried about the loss of the remaining jobs at the plant and a "possible 'domino effect' of further business losses in the Poughkeepsie area."[3] County Executive Lucille Pattison asked New York State's Governor Hugh Carey to help save Schatz, but received little encouragement. When efforts to persuade creditors to accept 34 cents—then 40 cents—for each dollar owed them failed, the creditors moved to force involuntary bankruptcy. At auction, a firm that had the reputation of being a liquidator, buying up businesses in order to sell their assets, successfully bid $7.3 million for Schatz's assets.

Over the course of successive Schatz layoffs, one worker's wife baked cakes for the men leaving in order to keep her mind off the hard times she saw ahead for many of them. She thought the postponements over the course of a year had been cruel to the men, alternately raising their hopes and dashing them. Her own husband "used to come home from work happy, but now he's on edge, snaps."[4] At age fifty-two, Robert Barnett couldn't envision what new employment he might find. For him, Schatz's closing was the destruction of a dream. An orphan who had spent his first seven years in Poughkeepsie's Children's Home, followed by twelve years in foster homes, Barnett in 1954 had landed a job at Schatz, a few blocks from the Children's Home. By 1980, this twenty-six-year employee stood to lose his $7.55 per hour job; he and his wife, who had raised three children, now faced the probable futility of their saving for a down payment on a ranch house at the edge of Rhinebeck.

While the layoffs provoked anger and disappointment, the few old-timers still working in the Fairview plant sometimes emphasized better times in the past. Fifty-seven-year-old tool inspector Ray Davis recalled his good paychecks over thirty-three years at Schatz. But another older worker felt sorry for the many "kids" among current employees. Although the company offered some workers lower-paying jobs instead of layoffs, most turned the offer down, fearing future job insecurity. Spouses who had not anticipated the loss of employment were shocked. Giovanni Indomenico's wife didn't say much; she just wanted to get out and move away.

During the next year, surviving employees worked a lot of overtime to convert all remaining raw materials into finished product. The men joked that the faster they worked, the sooner they would be out of a job. In March 1981, it was all over and the new owner of the building began looking for new occupants, offering unsuccessfully in 1983 to lease space for the county Department of Social Services. By 1988, local officials complained of the frequency of fires in the old plant buildings; in one fire, fifty employees of the Pleasant Valley Finishing Co. had to evacuate their shop.

## MANUFACTURING DECLINE

The pain for employees when major manufacturers closed their doors was an old story in Poughkeepsie, as elsewhere, and the reasons for closing varied. New to the late twentieth century was the sharp decline in the size of the manufacturing sector of the economy and the greater invasion of domestic markets by global competition. When manufacturers ceased to be efficient competitors for the volume production on which they had prospered previously, they often turned to niches of specialization. The post–World War II years saw dramatic transformation in many lines of manufacture, exemplified locally by IBM's shift from mechanical business machines to electronic computers.

Even smaller firms that previously served a regional market with kinds of manufacture that had remained little changed over long periods of time adapted to changing technology and market demands with fundamental transformation in what they produced. In Poughkeepsie, two Lumb brothers had opened a sash and blind factory right after the Civil War. The firm continued that line of manufacture for the next century as part of their business doing molding work for housing designed by architects. The Lumbs maintained a cabinet department complete with apprentice cabinetmakers. During World War II, they made gunstocks for the M1 carbines IBM produced in the town and also aircraft and rocket parts.

The firm's big new departure from its traditional molding manufacture came after the war when they began making Formica tops for Levi Strauss in Texas and then became deeply involved in the national market and in manufacturing for railroads. Using maple wood and balsa—both good insulators— the Lumbs made shoe beams for railroads to pick up the third rail. They made a lot of shipping tank bottoms for Kikkoman, the soy sauce producer. The Japanese firm Koshi became a big customer, especially on a project for wall and ceiling panels for railroad cars. That project, never completed, drove the Lumbs into bankruptcy because of their heavy investment in raw materials that they now could not use. Koshi then bought out the Lumbs and dropped all their production except for railroad cars.

Acquisition or relocation removed other manufacturers from the Poughkeepsie area in the 1990s. A Swiss firm purchased De Laval that had left the valley in 1989; its buildings in the town of LaGrange became the home of BOCES (Dutchess County's Board of Cooperative Educational Services). Fargo Manufacturing Co., maker of parts for the electric utility industry, had been a local company since 1912 when its owners sold Fargo to a Connecticut company in 1997. Craig Wolf observed, "Streamlining was Hubbell's strategy, i.e. moving Fargo's work mostly to Mexico."[5] Hippotronics, which made test instruments for the electric industry in Millerton, shut down in 1992, selling to the same Connecticut company that would shut down Fargo. Hippotronics that once had one hundred employees, fired its forty-five remaining workers. Some of the firm's work was moved to a Pennsylvania plant.

## IBM FACES COMPETITION

So long as IBM continued to prosper, townships near its plants in Dutchess and Ulster counties kept their advantage in lower unemployment and higher household incomes. Some signs of change after 1985, the peak year for IBM employment, could be read as worrisome. By 1986, orders began to decline in the worldwide information processing industry. While maintaining its policy of job security, the company in that year moved more than twelve thousand employees to new jobs or locations. In 1987, IBM used an early retirement incentive to reduce its American workforce by more than thirteen thousand employees.

By 1991, a company history, *50 Years in Poughkeepsie*, admitted in an otherwise upbeat account, "Still, the late 80s were difficult times for IBM, resulting in the consolidation of some plants and a reduction in the worldwide workforce."[6] In the summer of 1992, three thousand workers in the Hudson valley left company employment through "voluntary transitions." Reports of radical cuts to come in 1993 may well have led to a decrease in the average price of home sales in the last quarter of 1992.

Although businesses that served IBM and IBMers faced a contracting market, that change initially would be so gradual that the people of the valley didn't see the much bigger trouble soon to come. As late as 1992–1993, the single largest Poughkeepsie employer remained IBM with its 11,000 workers, followed in workforce size in the private business sector by the utility, Central Hudson, with 1,375. The two regional hospitals, Vassar Brothers and St. Francis, together employed 2,438, three private colleges employed 2,380, and the three levels of government employed 22,600, many of them public school teachers.

Who could imagine that the corporation that had brought so much affluence to Dutchess and Ulster would fail to remain on top of the industry it had dominated? Yet IBM was about to be overtaken by more nimble competitors in Silicon Valley using a technology that IBM had looked down upon except for its usefulness for memory. IBM had prospered in the 1960s and 1970s with the bipolar transistor that operated at a much faster speed than the alternative MOS (metal-oxide-semiconductor) transistor. But more MOS transistors could be put on an integrated circuit and they "could also be combined in circuit configurations using almost no power."[7]

MOS technology also permitted scaling down chips to progressively smaller dimensions to a point where MOS microprocessors "offered computing power that was close enough to the mainframe to affect its price."[8] IBM's prosperity had depended on the superior speed and reliability of the mainframe whose profits could absorb any costs, including inefficiencies in production and staffing. After Andrew Grove's Intel pioneered the fabrication of chips with thousands and later millions of MOS transistors, customers had new options "to meet their computer needs. They could use engineering workstations, or specialized computers with many microprocessors working together."[9]

## THE AWFUL DOWNSIZING

By 1990, some IBM customers were ready to consider cheaper alternatives when IBM launched Summit, its newest bipolar-based mainframe. Some models of Summit had list prices of more than $20 million. In the next few years, the company had to engage for the first time in mainframe history in price cutting, sometimes with discounts of as much as 50 percent. IBM lost market share not only to mainframe competitors but also to distributed systems based on networks of smaller machines. Sales were hurt by the economic recession of 1990–1991 and profits suffered from the costs of overstaffing in many departments. In 1993, IBM chose the radical and costly shift from bipolar technology to MOS for its mainframes. In the meantime, it eliminated thousands of workers in the mid-Hudson valley that had been the center for its bipolar semiconductor technology and its mainframe manufacture.

In 1985, IBM Poughkeepsie had employed 12,300 workers, the Kingston plant 7,142, and the East Fishkill facility11,600 for a total at the three Dutchess and Ulster county plant sites of 31,042 employees. By 1990, that total had dropped to 26,400 and by 1992 to 21,500. The next year saw a giant loss of jobs through layoffs. The company reported only 13,800 workers in 1993 and the next year IBM closed the big Kingston plant altogether. In 1996, IBM employment in the valley reached its lowest point with only 9,800 workers reported at Poughkeepsie and East Fishkill combined.

Meanwhile, the company brought in a new president, Louis Gerstner, who emphasized growth in software and services more than hardware and believed that networking was the wave of the future in computing. Arriving during the downsizing in April 1993, he sent a memo to "All IBM Colleagues" [employees], saying he would do all he could to get this necessary but "painful period behind us as quickly as possible, so that we can begin . . . building our business."[10] Contrary to the advice of investment bankers eager to help sell parts of the company, Gerstner's strategy was: "Keep the company together and not spin off the pieces. Reinvest in the mainframe. Remain in the core semiconductor technology business."[11] For this outsider president, "the least strategic but the most controversial [change was] paring back the paternalistic benefits structure. . . . Believe me, I would have loved to continue the employee country clubs and the no-cost medical plans."[12] Gerstner believed not only that the company could no longer afford the previous benefits, but also found them inappropriate to a "modern workforce" for the new IBM where jobs would not be guaranteed for life.

At its mid-Hudson sites, IBM notified those laid off in 1993 in common spaces en masse, not individually. An abrupt departure followed this notification. Some workers were allowed to return to their desks for fifteen minutes to collect personal belongings; others were not. Having heard rumors of downsizing for two years, those laid off had lived with anxiety. Now they became angry. Suddenly the benevolent paternalism for which the company had been famous disappeared and they found themselves stripped of the IBM employment they once thought they had for life. In subsequent "let your feelings out" sessions with non-IBM counselors, some of those laid off even "started to question the capitalist system which treats workers like machinery parts, get rid of them when they rust and you no longer need them."[13]

The prospects for IBMers who had counted on a lifetime career with the company looked grim: uproot their families and move to other IBM sites, retire early without any preparation, take jobs that paid much less, or try with some kind of self-employment to make a livelihood on their own. Because older workers were the most expensive for the company, the downsizing hit them most often. Peter Plavchan of LaGrange had been employed for twenty-one years when IBM laid him off, a double relief for the com-

pany since Plavchan had been organizer of a u
When such individuals alleged age discrimination
IBM denied any bias.

## TRANSITIONAL HELP FOR THOSE LAID OFF

Anticipating demoralization in the wake of the layoffs, IBM wanted to limit
the likelihood of a public "black eye" by providing those laid off with assistance
in making a transition to other employment. The laid-off were told by IBM
supervisors to report to an IBM location where counselors from outside the
company would see them. IBM had persuaded New York State to provide an
$8 million grant, bid out to an outplacement company, to fund a three-month
counseling and retraining program. Fred Nagel became director with ten to
twelve career counselors. Nagel previously had been a guidance director at Red
Hook High School where he had placed students in jobs as well as colleges.
The project rented the whole fourth floor of the Barney building on Main
Street in downtown Poughkeepsie, letting the laid off "park there, like a mini-
college with daily courses on networking, starting a new business, etc. On a
good day 160 people were using the service."[14] The amount of former IBM
employee traffic at the Barney building led many to call it the IBM building.
It was a short unhappy marriage of Main Street with the maker of mainframes.

Out of the twelve thousand laid off, three thousand were eligible for the
project. They came disproportionately from the middle- and upper-level ranks
of IBM employees; 75 percent of them held four-year degrees. At least fifteen
had PhDs, but Nagel found absolutely no market for them. A contemporary
rumor had Barnes & Noble booksellers saying, "We won't hire any PhDs,
because they're too smart to be happy with our kind of work."[15] So the advice
was keep the PhD off the resume unless the applicant wanted an insecure,
poorly paid, and often temporary adjunct position at a college.

Technical people and engineers with a sales background often did well,
seeing the job search as a sales exercise. Mechanical engineers also tended to
do well because their skills hadn't changed much over time; sometimes they
had to move elsewhere, as to auto manufacturers in Detroit. Electronic engineers, by contrast, frequently found that their college studies for that occupation had become obsolete. Some could only get marginal jobs with constantly
changing specifications and methods. Older workers, as always, had more difficulty finding comparable new employment, with many clinging to over-
lengthy resumes. Underprepared for starting their own businesses, they could
be suckers for fly-by-night schemes.

The laid off could elect to take courses at area colleges that stood to gain
financially from retraining them. The project spent $3.5 million in tuition
fees. A year's training for paralegal work usually cost $4,000, but Nagel
thought the colleges too often gave rosy pictures of subsequent job prospects

with overblown notions of remuneration, important legal work, and flexible scheduling. More important, he believed that the trainees would not find paralegal jobs in the mid-Hudson valley. If they did, they'd earn a pittance. Even in Westchester, paralegal work didn't pay well. Another short, oversold program for "network engineer" offered a Computer Network Administrative degree, but one had to leave the valley to find any jobs with that degree.

The project did pump $8 million of state money into the regional economy during its three-year life. With 70 percent rehired, the project also could boast a high placement rate, but only a small proportion reached their previous salary level in replacement jobs. Many took a one-third reduction in remuneration. A number of those laid off came back to IBM as "temps," so the company got some old hands for less than it had paid them previously. Those who fairly quickly moved elsewhere suffered in selling their homes in a locally depressed real estate market. Those who transferred to Texas or New Hampshire IBM jobs would face downsizings there and possibly selling their next homes at a loss. After twenty years employment at IBM in several IBM towns, Mike Nalasco lost his job in Poughkeepsie in the 1993 downsizing. He also lost his equity in the house he had just built after coming up from a former IBM site in Manassas, Virginia, where he had worked for a year. By 2002, he landed at IBM's biggest chip plant in Essex Junction, Vermont.

IBM would not only survive but prosper again in Dutchess County without, however, greatly increasing the total size of its workforce from the low of 1994. Whether the state and localities in Dutchess paid too much in trying to keep IBM from moving elsewhere remained an open question. National corporations for more than a century had played one community against another, and now, in a global age, localities around the world competed aggressively in offering better incentives for relocation. Even in its reduced state, IBM was generally viewed as a prize worth keeping, not least as a magnet for other high-tech firms. The incentives granted by state and local governments were substantial. IBM brought back a plant at East Fishkill, but got a tax write-off for fifteen years, paying no property tax at all for ten years. The Empire State Development Corporation gave IBM a $9 million grant to build its new chip plant there. IBM met the terms of this grant by hiring more than the required 5,348 employees by 2003, but at the same time the company downsized their microelectronics division.

Overall, the Pataki administration estimated that benefits given to IBM would total $475 million over ten years; in addition, state grants and loans provided the company with more than $28 million and it was eligible for $156 million in sales tax and other local benefits and exemptions. Dutchess County agreed to pay for two-thirds of the cost of constructing a 13-mile water pipeline capable of carrying eight million gallons a day from Poughkeepsie to East Fishkill where IBM needed a larger and secure water supply. IBM agreed to pay one-third of the $23 million price and to purchase half of the line's capacity.

In many respects, previously prosperous Dutchess County in the early 1990s paid a heavy price for its economic dependence on IBM. Even before the wave of retirements and layoffs began in the summer of 1992, the county experienced the largest increase in unemployment among nine Hudson Valley counties. Job weakening occurred across the board in manufacturing, service, and government. Dutchess's decline in manufacturing, dominated by the IBM cuts, contrasted with growth in jobs in Orange County, especially in distribution activities related to Stewart Airport near Newburgh. By the first quarter of 1993, Orange County replaced Dutchess in the top position on New York State's Business Activity Index. In a slowing national economy, several valley counties saw a decrease in their sales tax revenues, an indicator of retail sales, but only in Dutchess did revenues exceed a 5 percent decline.

In the meantime, travel to and from Poughkeepsie by air had become less easy. The Dutchess County Airport had been started in the 1930s by the U.S. Department of Commerce primarily as an emergency field. The airport flourished during IBM's heyday in the 1970s and early 1980s, in the wake of its triumph with the 360. Command Airways, which became American Eagle in 1986, offered direct flights to Syracuse, Utica, Boston, and other locations. This service disappeared before the 1990s. For IBMers and others at East Fishkill, Stewart Airport near Newburgh provided direct connections to Chicago and other cities, but passenger traffic at Stewart was up and down, leading to substitution of auxiliary carriers for major airlines. From 1990 to 1991, passengers rose from 191,971 to 401,820, remaining roughly at that level until declining to 361,210 in 1999 to 202,498 in 2001. The next five years brought some major improvements, especially jet flights with Southwest Airlines and Jet Blue, and a takeover of operations by the New York Port Authority to integrate its development within the metropolitan system.

## THE RIPPLE EFFECT OF IBM'S DOWNSIZING

The expected and dreaded ripple effect on local economies through decreased demand from IBM and IBMers did not loom large immediately. Delay reflected the temporary cushion of severance packages (up to one year's salaries for some retirees) and of job training stipends and unemployment insurance for those laid off. In the year after June 1992, loss of jobs in sectors other than manufacturing was limited to three hundred in wholesale and retail employment, three hundred in services, and four hundred in government. In Dutchess County, production work hours did rise dramatically as employers, uncertain of future demand, chose to increase the workday rather than hire new workers.

Home sales also rose sharply, accompanied in Dutchess, unlike other areas in the valley, by a steep decline in average home prices. Those who sold their homes not long after being laid off had the double disappointment of reduced value in what for many was their chief asset. In 1990, the average price for a single-family home was as high as $152,800, by 1994 it hit a low of $102,000. IBM also began a long-term process of emptying out the acres of land the company owned in Poughkeepsie, East Fishkill, and Lake Katrine in Ulster County. And it began withdrawing from its many acres of leased space in those locations and others like Wappingers and Fishkill. Tax revenues for these localities diminished accordingly.

By the end of 1993, unemployment in Dutchess hit a new yearly high: 8.2 percent. Analysis showed that for every IBM job lost, an additional one-third of a manufacturing job disappeared in Dutchess. In Ulster, that rose to three-fourths of a manufacturing job. Both counties continued to suffer in employment and wages compared to the rest of the valley as national economic recovery progressed. While the ripple effect varied in the valley, especially in job loss, the impact of IBM's massive downsizing spread through the region in the form of lessened consumer purchasing power. Business foreclosures soared; "the housing market collapsed; the Porsche dealer shut down."[16] In Dutchess County, both work hours and hourly pay declined in 1994, making Dutchess for the first time lowest in the region in hourly pay. The cost to governments of food stamps and medical assistance increased in the valley, perhaps due to fewer benefits from workplaces.

By 1996, however, the "dark days" were over. Both unemployment and use of food stamps decreased. Against the national trend of an increasing shift from manufacturing to services, Dutchess County's increase in employment included a 1,700 manufacturing job gain. But the manufacturing sectors of Dutchess, Ulster, and Westchester had shrunk, becoming, respectively, one-fourth, one-half, and one-fifth smaller than they were in 1992. The "new" IBM under Gerstner emphasized service to customers even more than hardware. IBM's continuing presence, however reduced in scale, in the towns of Poughkeepsie and East Fishkill did make it likely that "high tech" would remain important in Dutchess' future and in planning for it.

Overall, as the relative importance of the manufacturing sector decreased, Dutchess County, like New York State and the nation, moved toward a predominantly service economy. Subsequently, an unexpected influx of newcomers from Westchester County and New York City to the now cheaper Dutchess housing market made some observers wonder whether Dutchess might become primarily a bedroom extension for the metropolitan region. Even before 2000, the housing market tightened and prices rose. They continued to increase in the new century, with the average price for existing single-family detached houses rising from $225,217 in 2001 to $268,469 in 2002, making it harder for companies to bring in new employees from outside the county. A forty-year-old IBM engineer coming in from Nebraska for an IBM job in Dutchess paying $65,000 a year could not find a place to live; most new homes in the area cost $400,000 or more and older homes sold for about $260,000. Since banks required an income of $100,000 to be approved for a $300,000 home, most families needed to have two employed adults.

By 2005, the *Poughkeepsie Journal*'s reporter on area manufacturing, Craig Wolf, saw three possible paths for the mid-Hudson valley: "(1) a bedroom community for the New York Metropolitan area; (2) a growing high-tech center with abundant local jobs; (3) a high road of rising housing and other living costs and a low road of stagnant incomes for many people of ordinary means."[17] While job creation made the valley one of the stronger regions in New York State, with unemployment shrinking to 3.7 percent in 2005, the new jobs did not provide the same level of salary and benefits as IBM had in the past.

## BEGINNING THE TURNAROUND

How had Dutchess County managed to bounce back more quickly and effectively than anyone imagined? The clear lesson of the trauma of the 1993 downsizing seemed to be: diversify your regional economy. Strengthen already important sectors like tourism. Attract a variety of new businesses, including small ones, using all the means employed over many years like tax incentives and assistance finding sites, financing, and workforce. In 1906, Poughkeepsie's newly founded Chamber of Commerce had been forced to hustle to develop better means than the older Board of Trade employed. But, in 1993, Dutchess County already had in place one of New York State's Economic Development Corporations (EDC), created in 1977. The EDC in turn had spawned a county Tourist and Promotion Agency in 1984. The county also already participated in the state program of Empire Zones that certified sites for eligibility for tax and other incentives for relocating businesses; for example, in 1994, following IBM's downsizing, the Hudson valley received $60 million in state aid for economic development.

By 2005, diversification alone seemed an insufficient economic strategy for the future. IBM led the way toward a different emphasis on partnering between related businesses and clustering them in localities where they could serve each other more quickly and efficiently. In the early 1990s, IBM began its "partner friendly era" by joining with Motorola in a deal to develop chips. A former IBMer who later founded his own business in Poughkeepsie, Ricardo Fuentes, CEO of Matech, said this corporate partnering by IBM "was unheard of . . . it was like seeing the Pope in swim trunks."[18] But the then astonishing outreach by IBM became the precedent for more partnering and then clustering. For example, by the end of 1995, IBM had partnered with Cirrus Logic, Inc. in a new chip-making joint venture to form Micrus Corporation at the East Fishkill plant.

As Craig Wolf reported in 2005, Philips Semiconductors now ran a large older chip plant that it had bought from IBM. "Smaller companies lease space at IBM's East Fishkill Hudson Valley Research Park, given that name in late 1993 to help attract tenants. Other companies have taken space in a nearby business park, and IBM out sources much more often to independent contractors and vendors. Their employees typically earn less than IBMers with the same skills so IBM can achieve some lowering of benefit costs. Vendors who used to have one big customer in IBM either died because of it or diversified themselves to find a variety of customers. IBM now is an attraction for other businesses, rather than a barrier to them."[19] In short, the parts of Dutchess that IBM inhabited no longer resembled a company town, but the corporation continued to be the single largest influence in the county even though the proportion of county jobs it provided had fallen dramatically—from 23 percent in 1982 to 10 percent in 2001.

The company abandoned much of its former paternalism and leadership in benefits, ready as it had not been previously to compare its policies to that of other employers. IBM did continue to be generous in gifts and assistance to local institutions, but it could no longer count on automatic acquiescence of area municipalities in whatever it wished to do. When IBM wanted to expand its chip plant in East Fishkill with an annex in 2003, the town planning board came close to rejecting the expansion "because underground chemical pollution from decades earlier had inflamed the community."[20] The loss of tax revenues as IBM sold off many of its former properties in Dutchess did not improve the attitude of town officials toward the company. IBM moved aggressively to win tax reductions; in East Fishkill the company cut a deal that gave it a 15 percent assessment reduction in a locality where it paid more than 14 percent of the property revenue the town collected. But as Craig Wolf noted in 2002, "IBM still has a hefty share in tax rolls." In two areas of heavy residential concentration by IBMers, "Spackenkill school district IBM's $6.3 million payment is 37.2 percent of the total district tax levy and in East Fishkill the company pays more than 14 percent of the property revenue the town collects."[21]

In IBM's heyday before the 1990s, the corporation avoided a union presence and union voices. But, in 2002, Lee Conrad, the national coordinator of the union Alliance@IBM Communication Workers of America, Local 1701, observed, "The typical IBMer we all remember doesn't exist [anymore]." Noting that button-down white-collar men of "middle-aged demeanor, loyal to the company" were disappearing, Conrad thought that the company was trying to get rid of more senior employees.[22] More employees did have fewer years with IBM, but officials insisted that this shift resulted from the company's push to "remain competitive when technology was constantly changing." By 2002, half of the company's labor force had been with IBM less than five years, and the average age had dropped to between thirty-eight and forty-two. The younger workers no longer planned on a career at IBM and many came to IBM in mid-career, "often as a result of IBM taking over the information technology departments of established companies, like Price Waterhouse."[23]

The workplace atmosphere became more casual in dress and scheduling of working hours. Employees could vary the beginning of their IBM day within a four-hour time frame and spend up to two hours at lunch so long as they made up the extra time taken on the same day. Roughly one-third of IBMers did their work away from company facilities, whether "at home, at a customer's office, or on the road."[24] The gender and ethnic distribution of the workforce remained similar in the wake of downsizing. Men composed 69 percent in 1996 and 68 percent in 2002 and minorities—African American, Native American, Hispanic, and Asian—accounted for about one-fifth in both years.

Continuity in workforce composition no longer entailed cohesion in life off the job. As jobless IBMers moved elsewhere in search of employment, non-IBMers—often commuters to Westchester and metropolitan New York—bought the houses they vacated. The occupational mix of heads of household even in neighborhoods close to IBM facilities increased. Previous concentrations of as much as 80–90 percent IBMers on an individual street became a thing of the past, further diminishing the sense of a company town. Neighborhoods also became more settled as IBM no longer transferred its managers as frequently. A description of the Hagen Hills subdivision off Spackenkill Road in the town of Poughkeepsie in the fall of 2002 reflected the changes. "It's no longer a one-class society of IBM engineers and managers," reflected one resident of thirty-nine years and a veteran of forty-four years with IBM. Another Hagen Hills resident of thirty years added, "I don't think IBM has the loyalty it once had."[25]

IBM's vice-president for human resources did report a "shortage of people having the technical skills available in the geographic areas they are needed."[26] Similar shortages occurred in fields other than high-tech manufacturing as requirements for many jobs included more technical skills than in previous years. Local institutions of higher learning, especially community colleges, mobilized to try to meet these needs as they did elsewhere in the nation. Dutchess Community College cooperated with the Council of Industry of Southeastern New York to offer training and retraining, including courses in computer software training, management development, and medical claims administration. The Manufacturing and Technology Institute of BOCES created programs to train and retrain for specific kinds of employment. Marist College and IBM cooperated in a variety of ways after Vassar chose in 1970 not to create a proposed graduate center of science, technology, and human affairs.[27]

What the mid-Hudson valley did not have was a constellation of graduate-level research programs like the State University of New York at Albany and nearby Rensselaer Polytechnic offered to attract major public and private investment in cutting-edge research like the Nanotech project. Poughkeepsie entrepreneur Ricardo Fuentes commented in 2005 that currently the valley was a good place for small high-tech companies. But he feared that this advantage might not last as "the Internet, overnight delivery services, fiscal incentives, and the low cost of living in other areas of the country reduce the dependence on 'the ideal physical location.'" IBM's presence then would not be sufficient attraction, and Dutchess would need the "high density of local talent such as Silicon Valley, Austin, and the Research Triangle in North Carolina have. . . . Until I see a steady flow of science and technology graduates coming out of local schools—and the startups they will create—we won't reach the self-sustaining status necessary to support anything like a Silicon Valley."[28]

Another obstacle to attracting new high-tech ventures stemmed from the very success of Dutchess County in the major task of economic recovery after IBM's downsizing, filling up the physical spaces IBM vacated. In 2003, the head of the county's Economic Development Corporation, Ronald Coan, warned that municipalities had not zoned for high-tech use, that the county had few corporate or industrial parks, and those it did have "are either filled, too small to attract a big firm, contaminated by old industries, or too far from big roads."[29] A proposed corporate park adjacent to IBM's Hudson Valley Research Park and Interstate Highway 84 had aroused big turnouts at town meetings by those who wanted the site left as farms and wetlands, fearing the increased traffic and future spills that would worsen aquifer contamination.

## ATTRACTING AND KEEPING BUSINESSES

What did the outreach to businesses of the Dutchess County Economic Development Corporation (EDC) and other promotional groups yield? How much did area recruitment efforts contribute to the choice of Dutchess locations by individual companies like Hitachi Semiconductor, Rojan Electronics, Allied Electronics, and Conklin Instrument Corporation? Probably IBM's continuing presence in Dutchess, though much reduced, made it easier to appeal to smaller suppliers and high-tech firms and even some competitors. Most of the new businesses established in Dutchess and especially Ulster in the early years of the twenty-first century were small, employing less than fifty workers. Private firms employing fifty to one hundred accounted for 9,555 workers in Dutchess and 5,312 in Ulster in 2003.

Tax incentives in the Poughkeepsie Empire Zone helped keep a medium-sized manufacturer, Dorsey Metrology International, formerly Dorsey Gage, in the county. Incentives were crucial in attracting a major low-wage employer, GAP, to build a 2.3-million-square-foot distribution center in Fishkill. Opened in September 2000 and expanded the next year, this giant facility with nine hundred employees in 2003 speeded up commodity delivery by "direct-to-store" shipping.[30] Extensive automation and five daily shifts meant that you never saw the whole workforce at any time. GAP had no trouble finding workers at $10.50 an hour to start, although their work was heavy and monotonous. But the likelihood of attracting other low-wage employers decreased as housing costs in Dutchess rose with the influx of new residents at the end of the century.

In 2001, the two largest job generators in Dutchess County remained electronic equipment and manufacturing with 7,764 employees and industrial machinery and equipment manufacturing with 7,012. Their average wage was $78,467 and $91,620, respectively, compared to $35,195 and $32,790 for the next two largest job generators: health services and educational services. Health services added 1,910 workers between 1996 and 2001 compared to 1,154 in electronic equipment and only 397 in industrial machinery.

Across the river, Kingston, having lost its large IBM facility altogether in 1994, began its comeback with greater success in retailing for its hinterland. In Poughkeepsie, the decay of downtown in the wake of urban renewal, the arterials, and suburban shopping malls brought belated closure or flight of upscale clothing businesses like M. Shwartz and Up-to-Date, a remnant of the latter surviving in a shopping mall on Route 9. But the clothing merchants also suffered from changes in consumer taste and the coming of local branches of national chains like the Gap, Eddie Bauer, Talbot's and Joseph Banks.

Keeping and attracting business had always been a challenge for the valley's cities, but became even more so in the wake of IBM's downsizing. As manufacturing decreased, the importance of the non-profit sector in the local economy increased, as did the interest in tourism and other alternative ways to economic growth.

PART IV

# Postindustrial Poughkeepsie and the Valley

# SEVENTEEN

# The Nonprofit Sector Grows in Importance

COMPARED TO OTHER New York State counties, manufacturing, especially high tech, seemed likely to remain more important in Dutchess than in adjacent mid-Hudson counties because IBM still had facilities in Poughkeepsie and East Fishkill despite closing its earlier chip production line there in 1993. The company considered alternative sites for locating a new $3 billion 3-millimeter chip factory, but inclined toward remaining in its previous manufacturing area not too distant from its Yorktown Heights research laboratories. State and local governments offered $600 million in incentives to keep the new facility in East Fishkill. Planned to run twenty-four hours a day, seven days a week, the plant, opened in 2002, employed more than two thousand workers augmented by some 250 engineers and managers from partner companies, often from overseas.

## CHIPS AND SOFTWARE

"The few hundred people on the factory floor at any one time often had skills seemingly more suited to a research lab than to a production line: PhDs are numerous, and even machine operators with two-year degrees from technical schools must constantly upgrade their skills . . . plastic pods, riding on overhead tracks and carrying pristine silicone wafers [feed] hundreds of chip-making tools."[1] In 2006, one worker remembered dipping silicon wafers into chemicals by hand two decades earlier, a process now fully automated. Most of this new production went not to IBM as it had previously, but to other customers like video game makers. An observer of the regional economy noted that the cluster of high-tech-related firms at sites like East Fishkill did not create enough new jobs to offset the ongoing decline in traditional blue-collar manufacturing in upstate New York.

Moreover, the increased frequency of lower levels of education and of income among early twenty-first-century IBM workers no longer offered quite as much stimulus to the county's economy and to an expanding upper middle class in the region. Increasingly, manufacturing at IBM relied on technicians rather than on the engineers so numerous at IBM from the 1960s to the 1980s. More of the workforce had two-year associate degrees rather than the four- to five-year BA or BS degrees required to become engineers. For the future, this downward shift in educational requirements for employment could contribute to a more even distribution of Dutchess's population across income levels, unlike the earlier sharper gap between IBMers and non-IBMers.

But guesses about IBM's future impact on the mid-Hudson region remained hazardous, given its history of major transformations in direction. As *Barron's* noted in 2006, under CEO Sam Palmisano, "IBM is reinventing itself again. It's shed its disk-drive and personal-computer businesses to focus on less volatile operations with fatter margins, and has boosted productivity by slashing costs and spreading facilities around the globe. Welcome to the New Big Blue, the world's second-largest software company—quite a change from the hardware giant that invented the disk drive 50 years ago and lived high on the mainframe, or the service outfit it successfully morphed into under Gerstner—one whose revenues had stalled in recent years."[2] Each shift in focus entailed change in IBM's workforce, with outsourcing frequent.

The ongoing need in Dutchess for highly educated and well-paid professional workers in higher education and in the health care industry offered a greater sense of stability, as did the ongoing remarkable improvements in medical technology that increased demand for more highly skilled technicians. Those sectors, especially health care, previously had depended on many less skilled and often poorly paid employees; how far their situation would improve had yet to be determined in the early twenty-first century. All that seemed certain from looking back at the region's past was that its labor force would continue to adapt to new circumstances, and, at some historical moments, change shape dramatically, with losses for some workers and gains for others.

## HOSPITALS IN TRANSITION

Retailing on the scale of Fairacre Farms and the malls helped keep unemployment moderate in the valley. But the biggest area employers besides IBM continued to be federal, state, and local government, the regional utility, private educational institutions, and two hospitals. The two hospitals had combined staff of 2,438 in 1990. Yet they faced a shortage of nurses; the increasing proportion of foreign nurses and doctors in regional hospitals represented a dramatic national change in the American medical profession during the late twentieth century. With the continuing increase in expensive medical technology and the frequency of outpatient treatment, financial viability became a major issue for hospitals as did their increase in size and their problems of internal organization. Ron Mullahey, CEO of Vassar Brothers Hospital from 1985 to 2004, who had trained in the Hospital Management Program at Cornell University's business school, observed that "hospitals as we know them today are moving steadily and gradually to extinction."[3]

The desire to avoid hospitals' overhead expenses made it less likely that expensive technology would cluster there. A related and continuing worry for hospitals that wanted to maintain their economic base was that they were losing lower-end technology to nonhospital settings and so more urgently needed high-end technology. St. Francis Hospital tried to get a heart catheterization lab to do advanced diagnostics, but, if they succeeded, they then faced the universal problem of short lives for state-of-the-art status for new technology. The continuing need for increasingly advanced equipment did not provide sufficient time to depreciate the old equipment.

As medical technology became less invasive, it also drove decentralization of facilities. Even heart surgery could be done without breaking the chest bone, and laproscopic surgery became progressively widespread in usage. Describing genomic medicine as the new gold standard, Mullahey observed that when you know the right genes you can prevent disease. All of which made it probable that the practice of medicine increasingly could be conducted in ambulatory and other outpatient settings and even in doctors' offices with correspondingly less need for hospital beds. In the 1980s, for example, a cataract operation required an eight-day stay in the hospital where you had to lie completely still. In 2005, a patient was in and out in three hours from cataract surgery done in an ambulatory setting, miles from the nearest hospital.

## GROWTH OF GROUP MEDICAL PRACTICES

This new form of competition with hospitals posed by group practices run by doctors developed across the nation in the 1970s and boomed in the 1980s and after. As the incomes of physicians began to decline and medical schools turned out more specialists and fewer family practitioners, "the more entrepreneurial (or desperate) among them began purchasing the equipment and staff to offer everything from imaging to full-service surgical centers. Payers like it because it typically saves them money and patients like it because it's typically more convenient."[4] In the Hudson Valley as early as the 1960s, Howard Teitelbaum gathered together an array of doctors to occupy attractive offices in a five-story building. In 2006, the architecture of Westage center in Fishkill delighted those who could pay for services there, but many group practices still made do with much less elegant quarters.

The largest group centers or clinics resembled little hospitals, except that they could not take patients overnight. But, as private businesses, they did not have the financial drain of hospital emergency rooms that by law had to accept anyone who came seeking assistance. Nor did group centers have to accept Medicare or Medicaid. The larger practices that became the dominant trend across the United States by the late twentieth century could afford to hire professional administrators with MA degrees who were represented by a national Medical Group Management Association. In smaller group practices, a lead doctor managed on behalf of the other doctors, determining what the insurance companies would accept and supervising billings and collections.

To keep aggressive doctors from competing with them through independent group practices and attracting other doctors less enthusiastic about joining independent ventures, hospitals themselves often built specialty centers as joint ventures. Anyone who looked at the cityscape around surviving major hospital complexes in the early twenty-first century like Vassar Brothers Medical Center and St. Francis noticed how extensive the complexes had become, with new adjacent buildings housing groups of doctors with specialties like cardiology, cancer, gastroenterology, or urology. The strength of these specialties locally by 2005 contrasted sharply with the situation in 1985. A urology group had three members then, and twenty years later about twelve members. Dutchess County residents needing heart surgery in the 1980s most often went outside the county because nobody performed it at Vassar Brothers. As late as 2001, two-thirds drove to Westchester and one-third to Albany; by 2004, half stayed in Dutchess and the remaining half went to a variety of locations, including New York City. The Heart Center, advertising itself as "The Regional Leader in Cardiac Care," listed nineteen doctors in 2006 with offices at Poughkeepsie, Fishkill, New Paltz, New Windsor, and Sharon, Connecticut.

## HOSPITALS PARTNERSHIPS AND MERGERS

Meanwhile, hospitals needed to remake themselves. In gearing up for new specialties, outdated equipment urgently needed replacing in Ron Mullahey's first years as CEO at Vassar Brothers Hospital, not least to improve staff morale. Other improvements in infrastructure, in renovation and new construction, followed, and Mullahey spent a lot of time building up middle management at the renamed Vassar Brothers Medical Center. One means of cutting costs and improving service led the institution in a radically new direction, collaboration with another local hospital, St. Francis, in which each offered specialties not available at the partner. This division of labor expanded their patient base in their chosen specialties and avoided duplication and competition. In the partnership that began in 1991, Vassar Brothers took cardiology and cancer; St. Francis focused on orthopedics and neurosurgery, using the rehabilitation center they already had. The two hospitals created a new oversight board for the partnership and developed a fairness formula to balance out the monetary returns to each. Although both institutions remained independent, they felt "virtually" merged. They agreed that each should develop other affiliations and Mullahey hoped that St. Francis would develop a Catholic network with Benedictine Hospital in Kingston while Vassar Brothers worked "the secular side of the street."[5]

The arrangement satisfied St. Francis's board, but the archdiocese came to doubt its desirability. The ending of the nine-year partnership in 2000, however, resulted from a New York State antitrust action after a health maintenance organization—MVP HMO—that negotiated with them complained that the two hospitals were setting prices. A consent decree in the case specified that, regardless of community needs, there could be no cooperation between the two. The hospitals unhappily spent millions in lawyers' fees, but the cardinal archbishop of the New York archdiocese, concerned with issues of reproductive rights, was delighted with the resulting separation.

The potential usefulness of partnership between hospitals led to a new relationship for Vassar Brothers. Northern Dutchess Hospital in Rhinebeck had been struggling financially. It tried a connection with Kingston Hospital, then turned unsuccessfully to Benedictine Hospital in the same city. Knowing it could not survive alone, Northern Dutchess approached Vassar Brothers in 1998. These two merged in 1999 and became partners, together with Putnam Hospital in Carmel, in 2001 in a new holding company, Health Quest, creating a regional system. At one point, a relation with Butterfield Hospital in Cold Spring was considered. When that idea went nowhere, Butterfield turned to the hospital in Peekskill that ultimately closed them down. System building had its casualties like Butterfield, but the advantages of an expanded patient base for hospitals with strength in certain specialties perpetuated the trend as well as the creation of new specialty centers.

System building in medical centers added to the stimuli to regional consciousness and planning. (And the stimulation worked in the opposite direction as well when Arthur Weintraub, who began as a planner with Pattern for Progress in 1966, moved on to become president of the Northern Metropolitan Hospital Association.) Like all forms of bureaucratization, medical system building increased the number of white-collar workers. The county's labor force also was improved by the addition of highly educated and well-paid medical specialists. But, in 2006, valley hospitals remained a major provider of entry-level and correspondingly low-paid service jobs. They had not moved by that date to reduce the distance in earnings between staff members by creating training programs and ladders of upward mobility for these low-skilled workers, as Boston's major hospitals had done a few years before.

## THE CHAMBER OF COMMERCE AND UNITED WAY

Change in the relative importance of major employers accompanied IBM's downsizing, but area leaders' favorite organizations for dealing with most civic concerns and needs not addressed by local government and religious bodies continued to be the Chamber of Commerce, the Community Chest (renamed United Way), and service organizations like the Rotary. In a 1970 reputation study, thirty prominent area residents, selected for their reputed local influence, rated the Chamber as the most "influential" organization in Poughkeepsie and the Community Chest as second in "influence." The Chamber through its well-attended monthly contact breakfasts brought together businessmen, professionals, and, increasingly after World War II, staff from nonprofit organizations. Speakers were chosen to keep those attending well informed on topics deemed important for Poughkeepsie's present and future, especially opportunities for economic development. In the twenty-first century, speakers included a representative of the greenway, the regional plan important for future tourism as well as for local recreation.

The contact breakfast remained the single most important gathering place for community leaders of all kinds. A decade after the bounce back of the local economy from IBM's downsizing, the Poughkeepsie Area Chamber could proudly advertise on its Web site that job growth in Dutchess County had risen to thirty-fourth place on the Milken Institute's "Best Performing Cities" list for the nation in 2002 and held the highest place for New York State. Among two hundred metropolitan areas, it achieved fifth place in wage and salary growth and on a measure of high-tech business concentration it scored tenth.

The Community Chest had been area leaders' preferred means for aiding nonprofit service organizations since the 1930s. For four decades, the chairmen of its board of directors and the chair of its annual fund-raising campaign had been drawn from among prominent white residents, mostly Protestant males, beginning with Vassar College president Henry Noble MacCracken as the board's first chair. But, in 1970, a local Jewish merchant, Jonah Sherman, who had just served as president of the Chamber of Commerce, became chair of the Chest board. Jonah and his wife Joan went on to promote United Way internationally. After Sherman, an African American woman, Marie Tarver, then head of the Model Cities Program, served as chair.

Industrialists, financiers, and businesspeople composed 63 percent of board members in 1970, with clergy, journalists, and attorneys making up 12 percent, and others (mostly homemakers) 9 percent. The board had no representatives of organized labor or welfare agencies then. The most prominent members dominated the executive and budget committees and left the social planning division to homemakers and professionals. The choice of a clergyman as the chair of planning suggested that division's relative lack of importance in setting policy. But some broadening during the 1960s in the composition of the crucial grant-making budget committee revealed a trend toward a more socially diffuse set of gatekeepers. Officers of important local businesses would still be a majority of the United Way board by the end of the twentieth century, but with a wider range of religious, ethnic, and racial origins. The YMCA, Marist and Dutchess Community Colleges, and medical groups and hospitals would also be represented.

The Chest in 1970 made financial grants to a variety of local organizations, most serving cross-class clienteles like the YMCA, YWCA, and Boy and Girl Scouts. Chest leaders preferred to focus more on these and others of their traditional agencies, regarding local government and the Model Cities Program as having responsibility for "problems." Wishing to avoid conflicts, they usually made incremental changes in annual grants, allowing them, for example, to give the Neighborhood Services Organization (NSO) more money each year while reducing the NSO's share of the total budget. They also varied their appeals to different groups of fund-givers. Since blue-collar residents during the late 1960s and 1970s resented nontraditional causes like racism and poverty, in appealing to them, the Chest emphasized its help for the handicapped and for senior citizens. Since 1970, the Chest, becoming United Way, expanded its range to encourage ventures to provide better services for a diverse urban population, including the children of the Catherine Street Community Center and those in greatest need like the poor and working poor served by Dutchess Outreach.

One of the oldest community organizations in the city, Catherine Street Community Center has been an important resource in the lives of families and children since 1922. For decades, the center has been a safe haven where children work on their homework after school or learn ballet. In the twenty-first century, family programs under executive director Shirley Adams also focused on HIV/AIDS, providing case management for medical services and other social needs. An annual fund-raising event in honor of Dr. Martin Luther King, Jr.'s birthday developed into a gathering of over seven hundred city and county residents at the Civic Center where speakers urge communitywide reconciliation and present scholarships to local high school students.

Shirley Adams came to Poughkeepsie after working in the New York City mayor's office. She grew up in Alabama in a household where education was paramount. She was always around "women who were teachers or wanted to be teachers," she remarked.[6] Many women who have worked in agencies or volunteered in the city's or county's nonprofit organizations came from elsewhere, such as Adams, but, as often, many have been home-grown.

## MARY KEELEY AND DUTCHESS OUTREACH

Mary Keeley, Poughkeepsie-born and raised, was one of a number of local residents who became connected with or inspired by the war against poverty in the 1960s. Her efforts after 1974 focused on an outreach program, incorporated as Dutchess Outreach, Inc. in 1981, that became a continuing source of help for people dealing with "scores of problems—poor housing, sickness, drugs, hunger, family woes, poverty." As Keeley said in 1983, "I do think the poor are under super pressures just to keep living. You can see why [poverty] tears a family apart." Mary Keeley lost her own mother at age ten, but had had supportive "aunts and uncles on all sides."[7]

Her father scrimped to send Mary and her sister to Vassar College. When she graduated in 1941, she had law or the theater in mind. But marriage to Dr. James Keeley, a Poughkeepsie surgeon, and raising four children led her to pursue volunteer activities that over time became a career. Beginning in the 1960s, she served as president of Poughkeepsie's Board of Education and chairman of the city's Human Relations Committee and of the Model City Agency's Education Committee.

In 1974, Trinity United Methodist Church on South Hamilton Street launched a Neighborhood Outreach program, soon renamed the Satellite Citizens Center, with $5,500 from the Methodist Conference and with Mary Keeley as staff. Like others working with the poor at that time, she saw her role as that of welfare advocate, serving as guide and gateway to the social services her clients needed. Above all, she believed that the poor needed respect since so many of them found appealing for help humiliating. "A man this morning said he stood on the corner for half an hour before coming into the office. He had never had to ask for help before. . . . Many feel as if they have lost a battle, trying to stretch funds on rocketing rents, utilities, food and clothing bills."[8]

Finding money for even this modest venture remained problematic until 1981, leading to ups and downs in attempting to expand staff with a second person and a part-time bookkeeper. Trinity Church early on applied for money from Poughkeepsie's Community Development fund. In 1976, the Satellite Center financed the start of its Emergency Food Bank through the federally financed Dutchess County Committee on Equal Opportunity (DCCEO). When Community Development cut funds for all agencies, other churches helped with a special fund-raising drive in 1979. The year before, the First Congregational Church took responsibility for opening the Children's Clothes Closet.

Financial relief came with United Way's decision to accept the Satellite Center as a member in 1980, providing a regular funding beyond what its previous contributors could give. The center became incorporated as Dutchess Outreach in 1981. In 1982, it opened the Lunch Box, an instant success. Trinity Methodist, St. Paul's Episcopal, and St. John's Evangelical Lutheran churches collaborated on the Lunch Box, providing midday meals six days a week for those in need, with no eligibility requirements. Initially located at St. Paul's Church, across from the Catherine Street Center serving African Americans on Mansion Street, the program also received substantial grants from religious foundations. By 1986, Dutchess Outreach received its first FEMA funds for food and emergency assistance. At the end of the century, the Lunch Box had moved to the Family Partnership Center, not far away on North Hamilton Street. In 2003, the program served more than fifty thousand meals, adding another ten thousand in the next three years.

In 1985, Mary Keeley retired, but the example she set lived on in Dutchess Outreach. The *Poughkeepsie Journal* noted in 1983 how again and again she had "come to the rescue with food, clothes, advice and brisk, old-fashioned solicitude. She arranges rides, sorts clothes, accompanies clients to the welfare office and lugs groceries from supermarkets throughout the week. It's an unglamorous, never-ending business, which has kept her hopping in a 20-year fight against poverty." Noting that many clients come back again and again, she said, "You can't be judgmental in this job. . . . I can just suggest things; I'm not their mother, heaven knows!" Yet "calling out behind her as she heads for a client" she told the *Journal* reporter, "but I do know I have to go to Social Services or this gal will be in trouble."[9]

## LATEEF ISLAM AND THE
## FAMILY PARTNERSHIP CENTER

Introducing the county Department of Social Services or other public and private agencies to clients, or directing clients on how to find their way to the agencies that might help them had long been a problem for organizations helping residents who urgently needed assistance, but could not pay for it themselves. Often it meant going to a number of different locations without much guidance. In Dutchess County, that problem was greatly reduced in the 1990s. Distressed by the lack of coordination and duplication in their activities, Allen Thomas, head of Poughkeepsie's century-old Family Services agency, Emily Dyson, chair of his board of directors, and Lateef Islam, a remarkable presence among the city's African Americans, sought integration. They persuaded thirty caregiving organizations to join together, with the assistance of a $500,000 grant from the Dyson Foundation, to form the Family Partnership Center (FPC). The center made its headquarters in the large building on the edge of downtown previously occupied by the Poughkeepsie High School into the 1950s and then by Our Lady of Lourdes High School who moved out to Boardman Road in the town when IBM vacated their research and development laboratories in the late 1990s. With so many caregivers in the same building, an organization that needed to refer a client to another agency could, if that seemed desirable, have staff walk the client to its office for a personal introduction. More important, sharing the same building made the various staffs better informed about each other and their respective needs.

For its first Executive Director, the center in 1997 turned to Lateef Islam, who by then had become a legendary figure.[10] As African American and white leaders alike testified at his funeral in 2005, no one in the city's history had such a calming effect on racial tension and such an extraordinary capacity to move others to a host of good works without exhortation. A more than 400 pound giant of a man, Islam dwarfed others physically, yet simultaneously made them feel at ease. Unafraid himself, of everything from poverty to disability to race hatred, he built confidence in others. His booming voice and laughter made city streets friendlier as he passed through, as he often did during bad times with Mayor Colette Lafuente, who was half his size. On their frequent midnight walks, no one could miss his message: "No more violence. No more killing."[11]

Born in Brooklyn, Islam had been sent to Catholic schools by two women. But bad behavior brought ouster and further involvement in drugs and crime. A conviction for manslaughter sent him to Green Haven Prison in Dutchess County. Converted to Islam and accepted by fellow inmates as an imam, he undertook eleven years of coursework in Marist College's prisoner education program, leading to a degree in criminal justice. When he finished his sentence, Islam became a transitional counselor and head of the Marist program for another eleven years. His subsequent experience at the Family Partnership Center mixed his usual success in bringing people with disparate interests together in common causes along also with his lack of interest in and skills for administration. His legacy included specific goals like the creation of the Sadie Peterson Delaney African Roots Library at the FPC, assisted and carried on by Brian Riddell of Dutchess Outreach, and the wider gift of opening the eyes of many white citizens to the nature and causes of local racial tensions, as former County Executive Lucille Pattison testified at his funeral.

A more controversial issue than racism in voluntary associations was the demand for elimination of bias against homosexuals. The loss of one institutional supporter for United Way at the end of the century showed the difficulty it faced as a general fund-raiser because of conflicting values among its supporters. Individuals associated with Vassar College had played leading roles in the early days of the Chest, but, by the 1990s, neither the college's administration nor the faculty could approve the homophobia they saw in the national Boy Scouts organization's rejection of gay males as members. The United Way, however, continued to support the Scouts locally.

As a result, Vassar set up its own fund-raising organization, the Community Works Campaign, that gave 100 percent of the funds it collected to a smaller number of groups. While there was some overlap with United Way in recipients of grants, the college supported less traditional groups like the Rural and Migrant Ministry working on the right to collective bargaining, the Child Abuse Prevention Center, the African Roots Library at the Family Partnership Center, and a program sponsoring after-school support groups for adolescents who differ in sexual orientation or identity. Town and gown remained separate worlds with Poughkeepsians often describing Vassar as aloof, even though in every generation an important minority of the college had involved themselves actively in Poughkeepsie area affairs and activities. Some towns-people in turn participated gladly in a variety of cultural and other extracur-ricular activities on campus, but, in the general population, the sense of sepa-rate worlds remained.

DUTCHESS OUTREACH
TWENTY YEARS AFTER KEELEY

Another welcoming large man besides Lateef at the Family Partnership Cen-ter in the early twenty-first century was Brian Riddell, who directed the ongo-ing multiple activities of Dutchess Outreach, including the food pantry, deliv-ery of meals to the more recent constituency of homebound AIDS patients, and emergency assistance. Over time, religious assistance for the agency had diminished and, by 2005, the largest contributions to its $600,000 budget came from the federal Ryan White Title 1 program (federal assistance to Dutchess County for HIV/AIDS programs), as well as from United Way and some $90,000 from small contributions from about 3,500 supporters.

What remained constant was Mary Keeley's insistence that every indi-vidual be treated with dignity and respect. The program continued to attract volunteers ranging from college students to prominent citizens. Given the frequency of two wage-earner families in the early twenty-first century, the proportion of homemakers declined, as it did in so many other forms of vol-unteering. Among those served by the program, the disabled formed the largest proportion coming (no more than once a month) for a three-day sup-ply of groceries; their employment rate rose from 15 percent to 30 percent. The AIDS population—a new phenomenon since Outreach began—fluctu-ated, and the most recent immigrants, Mexicans, increased their share of those assisted from only 3 percent to 6 percent. The biggest shift was the increase in the number of welfare-to-work people whose earnings left them no safety margin. If they found themselves temporarily unable to afford their medication, rent, or utilities, they could turn to Outreach's emergency assis-tance program, available "for clients facing a one time shortfall due to an unexpected emergency."[12]

In 2005, Riddell saw a growing need for help in paying for medicine; Outreach's expenses for that purpose jumped from $3,000 to $25,000–30,000 annually. He also saw no letup in the tendency of both federal and state social services programs to resort to increasingly restrictive regulations, including the lowering of income caps and allowing administrators longer times to process applications. While the benefits from Medicaid had not changed, eli-gibility rules had. Failure to comply with requirements, like not showing up for an employment interview, resulted in "negative sanctions" that removed eligibility for forms of assistance. In New York State, the governor's budget for

2004, with the approval of Dutchess County's Commissioner of Social Services, permitted sanctioning the entire family, including children, for non-compliant behavior by an individual member.

## OTHER SERVICES, PUBLIC AND PRIVATE,
## FOR THE POOR AND THE ELDERLY

Located in the city of Poughkeepsie, the county Department of Social Services had a varied record over time in the way it treated the poor and working poor seeking assistance. The department's program for disabled persons cut across class lines with effective innovations; the department's funding in the early twenty-first century was reduced less than the funding for poverty assistance. Dealing with hunger in 1987, Social Services proved better than many other county departments in making people eligible for help, according to Professor Marque Miringoff. But it stood third from the bottom in actual provision of food stamps to those eligible. Less than 30 percent received stamps. Private charities doing both casework and advocacy tried, most often unsuccessfully, to get Social Services decisions overturned.

The Family Counseling Service of Dutchess County adopted the then new concept of a Family Advocacy Program in 1971. Lou Glasse, its first advocate, worked with families who needed helpful interference with hospitals, schools, police, and other services and authorities. She helped to initiate, then organize and train, volunteers for the Meals on Wheels program and worked with parents, audiology experts, and schools and school principals to develop a plan for educating the deaf and hard of hearing. In these and other projects, she became increasingly aware of the special problems of the elderly. After a series of *Poughkeepsie Journal* articles by Mimi McAndrew detailing those problems in October 1972 with editorial recommendation of a full-scale program to deal with them, County Executive William Bartles moved to fund an Office for the Aging in his budget. Soon after becoming the first director, Lou Glasse succeeded, after a tough round of questioning from the supervisors, in winning a commitment of $10,000 from the county in order to obtain $90,000 from the federal government to bring senior citizens to meal centers once a day for better food and socializing. In meeting this and a variety of other local needs, federal funding had become increasingly important.

Glasse served as director of the county agency on aging from 1973 to 1976 when Governor Carey appointed her as director of the New York State Office for the Aging. Her seven years' leadership there made her a widely sought consultant on women's health, aging and long-term care, and income security. She helped found the Older Women's League (OWL), serving as its president from 1985 to 1995. In 2006, the National Committee to Preserve Social Security and Medicare gave Glasse its Life Time Achievement Award.

Glasse's career as a social worker exemplified the expansion of services to help the less fortunate in the late twentieth century. Beginning in a private nonprofit agency, she moved from initiating advocacy of families needing assistance to becoming a public official seeking to attract federal funds to help the aged and to improve public policy affecting them. But she remained within the service sector of the economy. At the other end of the economic spectrum, a corporation like IBM shifted its primary focus from manufacturing computers to providing services to its clients. In the mid-Hudson valley, as in the nation, the services sector—both profit and nonprofit—now predominated, spanning the full range in scale from relatively small agencies like Dutchess County's Office of the Aging to the reduced giant IBM and to large hospital complexes. A similar span of occupations, from highly skilled and well-paid employees to the working poor, existed in private and public institutions of higher learning and in the largest employer of all, local governments responsible for public elementary and secondary education.

# EIGHTEEN

# Main Street Struggles to Return Amid Suburban Sprawl

IN THE AFTERMATH of massive urban renewal projects and civil unrest throughout urban America, and amid a changing social and economic landscape of suburban housing and shopping centers, cities attempted to reassert themselves as central places in the American landscape. By the mid-1980s, Poughkeepsie's Main Street no longer attracted crowds of shoppers to its pedestrian "mall" while much of the property along lower Main Street remained as vacant lots. Meanwhile the waterfront was cut off from the city by the North–South arterial and languished as underutilized parkland. The city administration appointed a variety of committees, commissions, and citizen advisory boards to study the situation. They recommended that the city hire consultants to assist them and, over the course of two decades, they produced a series of planning documents. Many of the committees and the subsequent reports were concerned with economic growth, while others focused on the physical fabric of the urban realm, including parks, open space, and public amenities.

## PERCEPTIONS OF MAIN STREET AND MAIN MALL

Even by the mid-1970s, it had become apparent that the construction of a pedestrian mall on Main Street, opened in 1973, had not maintained the previous economic or social vitality of downtown Poughkeepsie. Critics complained that parking was lacking and out of sight, the design had created too much vacant space, street furniture such as benches seemed too sparse, signage was limited and confusing, and store facades were unkempt. Although similar small upstate cities such as Corning and Ithaca had created interesting and commercially viable pedestrian main street malls with active public and private sector involvement, Poughkeepsie seemed to have only made a halfhearted attempt. Local citizens and visitors alike became disillusioned, fostering a widespread perception of the city as a depressed urban core. An opinion piece in the *Poughkeepsie Journal* in 1975 described one visitor's view:

> What's your favorite nightmare? . . . Well, for one unwitting businessman it is arriving in Poughkeepsie by train several hours after the sidewalks had been taken in. . . .
>
> Think about it folks. You're an absolute stranger with money in your pocket, used to the modern amenities of life, and expecting a semblance of civilization in the garden spot of the Mid-Hudson Valley. And, all of a sudden, you are standing in the haunted house that passes for a railroad station near the foot of Main Street as the witching hour approaches. . . .
>
> The [taxi] driver is friendly enough, although something less than enthusiastic. You tell him you want to go to the best hotel in the city. He chuckles in amusement as he tells you there isn't a hotel in the whole place. . . . You look out of the window as you are chauffeured up Main Street. Bleak, you tell yourself, almost like a bombed-out city. Where are all the people in this Hudson River metropolis?
>
> "That's the Main Mall," the driver points out as he swings the car right on Market Street. You look up the broad expanse and see nothing but lights. If this is the Main Mall, you ask yourself, what are the side streets like? . . . And so, there you are. A stranger in a city of ghostly buildings. A city without a hotel, and where a visitor who is willing to pay his way has to be careful about his demeanor in a late night watering spot. . . .
>
> In the light of day, the city doesn't look half so bad as it did the chilling night before. Nevertheless, you are glad when the train arrives and you can leave the place behind.[1]

The lack of a downtown hotel that so frustrated the visitor from New York City also concerned local businessmen. Ever since 1974, local developers including John Gartland, Jr. had struggled to line up the financing needed for a nine-story building with more than two hundred rooms. Planned for completion in 1979, it would be part of an ambitious "multi-use complex with a 3,000 seat convention center, 1,000 seat skating rink, 280,000 square feet of office space, and a two-story shopping mall with 80,000 square feet of retail space"[2] The hotel also would be across the street from the new Barney office building where IBM would be the major lessee.

In 1979, with cost estimates rising and a series of snags having stalled the hotel project, city officials met with Sheraton Inn developers to try to overcome the problems. By 1983, the preferred franchise shifted from Sheraton to Hilton and two years later shifted again to Wyndham. In its first year of operation, 1987–1988, an occupancy rate of only 30 percent fell well below Wyndham's projections and resulted in the hotel cutting its workforce from 170 to 135. In

1988, the *Poughkeepsie Journal* announced the latest change in franchise with the headline, "Goodbye, Wyndham, hello Radisson." By the end of the century, the hotel, still struggling to become profitable in a depressed downtown, would be sold to Joseph Bonura, Sr., who owned a restaurant and catering facility in Newburgh. No longer a national franchise, the hotel was renamed the Grand Hotel.

Throughout the 1970s and 1980s, vacant storefronts offered a depressing aspect to the downtown shopping district. Wallace's, one of the three largest clothing stores on Main Mall, shut its doors only one month after the visitor's opinion piece appeared in the newspaper and only one year after the opening of the mall. Poughkeepsians were awakened on the morning of April 29, 1975, by two headlines on the front page of the *Poughkeepsie Journal*: "Last American Troops Leaving, Copters Land in Saigon as Panic Grips Capital" announced the chaotic end of the Vietnam War, while "Wallace's to Close City Store" signified the demise of retail shopping along Main Street. Nationally and locally, Americans had reasons to be depressed.

Wallace's had opened in 1906 and its facade renovation during its expansion in 1941 was promoted as Poughkeepsie's "first modern-looking

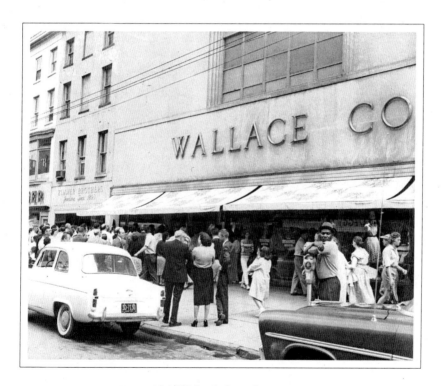

FIGURE 18.1. Wallace's department store, 1960

department store."[3] Various reasons were offered as to why the store closed; William Cahill, executive director of the Poughkeepsie Urban Renewal Agency, blamed it on a lack of sufficient parking. But Leonard G. Zimmer, president of Zimmer Brothers jewelry store that had been located on Main Street since 1893, thought it a matter of poor local management for a chain. Zimmer was upbeat about the potential for the mall and commented, "Our volume has increased substantially."[4] Nonetheless, Zimmer Brothers would soon move out of their downtown store to a new location in Arlington in the town of Poughkeepsie.

The year 1975 also saw the beginning of the end for Luckey, Platt, the largest department store in the mid-Hudson area. In that year, the firm went into Chapter 11 bankruptcy proceedings. It continued to operate during the latter half of the 1970s, while at the same time the owners opened a few satellite stores in the suburban shopping centers. The downtown Poughkeepsie store only used 10,000 of the building's 150,000 square feet; only the first floor remained open with limited merchandise staffed by just fifteen employees. In 1977, the county legislature rented out empty space on its upper floors for the Department of Social Services (DSS) "as a way of try-

FIGURE 18.2. Luckey, Platt & Co., "Men's Night," c. 1950

ing to aid the ailing department store, and thus help downtown Poughkeepsie."[5] The lease, however, had been negotiated by then county supervisor Edward C. Schueler, who had solicited a bribe from the building's
owner; Schueler later pleaded guilty to the charges and resigned. After their
move, DSS employees complained that the building's owner was irresponsi-
ble and that working conditions at the building had "approached intolerable."[6] On July 2, 1981, the company closed and locked its doors for good. As
the *Poughkeepsie Journal* observed the next day, "With no particular notice,
fanfare or funeral, Luckey, Platt and Co. quietly closed its Main Mall retail
store Thursday after 112 years of doing business to downtown Poughkeepsie. . . . The front doors to the once grandiose department store were locked
during the height of the shopping hour Thursday, with only a small, hand-
printed sign on the door announcing 'store closed.' Inside, there were lights
but no action. . . . One rack of clothes was still sitting in the store, toward
the rear, but most merchandise seemed to be gone."[7] Luckey, Platt had left
downtown Poughkeepsie. It had been the dominant retail establishment in
the mid-Hudson region for over a century and had occupied the largest
space along Poughkeepsie's Main Street. The empty building on the corner
of Main and Academy streets created an emptiness in the city's economic
and cultural claim to centrality.

FIGURE 18.3. Luckey, Platt & Co., "Christmas Lights," c. 1960

## MAIN MALL COMMISSION

Joseph Forman, chairman of the high-end women's clothing store Up-to-Date, and other downtown merchants attempted to reverse the slide. In 1983, Mayor Aposporos and the Common Council teamed up with the Downtown Council merchants to appoint a committee to focus on economic revitalization of the central business district. The original Main Mall Commission consisted of three businessmen who owned buildings or had stores on Main Street and two local citizens active in urban planning and development.[8] The commission was particularly concerned about the social and economic functions of the central business district. It appointed a subcommittee to promote the local businesses and immediately identified its main task as improving the "image" of Main Street and the "perceptions" of both shoppers and the employees of the shops. "There is a need," the marketing committee noted, "to get the employees and the storeowners to change their perceptions of the mall. If the employees project negative feelings about where they work the customers will have a difficult time thinking positively about it."[9]

The committee was equally frustrated with the image of the mall presented by the local press. "The press has to realize," they stressed, "that the advertisers on the mall are not only willing to support the press but are looking for their cooperation in balancing the public's perception of the mall and its stores." The mood on the mall, they suggested, was down. They concluded, "Present retailers are showing signs of wear and tear. They too need excitement, a sense that something positive is taking place and that business growth is once again possible." The perception of the downtown as an attractive and vibrant shopping district had been damaged, and, as in numerous small towns and cities across America, Main Street merchants and city administrations joined together to upgrade its image.[10]

In 1987, the Common Council, in partnership with the Main Mall Commission, hired the Washington, DC, planning firm of Hyett-Palma, Inc. to submit "A Business Enhancement Plan for Downtown Poughkeepsie, New York." Hyett-Palma prepared a "strategic plan" in association with Retail Consultant Services and the Real Estate Services Group that attempted to define a marketing plan for the commercial district. It was upbeat: "[D]owntown Poughkeepsie," they suggested, had "tremendous potential for enhanced economic development." But, they added, it would take cooperation among all the stakeholders as well as a good deal of effort. "Through a continuous public and private effort on the part of the citizens, the City of Poughkeepsie, merchants and property owners within the downtown area, the downtown can become the commercial district the people of Poughkeepsie desire and deserve."[11]

By the late 1980s, however, businesses on Main Mall struggled to survive. Vacant storefronts became increasingly apparent within the mix of retail shops and business offices. In a survey of ninety storefronts on Main Mall in 1986,

57 percent were retail shops, including thirteen food, nine clothing, five stationery, four jewelry, four shoe, and three photography; 32 percent provided service, such as banks, lawyers, dentists, and hair stylists; and 11 percent stood vacant. The latter accounted for 13 percent of the available 328,723 square footage fronting on Main Street, and included the former Luckey, Platt building, the largest space, and the buildings that had housed Woolworth's and Ehmer's butcher shop. An expanded survey two years later of 160 buildings along Main Street found eighteen vacant.

In 1991, M. Shwartz & Co., the last of the large department stores on Main Mall, closed. Retail shopping in downtown had reached its lowest point. In a storefront survey in 1997—a decade after the first survey—vacancies had increased to sixty-three on the first floors of the 160 buildings surveyed; ten of these had been documented in the previous surveys, indicating that approximately five vacancies occurred per year during the early 1990s. Of the more than forty retail shops that had existed at the time of the 1988 survey, only fourteen remained in 1997, with a total of only twenty-two on and off the Main Mall.

Downtown Poughkeepsie no longer served as a central place for retail shopping by the end of the twentieth century. The 1997 survey described Main Street as a declining urban place:

> In general, retail shops are the primary commercial use on the mall, although department stores have not stayed. Instead, small shops of 1000 square feet or less have stayed and new ones opened at the mall. Service-oriented businesses such as printing/copying businesses, hair salons, and travel services are the next largest category, followed by financial services and restaurants. Overall, the vacancies occur in large buildings, and increase from Garden Street east. The last two blocks in this area, the 400 and 500 blocks, are perhaps the most blighted. This area is characterized by vacant, boarded up buildings (some are fire damaged), large vacant lots, few commercial uses, and conversion of commercial storefronts to residential uses on the first floor. A few neighborhood commercial uses, such as delicatessens, convenience stores, and hair salons remain. The area is not visually connected to the Main Mall in part because it does not share the streetscape elements such as landscaping, brick sidewalks, and period lighting.[12]

The image of Poughkeepsie's downtown in the mid-1990s was not conducive to shopping or social gatherings. Main Mall seemed an empty and anonymous public space, with its many vacant storefronts, nonworking fountains, broken benches, poor lighting, and unkempt flowerbeds—not a vibrant and active social space.

The perception of Main Mall as unsafe became pervasive, especially in the city's white middle-class suburbs. Shoppers fled Main Mall for South Hills Mall located since 1976 south along Route 9 in the town of Poughkeepsie as well as the older strip malls such as the Poughkeepsie, Hudson, and Nine Mall plazas that had been constructed in the late 1950s. The opening of the Pough-keepsie Galleria in 1986, an enclosed mall adjacent to South Hills, added to the decline of major shopping in downtown Poughkeepsie.

A marketing survey for the proposed Galleria noted that of the 3.4 million square feet of retail space in Dutchess County in 1985, 7 percent was vacant; the report particularly mentioned downtown Poughkeepsie: "Most of the vacant space documented was in Main Mall and in Dutchess Mall [in Fishkill]. A common factor contributing to the high vacancies is each location's distance from affluent residential areas." Many Dutchess County residents traveled to White Plains in Westchester County or to New York City for fashionable clothing and other "high-end" goods. South Hills Mall provided the only competition favoring in-county shopping, they suggested. Their survey revealed the social characteristics of the typical suburban shopper. "Residents who visit South Hills Mall more frequently than average include females, those from households with children under age 18, those younger than age 45, and those from households with a male head employed in an upper white collar occupation." The survey attributed the lack of frequent shopping on Main Mall to limited parking and a lack of significant destination retailers (i.e., middle and high-end national stores). The Mall "may also suffer from perceptions of potential crime."

By the late 1980s, the perception that downtown Poughkeepsie was the place to shop was no longer as central as it had been prior to urban renewal. Shopping malls were in the suburbs and had lots of parking for the auto-centered consumer; even the renaming of the pedestrian Main Street as a "mall" seemed questionable. Nevertheless, Hyett-Palma argued to maintain the full name of Main Mall. According to the report, "A change of name at this point in time does not appear to be of value to the renewed economic development effort. In fact, due to the broad recognition the name MAIN MALL has within the community, a change of name may result in a loss of identity or signal that the area is seeking "fluff" approaches to enhancement."[13]

Instead, Hyett-Palma suggested a partial reopening of Main Street. In 1991, the city opened up the 300 block east of Hamilton to traffic. The Poughkeepsie Partnership, a joint public–private nonprofit organization between the Chamber of Commerce, the Common Council, and the mayor formed three years earlier, promoted the project. Other outside interests also argued for reopening the east end of the mall. Karl Ehmer, who had moved his meat store from his storefront along Main Street in the 300 block after construction of the mall, promised a substantial donation to assist in the costs of reopening the block. His promises to make a donation and to reopen his shop never materialized.

The Poughkeepsie Partnership viewed the reopening of the 300 block as a test to consider reopening Main Street altogether. As a test, it seemed partially successful. Several of the retail stores announced a slight increase in sales, the Dutchess County Health Department moved to an abandoned building to be closer to their clients, and a few new businesses opened up. Discussions over the next few years to fully open the mall to traffic bogged down, however, as differences among retailers and service providers stalled further action.

Efforts to market Main Mall as a retail shopping district eventually proved unsuccessful, and many of the businesses abandoned Main Street for nearby shopping centers or else went out of business altogether. Just a few years after the Hyett-Palma study in 1987, M. Shwartz and the upscale furniture store Danish Design would close down, Royal Tuxedoland was burned out, and Warshaw and Friedman's shoe stores faced stiff competition from national chains. Up-to-Date, Arax Photography, Capitol Bakery, and De's Jewelers established themselves in new stores outside the downtown. Long-standing nearby employers were also closing; for example, Western Printing closed its factory located on Route 9 across from Marist College in 1989. Locally owned small businesses throughout America were under siege, and Main Street bore the brunt of this economic upheaval.

## WATERFRONT ADVISORY COMMISSION

Efforts to revitalize Main Street were paralleled at the city's waterfront. A riverfront park had been proposed since the 1920s. Various proposals through the 1940s led to the purchase of the site at the foot of Main Street in 1954. In 1968 and 1974, the city allocated federal community development funds to refurbish the grounds and later dedicated them as Waryas Park. Boat docks and a playground were constructed. Climbing structures became a mosaic play sculpture "created by everyone."[14] The city engaged the Child Environment Design Institute, led by designer/artist David Aaron, to construct the playground. Aaron enlisted the help of 1,300 children from the elementary schools and the community day care center to assemble the mosaics. They were then placed on four large concrete sculptures that symbolized the city's past, including a ship, train, and portraits of locally important figures. The close involvement of the children meant that the structures had immense sentimental value to residents from all social classes and neighborhoods. Twenty years later, Ernestine Boone, an African American community leader, recalled. "Even the ones [children] who didn't do well, they could come back and look at it, point to this one positive thing in their life."[15]

The playground sculptures constituted a deep sense of community feeling for two generations of Poughkeepsians. When, in June 1999, they were demolished overnight by the city administration for reasons of legal liability, residents were horrified. Many who had worked on the project as children had become mothers who, with their own children, used the playground and they were upset and angry. A diverse group of citizens gathered at the site the next

FIGURE 18.4. Aerial view of waterfront, 1980

day. Mayor Colette Lafuente worked with them to establish a planning committee to create new sculptures over the next three years. As she remarked at the dedication of a sculpture of a whale, designed and constructed by artist Judy Sigunick, and decorated with colored tiles made by local schoolchildren and elderly residents, in October 2002, "Part of the community was gone. . . . It had to be brought back."[16] Public attitudes toward Poughkeepsie's waterfront after private industries abandoned the area continued to demand its use and river access for the whole community.

The development of the waterfront consumed the community's concern about the fate of the city for the latter half of the twentieth century. For years after the clearance of its former industries and docks, the riverfront had seemed a wasteland, and mirrored the physical decline of Main Street. Most of the river towns, such as Newburgh, Hudson, and Kingston, also had deteriorated waterfronts, and their economic decline had spurred the state to act by establishing a Coastal Management Program. Under this program, local municipalities were to create their own Local Waterfront Revitalization Plans (LWRPs).

In 1986, three years after the Main Mall Commission had been established, Mayor Thomas Aposporos and the Common Council appointed a small committee of local citizens to develop a plan for the revitalization of the city waterfront. With the assistance of the local planning firm, Matthew D. Rudikoff Associates, the Waterfront Advisory Committee (WAC) worked "diligently since then," and drafted a Local Waterfront Revitalization Program (LWRP) to submit to New York's Department of State for approval.[17] A decade later, a final draft was in place, having been revised by later WACs and officially accepted by a new mayor and common council.

In appointing the first WAC, Mayor Aposporos, who worked in real estate financing, realized that in the era after urban renewal, urban economic development required a reimagining of the cityscape. In addition, for the waterfront to return to its functional relationship to Main Street, it needed to become more publicly accessible. The final draft of the LWRP reflected these insights in its "vision statement":

> The City of Poughkeepsie's relationship with the Hudson River is one of its most important historical, cultural, economic and aesthetic resources. However, the Poughkeepsie Waterfront is underutilized in recent decades in terms of usage, enjoyment and economic benefits. We are missing an opportunity to bring people to the City as visitors and residents.
>
> To accomplish this, our vision is to create a riverfront that is a "front porch" of the City which respects the unique assets of the waterfront, that maintains and enhances public accessibility, that attracts private investment, creates jobs, and provides residents, tourists and visitors alike with an attractive and safe setting.[18]

Both the Waterfront Advisory Committee and the Main Mall Commission were concerned with how the city was perceived by the local community. Neither Main Street nor the waterfront were considered safe and attractive; the urban downtown was no longer seen as central to the community for its social or economic activities.

Urban crime and drugs were exploding in all of the nation's cities and Poughkeepsie was no exception. In 1993 alone, eleven young men were killed on the city's streets, while two years later another nine were added to the list; their names would be painted on a "Wall of Remembrance" on a building in the 400 block of Main Street along with more than a dozen others who also lost their lives during the decade. Drugs and the drug trade sparked much of the violence in the mid-Hudson cities during the 1980s. Due to the location of the cities of Newburgh, Beacon, and Poughkeepsie and their easy access to New York City, drug rings in New York City extended their market into the region. In Poughkeepsie, a large drug bust on December 17, 1994, joined 350 New York State troopers with city police in a dramatic raid that involved blocking off streets and using helicopters. Many Poughkeepsians felt that they were in a war zone, and the perception of the city's quality of life had reached a nadir.

PERCEPTION AT CENTURY'S END: DÉJÀ VU?

Spatial distribution of socioeconomic and ethnic groups both within and outside the borders of the city translated into different perceptions of the urban and nonurban scenes, especially of quality of life issues such as housing, economy, and crime.

In a 1995 study examining how the city was perceived by a variety of residents and nonresidents, distinct areas were identified according to their past or present uses. Certain landmarks stood out: the post office, Mid-Hudson Bridge, Civic Center, hotel, and train station offered visual points of reference and orientation. Both East–West and North–South arterials, including Route 9, composed a framework for both residents and nonresidents, while the downtown core, including Main Mall, remained somewhat obscure. "Attempts to make the Main Mall a central feature of the city's landscape have not been successful," observed the study.[19] "Eliminating traffic from Main Mall limits the imageability of the site since many Poughkeepsie residents image the city primarily from their cars . . . the arterial created an image of a hollow central corridor in which the Mall is lost." The study concluded that the "hollow" image combined "with a shift in commercialization to peripheral areas" hindered the Mall's success. It pointed to Upper Main Street whose image evoked particularly dark emotions and reflected back onto Main Mall:

FIGURE 18.5. Upper Main Street, 2000

"Main Mall eventually became imaged as the western end of perceived danger areas on upper Main Street." The most dangerous areas of the city, as perceived by both residents and nonresidents alike, was the Main Street corridor between the east and west arterials from Garden, Catherine, and Academy streets on the west to White Street on the east; the intersection of White and Main streets, locus of numerous drug-related episodes of violence, was found to be the most dangerous locale, while Mansion Square was also described in similar terms. Although the study sample was quite small, nevertheless the image of the city of Poughkeepsie in the 1990s as an urban wilderness was clearly shared by many residents and nonresidents alike.

Almost a quarter-century after the visitor's opinion essay published in the *Poughkeepsie Journal* in 1975, a reporter for the *New York Times* walked along Main Mall and wrote of his impressions. It was a crisp October day in 1998, much like the early spring evening of the previous writer, as the journalist observed the many vacant storefronts and spoke to a random selection of pedestrians, shop owners, and a local scholar. The journalist noted the continuing legacy of urban renewal and the limited retail space remaining on Main Street, which, he noted, gave the city a "clouded image."[20]

Demographic and economic data offered a bleak picture: the 1990 population of 28,844 "has declined by almost a third from a 1950 high," he recited, and added, "Of those remaining, 3 out of every ten never graduated from high school." Furthermore, "in all Poughkeepsie, only 111 families earn more than $150,000 annually." Unemployment was "about 6 percent," and the 1990 census listed 11.6 percent of families in poverty and only 21.8 percent of adults age twenty-five and over held a college degree.

The journalist's commentary offered an historical synopsis of many of the events that left their imprint on the urban landscape, from the loss of manufacturing since the middle of the twentieth century, including the devastating blow of IBM's downsizing in the early 1990s, to the demolition of buildings during urban renewal, and the state's decision to release "thousands of patients from psychiatric hospitals like the Hudson River Psychiatric Center here." This affected Poughkeepsie's Main Mall, he added, as "scores wound up homeless in downtown, where they scared off many remaining shoppers. As a result of this cascade of policy debacles," he continued, "Poughkeepsie has a threadbare statistical profile that is best crystallized by one fact: this city midway between Manhattan and Albany does not have a single supermarket."[21]

Indeed, the last supermarket in the city, a Grand Union at 690 Main Street, had closed its doors on March 7, 1992, six years prior to the journalist's remark. The loss of the supermarket created great difficulty in gaining reasonable access to food for the poor and elderly who lived in the Upper Main Street neighborhood. "For 40 years," the *Poughkeepsie Journal* lamented, "Grand Union—the last large grocery store in the City of Poughkeepsie—has been a saving grace of sorts for nearby senior citizens and low-income families, many of whom do not have cars, but live within walking distance of the store."[22] The national corporation had deemed the 24,000-square-foot grocery store as no longer profitable. Other, larger modernized supermarkets had been built in the town of Poughkeepsie, such as a Stop and Shop a few miles away. However, the public perception of the Grand Union and its location had deteriorated over the previous decade. Mayor Colette Lafuente suggested that the location suffered from high crime, while the poor management of the store resulted in produce that was "virtually inedible."[23]

Consolidation of stores by large supermarket chains was also cited as a reason for closing the Grand Union. In 1962, there had been six major supermarkets in the city of Poughkeepsie, four of them located along Main Street. Thirty years later, there were none. The megastores relocated on highways in the town, along Route 44 east of the city and south of the city along Route 9, including the addition of big-box Wal-Mart and BJ's wholesale food markets. The problem for city residents was that the grocery stores that had relocated in the town forced city residents to travel far to purchase food at reasonable cost; meanwhile, the city lost sales tax revenues. "All of the supermarkets moved out at the same time," recounted Mayor Lafuente, "then it dawned on everybody that there was nothing left."[24] At the turn of the twenty-first century, Casa Latina opened as a supermarket primarily selling to the immigrant Hispanic community; it located directly across Main Street from the former Grand Union that had become a Rite-Aid pharmacy, but had a limited range of stock and higher prices than larger supermarkets.

Access to fresh produce for city residents was not completely absent during the 1990s, although prices in small grocery stores were higher than in large supermarket chains. Frank Clark had opened The Main Mall Grocer in 1978 as a "green" corner store, with coffee and salad bar for downtown workers and shoppers. Unfortunately, due to the closing of nearby IBM offices in the Barney building in 1994 and the gradual decline of shopping along Main Mall, the store's customer base shrank and by the twenty-first century Clark worked a part-time job just to keep the store open. The store, according to Clark, was a community asset: "the *Cheers* without alcohol."[25] But, for family food purchases, city residents were forced to travel to the major grocery stores in the town. For many of the poor without access to a car, transportation was an extra cost, either for taxi service or on public buses that prohibited shopping carts and only permitted "4 bags of groceries per person."[26] Supermarkets as well as most retail shops had left the city for the suburbs.

A photograph of empty storefronts along a block of Main Mall in 1998 accompanied the *New York Times* description of a city living through the throes of deindustrialization and population decline. According to the *Times* journalist,

Poughkeepsie today is practically a tale of three cities—a ragged, partly industrial north side, a still genteel south side and a patchwork downtown

that is graced with isolated jewels like the Roosevelt-era post office and the
Bardavon Theater.

A visitor to a three-block pedestrian mall on Main Street can find an
anachronistic gem like Mary H. Abdoo's bridal shop, where for 47 years customers from all over the Northeast have tried on wedding dresses amid rose
plush drapery and wrought-iron seats. But the Main Street pedestrian mall,
where traffic was blocked off in the misguided notion that it would make
shopping more convenient, is now marked by empty storefronts.[27]

Change, nonetheless, was in the air. The railroad station had been renovated and was no longer a "haunted house" and a major hotel was in operation
in the center of downtown. Issues of crime and housing were being addressed.
Although the journalist's view from Main Mall in 1998 was of a city with a
"clouded image," a number of efforts by citizens, politicians, and investors
began to change the face of the city.

As abandoned buildings became affordable owner-occupied and rental
housing, crime decreased, and renewal activities along the waterfront began to
focus public attention on a potential urban renaissance, Police Chief Ronald
J. Knapp opined: "In 1996, people were screaming about homicides and
shootings," he said. "Now they're screaming about parking violations and college parties. Doesn't that say something?"[28] Three years later, at the beginning
of a new century, Main Street reopened to traffic. Downtown slowly returned
as a center of activity. But was it too late to change the perception of the city?

## SUBURBAN SPRAWL

As Poughkeepsie and all other cities in the Hudson valley tried to cope with
urban decline, an expanding population sought housing outside their boundaries, even beyond their older suburbs, such as the IBM-centered subdivisions
in the town of Poughkeepsie. Hundreds of new subdivisions began to cover
the former farmlands of Orange and Dutchess counties, while houses also rose
on three, five acre, and larger private lots sprawling across the landscape of the
mid-Hudson region. Most of these new residents continued their economic
and social ties to New York City or to the inner ring of suburbs from which
they came. "The boundaries of what people think of as the New York metropolitan area are being stretched," according to a front-page article in the *New
York Times* in April 1986.[29] Being more than 50 miles from Manhattan, those
who continued to work in the city endured two hours' commuting time on
roads "snarled with traffic . . . that they have little time to get involved with
civic affairs."

Longtime residents noticed the increased traffic on their narrow two-lane
roads, but other public infrastructure became strained as well. Volunteer fire
departments with little equipment, county sheriff's departments, water supplies,

waste management, and school systems were soon overburdened. Local officials in rural towns who had previously rejected "outside interference" began to consider assistance from county and regional planning agencies.

Meanwhile, many large corporations developed corporate headquarters in the outer fringe, such as IBM in northern Westchester County. A multinodal region of centers of business, shopping, and population emerged. The expanding population held little interest in the plight of the older cities in their midst, and there seemed to be few reasons to visit their downtowns. It would take two decades before the efforts of city administrations, investors, and local volunteers succeeded in changing their image.

NINETEEN

# Civic Identity and
# Social Change in the 1990s

RACIAL DISTRUST BECAME an important factor in the perception of urban downtowns throughout America during the 1970s and 1980s. In the aftermath of attempts at integration of businesses along many of America's main streets, civil rights marches, the murder of Martin Luther King, Jr., and television and newspaper headlines of urban riots in many major cities, race relations infused the everyday lives of ordinary citizens.

## A LANDSCAPE OF RACIAL UNREST

In Poughkeepsie and Dutchess County, multiracial community groups formed to attempt to deal with the interface between race, poverty, drugs, and street violence, such as the Enhancing Racial Harmony Project and its sub-group on criminal justice. At the same time, workshops on racial understanding for high school students from different towns were sponsored by the Eleanor Roosevelt Center at Val-Kill (ERVK).

Arts programs that engaged issues of racism and violence contributed to communitywide dialogue. Rodney Douglas, a native of Grenada who had moved to London to study theater and then to the United States in the early 1960s, founded the New Day Repertory Company in Poughkeepsie in 1963 with his wife Olive. They chose plays that had social and political content. "We have a mission," Rodney remarked after four decades, "We always choose plays that have social content. . . . It is through theater that I am fighting hatred."[1] New Day Repertory's repertoire was international; it was one of the first theater companies in America to perform the plays of the South African playwright Athol Fugard during the era of apartheid.

At the local level, Carole Wolf organized arts programs that focused on issues of race and social justice. Wolf established Mill Street Loft in 1981 as a not-for-profit, multiarts educational center based in the city of Poughkeep-sie. Mill Street Loft focused on building self-confidence and self-esteem through multiarts educational programs, job skills training, entrepreneurial activities, life skills, community revitalization, and economic development. Using the success of Project ABLE, an arts and creativity-based youth employment training program for low-income urban youth as a model, Mill Street Loft created PASWORD, an empowerment program for at-risk ado-lescent girls. Most of these urban-based programs focused on the city's poor and minority youth, although an annual summer arts camp drew young peo-ple from throughout the county.

These arts and community-based efforts organized within a complex regional context. The concentration of poor minority populations in the region's cities created a spatial framework that reinforced racial and ethnic stereotypes. Perceptions of many school districts and residential neighbor-hoods included racial, ethnic, and socioeconomic descriptors, while real estate agents, as gatekeepers, acted to maintain neighborhood differences. Although the number of incidents of racial discrimination and conflict in the region declined during the latter half of the twentieth century, the issue of racial intolerance and misunderstanding continued to slow social intercourse and the construction of a truly inclusive community.

## TAWANA BRAWLEY IN THE NATIONAL SPOTLIGHT

One such incident became a firestorm that reached beyond the region to become a three-year national news story. In 1987, Tawana Brawley, a young black woman, claimed that she had been abducted and raped by three white men. The alleged assault occurred in Wappingers Falls where she lived, with the ensuing court case tried at the county courthouse in downtown Pough-keepsie. Reporters from local and national newspapers and all major metro-politan television stations followed the high-profile case.

The length of time the story held high visibility in the news and the emo-tional power of the case offered the nation several conflicting perceptions of Poughkeepsie and the mid-Hudson valley; views of urban poverty, drugs, and racial discrimination mixed with small-town affairs and a bucolic countryside. Those views created a social landscape found throughout America in the 1980s. In metropolitan New York, the social and political atmosphere had reached a breaking point as a result of two deaths of young black men caused by white police. The Howard Beach case in the New York City area was at the top of the news in late 1987, while just across the Hudson River a similar inci-dent had recently occurred. In both cases, blacks and civil rights activists were upset at the resulting resolution of the cases, in particular the role of the police and justice system.

The situation in Dutchess County seemed similar: Sheriff Fred Scoralick did not have one full-time black on his staff of four hundred, while many incidents of overt racism were found in his supervision of the county jail. Most municipalities in Dutchess County depended on the sheriff's office for security. Even the few local police forces there had few, if any, blacks on the forces. Reporters from the *New York Times* described the local social environment of black–white relations in the context of the Brawley case:

> Poughkeepsie, best known as the home of Vassar College, is the hub and county seat. Most of the county's blacks live there. They are disproportionately poor and jobless, and few occupy positions of influence in the county; fewer still have positions of power. Of the county government's forty-three top administrators in 1987, only two were black, and there was only one black in the thirty-five member county legislature. Blacks were vastly underrepresented in every police agency, corporate management, school faculty, and civil hierarchy in the county; not a single black held a job in the county's fire, recreation, or parks departments. The district attorney had only two blacks on his staff of nineteen prosecutors, and there was only one black among ten full-time lawyers in the public defender's office, which counseled poor defendants in criminal cases. None of the county judges were black, and there was only one black justice of the peace in the local townships.[2]

A description of Wappingers Falls where the alleged rape took place also created a context that helped the national news audience understand the racial complexities of the case. It was described as "a quiet place" where the residents "work hard and raise families, live their lives, and die without much notice from the outside world . . . the village green, with its gazebo and benches, is free of litter." To the big city reporters in 1987, the village seemed like a throwback to the 1950s: "It is—almost absurdly—a vision out of Norman Rockwell or Thornton Wilder, a town where teenagers sip sodas in a drugstore with a zinc-topped fountain, where sleds course down hillsides in snowy winters and shouts rise from a swimming hole in hot leafy summers." It was small-town America, far removed from the problems of urban America. "On any afternoon in this pretty village in upstate New York," they mused, "the terrible problems of America—its racism and brutal crime, its betrayals of trust—seem little more than faraway echoes, like the drums on a distant battlefield."[3]

The cities of the mid-Hudson, however, were described in much darker tones. Newburgh was painted as a "tangle of streets ruled by crack peddlers, prostitutes and children with guns . . . some twenty-eight thousand people lived here, and a large percentage of them were hostages of poverty, living among criminals and addicts . . . [in] shattered tenements." The offices of the police department occupied, the *Times* reporters said, "a two-story brick fortress, that stood in the squalor like a relic of civilization in the jungle."[4] Even a decade later, Robert F. Kennedy, Jr., researching a pollution case that would "inaugurate" his career in environmental law, would describe mid-1980s Newburgh in depressing terms: "The historic city of Newburgh regularly leads the nation in virtually every criterion used to measure urban decay and is famed for producing local politicians with elastic ethics and a knack for plundering the public trust. The main thoroughfare, Broadway, is as squalid and dangerous as the worst streets in the South Bronx. In the words of the current police chief, Newburgh is a 'mean, sick, nasty, fetid little city.'"⁵ The city's waterfront was described as giving "new meaning to the word 'depressed.'" Junkyards and incinerators dominated the "once proud Hudson River vistas," while the remaining shoreline was described as "a defoliated and depopulated wasteland where truckers come for illicit sex and drug dealers sell their wares."

Newburgh's social relations mirrored the city's physical decay. In 1984, racial tensions were strained when the city attempted to sell public parkland and the city's boat ramp—the only public access to the Hudson River in Orange County—to "certain acquaintances of the mayor." During a visit to Newburgh to investigate the issue, Kennedy asked whether the public would still be able to use the boat ramp. The private developers replied, he reported, "with striking candor: 'We are not going to have spades drinking and screwing and swimming around our *new* boat ramp, if that's what you mean by the public!'" It was the moment, Kennedy recalled, when he realized that the "battle for the environment was the ultimate civil and human rights contest."⁶

The descriptions of Poughkeepsie by journalists at the time were less harsh and graphic, probably due to the fact that the city's downtown became perceived as safe, if a bit shabby. Many from the news media stayed at the Wyndham hotel during the Tawana Brawley trial and had coffee at Alex's restaurant, since both were just across Main or Market streets from the courthouse.

Television news coverage of rallies in both Newburgh and Poughkeepsie also presented differences between the two cities; a "dignified little gathering" of about 150 at the civic center in Poughkeepsie compared to the rage expressed by a large crowd in Newburgh. This rally, with fiery speeches that demanded a revolution by Louis Farrakhan, Al Sharpton, and C. Vernon Mason appeared on newscasts across the nation that evening. The Poughkeepsie event was not mentioned. Speeches by Clarence McGill, chairman of the Dutchess County Committee Against Racism, a recently formed interracial group, and Folami Gray, executive director of the Dutchess County Youth Bureau, were moderate in tone and asked for justice. Gray reminded the small crowd that racism existed in the county; she was, they all knew, the first black ever to be appointed to head a county department. Her appointment, by county executive Lucille Pattison, herself the first woman to be elected a county supervisor in New York State, had been well received by both white and black residents of the county. Previous efforts to address racial discrimination by the county legislature had been less than supportive. In 1984, Sherwood Thompson, a member of the county legislature from the city of Poughkeepsie and the only black ever to have been elected to that body, managed to get a bill passed establishing a human rights commission. However, it took over three years for the legislature to allot money for a director and a secretary and, even then, its powers remained only advisory. Meanwhile, two decades after the Brawley case, only two percent of the county's 540 sworn-in police officers were minorities. According to data compiled by the state Division of Criminal Justice Services in 2006, there were no blacks among the county sheriff's 146 officers, nor any black police officers in the towns of East Fishkill, Hyde Park, Rhinebeck, or Wappingers Falls. Of the four minorities on the town of Poughkeepsie force of 87, one was black, while three blacks were on the 101-member city police force.

The Tawana Brawley case brought unwanted national interest to the social and economic problems of Poughkeepsie and the Hudson valley region. The final judgment that the allegations were false and a hoax was an even greater bitter pill to swallow for many, especially white ethnic residents who had been unfairly placed, they felt, on the defensive for months. It would take over a decade for the emotional wounds and social scars to heal. Unfortunately, the city remained a locus of racial concern; although the incident allegedly occurred miles from downtown Poughkeepsie, a perceptual cloud hung over the city with respect to black–white relations that was reinforced by the growth of an urban Hispanic population.

## DEMOGRAPHICS

In the latter decades of the twentieth century, the population of the mid-Hudson region grew, and, like the century before, changed in composition and settlement pattern. The counties and towns grew whereas the urban centers declined. Between 1980 and 1990, the population of Dutchess County increased by about 6 percent to 259,462, while the city of Poughkeepsie decreased by about 3 percent to 28,844. Indeed, from 1960 to 1990, all four mid-Hudson cities had declined: Poughkeepsie's 1990 population had declined by −24.7 percent; Beacon's 1990 population of 13,243 had declined by −4.9 percent; Kingston's 1990 population of 23,095 had been decimated by IBM's closure by −21.1 percent; while Newburgh's 1990 population of 26,454 had also decreased by −14.0 percent. The growth outside the cities was fairly homogeneous socioeconomically. Most minority racial and ethnic groups and lower income households remained in core urban areas, whereas middle-class whites moved out into the towns and moved into the area from other parts of the metropolitan New York region or elsewhere.

Although sharing the same name of Poughkeepsie, city and town were significantly different. Certain services were shared, such as some water and sewer and cable television as well as the library, while each had separate elected and appointed governments, fire and police departments, and school districts. IBM and the major shopping plazas were in the town, while in the city were offices providing automobile licenses and welfare services, as well as the cultural venues of the Civic Center, Bardavon, and The Chance nightclub. Federal, state, and county government offices were all located in the city, adding to the city's budgetary burden as they and other not-for-profit agencies and religious organizations constituted over 60 percent of city properties off the tax rolls.

Populations were also distinct. In 1990, the population of the town was 40,143, over ten thousand greater than the city's 28,844. Households were more likely to be composed of singles and elderly in the city who lived in closer proximity to each other. The city had a density of 5,605 persons per square mile compared to the town's 1,396. Socioeconomic differences were equally striking: according to the 1990 census, family incomes in the city averaged $34,211 while town families averaged $53,543. In the city, 15 percent lived below the poverty line in 1990, while only 3.5 percent of town dwellers did. Life was much more difficult for city children as the census indicated that 24 percent lived in poverty compared to 4.4 percent of town children. Blacks constituted 32 percent of the city population and whites 65 percent, whereas blacks only constituted 5.6 percent of the town population that had a majority of 90 percent whites. This racial and socioeconomic disparity between the city and the town increased in a comparison between enrollments in city schools and the Arlington and Spackenkill school districts: in 1993, blacks constituted 61 percent of the students in the Poughkeepsie school district, but less than 10 percent in Arlington. Twenty-three percent of the city's black students came from families living below the poverty line. The city provided no school transportation for middle and high school students; they either walked or paid to ride city buses.

At the end of the twentieth century, the differences between city and town and county entailed differences of perception about the city; meanwhile, the spatial distribution of the city's population itself was quite varied. An east–west corridor along Main Street and the East–West arterials roughly divided the city into a largely white population on the south side and more ethnically mixed neighborhoods on the north side. The majority of the city's black population lived on the north side. Until the establishment of a program to integrate the elementary schools in 1970, those schools on the north side such as Warring and Morse enrolled over two-thirds minority students, while Krieger School on the south side in the Eighth Ward had less than 3 percent. Two decades later, as a result of busing and the creation of magnet schools, the city's elementary schools were more integrated, although the changing demographics citywide meant that the middle and high school enrolled a majority of minority students.

Blacks in Poughkeepsie were also disproportionately poorer than whites, with 22 percent of the black population in 1990 living below the poverty line compared to 10 percent of whites. The majority of the city's rental units and rooming houses were similarly located on the north side and along the east–west corridor along Main Street between the arterials. This housing became available for poor migrants to the city, both rural white poor seeking welfare and health services from the county's department of social services located on Market Street and foreign migrants, such as Latinos, seeking jobs in the area.

After World War II, a substantial Afro-Caribbean population immigrated from the islands, some by way of Great Britain. Some became professionals, nurses, white-collar workers, or IBM employees. Others had been migrant farm workers who remained in the valley and made it their home. Many came directly from their home island to the Hudson Valley and others relocated from New York City or other urban places in the United States. The majority were Jamaicans, and by 1980 had organized a cricket club with a clubhouse on the corner of Pershing and Cottage avenues with a field and pitch across the street next to the railroad line. Restaurants selling jerk chicken, patties, curried goat, and other Caribbean food located on the north side and in the Main Street corridor, with signs in the black and gold of the Jamaican flag.

Throughout the mid-Hudson region, African Americans remained clustered in the cities, and the number of "foreign-born" also increased, even as the cities' overall populations decreased. In Poughkeepsie, from 1980 to 1990, the number of foreign-born grew to 2,878, or 10 percent of the population; many were new immigrants from Mexico, while the number increased dramatically over the next decade, especially among undocumented migrants.

## NEW IMMIGRANTS: MEXICANS

Migration to Poughkeepsie has always been about economic and social change. As we have indicated in previous chapters, there are countless stories of men, women, and families who have immigrated to the United States and found their way to Poughkeepsie with hopes of a better future. In the early and mid-nineteenth century, immigrants arrived primarily from England, Ireland, and Germany, while in the late nineteenth and early twentieth centuries, the majority of immigrants were from Italy and central and eastern Europe. After World War II, the origins of most immigrants changed again to include the Caribbean, south and central America, the Middle East, and south and eastern Asia. Migrants from the southern half of the Western hemisphere initially located in the city, while those from Asia primarily lived elsewhere in the county.

Hispanic migration to Newburgh and Beacon was under way by the 1970s. The newcomers came primarily from Puerto Rico in the early stages; in later decades, other Latinos from Central and South America also moved north from New York City into the mid-Hudson valley. During the 1990s, the Hispanic population increased by 85 percent in Dutchess County and 60 percent in Ulster County, and had doubled to 6 percent of the total population of both counties by 2000. According to the U.S. Census, persons of Hispanic origin in Dutchess County almost doubled from 9,765 in 1990 to 18,060 in 2000 and by an additional 43.8 percent to 25,976 in 2007. Many more were undocumented. The new Hispanic migrants primarily settled in and around the Main Street corridors of Beacon and Poughkeepsie. In Beacon, Puerto Ricans made up 60 percent of the Hispanic population, while in Poughkeepsie, Mexicans accounted for well over half of the ethnic group.

Immigrants from Mexico to Poughkeepsie in the last two decades of the twentieth century came almost exclusively from the Mexican state of Oaxaca. Like many of the early Italian immigrants to the city and county who emigrated from a relatively few villages in southern Italy and Sicily, the Oaxacans established a chain migration of friends and relatives from a limited number of villages. This village–city relationship became perceptually reorganized by the migrants themselves and their families back in Oaxaca, thought of as a singular place, with known social spaces where they lived, worked, shopped, and socialized.[7] El Bracero, a Mexican restaurant along Main Street, became the first place of contact for many of the Oaxacans when they first arrived in the city.

Honorio "Pie" Rodriguez, co-owner of El Bracero, has claimed that he was the first Oaxacan migrant in Poughkeepsie. He worked for several years in New York City and came to Poughkeepsie in 1977 when his employer opened the Majestic Diner where he worked for a few more years. By 1991, he had saved enough money to bring his family north and open his own restaurant. Rodriguez had come from La Cienaga, a Oaxacan village of 3,000. According to one estimate, close to "a quarter of La Cienaga's adult men worked in the Poughkeepsie area by the 1990s."[8] The population of the village of San Agustin is similar; its list of "active citizens" of men of working age was 750 in the mid-1990s, "most of whom reside[d] temporarily in Poughkeepsie."[9] The men who emigrated to Poughkeepsie constituted about 23 percent of the village, and left behind a "village of women," children, and the elderly.[10] Zaachila, a third small village in Oaxaca, is similarly a place of origin for the city's Mexicans. For the migrants to the Northeast from these villages, Poughkeepsie has been the "central community. New migrants nearly always arrive first to Poughkeepsie, the location with by far the largest concentration of villagers. . . . Poughkeepsie serves the role of 'home base' . . . migrants share information such as job and housing opportunities, as well as the most recent gossip of events in Poughkeepsie, the village, and elsewhere."[11] The first stop for many arriving for the first time in the city has been El Bracero, where the new migrants can learn of possible jobs and housing options.

During the 1980s and 1990s, young Mexican men found work washing dishes in restaurant kitchens and on landscaping crews. Many lived together in apartments, living, "as they say in the village," as "amontonados," or as "many people piled on top of each other."[12] Many of these apartments were left in poor condition by absentee landlords and were located in areas of the city that were known for drugs and violence during the previous decades. By the latter half of the 1990s, many migrants had been able to bring their families along and had spread out from the near north side into safer and more well-managed housing.

The Mexican community grew in the 1990s and became more "visible" throughout the city and the town. The Galleria Mall became an important gathering place for shopping for clothing and electronic gifts to bring back to their relatives in the villages as well as for socializing. Informal games of soccer eventually resulted in club teams, with individual uniforms in an organized *Liga Independiente de Futbol Asociado*, that play their games on Lincoln field, home of the city's youth soccer club.

As the community matured during the 1990s, various social services helped to stabilize the families; health services hired Spanish speakers, ESL classes began, Christ Church Episcopal and St. Mary's Roman Catholic churches instituted *misa espanol*, and children attended city schools. In some of the elementary schools, such as Clinton Elementary School on Montgomery Street across from Christ Church, boys and girls of Mexican parentage began to constitute a significant presence.

In the early decades of the twenty-first century, Poughkeepsie's Hispanic population, primarily of Mexican origin, constituted between 20 and 25 percent of its total.[13] The Hispanic community concentrated in the central core area of the city's downtown along the Main Street corridor. In 2000, the median household income in this area of the city was the lowest in the city, only $15,758 compared to $29,389 for the entire city and $54,086 for Dutchess County. It was also an economically depressed landscape. The 1997 survey of storefront vacancies had shown few shops and many abandoned and vacant buildings. For many poor migrants, however, it became a landscape of opportunity. Housing, although initially of poor quality, was available. Initial rents for vacant storefronts were low enough for Spanish-speaking entrepreneurs to sell groceries, CDs, telephone calling cards, and money orders to fellow nationals.

Main Street began to reflect the Hispanic presence. A "Latino landscape" was particularly evident in the commercial streetscape, according to social geographer Brian Godfrey. "The explanation." he wrote, lay "in the newness of the Latino immigration, the low-income and renter status of most immigrants, and the city's lack of a previous Hispanic presence."[14] An "aspiring Latino entrepreneurial class" began to open shops along Main Street among the mostly vacant storefronts; soon there were more than two dozen Spanish-language businesses, including nine restaurants, eight variety stores advertising money transfers to Latin America, three grocery stores, two *panaderias* or bakeries, two delicatessens, and a hair salon. Much of the signage, window treatments, awnings, and facades reflected Mexican heritage, as in the use of the colors of the Mexican flag, similar to the painted signs using the colors of the Italian flag by merchants in Mount Carmel Square neighborhood. The

FIGURE 19.1. Aerial view of Main Street corridor, looking west, c. 1998

two small neighborhoods visually promoted their urban ethnic character for economic reasons as well as community identity.

The Latino community became much better known to the greater Poughkeepsie community after a hit-and-run car accident on April 10, 1998, killed Jaime Gil Tenorio. Tenorio was a thirty-two-year-old undocumented migrant who worked in landscaping to support a wife and four children who remained back in Oaxaca. K. Skip Mannain, a city police detective who had investigated the case, arranged to transport Tenorio's body back to his village for burial, and with the support of local churches and newspapers, over two thousand local donors raised $22,583. Skip and a team assembled by the *Poughkeepsie Journal* delivered the gift to the family. It was a turning point in terms of perception and local acceptance according to the *Poughkeepsie Journal*. National newspapers also reported on the story. "Detective's Kindness Helps Awaken City: After a Death, Poughkeepsie Notices Its 3,000 Mexicans and Their Roots" headlined the *New York Times*. The paper quoted Peter Leonard, a Vassar College professor and columnist for the *Poughkeepsie Journal* who accompanied Mannain, "Until the accident, the climate in Poughkeepsie had been indifferent or hostile. But in the accident's aftermath," he and local Mexicans said, "the people of Poughkeepsie have grown curious and friendly" about the expanding Mexican American population in the area.[15] Many other national news organizations reported on the story; *People* magazine covered the trip to Oaxaca and

FIGURE 19.2. Aerial view of Main Street corridor, looking east, c. 1998

"Detective Skip," as he was affectionately called in San Agustin, was interviewed by newscasters and Oprah Winfrey. The National Association of Police Organizations also named Mannain one of the country's "Top Cops."

Mannain compared Poughkeepsie's residents to the new immigrants, "There's an awful lot of good people in this area. There are illegals here, but most of them are working. My heritage is that of immigrants. We're all immigrants, unless we're American Indians. . . . But this is still America, the land of dreams."[16] Leonard noted the parallels to earlier migrations, and added a function for the city in developing a sense of civic responsibility: "The Mexicans also come from a climate and culture that encourages great use of outdoor civic space. The life of Mexican cities revolves around the community plaza or *zocolo*. This rich civic life," he continued, "translates into greater public safety and the sheer joy of publicness. You can see this on any Sunday summer afternoon at Waryas Park where Mexican families are out enjoying barbeques, music and soccer."[17]

## NEW IMMIGRANTS: ASIANS

The Mid-Hudson region also became a home for a number of south and east Asians in the latter three decades of the twentieth century. A few of the churches associated with the Dutchess County Interfaith Council assisted in the resettlement of southeast Asian refugees after the Vietnam War in the 1970s. Christ Episcopal Church helped the Oudom family from Laos find lodging in the Rip Van Winkle apartments on lower Main Street. A former official in the Laos government, Khantorn Oudom first began work as a janitor at Dutchess Community College and soon thereafter at a factory job in Pawling, while his wife Bouachine worked as a seamstress. Their six children all attended schools in Poughkeepsie, and although they had learned English as a second language in the refugee camp in Thailand before arriving in America, they all quickly became fluent and at the top of their classes. After a few years, the family had fully entered the middle class: they moved from their subsidized apartment to a new home on the south side of the city near Spratt Park; the children went to college; they entered the medical and health professions, engineering, and the military.

In contrast to the Latino influx, the Asian population grew more modestly in numbers, as individual families, often highly educated, were recruited to professional jobs in the region. Opportunities in the medical, health, and educational professions as well as in engineering and computer development at IBM, Texaco, and other high-tech industries drew hundreds of Koreans, Chinese, Indians, and Japanese to Dutchess County. Their occupations were in the middle- and upper-income brackets and most all chose to live in new housing far from downtown Poughkeepsie. The churches and religious and cultural institutions that they organized were also close to their residences in the suburban towns near IBM facilities. For example, the Hindu Samaj Center, Mid-Hudson Chinese Christian Church, Gurudwara Mid-Hudson Sikh Cultural Society, Majid Al-Noor Mid-Hudson Islamic Association, and the Kagyu Thubten Choling Center all located in Wappingers Falls, while the Mid-Hudson Korean United Methodist Church relocated from a small church on the corner of Cherry and Forbus streets in the city to a new larger building in the town of Poughkeepsie. New congregations often began meeting in the city as did the Korean Methodists; for example, the Jordanian Orthodox Christian congregation has been one of several small groups that have been housed in the First Presbyterian Church in downtown Poughkeepsie.

Asians constituted 3.4 percent of the county's population in the beginning of the twenty-first century, having increased 33 percent from 2000 to 2007, with over 9,500 self-declared in the U.S. Census. The largest national group was the Chinese with close to 3,800 enumerated in 2005, while Asian Indians were just below 2,000, Koreans at nearly 1,200, and Vietnamese 1,100.

## SOCIAL AND PHYSICAL RENEWAL

In 1991, the city entered into an agreement with the U.S. Department of Justice to participate in a comprehensive strategy for community revitalization, called the Weed and Seed Initiative. The objective of the effort was to establish a partnership between police, community service organizations, the private sector, and local residents to prevent drug-related violence and develop strategies to prevent further disinvestment. Community policing efforts over the decade began to show results; for example, the number of reported shootings in the city in 1994 compared to 1999 fell from fifty to eleven.

Crime, violence, and other drug-related activities remained endemic to a few particular neighborhoods on the north side and in the Main Street corridor. Garden Street, between Mill and Mansion streets, contained many boarded-up buildings where many criminal activities occurred. The Weed and Seed program offered funding to address this area of urban physical blight. In 1996, the city donated city-owned properties on Garden Street to Hudson River Housing (HRH), a Neighborhood Preservation Company founded in 1982 to promote home ownership and provide shelter for residents in need. "The idea for the organization . . . started after an intern at Vassar Brothers Medical Center saw there was nowhere for many of the hospital patients to stay once they were discharged," according to former county executive Lucille Pattison.[18] In 1979, a task force was set up, and the members met regularly in the office of former *Poughkeepsie Journal* publisher Richard Wager, the first board president. The *Journal* is part of the Gannett newspaper chain and Wager was able to secure funding to open Gannett House in the former Dutchess Motel on South Road (Route 9) in January 1984.

In the last two decades of the twentieth century, HRH took over operation of the homeless shelter that had been started by volunteers at Christ Episcopal Church, then moved to the Salvation Army before having permanent quarters for twelve beds at Hillcrest House on the grounds of Hudson River Psychiatric Hospital; the number of available beds rose to sixty in 2006. HRH also offered transitional housing in apartments at Hillcrest House. Over this period, HRH created nearly three hundred apartments and more than thirty affordable home ownership opportunities. Owning a home should be available to everyone, according to HRH executive director Gail Webster.

But neighborhood renewal was more than bricks and mortar. HRH helped to create a grassroots community organization that included the expertise of local banks, churches, and schools alongside home owners in the neighborhood. Susan Guerrina, local home owner and resident activist reported that the success of the Garden Street project resulted from the dedication of local home owners who had a vested interest in maintaining properties and stabilizing the neighborhood. "They join neighborhood crime watches and block associations," she wrote, and added that absentee landlords were a major source of the problem in the neglect of buildings and whole neighborhoods. In the process of renovating her own home on Garden Street just north of Mansion Street, she recalled the remarks of Kevin O'Connor from HRH: "Increasing owner occupancy is key to neighborhood stability."[19]

New immigrants reinvigorated local commerce; developers and government agencies restored storefronts and apartments along Main Street; and not-for-profit organizations revitalized cultural activities. Nonetheless, social discourse between urban and nonurban residents remained discordant. A full urban renaissance would require reimagining these relationships; where social and physical space interact, history is recalled and a future created.

TWENTY

# City and Region at the End of the Twentieth Century

THE POUGHKEEPSIE URBAN REGION has been the center of the Hudson River valley for the past two centuries. The city is the county seat for Dutchess County, while many of its businesses function throughout the other counties of the mid-Hudson region. Wholesale distribution businesses, such as EFCO, which has supplied products used in the baking industry, including cake mixes, fillings, and toppings since 1928, as well as banks and legal firms, include the region as their trade area. The regional transportation network facilitated the central role of Poughkeepsie in the region's economy.

## REGIONAL CONSCIOUSNESS AND PLANNING

A consciousness that the Poughkeepsie urban region was central to the mid-Hudson valley had early roots in the business community. In 1910, "some Poughkeepsie factory entrepreneurs" created the Mid-Hudson Industrial Association that subsequently became the Council of Industry of Southeastern New York, a privately funded nonprofit association.[1] It grew in the 1930s and 1940s, reaching across the Hudson for new members and undertaking programs like training supervisors that could only be offered with the critical mass of businesses that a region provided. In the meantime, the Regional Plan Association (RPA) had projected a rapid expansion outward of metropolitan New York; that growth did come, but not as rapidly as expected. The association's plan for growth, however, remained the primary influence on planners' thinking about the region. In December 1973, the RPA and Mid-Hudson Pattern for Progress released a joint Mid-Hudson Development Guide that urged, "no growth sections . . . development channeled into urban corridor" and recommended that a quarter of the land be kept in "public open space," with "measures to preserve farm areas" and with "seven growth centers for urban activities." So much emphasis on space proved controversial with businessmen and developers especially.[2]

Mid-Hudson Pattern for Progress, a nonprofit planning group founded in 1964, covered nine counties. The inspiration for Pattern grew out of a conference organized by Lee Sillin, the CEO of Central Hudson Gas and Electric, one of the biggest employers in the valley, and the president of the State University of New York at New Paltz. Pattern looked for member institutions and businesses that had a regional interest, like utilities; forty years after its founding, by 2004, it had more than four hundred members. Pattern's work was to be based on research, focused on issues, and staffed by individuals having at least postgraduate degrees. They early became advocates.

In 1968, for example, they played an important role in bringing about what many in Newburgh thought to be Mission Impossible: persuading the city's mayor and council to undertake the first project of Governor Rockefeller's new Urban Development Corporation headed by Ed Logue of Boston, the Robert Moses of his day. In that year of national crises, generally quiet Newburgh had enough rumblings of discontent among local African Americans that Rockefeller, then hoping to run for president of the United States, wanted to mitigate. Newburgh's mayor, a plumber, resisted putting the all-white council together with the head of the local NAACP for discussion. But with Pattern's assistance, the meeting happened with the ultimate result that a limited amount of affordable housing was made available to local blacks.

Another intervention had a less happy ending. A 1971 Pattern study of Stewart Airport, just outside of Newburgh, considered whether aviation demand, economic potential, and environmental impact would justify the desire of Governor Rockefeller and the Metropolitan Transportation Association's Dr. William Ronan to make Stewart New York City's fourth jetport. Community groups worried that a large airport would ruin the valley. Both sides hoped that Pattern's study would support them; both were deeply disappointed that it did not. Even Pattern's board split over the conflict between economic and environmental concerns. It would be another thirty-five years before work would begin to construct a highway interchange connecting the airport to the New York State Thruway and a takeover of Stewart by New York Port Authority as the fourth major airport in the metropolitan region.

By the end of the century, another regional organization, Hudson Valley Economic Development Corporation, covering eight counties, complemented the work of Pattern for Progress. It had begun as Team Hudson Valley, a volunteer group without staff or funding that accomplished little. The then chairman of Central Hudson pushed for a more aggressive marketing approach to scouting for big space users, leaving local agencies to recruit businesses with smaller land use requirements. Both regional and local organizations sought to take advantage of the physical attractiveness of the valley's topography for potential residents and investors. In trying to lure new businesses, they emphasized the region, not the locality, as the *Poughkeepsie Journal* reported: "Regional consciousness is spreading in the Hudson Valley."[3]

## A REGIONAL FABRIC OF CITY AND COUNTRYSIDE

From the 1920s through the 1960s, urban historian and public intellectual Lewis Mumford promoted regional planning in the New York metropolitan area as an integration of economic, social, and ecological features. Mumford, a resident of Amenia, a small town in southeastern Dutchess County, had his regional planning canvas encompass both rural and urban landscapes, with the city as its magnet.

> To define human areas, one must seek, not the periphery alone but the center . . . in human culture generally, the urban spheres of attraction become geographic facts of utmost importance: for the urban center tends to focus the flow of energies, men, and goods that passes through a region . . . exerting a close and controlling influence over the development of region as a dynamic reality.[4]

Mumford's early efforts with the Regional Plan Association (RPA) primarily focused on knitting together the physical infrastructure of the New York metropolitan area to promote economic development. But he was also interested in the historical social framework and the natural environment. The Hudson River valley exemplified these characteristics and could clearly be defined as a region. Mumford realized that its cultural history was deep and resonated with the origins of the nation, while its geographic boundaries of watershed, fauna, flora, and topography were apparent. The interface between the natural and cultural landscapes engaged Mumford and his colleagues at the RPA as they discerned the effects of the changing and expanding urban realm during the middle of the twentieth century. Mumford warned of the impact of the automobile and the highway and the development of an auto-centered landscape; he posited that modernization and technology were creating a gap between society and the environment in an early description of sprawl: "in the act of expanding indefinitely, in response to the 'thrust of technology' and the desire for immediate profit, one metropolis will merge physically with its neighbor. In that merging each metropolis will lose the neighboring landscape that served it for education and recreation, along with its residue of urban individuality."[5]

The RPA promoted several ideas to forestall the predicted future of an unstructured and featureless landscape, uninterested in local history or ecology. Their overall approach was comprehensive regional planning. They encouraged the development of plans that integrated economic development, transportation networks, and other physical infrastructure, such as water quantity and quality. Various efforts at comprehensive planning for the Hudson River valley were proposed and implemented over the latter half of the century.

In 1965, at the urging of his brother and avid conservationist Laurance, Governor Nelson Rockefeller appointed the Hudson River Valley Commission (HRVC) to conduct a survey of the valley corridor from New York City to the Adirondacks and report to the state legislature with proposals to protect the region's scenic, historic, and cultural resources. In their first report a year later, the commission recommended that a bi-state–federal compact be formed, and the commission itself become permanent. It would have the authority "to review plans for government and government-aided projects which would have substantial effect on the Valley [and] would also review applications for government licenses for major private projects, such as the construction of utility plants."[6] The HRVC reviewed many development plans over the next few years, including the redesign of the electricity generating plant built by Central Hudson on Danskammer Point in Newburgh. HRVC also surveyed the scenic, historic, and cultural resources of the valley; these data became useful as development pressures became more intense toward the end of the century.

Political pressure against comprehensive regional planning from local municipalities throughout the valley led to the eventual demise of the HRVC by 1976. Yet, paradoxically, the bicentennial year also led to increased interest in the historical, cultural, and scenic values of the regional landscape. In 1978, the New York State Department of Environmental Conservation (NYS DEC) created a Hudson River Study Advisory Committee "to develop a program for the preservation and protection of the Valley's scenic, recreational, and ecological values."[7] Local citizen groups also emerged to offer advice to their municipalities about land use issues; for example, in Hyde Park, the local Visual Environment Committee attempted to educate its elected and appointed officials on the need for planning through its support for a documentary film on the town's history and rapidly changing landscape. Local municipalities also began to cooperate in protecting their historic properties and integrating them into their master plans. From 1980 to 1983, the Hudson River Shorelands Task Force worked with the Dutchess County towns of Hyde Park, Rhinebeck, and Red Hook and the Columbia County towns of Clermont and Germantown to develop guidelines for the management of New York State's first officially designated scenic district, "The Mid-Hudson Historic Shorelands Scenic Area."[8]

Meanwhile, the Regional Plan Association worked with counties in the mid-Hudson region to develop plans to integrate urban growth and environmental conservation, such as *The Mid-Hudson: A Development Guide—shaping urban growth to expand opportunities and conserve the environment* (1973). Specific projects were also proposed by RPA. In an attempt to integrate regions as well as to maintain a distinction between natural and human spaces, a series of hiking trails was conceptualized. Mumford's colleague Benton MacKaye mapped out the Appalachian Trail that has come to symbolize one of the late twentieth century's major efforts at offering individual contact with nature. The Hudson valley greenway would be created by century's end.

## COMMUNITY AND REGIONAL PLANNING

In 1978, county executive Lucille Pattison was elected as a reform candidate after the corruption charges against and resignation of Edward Schueler. Pattison was the first woman to be elected to such a high political office in the state; she was also a Democrat in a Republican county. During her tenure, efforts were made to bridge the gulf between the concerns of the rural and suburban towns with the massive urban problems of the cities of Beacon and Poughkeepsie. Social issues such as poverty, racism, teenage motherhood, and domestic violence rose in importance, even while jobs growth, road maintenance, water quality and supply, and sewage treatment and trash disposal remained significant problems. Tackling the social, economic, and environmental issues over the course of more than a decade, she helped establish the county's Human Rights Commission and the Resource Recovery Agency. One of her first appointments was Kenneth Toole as Commissioner of Planning.

Ken Toole began at the Dutchess County Department of Planning in 1965 and was Commissioner Henry H. J. Heissenbuttel's deputy until Heissenbuttel's untimely death in 1978. Heissenbuttel and Toole were both responsible for the development of a regional planning focus through a series of citizen conferences and publications that assisted local and county land use decision-making, as in *The Future of Dutchess County* published in 1972. Heissenbuttel's emphasis on central places, such as village centers and urban cores, became fundamental to county planning for the next thirty years. His conceptual framework that a land use pattern that distinguished between city, village, and countryside enhanced economic growth and supported social communities would evolve as a core value of "Smart Growth" planning by national planners over the decades.

Building community was central to Heissenbuttel's planning effort. The problems in Poughkeepsie, however, were difficult, since land use issues were quite different between the city and the other municipalities in the county. According to Toole, "The city was such a different environment from the rest of the county. It was unique in that it was much more diverse with urban renewal and eventually community development money. . . . The functions were very different in that we were involved with communities that were very rural in nature."[9] A major aspect of the county's planning work was "to control strip zoning," he added. As retailing left Poughkeepsie's Main Street and reestablished along Route 9 and other highways, it also impacted the village centers. And, as stores spread out into the formerly rural landscape, so, too, did residential subdivisions and exurban sprawl. Communities lost much of their social coherence and sense of history.

For two decades, development seemed to outpace planning. In 1987, a report on land use and community development described "an overall pattern of development in Dutchess County that is increasingly fragmented and hap-hazard . . . which, if unchecked, will continue to consume large areas of land, threaten the county's natural resources, increase the cost of providing services and facilities, decrease the efficiency of the transportation network, and con-flict with agricultural activities in the county."[10] As noted in chapter 18, sprawl had emerged as a significant land use problem. The report defined sprawl as "characterized by the separation of residential, commercial, industrial and cul-tural activities, the increased dependence on the automobile as the dominant means of transportation, and the conversion of large quantities of land from agricultural and open space uses to residential, commercial and industrial uses." To rein in sprawl and reinforce community identity, the county should plan, it argued, "to support the existing community centers within the county, which range from the urban centers of Poughkeepsie and Beacon to town, vil-lage and hamlet centers found throughout the county."

As a creative approach to address the problem of social fragmentation and community identity, Heissenbuttel and Toole early on integrated the perspec-tives and efforts of historic preservation and arts organizations in the devel-opment of community-based planning along with traditional planning con-cepts. One effort was *Landmarks of Dutchess County, 1683–1867*, an inventory of significant structures and landscapes for the Architecture Worth Saving in New York State project of the New York State Council on the Arts in 1968–1969. Although this work only included several sites and the historic district of large Victorian-era residences on Academy Street and Garfield Place in the city of Poughkeepsie, it nevertheless gave impetus to create a Landmarks Association that worked to preserve the working-class homes and streetscape along Union Street that had been slated for urban removal. As Toole remarked, "We reversed the trend of demolition," which was then a national program of massive urban change, to projects that would rehabilitate ageing structures in place and preserve whole neighborhoods.

## GREENWAYS

The combined interests of historic preservationists and environmental con-servationists that emerged after the Storm King battle in the 1960s and focused on regional planning in the Hudson River Valley Commission in the 1970s and the Hudson River Shorelands Task Force in the early 1980s solid-ified in the late 1980s with plans for the Hudson Valley greenway. The green-way project to link municipalities from New York City to Albany with a trail along the banks of the Hudson River began to take shape after a national conference in 1987 of the President's Commission on American Outdoors. In a book on the historical antecedents of the "movement" to create greenways across the nation, Charles E. Little noted the work of Frederick Law Olmsted and Calvert Vaux in New York and Boston and the development of the parkways outside these cities into the countryside. The greenway movement in the 1980s, according to Little, built on this foundation and the regional environmental consciousness of the post-Earth Day decades through the hard work of local conservationists and environmental planners. In the Hudson valley, former members of the HRVC and activists in regional environmental organizations joined forces to formulate a greenway plan for the valley.

Laurance S. Rockefeller, former chair of HRVC, introduced a report "prepared by a group of citizens concerned with the future of the Hudson River Valley" in 1988 titled *Greenways in the Hudson River Valley: A New Strategy for Preserving an American Treasure.*[11] He noted the efforts of his brother, Governor Nelson A. Rockefeller, and the then-current governor Mario Cuomo, in promoting the preservation of open space through public and private efforts. The report, according to Rockefeller, "is entirely unofficial. It is the work of a group of citizens who care about the Hudson, who know something about it, and who have had some responsibility for it in public and private capacities. . . . This long tradition of American citizen action applies particularly to the Hudson."[12]

Numerous private, nonprofit environmental organizations were involved in the early discussions to create a Hudson Valley greenway, including: Historic Hudson Valley; Sleepy Hollow Restorations, Inc.; Jackson Hole Preserve, Inc.; Hudson River Valley Association; The Conservation Fund; and Scenic Hudson, Inc., whose executive director, Klara B. Sauer, was particularly active. She had, she admitted, "missionary zeal."[13] In *Greenways for America*, author Charles Little commented that Sauer "created much of the intellectual foundation and civic support for the most ambitious greenway project in America—the Hudson River Valley Greenway."[14] Little offered a brief personal history of Sauer's migration from Hanover, Germany, to Poughkeepsie, her gaining a BA from Vassar College at the age of thirty-four, and her subsequent role at Scenic Hudson. From the first planning conference in 1988 to the Hudson River Valley Greenway Act of 1991 and design of the Council and Conservancy, to the nomination of the Hudson as one of America's first Heritage Rivers in 1997, Sauer was an active and effective advocate.

The "six-year project," according to Sauer, involved numerous individuals from nonprofit environmental organizations and state agencies, such as NYS DEC and the Office of Parks, Recreation, and Historic Preservation, as well as state political leaders. Dave Sampson, a lawyer in the capital district, and Fran Dunwell from Scenic Hudson's Poughkeepsie office, creatively structured the greenway into a Conservancy that focused on land use issues and a Compact that linked close to three hundred municipalities and encouraged them all to join in the effort. Scenic Hudson led the public relations effort with public presentations and booklets published by New York State Council on the Arts in 1988 and by the National Park Service in 1989. Frances Reese, then-president of Scenic Hudson, was on the Board of Trustees for Marist College and she persuaded college president Dennis Murray to have the Marist Opinion Poll under the direction of Professor Lee Miringoff investigate interest in the development of a greenway; 75 percent were positive to the "idea."

The next year Henry Diamond "crafted" legislation for state funding. From the mid-Hudson, Maurice Hinchey led the effort in the state assembly while Jay Rolison championed the regional effort in the state senate. Governor Pataki appointed Dave Sampson to chair a panel that held hearings throughout the valley. "To get it accepted by the legislature," Sauer recalled, the greenway was promoted as being "good for the economy because it attracts tourists. Tourists," she added, "like to come to places where the underlying features are attractive," particularly historic resources such as "landscapes, mansions or villages." The legislature passed the legislation late in the session, but Pataki hesitated to sign it into law. According to Sauer, Richard Wager, publisher of the *Poughkeepsie Journal*, called Pataki and reminded him that the regional economy was changing from an industrial base to a postindustrial one dependent on tourism. Sauer quoted Wager as saying to the governor, "IBM is fading. This is the only thing in town." "So," Sauer added, Dick Wager "saved it," and the governor signed the bill at 4:30 P.M. on December 31. Sampson was appointed the first executive director, Dutchess County was the first county to sign on to the Compact, and the greenway trail across the Beacon-Newburgh bridge along I-84 linking the two cities would be among the first trails generated by the state program. By century's end, Hinchey would take his political acumen and expertise on environmental matters to the U.S. Congress, representing rural Ulster County and the cities of Kingston and Poughkeepsie.

## RURAL LAND USE CHANGE

In the latter half of the twentieth century, the rural landscape of the mid-Hudson valley was transformed. The American Farmland Trust identified the region as "the tenth most threatened agricultural region in the nation" in 1997.[15] From 1982 to 1997, there was a 30 percent increase of rural land converted to urban development. However, the region's population grew only by 2.6 percent over those same years, "resulting in urban sprawl in the form of reduced density."[16] From 1987 to 1997, the mid-Hudson lost 78,802 acres, or 18 percent of land in farms, by conversion to other uses. This represented a loss of 522 farms, or 17 percent of the total number of farms in the region.

By 1986, the alarm had been raised. A series of articles in the *Poughkeepsie Journal* in August 1986 chronicled a number of families in Dutchess and Ulster counties with generations of farming experience who were facing difficult decisions about their futures in agriculture. "Auctioneers pushing cows and tractors shout what many fear for local, full-time farms: 'going once . . . going twice . . . gone.' There is a future for farmers in Dutchess County, but it is not in milking cows or making a full-time living off the land, agreed farmers and farm experts."[17] Fruit growers in Ulster County were similarly under severe financial pressures in the mid-1980s. Many reacted to the increased value for land by selling off house lots or subdividing their entire orchard, while a few sold out to vintners and shifted their crops from apples to grapes.

Throughout the Hudson Valley during the 1980s and 1990s, types of agriculture changed from low-value commodities such as dairy, corn, and hay that used extensive acreage to high-value and land-intensive uses such as vegetables, vineyards, and nurseries and greenhouses. The loss of large-scale commercial agriculture also coincided with a decline in the agricultural service and supply infrastructure. In Dutchess County, for example, the number of tractor dealers and other agricultural suppliers declined from 50 to 24, (or −53 percent) from 1993 to 2000, although certain services increased such as veterinarians, who increased from 222 to 302. Veterinary services, like nursery supplies, coincided with the growth of sprawl.

In 1925, of Dutchess County's 352,000 acres, 63 percent was classified as farmland; sixty years later it was less than 27 percent. In 1997, farmland accounted for 106,749 acres in the county. Dairy farms formerly constituted the major agricultural land use in the county, but their number declined rapidly from 320 in 1960 to 275 in 1972, 155 in 1980, 90 at the end of that decade, and 64 by the end of the century. Only 42 commercial dairy farms remained in the county in 2000, with an additional loss of four over the ensuing three years. The number of milk cows also decreased substantially; from 1983 to 2000 the number fell 60 percent from 13,500 in 1983 to approximately 5,000 in 1992 and less than 2,500 in 2000.

The decline in dairy farming resulted from both external and internal factors. Nationally, the vagaries of federal price supports for milk often had an effect on local farmers' ability to remain economically viable. National and international competition for various commodities undercut the profitability of many regional products. Apple orchards in both Ulster and Dutchess counties competed against the production from the states of Washington and Michigan during the 1980s and 1990s, only to have vast quantities of apples and apple juice shipped to the regional farmers' traditional markets in the metropolitan New York area from China and other countries. Meanwhile, natural forces also affected vegetable crops and orchards; for example, erratic weather in the four years at the end of the century precipitated the loss of nearly half of the region's apple orchard acreage. Increased property taxes in many of the towns, or changes within families to discontinue farming, led to many decisions to sell farmland for exurban residential development. According to information from the National Resource Inventory conducted between 1992 and 1997, Americans lose 3,193,200 acres of land every year to poorly planned development.

Most of the conversion of rural open space resulted from a loss of farmland to other uses, such as housing and other nonagricultural purposes. Fields that grew corn in the 1960s sprouted raised ranches thirty years later.

Not all rural land converted to nonagricultural uses; some changes in activity reflected new investment by a social class as involved in self-interest as in profit. In 1989, there were forty thoroughbred horse farms that had been established on former dairy farms, as well as twenty-five purebred breeding operations for beef cattle. Sheep farming also increased during the 1970s and 1980s, while truck farming of vegetables and nursery and greenhouse sales increased by 300 percent as the county's population grew.

Despite the loss of farms and acreage, agriculture remained the largest single user of land in Dutchess County and an important sector in the economy. Withstanding a loss in the number of farms from 613 in 1987 to 539 in 1997, there was a small increase in part-time, or "hobby" farms at the turn of the twenty-first century. Agriculture employed about 3,500: 1,500 on farms and 2,000 in providing goods and services to farmers. The 1997 USDA Census of Agriculture reported that about one-half of the county's agricultural economy came from the sale of crops (including field crops, greenhouse and nursery crops, fruit including tree crops, and vegetables), while the other half came from the sale of livestock and livestock products (including milk, cows, calves, horses, ponies, eggs, sheep, goats, and their products). By 2000, the vegetable and nursery-greenhouse sector accounted for 40 percent of production. One area of growth at the end of the century was in specialty farming, such as vineyards and the equine industry, and led to an increase in veterinarians, feed stores, and tack shops.

Consumer interest in purchasing local foods, from organically grown tomatoes to grass-fed beef and free-range chicken, has also opened up new venues for regional agriculture. Hudson Valley Fresh was one of the more successful ventures. A local dairy cooperative initiated by Dr. Samuel Simon, a former orthopedic surgeon whose office was in the city of Poughkeepsie, marketed its milk as locally produced from family-owned farms in Dutchess and Columbia counties and delivered fresh to local markets such as Adams Fairacre Farms. Adams food stores were instrumental in developing a market for locally grown or produced foods, such as salsas and barbeque sauces made and packaged at Poughkeepsie's Food Works. Food Works was housed in the former Woolworth's building on Main Street with industrial kitchens for small start-ups. It also served as a center where urban youth learn culinary trade skills and entrepreneurial business operations.

## COMMUNITY SUPPORTED AGRICULTURE

Outside of commercial farming, cooperatives continued to grow crops on small plots of land in the mid-Hudson region. Community Supported Agriculture

(CSA) farming arrangements sprouted up throughout the region during the last decade of the twentieth century. Farmers established CSAs to provide food directly to consumers, either through devoting all or part of the grower's farm and selling shares in the harvest or having a core group of members hire a farmer and rent or buy land for the farm and divide the harvest among the membership. Members often also assist in the planting and harvesting of the crops, and affirm their sense of community by supplying homeless shelters and other social service agencies with fresh produce for their soup kitchens and food pantries.

Twenty CSAs emerged during 1990s in the mid-Hudson counties of Dutchess, Ulster, Orange, and Columbia. In 1998, the Poughkeepsie Farm Project (PFP) became the first urban CSA. A core group of city and town residents established PFP on 10 acres of Vassar College's farm and hired Dan Guenther away from Phillies Bridge farm in Ulster County where he had been the farmer. PFP grew rapidly to a membership of over two hundred shares of approximately 150 families; its mission included both an educational component on urban food security as well as outreach offerings of its organically grown produce to the city's homeless shelter, food pantry, and the Lunch Box at the Family Partnership Center. Five years after creating PFP, Guenther left to start up another local farm across the river in Ulster County and PFP hired Wendy and Asher Burkhart-Spiegel as their growers. Although the urban focus of PFP was unusual, all CSAs in the region enabled farming to continue to maintain open space.

In the city of Poughkeepsie, a few local residents began growing their own vegetables and flowers in community gardens in their neighborhoods. Growing one's own was not new in the 1990s, as many residents, particularly Italian-Americans in the Mount Carmel neighborhood, had backyard gardens for over a century. Vassar College had also offered small plots of land for individuals to garden on its abandoned farm since the 1960s. However, the organization of community gardens on vacant lots in the city was a new phenomenon in cities all across America in the late twentieth century.

Two community gardens created in the late 1990s in Poughkeepsie constituted spaces where neighbors gathered to share stories and renew their spirits while growing fresh produce for their tables. Cleaning the vacant lots of trash and debris also promoted safer environments. For example, in the initial cleanup of a lot on the corner of South Hamilton and Montgomery streets in 1996 by the newly formed Trinity Neighborhood Association with assistance from AmeriCorps volunteers, "countless bags of needles" were gathered and disposed of, and quickly led to a decline in drug-related activity in the immediate area.[18] The cleanup of the Poughkeepsie Community Gardening Association lot under the Railroad Bridge in the Mount Carmel neighborhood produced many truckloads of trash, but similarly led to a more safe and beautiful environment that also offered personal food security and a sense of community for the gardeners involved.

In contrast to community gardening projects in major cities such as New York, Boston, and Philadelphia, however, the small citizen-inspired efforts in Poughkeepsie faced difficulties in surviving. Nevertheless, the community garden movement indicated the concerns of many urban dwellers in personal food security and neighborhood safety and availability of open spaces for recreation and enabling a sense of community.

Other strategies to retain open space have included agritourism and land trusts. Pick-your-own farms and orchards have had success as regional farmers have faced increasing competition from industrial farms in the West and from foreign sources. Carloads of people have come from the metropolitan New York area to pick seasonal crops such as strawberries and blueberries, tree crops such as apples and cherries, and a Halloween pumpkin or a Christmas tree. Roadside stands, farm markets, and on-farm entertainment such as hayrides and corn mazes added to farm incomes. At the beginning of the twenty-first century, there were over 200 on-farm venues and two dozen farmer's markets in the four mid-Hudson counties of Columbia, Dutchess, Orange, and Ulster. The wine industry mapped out two wine trails that include wine and regional food tasting; over 10,000 visitors a year visited the vineyards by the end of the century. The equine industry similarly integrated tourism, recreation, and agriculture with various activities including shows, polo events, fox hunts, and trail rides through pastoral landscapes with scenic vistas.

## OPEN SPACE PRESERVATION: PUBLIC AND PRIVATE

Traveling through the Hudson Valley countryside and to the mountains for long stays at Victorian-style resorts was not in fashion by the mid-twentieth century. Tourist tastes had changed. Many of the enormous mountain house resorts such as the Catskill and Kaaterskill hotels declined and were abandoned, although other establishments adapted and grew as ethnic summer camps. To accommodate an increased interest in motorized touring and camping, New York State expanded its holdings within the existing Catskill Forest Preserve for public campgrounds. In 1930, the state began development of 2,800 acres at North Lake, later expanded in 1961 and 1962 to include over 500 acres, including South Lake of the former Catskill Mountain House property. NYS DEC burned the remains of the crumbling relic in January 1963 and opened up the prospect view to the public.

In the decades following World War II, the state acquired another of the great mountain house properties. In 1879, Alfred H. Smiley opened the first of two mountain houses at Lake Minnewaska, just 5 miles to the south on the Shawangunk ridge of Lake Mohonk where his brother Albert had begun operating Mohonk Mountain House. From the late nineteenth century until the 1950s, the two branches of the Quaker Smiley family served as both hotelkeepers and stewards of the Shawangunks, a low-lying ridge of distinctive white conglomerate rock surrounded by three brilliantly pure rainwater lakes—Mohonk, Minnewaska, and Awosting—and crowned with pitch pine and blueberries.

In keeping with their Quaker values, the Smileys attracted a clientele who came to enjoy the serenity, natural beauty, and carriage roads and trails for hiking and contemplation of nature. The Smileys of Mohonk have maintained that tradition into the twenty-first century with some concessions to changed expectations of resorts. By the 1950s, however, the Smileys of Minnewaska wished to leave the hotel business and sold both Cliff House and Wildmere hotels and some 10,000 acres to Kenneth Phillips, Sr., the resort's general manager. Phillips proceeded to update the facility by adding a golf course in 1957 and "Ski Minne," a downhill ski area, in 1963. However, the increasing costs of maintaining the old, wooden hotels and escalating taxes forced Phillips in 1969 to sell 6,725 acres, including Lake Awosting, to the Palisades Interstate Park Commission (PIPC) for a state park.

The Phillips family hoped to develop a more modern resort at Lake Minnewaska, but the century-old structures were too costly to repair or upgrade, while heating costs became too expensive during the oil crisis of the 1970s. Phillips filed for bankruptcy in 1976; Cliff House burned down in 1978 and Wildmere, which had closed at the end of its one-hundredth season in 1979, later also burned down.

Meanwhile, the Marriott Corporation had contracted with Phillips to purchase the property and construct a modern resort, including a four-hundred-room hotel on the previous site of Wildmere and three hundred condominiums on the previous site of Cliff House overlooking the valley below. Local citizens and environmentalists filed numerous lawsuits opposing the impact of Marriott's proposed new resort; among a variety of ecological issues was the question of the modern requirements for a sufficient water supply, while a major political issue questioned the public's rights to access the trails that connected the private resort land with the state park.

After seven years of court battles and mounting legal costs, Marriott dropped its plans. In 1985, Phillips did agree, except for the financing, to a deal for state acquisition with the Nature Conservancy, the Open Space Institute, and Nash Castro, executive director of the Palisades Interstate Park Commission. Months of frustrating and adversarial negotiations ensued and in the end the state used eminent domain proceedings to acquire the remaining property in 1987 for a purchase price of $3 million, an amount offered previously but rejected by Phillips. Minnewaska State Park was opened as a "park-preserve" as part of the PIPC in 1993.

The Smiley brothers' legacy of private open-space preservation and recreation management remained on the more than 8,000 acres of Mohonk Mountain House. Mohonk, like Minnewaska, faced difficult times during the Depression era and the post–World War II period when mountain resort tourism declined. Mohonk retained its Quaker heritage and rustic mountain house flavor for many years, but also adjusted slowly to some building improvements and accommodating automobile parking in the 1920s, eventually allowing them up to the Mountain House in the 1970s.

In an effort to preserve most of its landscape as open space, Mohonk created a private land trust of over 5,000 acres surrounding 2,000 acres containing the hotel, gardens, and lake. One of the earliest examples of a private land trust in the mid-Hudson region, the Mohonk Trust was established in 1963. Two decades later and renamed the Mohonk Preserve, it had control of over 6,500 acres by the end of the century and constituted the largest private land preserve in New York State. With over 150,000 visitors a year and nationally known by rock climbers for its sheer rock cliffs and by hikers for its nineteenth-century carriage roads, the organization developed a reputation as a significant site for ecological research and environmental education.

Most land trusts developed during the latter half of the twentieth century in response to increased exurban residential growth. The Dutchess Land Conservancy, established in 1985, focused on protecting open space as a countryside amenity while maintaining it as a working landscape. Development rights were purchased to enable the landowner to continue to farm, while future development, perceived as sprawl, would be curtailed. From 1985 to 2000, the Conservancy worked with 148 landowners and protected 13,000 acres in the county's eastern lands. Smaller private land trusts were established in the 1990s to protect endangered landscapes and watersheds throughout the local area and by 2004 there were ten managed land trusts in the region that conserved 22,472 acres of farmland, while in the ten counties of the Hudson valley region the total number of land trusts was twenty-six, protecting over 57,000 acres.

## BALANCING RURAL AND URBAN ISSUES

National and regional environmental organizations became active in land protection. The Nature Conservancy and Open Space Institute purchased hundreds of acres that were donated to the state park system or to locally based land protection organizations for management. Scenic Hudson became a holder of conservation easements and development rights to protect over 17,000 acres in the mid-Hudson region. Over the years, they purchased over a thousand acres with scenic views of the Hudson River or along the river's shore for public access, and created or enhanced over two dozen local parks and preserves, such as the 120-acre Poets' Walk Romantic Landscape Park in Red Hook that opened in 1996. Scenic Hudson's efforts in urban waterfront revitalization generated numerous parks and walkways along the river's shore, including the 25-acre Beacon Landing Park in Beacon, while they also offered legal and design expertise to numerous waterfront communities throughout the 1980s and 1990s. This included Poughkeepsie's Waterfront Advisory Committee (WAC) and Local Waterfront Revitalization Plan (LWRP).

Urban and rural issues merged as regional land use and economic growth were concerns of city and county; the Main Streets of Poughkeepsie and Beacon as well as the landscapes and economic histories of the rural towns and villages were changing. The social organization that formed community, whether in the cities or the towns, needed as much attention as the conservation of the environment, the development of the physical infrastructure, or the growth of the economy. Cities remained central to civic life, where the private sphere of the suburb and the countryside interacts with the public sphere of commerce and politics.

TWENTY-ONE

# Main Street and the
# Twenty-first Century Cultural Landscape

URBAN AND REGIONAL PLANNING at the close of the twentieth century increasingly focused on quality-of-life issues. Perceptions of the region and its cities, towns, and neighborhoods continued to include concern for economic development and containment of crime, while they turned toward the preservation of open space, historic sites, and urban streetscapes. The social and cultural landscapes of the valley's main streets, waterfronts, and residential neighborhoods became as important to overall regional health as the rural and natural landscapes. The history and future of both town and country were interconnected. A national effort to preserve both natural landscapes and historic sites emerged in the 1970s and 1980s, and would expand to urban neighborhoods and streetscapes after the bicentennial as the National Trust for Historic Preservation established a Main Street project. Private and public efforts in the Hudson River valley would lead to its designation as the "Landscape that Defines America" by the U.S. Congress in 1997. In the mid-Hudson region, private and public sectors were involved: citizen groups placed sites and districts on the National Register, while individual counties and the state generated surveys of historic resources and developed preservation plans.

## HERITAGE TOURISM

Published in 1969, *Landmarks of Dutchess County, 1683–1867: Architecture Worth Saving in New York State* identified ninety-three notable structures that formed a foundation for the county's social and cultural history. There were estate houses, barns, churches, meetinghouses, iron furnaces, charcoal kilns, inns, colleges, and designed landscapes. Prepared by the Dutchess County Planning Board and published by the New York State Council on the Arts, the volume initiated an interest in the county's architectural and cultural history as having an evolving role in regional economic development through heritage tourism. In the same year, the Hudson River Valley Commission published *Historic Resources of the Hudson*, an inventory of over 1,650 sites in the fourteen counties and 300 miles of its jurisdiction.

HRVC's inventory and the various county surveys during the 1960s and 1970s documented tangible resources that constructed a sense of place for valley residents. According to HRVC, the structures and sites were useful for planning as sources of aesthetic designs and as economic resources in the postindustrial economy. However, in considering the economic development potential of the historic landscape, HRVC noted unhappily that few of the "millions of persons" who "were lured through the Valley" on their way to World Fairs held in Montreal and New York City in the 1960s visited sites or stayed overnight in the area. The inventory and surveys were the first stage in planning for an economy based on heritage tourism. HRVC promoted "the scenic beauty of the Valley and its dynamic history" as making the valley "potentially one of the major tourist areas of the country."

Looking to the future, HRVC saw a network of natural and cultural settings as establishing a new economy: "When, in a few years, the Hudson River again becomes pure, and boating, fishing and swimming are added to the lists of visitor attractions, the tourist industry might well become a prime source of economic activity." The report argued for preservation in contrast to urban removal for the cities of the region: "This new income will not flow to areas that have allowed their old sections to remain slums, nor to cities that have been rebuilt in a sterile way. It will go to the places that have retained their freshness, their uniqueness, their charm."[1]

Local citizen action to preserve their historic resources grew rapidly after the bicentennial. Both Poughkeepsie and Hudson reduced their urban renewal projects in efforts to retain neighborhoods and Main Street architecture. Hudson River Heritage organized in the towns of Rhinebeck and Red Hook to preserve the landscapes and estates stretching from the Roosevelt and Vanderbilt National Parks and Mills Mansion in Hyde Park to the New York State site of Olana in Columbia County. In 1980, the private properties were linked to form the longest contiguous historic and scenic district in the nation. Descriptions of the more than 20 miles of historic countryside encouraged tourism, as according to John Russell, English art historian and art critic for the *New York Times*, who wrote in 1980, "It is as civilized a countryside as we can hope to see."[2]

Many of the estate properties, however, were in great need of repair. A few had already been abandoned and pressures to subdivide their large acreage were growing. The National Historic Register listing promoted interest in the properties both for their value in national and regional cultural history as well as for their use as potential heritage tourism sites. Montgomery Place would be purchased by Rockefeller's Hudson River Valley Association and, after expensive renovations, opened to visitors. Wilderstein was similarly acquired by a private not-for-profit organization called Wilderstein Preservation, Inc. with the goal of restoration of the house, carriage barn, and grounds, making them available for public visitation. The last owner of Wilderstein, Miss Margaret "Daisy" Suckley, a distant cousin of Franklin Delano Roosevelt, lived in the house until her death at one hundred years old. In 1983, at age ninety-one, she commented on the financial burden associated with maintaining "the hulking Victorian mansion": "We haven't had much money to fix it, so we left it." As she looked around her sitting room at the peeling wallpaper, she added, "If you can't paper it, you can't paper it. No sense in making yourself miserable about it."[3]

Later in the twentieth century, the river valley landscape became nationally recognized for its scenic beauty and historic resources. The river was declared one of the first National Heritage Rivers in 1988 and the valley a National Heritage Area in 1996. By the end of the century, an estimated twenty-five million visitors a year translated into a regional economic impact of $600 million to $936 million during the summer and fall high-traffic months, according to the Marist College Bureau of Economic Research.

## SPRINGSIDE

The major national and state historic resources in the region attracted most attention as destinations for heritage tourism. Meanwhile, local citizens were equally active in saving other lesser-known sites. For example, the *Landmarks of Dutchess County* survey included Springside, an historic landscape in the city of Poughkeepsie that had been abandoned and was relatively unknown to the public at that time. Springside had been placed on the National Register of Historic Places in 1969, yet was not as publicly heralded as Locust Grove, the former home of Samuel F. B. Morse, located nearby, south along Route 9 in the town. Matthew Vassar, local entrepreneur, philanthropist, and founder of Vassar College built Springside as his summer home and farm. Springside's honor as one of America's earliest designated National Landmarks was not due, however, to Vassar's historical significance; rather, its structures and landscape were designated together as the only known extant landscape designed by America's first major landscape designer Andrew Jackson Downing. Downing and his partner Calvert Vaux were the architects of the buildings and grounds of Springside from 1850 to 1852. They were all designed in the Romantic style that Downing had promulgated in his writings during the previous decade. By the mid-twentieth century, however, the property had been abandoned, barns and cottage were in poor repair, and brush and second growth had taken over the landscape.

One week after it was designated a national landmark, Springside's carriage house, designed by Downing, burned to the ground. It was a devastating loss for architectural historians and was cited as a national example of the problems of America's interest in economic growth at the cost of any concern for history by *New York Times* critic Ada Louise Huxtable.[4] One year later, the city rezoned the parcel to allow the development of an apartment complex by the then-owner Robert S. Ackerman. The project would have obliterated the historic landscape garden, although the plans were not executed.

Ackerman proposed a 190-unit condominium development a decade later. Local preservationists successfully halted development on the site after a protracted battle with the city planning board and the developers led by two organizations, the Hudson River Sloop Clearwater and Hudson River Heritage, and five local citizens. They hired local environmental lawyer Robert C. Stover and Robert M. Toole, a landscape architect from Saratoga Springs who specialized in historic landscape analysis, and began legal proceedings in an effort to stop the development.

An agreement was finally reached in 1985 between Ackerman and John Mylod, executive director of Clearwater, that resulted in the historically significant 20 acres being donated to a nonprofit entity Springside Landscape, Inc., with the remaining half of the property left available for condominiums. Mylod and local preservationist Virginia Hancock would lead a small group of volunteers into the twenty-first century as they cleared over forty years of undergrowth, organized conservation efforts to save a few of the century-old hemlock trees that were attacked by *wooly adelgid*, and raised funds to maintain the porter's lodge, the only remaining Downing-era structure. Rather than "Doomsday," as Huxtable lamented, the loss of some of the structures and the near-loss of the entire landscape led to a community-inspired effort to preserve the landmark and to promote its existence to the very architectural and landscape historians who had previously neglected Downing's role in creating a national domesticated landscape.

John Mylod combined both a knowledge and affinity for cultural heritage and natural history in the task of saving Springside. His father, a prominent lawyer in Poughkeepsie, also collected and wrote local history. John became a commercial shad fisherman, and later led the environmental organization Hudson River Sloop Clearwater, Inc. for over twenty years. He and his family have long been active in community affairs. Their knowledge of the city's history has been reflected in the revitalization of the waterfront and Main Street as well as the role of the Fall Kill in the development of the city, and specific historic sites such as Springside.

## CITIZENS CREATE A NEW NEIGHBORHOOD PARK

Parks and playgrounds are important urban amenity spaces, while trees and stream corridors offer important green spaces for habitat and pleasure. In 1978, Poughkeepsie adopted a municipal tree ordinance that established a shade tree commission; the city was subsequently declared as New York State's oldest, continuously certified "Tree City."

A community effort in 2000 to preserve the state champion butternut tree created a new park on less than an acre of open space on the corner of Forbus and Cherry streets, one block from the high school. The preservation effort began in an attempt to stop the owner of the parcel from subdividing it into a number of house lots. A physical confrontation between Robin Poritzky plus other neighbors who lived across the street and men with chain saws set to cut down the trees on the property eventually led to the discovery of the importance of the butternut tree and the subsequent establishment of the Forbus Butternut Association, a private preservation group to negotiate with the land owner and eventually purchase the lots surrounding the tree as a public-private park. When the citizens group applied to the city for financial assistance to purchase the lots, a debate ensued between Common Council members. Robert Bossi argued for the right of the land owner to cut trees on his private property and build neighborhood houses, and he thought that the people in the neighborhood "have more important things to think about than the survival of the butternut tree."[5] Other Council members disagreed with Bossi and voted to grant the association funds. Mayor Lafuente remarked, "I think we will be preserving a major part of Poughkeepsie's history. It will continue to be an asset to the neighborhood and the city." Common Council Chairman Thomas O'Neill concurred, "I think, as a grassroots neighborhood organization, their request is deserving of a hearing."

In an ironic twist on the question of citizen participation in focusing on urban quality-of-life concerns, the November 2003 Poughkeepsie mayoral race pitted Bossi against Nancy Cozean, former vice-president of the Forbus Butternut Association. Two visions of the urban community were offered. One hearkened back to the industrial city of working families and busy shops along Main Street on Thursday evenings. The other was a postindustrial vision that considered new lifestyles and quality-of-life issues. In her successful campaign, Cozean noted the role of historic houses and landscapes, and neighborhood beauty and "neighborliness," as "tangible assets" of community pride. "History," she added, "makes the city feel its worth. . . . We need to explore ways to balance progress with preservation."

## CREATIVITY AND REGIONAL REVITALIZATION

Revitalization efforts in the twenty-first century have attempted to focus postindustrial productive energies into clusters of human and social capital. Regional planning agencies in the Hudson valley have mapped clusters of technological innovation and creativity from the worldwide offices of IBM in Westchester County north to IBM's chip and mainframe plants in Fishkill and Poughkeepsie and associated electronics firms in Dutchess County to the nanotechnology laboratories centered in the capital region of Albany and Rensselaer counties. In a study of over three hundred urban economic regions across the United States, Dutchess County was rated seventh in technological innovation, reflecting the large number of patents generated by IBM and other regional firms. The county was also rated twenty-fifth in "creativity," with a third of its workforce engaged in technical, professional, or artistic endeavors. Regions with such high values will thrive, "because creative people want to live there."[6]

Economic growth in the twenty-first-century, according to that study, will be associated with the energizing of clusters of human resources in existing urban regions. In the first decade of the new century, creative efforts to revitalize the vitality of the Hudson valley's downtown districts have included significant investments in the cultural landscape through historic preservation and the arts. Theaters have been refurbished; art galleries, antiques shops, clubs, and restaurants have opened. "The economy itself increasingly takes form around real concentrations of people in real places."[7] The cities of the mid-Hudson valley are real places.

## COMMUNITY AND THE ARTS: POUGHKEEPSIE

Artists and craftspersons have looked to the Hudson valley and Catskill region landscapes for inspiration throughout the nineteenth and twentieth centuries. Like Hudson River school artists Thomas Cole and Frederic Church, they have built their homes and studios in the area, while artist colonies have flourished, declined, and re-formed throughout the countryside. At the turn of the twentieth century, a group of artists formed a community called Byrdcliffe in Woodstock that, by mid-century, had introduced many artists to the region. In the heady days of the 1960s, Woodstock emerged as a center of aspiring artists, craftspersons, and musicians. Artists also joined together in marketing cooperatives in cities and towns as cultural tourism developed in the region.

In the latter half of the twentieth century, architectural preservation, environmental conservation, and the arts forged common bonds in urban revitalization efforts throughout the Hudson valley. Artists and arts organizations formed the human capital that, combined with economic capital, have sparked revitalization along urban main streets.

In the 1980s, a group of painters, sculptors, and crafts artisans operated a gallery in Poughkeepsie's old city hall on Main Street, just east of Market Street and the County Court House. The group helped to rehabilitate the abandoned historic structure, and although its sales taxes to the city's coffers were rather meager, the gallery was a harbinger of the potential impact that the arts community could have on urban revitalization. The cooperative lasted a few years until the city returned the building to use for several of its offices.

Later, Dutchess Community College and the Dutchess County Arts Council would hold annual arts and crafts fairs as venues for regional artists.

In the following decade, and further along lower Main Street, art galleries and arts programming at the Cunneen-Hackett Cultural Center provided an optimistic perspective on other efforts of physical and social renewal. Lorraine Kessler opened an art gallery at 196 Main Street in the early 1990s. She created a sculpture park in the summer of 1993 in a vacant lot next door on the corner of Main and South Bridge streets that had been cleared through urban renewal. The next year another gallery opened up next door to Kessler's, which, with Cunneen-Hackett across the street, began to establish interest in the development of an arts corridor along lower Main Street. An economic renaissance would eventually arrive after much struggle; Albert Shahanian became principal owner of both galleries and served as an anchor for revitalization efforts using the visual arts in a supporting role to economic investment.

Rehabilitation efforts along Poughkeepsie's Main Street were enhanced by visual artists who painted a number of murals on the sides of buildings. Murals by artists Franc Palaia and Nestor Madalengoitia became visual signifiers of economic, social, and physical revitalization. Many of the murals focused on the city's local history helped to reimagine several of the restored and historicized building facades. Seth Nadel, another Poughkeepsie artist, painted murals inside the County Court House and the former Barney building, renamed the Commerce building and home to the Chamber of Commerce.

"Music and Art are not simply 'frills,' but crucial components to a successful community," according to Virginia Hancock as she considered the developments along lower Main Street and throughout the city in her role as president of the board of directors of the Cunneen-Hackett Cultural Center in 1994.[8] Chris Silva became executive director of the Bardavon Theater that year and fulfilled Hancock's message. The preservation of the Bardavon in downtown Poughkeepsie was crucial to the role of the city as the cultural center of the mid-Hudson region. Both the Bardavon and the Mid-Hudson Civic Center were the two major performance venues for music, theater, and dance.

Silva established the Bardavon as a major community resource. He increased visitation from 40,000 annually when he arrived to 120,000 by the turn of the century. He scheduled high-quality performances and acts that appealed to diverse audiences who drove into the city center from the suburbs. The image of the urban downtown began to improve as a social space. Silva's efforts at rebuilding the city's image involved events where the city itself was the stage to be celebrated. He became the organizer and chief civic force behind the Hudson Arts Festival held at Waryas Park with the Hudson River as backdrop during the summer and fall, and the "Festival of Lights"—complete with fireworks—on the first Friday in December. As he recalled more than a decade later, "We created it many years ago to help bring light into the darkest time of the year and also, to help stimulate getting people down and into the city. Back then, the city was still perceived as a scary place to go."[9] He added, "The city has come a very, very, long way in that amount of time." Silva's city as theater invited both residents and visitors to become participants, not simply spectators; these events would ultimately renew the vitality of the urban core.

Throughout the 1980s and 1990s, the city and the Dutchess County Arts Council sponsored arts and food festivals designed to encourage residents and nonresidents to visit Main Mall or the waterfront. Ethnic festivals promoted exotic foods and music, while general holiday events, such as the Fourth of July celebrations, brought thousands of people to Waryas Park for fireworks displays. John Flowers, an African American community activist, organized multiracial events such as the "Olde Fashioned Easter Egg Hunt" that would bring over 2,000 children and families to Waryas Park to hunt for 14,000 eggs. Such events proved that there was safety in numbers and excitement in communal gatherings.

Besides the Bardavon, other cultural centers in the city were equally engaged in using the arts to revitalize Poughkeepsie's image. Barrett Arts Center, located in the former home of Tom Barrett, an "Ash Can" style artist of urban scenes in Poughkeepsie in the 1920s and 1930s on Noxon Street, one block from Adriance Library, held painting classes and exhibits for many years. In the 1990s, Jeep Johnson, a sculptor and Barrett's executive director, expanded the art center's efforts further into the city's revitalization efforts. A City Arts Partnership (CAP) formed to stimulate more venues in the downtown area for artists by encouraging visitation through the organization of an Art Hop linking the various venues by a "trolley" along Main Street.[10] The Barrett Clay Center would also open later in a rehabilitated building in the 400 block along upper Main Street. The city embraced the arts as essential to its redevelopment efforts, and a number of artists' studios would be built in the upper floors of rehabilitated buildings along Main Street in the twenty-first century.

Children's arts education outside the schools became integrated into Poughkeepsie's revitalization. The focus of Mill Street Loft's arts work on at-risk youth has been described in chapter 19. Another youth-empowerment organization, the Children's Media Project, began in 1994 as an extension of local arts education. Located on Academy Street south of Main Street, CMP developed videos to combat violence and drugs in local high schools, and partnered with higher education institutions in the region to study specific urban issues in Poughkeepsie. For younger children, the Children's Museum began as an effort in arts and science education by volunteers throughout the county. Located initially in empty store space in South Hills Mall in 1993, the museum moved to Poughkeepsie's waterfront eleven years later. It took up space formerly occupied by a restaurant that had restored a nineteenth-century dye works building on Water Street at the mouth of the Fall Kill. The move enabled the museum to expand its programs and exhibits; the public function of the building encouraged thousands of visitors to revise their perceptions of the city and become familiar with the waterfront as an amenity.

Increased public use of the waterfront encouraged developments among nearby restaurants. The Riverfront Restaurant Association promoted the area and registered profitable growth by the turn of the century. These restaurants, including River Station, Spanky's, and Brown Derby (renamed 91 Main), were joined by Mohoney's Irish Pub and Amici's that opened in Dooley Square, the former J. D. Johnson building at the train station, and the Grandview and Shadows, overlooking the Hudson River along the waterfront on the site of the defunct sewer treatment plant and adjacent to the former site of the De Laval plant. The Bonura family, owners and operators of the Grand Hotel in Poughkeepsie's downtown, developed the latter restaurant and catering facility.

## REVITALIZATION OF COMMUNITY THROUGH THE ARTS: HUDSON

The mid-Hudson's other riverfront cities also embraced historic preservation and the arts as an important strategy in their revitalization plans. Newburgh and Kingston focused on some architectural restoration and the development of restaurants along the riverfront, while Hudson's and Beacon's revitalization strategies centered more on the arts community.

Hudson's revitalization efforts took a small nineteenth-century city from a depressed economy in the mid-twentieth century to one based primarily on the arts in the twenty-first century. Middle-class newcomers and new investment changed the face of Hudson's main thoroughfare, Warren Street, as well as housing in many neighborhoods. Many of the neighborhoods had become severely blighted, as were many buildings on Warren Street. Most retail shops had abandoned their storefronts on Warren Street and migrated to shopping centers to the north of the city along Route 9. But the structures themselves retained particular historical resonance, indicated by their inclusion as a Historic District on the National Register of Historic Places. Numerous studies in the 1960s and 1970s suggested that Warren Street was worthy of rehabilitation and could form the core of the city's efforts at revitalization.

In the mid-1970s, Hudson's urban renewal agency enacted a facade easement program with federal funds to preserve the image of Warren Street and encouraged private investors to rehabilitate a few of the historic structures. Most investors sought to renovate the buildings for apartments, but, by the late 1980s, the storefronts began to be rented or purchased by antiques dealers for their historic ambiance and low rates.

In the 1980s, Columbia County had become a destination for Manhattanites who wanted to own a house in the country. Columbia County properties were significantly cheaper than similar countryside opportunities in rapidly exurbanizing Dutchess County. Some of these newcomers were involved in the arts, and became quite interested in the Main Street image of Hudson. By 1991, the primary use of Warren Street's storefronts was associated with antiques; for example, in a survey of eighty-seven storefronts, twenty-two were vacant while twenty-four were devoted to antiques retailing. The number of antiques dealers continued to grow and by the end of the century, more than forty antiques dealers had located on Warren Street.

The improved image of Hudson's "Main Street" resulted in a confluence of the arts at century's end. Warren Street's physical rehabilitation and economic revitalization led to a sense of community that emerged among both newcomers and old-timers. This would be tested in the twenty-first century when an international cement company proposed to construct a massive cement plant in the town on the edge of the city boundaries.

In the first years of the twenty-first century, the views from Olana and the city of Hudson were once again at the heart of a debate over the proposed construction of a massive cement plant on the border of the city in the town of Greenport. A local citizens organization called the Friends of Hudson (FOH), which together with other local citizens from the village of Claverack, the Olana Partnership, and environmental organizations such as Scenic Hudson opposed the project.

The proposed plan by St. Lawrence Cement (SLC), the second largest cement producer in the world, would have covered 1,800 acres, an area 20 percent larger than the city of Hudson. The facility itself was to have a 406-foot (forty-story) tall smokestack; the plume from the smokestack was projected to extend as far as 6 miles, while the extension of the dock area would have eliminated most of Hudson's newly renovated waterfront park.

After six years of debate by SLC and many workers in the community in favor and regional environmental and tourism organizations and local citizens in opposition, the state denied the company permits to proceed. The permit denial was based on issues of economics, heritage tourism, aesthetics, and quality of life. The changing nature of the regional economy was cited in the rejection of SLC's claims for increased industrial development. Rather, according to the state's decision, Hudson's urban planning documents promoted the city's commitment to a new economic future: "Based on this review of Hudson's past planning and implementation activities, it is clear that the City's waterfront has been and will continue to be transformed from a private industrial waterfront to a public waterfront for boating, tourism, commercial and other compatible uses. These uses are in direct competition with SLC's proposed industrial riverfront facilities."[11] SLC's proposal, in other words, was incompatible with the new economy. The decision also reflected on how the proposed industrial project would adversely affect the community's definition of its own character. Hudson's historic and cultural landscape had shaped its identity and would form the basis for its future economy.

## MAIN STREET REVITALIZATION
## AND THE ARTS: BEACON

Arts community investment in the revitalization of the city of Beacon has been the most direct of the region's cities. Dia:Beacon, a major museum of contemporary art, opened in 2003. Arts journals and major news outlets, such as the *New York Times*, wrote numerous articles that would attract thousands of visitors over the next few years to the museum, and some to shops along Main Street. The opening stimulated real estate investment in Beacon's deteriorated housing stock and Victorian Main Street. Galleries, restaurants, and other shops catering to tourists and a growing artistic population opened in formerly abandoned storefronts along Main Street. Local citizens, spurred on by local resident Pete Seeger and the Beacon affiliate of the Hudson River Sloop Clearwater environmental organization, restored a public park at Beacon Landing on the waterfront. Scenic Hudson invested in waterfront property and worked with investors planning a new housing development along the shore; the land preservation organization also worked with the city to develop a park on historic Mount Beacon.

Beacon:Dia was not alone in focusing the arts community on Beacon. Interest in older Beacon properties grew during the 1970s and 1980s. The Howland Cultural Center, like Cunneen-Hackett in Poughkeepsie, had been an important center for the arts since 1976 when it occupied the former city library on Main Street. A decade later, Tallix Foundry opened nearby as the first major fine arts investment that would become profitable and internationally known. One of their projects was a replica of Leonardo da Vinci's *Il Cavallo*, a 24-foot, 15-ton bronze sculpture of a horse that would be installed in a public park in Milan, Italy. Its production received wide news coverage, much of which introduced Beacon to a wider audience interested in the arts and urban revitalization. In the early 1990s, the film *Nobody's Fool*, from the novel of the same name by Richard Russo, starring Paul Newman and Jessica Tandy, was filmed using sites in downtown Beacon, as well as other venues in Poughkeepsie and Hudson.

At the end of the century, Dia:Beacon's purchase of the former Nabisco box factory became the major catalyst for increased real estate investment along Main Street. Leonard Riggio, CEO of Barnes & Noble and chairman of the board and "patron" of Dia:Beacon, also purchased Beacon's former high school and established the Beacon Cultural Foundation and Bulldog Studios as a collection of artists studios and cheap living units. Other newcomers purchased buildings along Main Street, adding properties to the city's tax rolls. Clara Lou Gould, mayor of Beacon, was ecstatic: "The Arts are industry, the Arts are education, the Arts are tourist destination . . . the Arts are definitely economic development. We welcome the Dia Center for the Arts to our community and look forward to the very positive impact they will have."[12]

Dia Foundation's choice of Beacon was determined by the availability of the empty Nabisco factory. Built in 1929 of concrete and steel with solid wood floors, its location next to the railroad and a Metro-North train stop was ideal, according to Michael Govan, Director of Dia:Beacon, who marveled, "Who could ask for anything more!" He added that it was the first building that he had seen "with enough space and light to do justice" to their collection.[13] Dia's collection of contemporary art by such artists as Andy Warhol, Dan Flavin, Donald Judd, Richard Serra, Robert Smithson, and others was extensive so that Govan, with major funding from Riggio, was searching for a space large enough to hold and exhibit the pieces as a permanent collection. Lee Balter, CEO of Tallix Foundry, introduced Govan to Beacon and the empty Nabisco building. Balter would later involve Minetta Brook, an arts organization headed by Diane Shamash and based in New York City that would initiate public arts projects throughout the Hudson valley.

The museum's place as a catalyst for the city's redevelopment had roots in previous urban arts-based revitalization efforts in other cities in America. Individuals in the New York arts community associated with the Dia foundation were also directly involved in the development of the Massachusetts Museum of Contemporary Art (MassMOCA). MassMOCA originated as an art museum with a specifically urban revitalization agenda in North Adams, Massachusetts, a defunct mill town and one of the poorest in the state of Massachusetts. The MassMOCA model, according to a study by the Ford Foundation, showed "how the museum's 1999 opening helped the town revive its empty Main Street and attract jobs."[14]

The revitalization of the east end of Beacon's Main Street followed the arts-based development model in the first years of the twenty-first century, although the west end languished. As described in the *Poughkeepsie Journal* in April 1999 after the opening of Dia:Beacon: "First it was the American Revolution. Then came the industrial revolution. Today, it's a cultural revolution that is leading a rebirth of the city of Beacon."[15] Beacon also received greater visibility in its revitalization efforts from the metropolitan New York arts community and the state's environmental science community. The arts organization Minetta Brook included the city as one of its sites for public art in the mid-Hudson valley with its Watershed project at Beacon Landing, while Governor Pataki chose Denning's Point as the site for the Estuaries Research Center, later named the Beacon Institute.

## PUBLIC OR PRIVATE COMMUNITY?

As the new century began, Beacon's Main Street and the main streets of Hudson and Poughkeepsie were in the process of revitalization through the combined efforts of the arts and preservation communities. Revitalization efforts also focused on the urban waterfronts. However, would public space become privatized, thus limiting public access to the Hudson River? And, would economic and social vitality return to the urban centers as well?

Economic development efforts during the twenty-first century would contend with balancing private and public access and perceptions of the aesthetic and historic landscape. Scale and function would become important issues in decisions affecting waterfront development, as indicated in the state's decision to deny a permit to construct the St. Lawrence Cement plant and associated dock facilities. Across the river in Kingston, a proposal to construct over two thousand units of residential housing would arouse similar concerns about scale and access, "complicated by the enormity of the site—more than 500 acres spanning a mile of riverfront."[16]

Along with scale and riverfront access, city residents have been concerned with housing affordability. Although increasing urban density can be a strategy to slow suburban sprawl, many of the proposals have focused on a privatized waterfront apart from the public sphere of the urban downtown. "Some of the housing proposals are so ambitious," according to a 2005 article in the *New York Times*, "that they would create villages within villages, leading to dramatic population increases and, some critics charge, a total change in the character of the towns."[17] A "New Urbanism" proposal for Newburgh's waterfront, as well as the Kingston Landing project, would present such concerns for the twenty-first century; facing the river and separated from the city's main street, how would such residential and mixed-use developments relate to the older urban core? For all the Hudson valley's riverfront communities, the future of their Main Streets and downtowns, and their very urban consciousness and history of social, economic and political centrality, would be at stake.

EPILOGUE

# Main Street Revisited

---

... story is at the heart of history. ... Stories have consequences.
If cities are seen as treasures of civilization, they will be made
treasures through cultivation. If cities are seen as degraded, they
will be made so through neglect.

—Anne Whiston Spirn, 1988

OVER THE COURSE of the twentieth century, the cities of the Hudson River
valley, like most urban areas in the Rust Belt region of the Northeastern
United States, endured deindustrialization as well as growth in the "new economy"; demographic shifts in size, socioeconomic conditions, and ethnic backgrounds; destruction of residential neighborhoods, and wholesale changes to
physical infrastructure such as transportation. Cities in the mid-Hudson
region concentrated minority populations and poverty, while economic activities in most sectors, including manufacturing such as IBM and retail such as
shopping centers, all located outside urban boundaries. New housing construction spread through the countryside as suburbs and exurbs. The perception of the cities' downtowns and main streets as central to the life and livelihoods of the region disappeared.

The cities responded with a diverse menu of strategies to halt the
decline and revitalize their cores. Urban renewal projects and Model Cities
programs had a lasting effect on the images of the cities. Cities focused on
reimagining their primary physical assets, their main streets, waterfronts,
and historic architecture, in some cases attempting to correct perceived
mistakes. While the business community focused on attracting new businesses, the city administration and the larger community focused on public safety and image and the "new economy"—the arts, historic preservation, and the environment.

FIGURE E.1. Main Street reopening, 2001

## MAIN STREET POUGHKEEPSIE

Poughkeepsie's Main Street reopened to traffic on Saturday, November 8, 2001, with a parade and ceremonial ribbon cutting. Mayor Colette Lafuente was particularly pleased, as she said, "This is the best thing that could happen. . . . This beginning is great and soon there will be more and more people down here."[1] Business owners along Main Street hoped for greater visibility and more customers, while advocates of affordable housing looked forward to more apartments in the soon-to-be restored buildings. Unlike earlier downtown developers, some now expected residential occupancy of the upper floors to come first, providing a potential clientele to attract shopkeepers to move into the ground floors. Investors saw opportunities in renting out rehabilitated storefront properties, and construction workers planned for jobs.

Hope for a new beginning for Poughkeepsie's downtown was in the air. The reopening of Main Street came just two months after the destruction of the World Trade Center in New York City. The shock waves of that day were felt throughout the nation and locally; Juan Lafuente, the husband of Poughkeepsie's mayor, was among those lost, along with a number of others from the region. As during the race riots and drug-related crime waves of the previous century, many Americans thought about the health of their cities pessimistically. Rebuilding lower Manhattan would be a sign of the nation's stature in the world; revitalizing the mid-sized cities of the Hudson valley might even be more difficult, as it would test the entire social fabric of the region and require overcoming the pessimism about urban renewal since the 1970s.

What would be the role of urban downtowns in the twenty-first century? The deindustrialization of America in the twentieth century removed the main sources of employment from the urban tax base. Each of the Hudson valley cities suffered these economic losses. Throughout the nineteenth century, the city of Poughkeepsie held all the major industries within its borders, along the waterfront and railroad on the north side. By the middle of the twentieth century, most of these industries had either died or moved out of the city where new industries, such as IBM, located. In the latter half of the twentieth century, IBM expanded to other locations in the towns of Poughkeepsie and Fishkill, along with several electronics firms and wholesale distributors, such as Gap, following the economic forces and spatial strategies of the new economy.

Retail followed suit. Poughkeepsie's Main Street was the hub of commerce from the eighteenth century, through the nineteenth century and into the first half of the twentieth century. As shopping centers and fast food retailers followed the auto-centered suburbanization of the countryside in the immediate post–World War II period, retail clusters developed along Route 9, first at South Hills Mall and later the Galleria. At the end of the twentieth century, all the department stores and mid- and high-end clothing stores had left Main Street, even as the city attempted to retain them through the construction of a pedestrian mall. Even after the reopening of Main Street in the early years of the twenty-first century, there was not a Starbucks, Barnes & Noble bookstore, or supermarket on Main Street, or anywhere nearby in the city, although all were in the town.

The decline of activity in the downtowns of America's cities severely changed their role in building and maintaining community. Reminiscences by older residents of Poughkeepsie recall the vitality of Main Street before urban renewal in the 1960s and 1970s. Personal anecdotes revealed a sense of pride in local citizenship. Much of this was lost during the latter half of the twentieth century. Urban renewal had cleared away many of the shops and neighborhoods that had been their social landscape; some recalled that their own homes, backyards, or tree-lined streets became vacant lots or arterial highways. Their personal world had been fragmented, even made unsafe; they spoke of a community that became more stratified and polarized, and of boarded-up buildings, drugs, and crime that distanced them from the physical space of the city and even their own neighborhoods. The reopening of Main Street and revitalization of the waterfront, however, rekindled hope and pride in the city for these Poughkeepsians. They remained in the city and looked forward to its future with reserved optimism. But the social landscape of the city and the county had changed.

Cities were no longer the major centers of population. The population of Poughkeepsie peaked in 1950 and declined for the rest of the twentieth century, with limited growth by 2000, once again reaching 30,000 in the first decade of the twenty-first century, although still not the height achieved during mid-century. Meanwhile, as the valley's population grew, so, too, did the minority segment as a percentage of the total population. In Dutchess County, from 1990 to 2007, the minority population increased from 12 to 23 percent of the population. Between 2000 and 2007 the Asian population increased 33 percent and the Hispanic population grew by 43.8 percent.

Demographic and socioeconomic spatial differences between cities and their hinterlands expanded. In contrast to the nineteenth century, most new European and Asian immigrants to the region preferred to live outside urban centers. The great majority of the black and Hispanic populations lived in the cities, while whites and other minorities and professionals resided in the suburbs and exurbs.

A wealth gap among households similarly grew during the latter half of the twentieth century, becoming clearly visible in its spatial distribution. Although the majority of Dutchess County households were declared middle class with household incomes between $50,000 and $200,000 in the 2000 census, they primarily lived outside the cities, while the poor and low-income households lived in urban centers. That contrast continued to cast its shadow over Poughkeepsie. Well into the twenty-first century, the Family Partnership Center continued to supplement the supplies of hundreds of families from a free food pantry while serving daily lunches to hundreds more at the Lunch Box. Beds at the Homeless Shelter remained occupied. Local churches developed programs to assist many of the unemployed as well as discuss local and national issues through a Justice for All speaker forum.

Urban and suburban areas reacted to regional shifts and continuities in society and economy. Some areas of the city changed in reputation as they did elsewhere in the nation when gentrification occurred. At the midpoint in the first decade of the twenty-first century, a turnaround in Poughkeepsie's population had begun as rentals increased in rehabilitated buildings in the Main Street corridor.

In Dutchess County, many middle-class families manifested an anti-urban bias in their perceptions of advantages and disadvantages of school districts. Schools in both Beacon and Poughkeepsie struggled with greater percentages of students who were from families grappling with complex economic and social challenges, often with English as a second language or other learning handicaps. Real estate brokers steered middle-class newcomers to housing outside city districts. Even though school taxes were higher and children endured long trips on school buses as they commuted to school, college-trained parents focused on the social and cultural differences associated with place and community and chose homogeneity over diversity.

Of course, not all housing choices reflected concern over schooling. The majority of housing units in the cities predate World War II. Newer single-family homes on larger lots would be found in the suburbs or exurbs. Also, shopping was closer to the auto-centered suburban residences, and images of high crime rates in urban areas persisted. For these and other reasons, population growth in the mid-Hudson resulted in sprawl. By the early years of the twenty-first century, the population of Dutchess County reached over 290,000; almost all the growth was in the southern towns encompassing IBM, shopping malls, and proximity to the Taconic Parkway.

Social and administrative services remained clustered in city centers. Poughkeepsie, as the capital of Dutchess County, retained the urban functions in legal affairs, banking, and government. Not-for-profit organizations also clustered in the urban centers. The postindustrial economy has increased work in the service sector and urban land uses have followed that trend. Unfortunately for the urban tax base, these organizations and agencies do not pay property taxes and they place additional burdens on the cities for police, fire, and physical infrastructure. Similar disparities occur throughout the region between urban and suburban school districts, whereas cultural institutions, such as the Bardavon in Poughkeepsie and UPAC in Kingston as well as a host of art galleries, music venues, and restaurants maintain the role of cities as centers of culture and the arts.

The cities of the mid-Hudson region turned to the arts as a major feature of their Main Street revitalization strategies. New York State Assemblyman Kevin Cahill of Kingston commented on the growth of galleries, theaters, clubs, and restaurants in the downtowns of Kingston, Beacon, Hudson, and Poughkeepsie, as he factored in their economic impact, "I don't make a distinction between arts and commerce—I think they are one and the same," he said. "In Woodstock, arts were integral to the founding of the community. It's easy to talk about the arts in Woodstock—there's no disconnect. People don't necessarily see their importance in Kingston. But as a post-industrial river town, Kingston needs the arts. While IBM may be gone, there is a new IBM in Kingston—the arts community."[2]

FIGURE E.2. Main Street mural, painted by Franc Palaia, c. 2002

In Poughkeepsie, the reopening of Main Street led to a great deal of investment in the many buildings that had been abandoned during the Main Mall era. Over seventy retail, restaurant, and service businesses opened in the years following reopening of the street to two-way traffic, sales tax revenues increased, and apartments were rented. The city invested some public funds in lighting and streetscape beautification as well as locating a new public safety building in the middle of the often crime-infested 400 block.

Many of the buildings along Main Street had deteriorated to such a degree that rehabilitation was questionable, yet creative entrepreneurs in construction and real estate took on the challenges. The roof and floors of the Luckey, Platt building had collapsed during years of neglect, but the building was rebuilt, leaving its historic facade intact facing onto Main Street. Abandoned mills and factories along the Fall Kill were planned as new apartments, including the former Poughkeepsie Underwear Factory on White Street between Main Street and the westbound arterial. Close to the waterfall at the mouth of the Fall Kill, the Pelton mill building on Mill Street across from Mount Carmel Church was gentrified into new apartments, while similar plans were made for the Piano factory on Water Street across from the Children's Museum.

Revitalization of Main Street paralleled efforts along Poughkeepsie's waterfront with the opening of the Children's Museum, enhancement of Waryas Park with a music pavilion and a walkway along the shore as part of the greenway trail, and the opening of a restaurant and catering facility on the site of the former sewage treatment plant. After years of negotiation between various developers and the city over proposals to develop formerly industrial waterfront properties that had been cleared by urban renewal, such as the De Laval factory, Joseph Bonura, Sr., owner of the Grand Hotel in the city's downtown, proposed a plan for a restaurant and catering facility that met many of the economic needs and architectural and landscaping priorities acceptable to the community. The businesses opened with great fanfare during the winter of 2006–2007.

## REGIONAL CONNECTIONS TO NEW YORK METROPOLITAN AREA

Reopening Main Street to traffic was an important phase of the city's transportation strategy. The beginning of the twenty-first century also saw the restoration of the train station, making a walkway from Main Street and locating a bus terminal to create a multipurpose transit station. Metro-North also completed the construction of a three-story parking garage as well as many more parking spaces along nearby Rinaldi Boulevard. Retail businesses opened up next to the train station in Dooley Square, the former J. D. Johnson plumbing supply building.

FIGURE E.3. Aerial view of Poughkeepsie waterfront, c. 2002

Commuting from Dutchess County to Westchester County and the New York metropolitan area increased throughout the 1990s, both by automobile and by train. By the beginning of the twenty-first century, over 39,000 workers commuted to jobs outside the county. Ridership on Metro-North doubled from 1985 to 1994 and doubled again a decade later. The Dutchess County workforce increasingly commuted to jobs outside the county, particularly to work in sectors, such as finance and service, of the new economy. External forces suggested that the area was becoming a bedroom community, while efforts within the business and education communities promoted a "Tech Valley." Within the county, IBM remained the single most important firm, employing over 10,000 on average from 1995 to 2006, topping 11,000 in 2007, while a clustering of firms developing innovative technologies, including nanotechnology, located in the valley from Westchester County northward to Albany.

Population growth in the mid-Hudson region increased dramatically after the events of September 11, 2001. Many New York City residents decided to move out of Manhattan apartments to single-family homes in rural and semirural towns in Orange, Ulster, Dutchess, and Columbia counties. Some converted the "summer homes" they had purchased prior to 9/11 into primary residences, while others sought contemporary homes in new subdivisions. A landscape of sprawl emerged with the new houses built on large lots in former farmlands or orchards, and households with two or more vehicles. Most kept their jobs in the city and commuted by auto, train, or bus, although as gasoline prices increased sharply in 2008, many stayed at home working electronically and traveling to the city only once or twice a week.

Work was not the only tie that brought residents of the outer ring of mid-Hudson counties into closer connection with inner ring suburban counties such as Westchester County and New York City. High-end retail shopping concentrated in the city as well as a few major suburban shopping malls, and the cultural and arts venues for music, theater, and museums remained powerful draws for the former cosmopolites. New York City newspapers, such as the *New York Times*, had a significant circulation and were sold in local groceries alongside regional newspapers such as the *Poughkeepsie Journal*. Major television networks were based in New York City, although AM radio continued as important sources of local communication. On FM, national public radio station WAMC broadcast from Albany through affiliates throughout the mid-Hudson.

The primary regional economic and social connectivity was south toward New York City and the New York metropolitan area. To the north, Albany and the capital district also exerted influence on the mid-Hudson. State policies and finances impacted school districts, infrastructure, and economic development in all the counties, although Albany and its services offered little more than counties to the south. The majority of the region's air travelers used airports in the New York metropolitan area rather than Albany, even as the regional airport at Stewart in Newburgh struggled to become a fourth major airport in the greater New York area alongside Newark, LaGuardia, and JFK. For Poughkeepsians, the mid-Hudson valley region was interconnected with and interdependent on the greater New York metropolitan area. The plans and ideas of Lewis Mumford and the RPA in the 1930s and 1940s had evolved into an interconnected regional network by the beginning of the twenty-first century. Yet consciousness of a four-county region still prevailed in countryside and modest urban centers.

## URBAN CORE REVITALIZATION

The perception of Poughkeepsie as a vital center of activity improved after the opening of Main Street and other major thoroughfares such as Hamilton Street to two-way traffic. Pedestrian traffic also increased as did use of Waryas Park, with its skateboard park and the Children's Museum at the waterfront. When Colette Lafuente was elected mayor in 1997, she focused much of her mayoralty on controlling crime in the city. By the end of her term in 2003, the crime rate had substantially decreased; this was in line with other cities, such as New York, and resulted in the overcrowding of the many state prisons scattered around the Hudson valley, as well as the Dutchess County jail located on North Hamilton Street in Poughkeepsie. This prison population was overwhelmingly black, Latino, and poor, and with the closing down of the Hudson River Psychiatric Hospital many have been incarcerated with severe mental health problems.

With Main Street reopened and criminal activity diminished, citizen efforts in the preservation of the city's historic fabric refocused interest on the visual image of the urban core. Lafuente's successor as mayor, Nancy Cozean, promoted the preservation and restoration of the city's historic architecture as a marketing strategy to encourage new business investment. Street trees and parks offered visual renewal to the urban scene. However, the unhappy legacy of much urban renewal demolition during the 1960s and 1970s remained visible just behind Main Street in the vast parking lot next to the west arterial and in the empty spaces between the formerly continuous physical fabric of once fashionable Mill Street, now occupied mostly by professional offices. On upper Main Street, the city developed an infill strategy with the construction of a safety building housing special units of the police department focused on community and neighborhood concerns.

Hudson Valley communities promoted their own and the region's historic resources in their efforts in social and economic development. Heritage tourism promised to be a new engine of economic growth in the twenty-first century, balanced with "clean" high-value-added industries, such as IBM and similar high-technology firms. The region's economic future would be dependent on

assuring that the cultural and natural landscape presented a pattern of sustain-
ability and harmony. But that hope faced the relentless challenge of new residential subdivisions as developers followed the usual preference of Americans
for their own private lot and freestanding house. Sprawl remained king
throughout Dutchess County, swallowing up hamlets and villages as it progressed. In a 2007 study, a "predominance of single-family homes," on large lots
"in isolation," of "larger homes that house smaller families," and auto-depen-
dent, led to increased travel time to work and "fewer options" for shopping,
"civic services and other community amenities."[3] Also, early in the twenty-first-
century, cleanup of the Hudson River and its shoreline led to a boom in housing developments. Public access to the river would again be threatened. As an
editorial in the *New York Times* in 2005 remarked with concern: "Rescuing the
riverbank from polluting factories only to seal it off again with endless acres of
ill-planned luxury housing would be the hollowest of victories."[4]

The Storm King battle in the 1960s and 1970s presaged other environmental struggles between the industrial and postindustrial economies. The final deci-

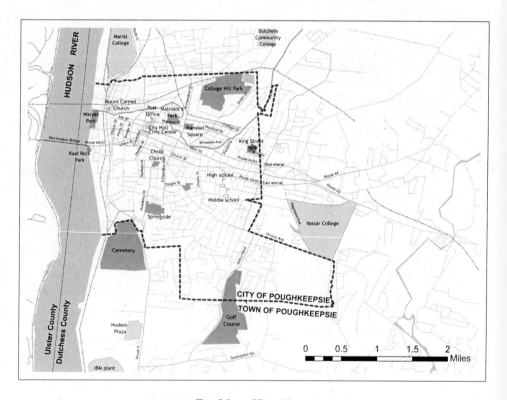

FIGURE E.4. Map of Poughkeepsie, 2007

sions that led to the cancellation of the hydropower plant on Storm King Mountain were based on the environmental impacts of the project on the mountain, in the Hudson River, and to the aesthetic landscape. The appeals court also admitted testimony by citizen groups not directly affected economically by the proposal. Proposals to construct major industrial complexes later in the century and in the twenty-first century, such as the planned massive cement plant near Hudson, met with similar defeat. Permit denials would be based on the inability of the potential developers to sufficiently mitigate unacceptable environmental impacts, such as on the views from Olana, or recognize that economic development and urban revitalization in the Hudson Valley was in a postindustrial era.

FIGURE E.5. Fireworks at Waryas Park on the waterfront, c. 2005

## THE VALLEY'S MAIN STREETS

The social and economic plans of the cities of the Hudson River Valley reflected the twenty-first-century demands of the new economy. Heritage tourism and high-technology linkages between IBM and affiliated firms from Westchester County north to Albany would frame the region's economic development. Quality-of-life issues included hopes of improving the valley's social and physical environment and a reenvisioning of the urban realm.

In an age of sprawl, reviving Main Street might consolidate community, at least for those residents drawn to its new cultural and artistic offerings. Increasing residential density could also begin to address national issues involving energy and climate. However, like other American cities and small towns that have transformed their main streets into specialized retail and service centers, Main Street seemed less likely to attract the throngs of shoppers from every social class that figure in the reminiscences of long-time residents recalling downtown Poughkeepsie in the early and mid-twentieth century.

Nonetheless, the many small-scale changes to the streetscape and the social and economic life of the city's downtown, such as a weekly farmers' market, bistro, and artists' studios, could be seen as evidence of a reemergence of a sense of place. "With new shops opening, people are returning to the city," touted the *Poughkeepsie Journal* two years after the reopening of Main Street.[5] But, according to Naomi Goldberg, who with her husband owned two card and variety shops on Main Street from 1958 to 2007, the success of the city depended on "a total package, including developing the waterfront and providing transportation to businesses uptown to make the city a destination place."[6]

In the twenty-first century, Main Street's revival would be influenced by changes in the region's economy and demography. Regional shifts in economic and cultural resources would affect the images of the cities. The question for the twenty-first century for each city, whether Beacon, Newburgh, Kingston, Hudson, or Poughkeepsie, would be whether their efforts to regain their historic sense of place, and of centrality for the region's political, economic, social, and cultural life would succeed. Whatever the answer to that question, the previous history of the region and its cities made it probable that they would be adapting to major change in their future as they had in the past.

# Notes

## CHAPTER ONE. THE VALLEY SETTING

1. Wallace Bruce, *The Hudson River by Daylight* (New York, 1884), 40.

2. James Fenimore Cooper (1823) quoted in Roland Van Zandt, "The Setting," in Bonnie Marranca, *A Hudson Valley Reader* (Woodstock, NY, 1991), 260.

3. Harriet Martineau (1835), quoted in Roland Van Zandt, *Chronicles of the Hudson: Three Centuries of Travelers' Accounts* (New Brunswick, NJ, 1971), 217.

4. Jacquetta M. Haley, ed., *Pleasure Grounds: Andrew Jackson Downing and Montgomery Place* (Tarrytown, NY, 1988), 11.

5. Klara Sauer, "Protecting Landscape Is Our Destiny," *The Hudson Valley: Our Heritage, Our Future*, edited by Margaretta Downey (Poughkeepsie, NY, 2000), 127.

6. Henry Cassidy, "Francis Rombout and the Early Settlement of Dutchess County," in Joyce Ghee, Melodye Kaltz, William McDermott, Richard Wiles, eds., *Transformations of an American County: Dutchess County, New York, 1683–1983* (Poughkeepsie, NY, 1986), 23.

7. Ibid., 8.

8. R. K. McGregor, "Settlement Variation and Cultural Adaptation in the Immigration History of Colonial New York," *New York History*, 73 (April 1992), 194.

9. Martin Bruegel, *Farm, Shop, Landing: The Rise of a Market Society in the Hudson Valley, 1780–1860* (Durham, NC, 2002), 23.

10. Martha Collins Bayne, *County at Large* (Poughkeepsie, NY, 1937), 55.

11. Michael Groth, "Laboring for Freedom in Dutchess County," in Myra Armstead, ed., *Mighty Change, Tall Within: Black Identity in the Hudson Valley* (Albany, NY, 2003), 62.

12. "Diary of Vincent Morgan Townsend, 1812–1896, Clapp Hill, LaGrange" (Typescript, Local History Room, Adriance Library), 1–2 (December 26–27, 1833).

13. D. W. Meinig, "Geography of Expansion, 1785–1855," in John Thompson, *Geography of New York State* (Syracuse, NY, 1966), 169.

## CHAPTER TWO. POUGHKEEPSIE
## GROWS FROM VILLAGE TO CITY

1. Cynthia Kerner, "Patrician Womanhood in the Early Republic: The 'Reminiscences' of Janet Livingston Montgomery," *New York History*, 73 (October 1992), 391.

2. Quoted in Carl Carmer, *The Hudson* (New York, 1939), 163.

3. Michael Groth, *Forging Freedom in the Mid-Hudson Valley: The End of Slavery and the Formation of a Free African American Community in Dutchess County, New York* (Ann Arbor, 2002), 293–294.

4. Quoted in Daniel Klein and John Majewski, "Plank Road Fever in Antebellum America: New York State Origins," *New York History*, 75 (1994), 57–58.

5. Collegiate student quoted in *Dutchess County Historical Society Yearbook*, 36 (1951), 47.

6. Mary Amesbury, "Political Nativism in Dutchess County from 1845–1848" (Vassar College, senior thesis, 1957), 53–54.

7. Clyde and Sally Griffen, *Natives and Newcomers: The Ordering of Opportunity in Mid-Nineteenth-Century Poughkeepsie* (Cambridge, Mass., 1978), 29.

8. Ibid., 44.

9. Edmund Platt, *The Eagle's History of Poughkeepsie from the Earliest Settlements 1683 to 1905* (Poughkeepsie, NY, 1905), 143.

10. *Poughkeepsie Daily Eagle*, March 23, 1879.

11. Griffen, *Natives and Newcomers*, 175.

12. Ibid., 35.

13. O. E. David, "Gail Borden," in the History section of the Borden, Inc. Web site.

## CHAPTER THREE. IMPROVEMENTS AND CONFLICTS
## IN THE LATE NINETEENTH CENTURY

1. Clyde Griffen, "Matthew Vassar," *American National Biography*, 22 (New York, 1999), 284.

2. Platt, *Eagle's History*, 193.

3. Ibid., 208.

4. Griffen, *Natives and Newcomers*, 1.

5. Wilson Poucher, "Poughkeepsie's Water Supply, 1799–1923," *Dutchess County Historical Society Yearbook*, 27 (1942), 66.

6. Platt, *Eagle's History*, 237–39.

7. American Guide Series, *Dutchess County* (Philadelphia, 1937), 36–37.

8. Ibid., 42.

9. Ibid., 154.

10. *A Tale of Fifty Years: Luckey, Platt & Co., 1869–1919* (Poughkeepsie, NY, 1919), 15.

11. *Poughkeepsie Daily Eagle*, July 17 and July 23, 1877.

12. Griffen, *Natives and Newcomers*, 39.

13. *Poughkeepsie Daily Eagle*, January 18, 1862, and August 31, 1863.

14. Clyde Griffen, ed., *New Perspectives on Poughkeepsie's Past* (Poughkeepsie, NY, 1988), 137.

15. *Poughkeepsie Daily Eagle*, April 2, 1877.

16. Vincent Scully, *American Architecture and Urbanism* (New York, 1969), 88.

17. Letter from Church to fellow Hudson valley artist Erastus Dow Palmer in 1884, quoted in David C. Huntington, *The Landscapes of Frederic Edwin Church: Vision of an American Era* (NY, 1966), 116; James Anthony Ryan, "Frederic Church's Olana: Architecture and Landscape as Art," in Franklin Kelly, ed., *Frederic Edwin Church* (Washington, DC, 1989), 147; and Robert M. Toole, "The Art of the Landscape Gardener: Frederic Church at Olana," in *The Hudson River Valley Review*, 21, 1 (Autumn 2004), 58.

## CHAPTER FOUR. THE CITYSCAPE AT THE TURN OF THE TWENTIETH CENTURY

1. Edward Hagaman Hall, ed., *The Hudson-Fulton Celebration 1909* (The Fourth Annual Report of the Hudson-Fulton Celebration Commission to the Legislature of the State of New York.), Vol. II (Albany, NY, 1910), 950.

2. Ibid., 943, 941. Also, "Immense Crowd at Hudson-Fulton Religious Exercises," *Poughkeepsie Daily Eagle*, October 4, 1909, and "Hudson-Fulton Celebration Here a Bright Page in City's History," ibid., October 5, 1909. See also: James L. Lumb, "The Big Parade," *Dutchess County Historical Society Yearbook*, 69 (1979), 98–111.

3. *Poughkeepsie Sunday New Yorker*, October 3, 1954. Also, Charles Benjamin, "Poughkeepsie Horse Cars," *DCHS Yearbook*, 70 (1985), 59–64.

4. Francis Goldsmith, "Poughkeepsie Trolley Ride" (5 page mss, April 1956) in Adriance Memorial Library Local History Room.

5. *Poughkeepsie Journal*, May 28, 1950.

6. Jeanne B. Opdycke, *City of Poughkeepsie Walking & Driving Guide* (Poughkeepsie, NY, 1977), 8.

7. William B. Rhoads, "Poughkeepsie's Architectural Styles, 1835–1940: Anarchy or Decorum?" in Griffen, ed., *New Perspectives*, 30.

8. *National Register Inventory* forms for Luckey, Platt and Platt, *Eagle's History*, 206, located in Dutchess County Department of Planning Library.

9. Helen Thompson, *A Report of a Housing Survey in the City of Poughkeepsie* (Poughkeepsie, NY, 1919), 6.

10. *Poughkeepsie Evening Star and Enterprise*, July 18, 1928.

11. Quoted in Opdycke, *Guide*, 23.

12. Thompson, *Housing Survey*, 21–22.

13. Sandra Piotti Ponte, "The Catholic Church and the Southern Italian Immigrant" (American Culture senior thesis, Vassar College), 198.

14. Opdycke, *Guide*, 53.

15. Quoted in ibid., 52–53.

16. Helen Wilkinson Reynolds, ed., *The Records of Christ Church, Poughkeepsie, New York* (Poughkeepsie, NY, 1911),

17. Rhoads, "Poughkeepsie's Architectural Styles," 30.

18. Platt, *Eagle's History*, 260, and *National Register* records.

## CHAPTER FIVE. A NEW WAVE OF IMMIGRANTS CHANGES THE CITIZENRY

1. Louis Zuccarello, "The Catholic Community in Poughkeepsie 1870–1900: The Period of Testing," in Griffen, ed., *New Perspectives*, 112.

2. Sandra Piotti Ponte, "The Catholic Church and the Southern Italian Immigrant." (American Culture senior thesis, Vassar College, 1989), 200. See also "Italians to Celebrate Mt. Carmel Feast," *Poughkeepsie Enterprise*, June 6, 1912.

3. Ponte, "Southern Italian Immigrant," 207.

4. Tony di Rosa, *El Pibe* (Buenos Aires, 1991), 75.

5. Ponte, "Southern Italian Immigrant," 195.

6. Quoted in Zuccarello, "Catholic Community," 107.

7. Christine Chiu, "Polish Community in Poughkeepsie" (Vassar College, history essay, 1986), 28.

8. Ibid., 29.

9. Ibid., 18.

10. Ibid., 26.

11. Eva Goldin, *The Jewish Community of Poughkeepsie, New York: An Anecdotal History* (Poughkeepsie, NY, 1982), 137–38 on the Rosenthals.

12. *Annual Report of the Executive Secretary of the Women's City and County Club* (May 23, 1921), 10–11. Local History Room, Adriance Library.

13. Speaking at an Italian dinner, their cosmopolitan college president, Henry Noble MacCracken, worried about the effects of federal legislation restricting immigration.

14. Michael Schroeder, "The Dutchess County Defense Council (April 1917 to November 1920)" (Vassar College, history senior thesis, 1982), 12.

15. *Poughkeepsie Eagle-News*, July 28, 1924.

16. Lawrence H. Mamiya and Patricia A. Karouma, eds., *For Their Courage and For Their Struggles* (The Black Oral History Project of Poughkeepsie, NY, 1978), 51, 59.

17. Ibid., 48.

18. Tom Buggy, *Golf's Lady of the Hudson: A Centennial History of Dutchess Golf and Country Club* (Basking Ridge, NJ, 1998), 12.

19. Ibid., 67.

20. Printed announcements for the Tennis Club's Vaudeville Night, November 27, 1916. Adriance Library.

## CHAPTER SIX. MUNICIPAL REFORM
## AND URBAN PLANNING

1. Platt, *Eagle's History*, 260.

2. Ellen M. Litwicki, *America's Public Holidays, 1865–1920* (Washington, DC, 2000), 194. Also, Robert Haven Schauffler, *Arbor Day* (New York, 1909), 8; and John Bodnar, *Remaking America: Public Memory, Commemoration, and Patriotism in the Twentieth Century* (Princeton, 1952).

3. *Poughkeepsie Eagle*, April 10, 1897.

4. Quoted in Nicholas Adams and Bonnie Smith, eds., *History and the Texture of Modern Life: Selected Essays, Lucy Maynard Salmon* (Philadelphia, 2001), 8.

5. From "Main Street" in ibid., 89.

6. Ibid., 16–17.

7. New York *Evening Post*, January 11, 1905. See also Miss Salmon's undated typescript, "Do It for Poughkeepsie," no doubt created for the 1911 "Cleanup Campaign" in Salmon papers, Special Collections, Vassar College Library.

8. See especially Folders 57:10, 57:11, and 57:13 in the Salmon Papers.

9. See Miss Salmon's book of clippings, 1902–1908, in Salmon papers, her scrapbook of clippings from the Poughkeepsie *Daily Eagle* for 1898–1904 in Poughkeepsie Document Box, Local History Room, Adriance Memorial Library, Poughkeepsie, NY.

10. *The Enterprise*, October 25, 1906.

11. Ibid., October 27, 1906.

12. *Sunday Courier*, June 9, 1912.

13. Letter from "Poughkeepsian" in the *Daily Eagle* (undated clipping in 1902–1908 scrapbook).

14. *The Enterprise*, November 9, 1906.

15. Ibid., March 16, 1916.

16. Ibid., April 7, 1908.

17. See Salmon's clipping from the *New York Tribune*, July 19, 1908, on Nolen's plan for beautification of Montclair, New Jersey. Also, Jon Teaford, *The Twentieth-Century American City* (2nd edition, Baltimore, 1993), 67–68.

18. "Main Street" in Adams and Smith, eds., *History*, 90–91.

19. *Daily Eagle*, May 11, 1908.

20. New York *Evening Post*, November 4, 1908.

21. Untitled and undated clipping reporting Miss Salmon's talk to the YWCA in the 1902–1908 Scrapbook.

22. *Daily Eagle*, October 3, 1908.

23. See the printed handout dated January 17, 1907, for the conferences on city affairs, and Salmon's notes on representation of local organizations at the conferences. Salmon Papers.

24. Howard Platt of the Chamber of Commerce to Salmon, April 28, 1910. Louise Fargo Brown, *Apostle of Democracy: The Life of Lucy Maynard Salmon* (New York, 1943), 210–12.

25. *Evening Enterprise*, July 14, 1914.

26. Poughkeepsie *Eagle*, March 2, 1909.

27. *Eagle-News*, June 9, 1916.,

28. Eva Boice, "Woman Suffrage, Vassar College, and Laura Johnson Wylie," *The Hudson River Valley Review*, 20 (Spring 2004), 42.

29. Ibid., 43.

30. Women's City and County Club, *Annual Report for 1921*, 4–5. Adriance Library.

31. Ibid., 8.

32. Ibid., 7.

33. *Summary of Undertakings and Accomplishments of the Poughkeepsie Chamber of Commerce, March 1918.* Courtesy of Jonah Sherman, from his collection of materials on the city's history.

34. *A Plan for the Improvement and Extension of Poughkeepsie, New York: Prepared by Myron Howard West and Staff of the American Park Builders* (Chicago, 1924), 15–16.

35. Nancy Mack, "Poughkeepsie: A Case Study of Planning and Zoning in the 1920s (Vassar College, history senior thesis, 1983), 65, 48.

## CHAPTER SEVEN. CHANGES TO THE
## SPACE ECONOMY BETWEEN THE WARS

1. Carolyn Burke, *Lee Miller: A Life* (New York, 2005), 9.

2. Elizabeth Carter, "Special Report: Bridging the Hudson," *Poughkeepsie Journal*, August 23, 1980, 1.

3. William R. Corwine, "Historical Sketch of the Events Leading Up to the Building of the Mid-Hudson Bridge at Poughkeepsie, New York." Poughkeepsie, NY, 1925 (mss Adriance Library collection).

4. "Poughkeepsie—Highland Bridge Opening Celebration Committee" flyer, August 19, 1930 (Adriance Library collection).

5. "15,000 Persons Attend Dedication of New Bridge," *Poughkeepsie Eagle-News*, August 26, 1930, 1. Photographs from Franklin Delano Roosevelt Library reprinted in *Poughkeepsie Journal*, August 23, 1980, 3; and Joyce C. Ghee and Joan Spence, *Poughkeepsie: Halfway Up the Hudson* (Dover, NH, 1997), 34.

6. "Opening Celebration—Woodcliff Pleasure Park," advertisement in *Poughkeepsie Eagle-News*, August 25, 1930.

7. Elizabeth Carter. op. cit. 1.

8. *Poughkeepsie Eagle-News* (August 26, 1930), 2.

9. "The Vision Is Realized," *Poughkeepsie Eagle-News*, August 25, 1930, 6.

10. "The New Bridge," *Sunday Courier*, August 24, 1930, 6.

11. Quoted in Robert O. Binnewies, *Palisades: 100,000 Acres in 100 Years* (New York, 2001), 144. Further information on construction and finances in Henry J. Stanton, "Hudson Spans Rise in Homage to Car," *The Hudson Valley: Our Heritage, Our Future* (Poughkeepsie, NY, 2000), 142,

12. "Freeways Are Now Urged," *New York Times*, December 13, 1936.

13. Binnewies, op. cit., 235; he continued: "The parkway is a design success, living up to expectations that a major roadway could be constructed in a manner that rested gently on the land, presenting motorists with a green corridor looping along the contours of rolling terrain, passing under stone bridges of elegant style, meandering through a linear park of trees and flowers, avoiding the typical recipes for road building that too often result in dull troughs."

14. *Westchester County Park Commission Report, 1931*, quoted in "Taconic State Parkway: Historic Overview," http://www.nycroads.com/roads/taconic.

15. Taconic State Park Commission brochure on opening of parkway extension to Dutchess-Columbia County line (October 17, 1949), reprinted in Robert Moses, *Public Works: A Dangerous Trade* (New York, 1970), 140.

16. Martha Collins Bayne, *County at Large* (Poughkeepsie, NY, 1937), 49.

17. *Sunday Courier*, editorial, June 11, 1939.

18. Henry Noble MacCracken, "Vassar's Social Laboratory," *Vassar Alumnae Magazine*, vol. 26, no. 4 (March, 1941), 6.

19. "200,000 to be in City Today," *Poughkeepsie Eagle-News*, June 10, 1939, 14.

20. William B. Rhoads, "Poughkeepsie's Architectural Styles 1835–1940: Anarchy or Decorum?" in Griffen, ed., *New Perspectives on Poughkeepsie's Past*, 33.

21. Quoted in Cynthia M. Koch and Lynn A. Bassanese, "Roosevelt and His Library," in Nancy Fogel, ed., *FDR at Home* (Poughkeepsie, NY, 2005), 97.

22. Editorial, *Beacon News*, October 14, 1937, 4, quoted in Bernice L.Thomas, *The Stamp of FDR: NewDeal Post Offices in the Mid-Hudson Valley* (Fleischmanns, NY, 2002), 13.

23. As reported in the *New York Times*, November 3, 1936 and quoted in William B. Rhoads, "The President and the Sesquicentennial of the Constitution: Franklin Roosevelt's Monument in Poughkeepsie," *New York History*, 71, 3 (July 1990), 320.

24. Ibid., 321.

25. Rhoads, "Poughkeepsie's Architectural Styles," op. cit., 32.

26. Kevin Gallagher, "The President as Local Historian," *New York History*, 54, 2 (April 1983), 152.

27. Copy of March 14, 1946 letter in Frederick A. Smith collection, FDR Library. See also "Hyde Park Proposed as Site for United Nations Home," *New York Post*, September 18, 1945, 5.

## CHAPTER EIGHT. BUSINESS AND LABOR IN THE 1920s AND 1930s

1. Mabel Newcomer, "The Little Businessman: A Study of Business Proprietors in Poughkeepsie, New York," *Business History Review*, (1961), 487.

2. Fitchett Brothers' handbill, titled "Opening Tomorrow: The Mid-Hudson Area's Most Modern Dairy Plant," Fitchett family papers.

3. M. V. Fuller, "The Rejuvenation of Poughkeepsie" *The American City*, 4 (January 1911), 4.

4. Poughkeepsie Eagle, *50th Anniversary Edition*, June 1911, 2 and passim.

5. Florence Brewer, *Choosing an Occupation: The Kinds of Work That Are Open to Women in Poughkeepsie* (Poughkeepsie, NY, 1910), 33.

6. *Poughkeepsie Eagle*, March 4, 1903.

7. Schatz Company Scrapbooks, Adriance Library. The first scrapbook is titled "Federal: S & Co. News, 1918 to 1945." P. 2 is a copy of a typescript page titled "Labor Day Program—1903: The Separator Company Troubles.

8. Ibid.

9. Ibid.

10. *Poughkeepsie Eagle*, April 4, 1927.

11. *The Truth*, January 7, 1927.

12. *Sunday Courier*, January 9, 1927.

13. Editorial, *Poughkeepsie Daily Eagle*, February 18, 1910.

14. Martha Collins Bayne, *County at Large* (Poughkeepsie, NY, 1937), 22, 80.

15. Mamiya and Karouma, *For Their Courage and For Their Struggles*, 32.

16. Peter Edman, "A History of the Curriculum in the Poughkeepsie City School District, 1843–1929," *Dutchess County Historical Society Yearbook*, 70 (1985), 90.

17. Robert and Helen Lynd, *Middletown* (New York, 1929), 170.

18. Bayne, *County at Large*, 21–22.

19. Ibid., 21.

20. Henry Noble MacCracken, *Blithe Dutchess: The Flowering of an American County from 1812* (New York, 1958), 205.

21. R. G. and A. R. Hutchinson and Mabel Newcomer, "A Study in Business Mortality: Length of Life of Business Enterprises in Poughkeepsie, New York, 1843–1936," *American Economic Review*, 27 (September 1938), 510.

22. Clipping dated April 24, 1939, in Schatz Federal Bearing Scrapbook, Vol. 1.

23. *Poughkeepsie Sunday New Yorker*, January 16, 1944.

24. *Highland News*, December 2, 1945.

25. Clipping dated November 16, 1945, in Schatz Federal Bearing Scrapbook, Vol. 1.

26. Interview with Jesse Effron, Decenber 16, 2003.

## CHAPTER NINE. DEPRESSION IN FDR'S HOME COUNTY

1. Ronald Samuelson, "Newspaper Coverage of the Great Depression and the New Deal in Dutchess County, New York: The Election of 1932 and the Hundred Days" (Vassar College, history senior thesis, 1992), 12.

2. *Industrial Survey of the City of Poughkeepsie, Poughkeepsie Chamber of Commerce, 1930*, 38.

3. Jack Lippmann, "The Depression Comes to Poughkeepsie, 1930–1936," *Dutchess County Historical Society Yearbook* (1981), 95.

4. Ibid., 97.

5. Ibid., 100.

6. Ibid., 98.

7. Ibid.

8. Ibid., 102.

9. *Poughkeepsie Eagle-News*, December 21, 1931.

10. Lippmann, "Depression," 117.

11. Samuelson, "Newspaper Coverage," 5.

12. "Modernize Main Street," *Architectural Forum* (July 1935), 51; noted in Hans Wirz and Richard Striner, *Washington Deco: Art Deco Design in the Nation's Capitol* (Washington, DC, 1984), 71.

13. Quoted from *52 Designs to Modernize Main Street with Glass* in Alison Isenberg, *Downtown America: A History of the Place and the People Who Made It* (Chicago, 2004), 146.

14. Ada Louise Huxtable, *Architecture Anyone? Cautionary Tales of the Building Art* (Berkeley, 1986), 313–15; originally published as "The Death of the Five-and-Ten," in the *New York Times*, November 8, 1979.

15. Jean Maddern Pitrone, *F. W. Woolworth and the American Five and Dime* (Jefferson, NC, 2003), 193.

16. *American Guide*, op. cit., 37.

17. Martha Collins Bayne, *County at Large*, (Poughkeepsie, NY, 1937), 173.

18. Pete Bergamo, "Paramount Memories (Redux)," *Marquee: The Journal of the Theatre Historical Society*, 36, 2 (Second Quarter 2004), 11–12.

19. Quoted in Annon Adams, "Juliet Theatre: A Rags to Riches Story," *Marquee*, 36, 2 (Second Quarter 2004), 4.

20. Bernard Weisberger, a memoir in four extended e-mails, 2003.

21. David Montgomery, "The Poughkeepsie Regatta, 1895–1915" (Vassar College, history senior thesis, 1990), 40.

22. Ibid., 35.

23. "New York Excursionists Riot at Woodcliff Park," *Poughkeepsie Eagle-News*, August 11, 1941, 1.

24. Ibid.

25. Allen Weinreb, "Staatsburgh: The History of the Lewis-Livingston-Mills Estate" (draft, August 1999).

26. Bayne, *County at Large*, 64.

27. Ibid., 63.

28. Henry Noble MacCracken, *Blithe Dutchess: The Flowering of an American County from 1812* (New York, 1958), 147.

29. Bayne, *County at Large*, 58.

30. Ibid., 60,

31. Clipping dated November 15, 1939, in Schatz Federal Bearing Scrapbook, Vol. 1.

## CHAPTER TEN. TECHNOLOGICAL REVOLUTION TRANSFORMS THE REGION: IBM

1. MacCracken, *Blithe Dutchess*, 204.

2. "Civic Conference Notebook" (1943), Adriance Memorial Library.

3. Songs #5 and #67 in IBM, *Songs of the I. B. M.* (1931 edition), 6, 29.

4. Typescript of interview with Charles Lawson in Naples, Florida, February 2002, 3–5.

5. Katherine Fishman, *The Computer Establishment* (New York, 1981), 80.

6. Julia Kennedy, "IBM in Dutchess County: A Postwar History of Prosperity" (Vassar College, history senior thesis, 1995), 31.

7. IBM, *Thirty Years of Management Briefings, 1958–1988* (Armonk, NY, 1988), 18.

8. Thomas Watson, Jr., *Father, Son & Company* (New York, 1990), 206.

9. Fishman, *Computer Establishment*, 120.

10. Typescript of interview with Ray Boedecker, December 12, 2001, 2,4.

11. Fishman, *Computer Establishment*, 84.

12. IBM, *Management Briefings*, 17.

## CHAPTER ELEVEN. IBM TRIUMPHS WITH THE 360 MAINFRAME COMPUTER

1. *Poughkeepsie Journal*, September 22, 2002.

2. IBM, *Management Briefings*, 84.

3. Emerson Pugh, Lyle Johnson, and John Palmer, *IBM's 360 and Early 370 Systems* (Cambridge, 1990), 632.

4. Ross Bassett, *To the Digital Age: Research Labs, Start-up Companies, and the Rise of MOS Technology* (Baltimore, 2002), 236.

5. Quoted in Kennedy, "IBM in Dutchess County," 22.

6. Lawrence Mamiya and Patricia Karouma, *For Their Courage and For Their Struggles: The Black Oral History Project of Poughkeepsie, New York* (Poughkeepsie, NY, 1978), 32.

7. IBM, *Management Briefings*, 64.

8. Mary Flad, Steve Iko, and Louis Lipschutz quoted in Kennedy, "IBM in Dutchess County," 23–24.

9. Burt Gold, personal communication.

## CHAPTER TWELVE. THE QUEST FOR INNER-CITY REVITALIZATION: URBAN RENEWAL

1. Jane Holtz Kay, *Asphalt Nation: How the Automobile Took Over America and How We Can Take it Back* (Berkeley, 1977), 245.

2. *New York Times*, February 10, 1964, quoted in Sandra Opdycke, "With Prosperity All Around: Urban Issues in Poughkeepsie, N.Y., 1950–1980," *Dutchess County Historical Society Yearbook*, vol. 75 (1990), 69.

3. Ibid.

4. Clay MacShane, *Down the Asphalt Path: The Automobile and the American City* (New York, 1994), 193.

5. Quoted in Kay, *Asphalt Nation*, 215.

6. *Poughkeepsie New Yorker*, January 13, 1950, p. 1, quoted in Opdycke, 64.

7. Candeub & Fleissig, *Master Plan Report No. 4: Traffic Plan* (Poughkeepsie, NY, February, 1960), 8.

8. City Planning Board, *East–West Arterial* (Poughkeepsie, NY, 1966), 3.

9. Kay, *Asphalt Nation*, 73.

10. *Minutes*, Shade Tree Commission (September 11, 1978).

11. "City Artery Plan 'Horrible' Says Pastor of St. Mary's," *Poughkeepsie Journal*, February 21, 1966.

12. *Poughkeepsie Journal*, November 8, 1956.

13. O. Wayne Noble, Associates, *West View General Neighborhood Renewal Plan*, January 1964, p. 20, quoted in Opdycke, 67.

14. Quoted in Gerry Raker, "Main Street U. S. A.," *Poughkeepsie Journal*, December 5, 1971, 1–F.

15. Quoted in "Van Kleeck's Store Closing, in Same Family Since 1799," *Poughkeepsie Journal*, August 2, 1960, 1.

16. Robert D. King, quoted in *Poughkeepsie Journal*, September 19, 1965, 22.

17. Quoted in Kay, *Asphalt Nation*, 269.

18. Candeub & Fleissig, *Master Plan Report No. 5: Central Business District* (Poughkeepsie, NY, April, 1960), p. 12; emphasis in original.

19. *Sunday New Yorker*, April 24, 1955.

20. Leon R. Bloom, "Remarks for Urban Renewal Task Force," *A Total Approach to Renewal: Urban Renewal Task Force Visit, May 26, 1966* (Poughkeepsie, NY, 1966), 2.

21. Kevin Klose, "City of 55,000 Forecast by 1985 with Urban Renewal," *Poughkeepsie Journal*, September 19, 1965, 22.

22. *Poughkeepsie Journal*, September 18, 1965.

23. *Poughkeepsie Journal*, June 23, 1972, editorial, 4.

24. Quoted in Susan Bronson, "Lindsay: Nation's Fate Depends on its Cities," *Poughkeepsie Journal*, June 25, 1972, 1.

25. *Poughkeepsie New Yorker*, August 18, 1959.

26. Candeub & Fleissig, *Master Plan Report No. 5*, 31.

27. *Poughkeepsie Journal*, September 17, 1969.

28. *Poughkeepsie Journal*, November 7, 1969.

29. *Poughkeepsie Journal*, April 20, 1972.

30. Mayor's Task Force on the Mall, *Report* (Poughkeepsie, NY, 1972).

31. Llewelyn-Davies Associates, *Comprehensive Plan for Poughkeepsie, Vol. 1: Poughkeepsie Today* (Poughkeepsie, NY, 1974), 107.

32. Opdycke, "With Prosperity All Around," 72; store vacancies and department store problems, ibid., from *New York Times*, June 15, 1975, 27.

33. Llewelyn-Davies, *Poughkeepsie Today*, 31.

34. Candeub & Fleissig, *General Development Plan*, 9.

35. Kenneth Toole, interview July 24, 2006, Brewster, Massachusetts.

36. Leon Bloom, "Remarks for Urban Renewal Task Force;" also see PURA's 1971 annual report, published as an advertisement in the *Poughkeepsie Journal*, August 29, 1972, 15.

37. "Riverview: A New Concept in Residential Design," in *Ground Breaking for Rip Van Winkle House* (Poughkeepsie, NY, 1988), 5.

## CHAPTER THIRTEEN. SOCIAL PLANNING— THE MODEL CITIES EXPERIMENT

1. John A. Jakle and David Wilson, *Derelict Landscapes: The Wasting of America's Built Environment* (Savage, MD, 1992), 143.

2. Richard W. Mitchell, mayor, letter dated April 27, 1967, in *Poughkeepsie Model Cities Proposal* (April 1967).

3. *Poughkeepsie Model Cities Proposal* (April 1967), Part I, Section A.

4. Ibid., Part I, Section B; Pershing Avenue description in Part II, Section B, 1.

5. Updated documentation of the original proposal, "The Model City Area Problem Analysis" (September 24, 1968).

6. *Poughkeepsie Model Cities Proposal*, Part I, Section C, 2.

7. *Model Cities Program "First Year Action Program" Volume I* (April 28, 1969), Part I-3.

8. Ibid.

9. Mamiya and Kaurouma, eds., *For Their Courage and For Their Struggles*, 59.

10. *Model City Problem Analysis* (September 24, 1968), 7.

11. Opdycke, "With Prosperity All Around," 70.

12. Joan Sherman, "Social Planning and Economic Power" (MA thesis, Sarah Lawrence College, April 1971), 46–47.

13. Kenneth R. Toole, interview, July 24, 2006.

14. Affidavit of Kenneth R. Toole deposition (Robert E. Ferguson, attorney-at-law, Poughkeepsie, NY, June 23, 1976).

15. Ibid., 8.

16. Summons by PHDC as plaintiff to City of Poughkeepsie and members of the Common Council (Robert E. Ferguson, attorney, June 23, 1976), 4.

17. Peter Sleight, "Firm to Buy Apple Hill, Despite City Moves," *Poughkeepsie Journal*, May 19, 1976, 37.

18. The votes are recorded in "Summons," p. 4. Maps of the concentration of black families in 1970, substandard residential housing, and percentage of overcrowded residential units are found in Llewelyn-Davies Associates, *Comprehensive Plan for Poughkeepsie: Poughkeepsie Today, Volume One* (1974).

19. Peter Sleight, "City Housing Group Vows Continued Fight," *Poughkeepsie Journal*, November 9, 1976, p. 14; see also Peter Sleight, "Judge Dismisses City Housing Suit," *Poughkeepsie Journal*, November 8, 1976,13.

20. "Urban Renewal: Stormy Session," *Poughkeepsie Journal*, March 31, 1970; see also a letter in favor of retention and rehabilitation of the Gate Street neighborhood supporting the residents, written to John Boyle, chairman of the Model City Area Council IV, by Clyde Griffen (July 15, 1970).

21. *Poughkeepsie Journal*, February 18, 1971.

22. The term "urbanistic" is found in a letter from Mark Lawton, director of the New York State Historic Trust to James A. Woodwell, executive director of PURA (October 15, 1970).

23. Quoted in Kim Gantz, "The current problem of the Union Street area in Poughkeepsie, New York," a student paper prepared at Vassar College in May, 1971 and included in Dutchess County Landmarks, *Union Street*.

24. Dutchess County Landmarks Association, "National Register of Historic Places Inventory-Nomination Form," (May 1971), 2.

25. William Theyson, "Historic Union Street Today," submitted to the 1982 HUD National Recognition Program for Community Development Partnerships, quoted in Virginia Maltese, "Gentrification in Poughkeepsie? The Union Street Experience" (Vassar College, BA thesis, 1986), 34.

26. R. DeFillippo, "Old-timers Question Cost of Facelift," *Poughkeepsie Journal*, April 29, 1984, 16A.

27. Louis Greenspan, one of the three partners, quoted in "Bardavon Owners Eyeing Demolition," *Poughkeepsie Journal*, July 28, 1976, reported in Jesse Effron, "The Bardavon 1869 Opera House: A History," *Marquee*, 13 (Second Quarter 1981), 7.

28. Michelle J. Lee, "Dunwell's Legacy: Bardavon," *Poughkeepsie Journal*, March 15, 2006, D-1.

29. Opdycke, "With Prosperity All Around," 73.

30. Jon C. Teaford, *The Rough Road to Renaissance* (Baltimore, 1990), 309–310.

## CHAPTER FOURTEEN. ISSUES AND CAUSES OF THE 1960s

1. "Why Vassar Picketed," *Miscellany News*, March 23, 1960.

2. "Ministers Urge Closer Supervision of Young People After Disturbance," *Poughkeepsie Journal*, July 28, 1967, 1; see also *New York Times*, July 28, 1967, 12, and July 30, 1967, 1 and 43.

3. Richard K. Wager, "A City Honors Dr. King," *Poughkeepsie Journal*, April 8, 1968, 1.

4. "Mitchell Vows Programs to Match Dr. King's Dream," Ibid.

5. Lawrence Mamiya and Lorraine Roberts, "A Historical Overview of the Black Community in Poughkeepsie," in Clyde Griffen, ed., *New Perspectives on Poughkeepsie's Past: Essays to Honor Edmund Platt* (Poughkeepsie, NY, 1987), 93.

6. *New York Times*, January 10, 2007.

7. Mamiya and Karouma, eds., *For Their Courage and For Their Struggles*, 31.

8. Ibid., 65–66.

9. Ibid., 27.

10. Typescript of interview with Lou Glasse, April 15, 2004, and "The Good Neighbor Pledge" sign-up sheet.

11. Timothy Leary, *Flashbacks: An Autobiography* (Los Angeles, 1982), 187.

12. Ibid., 197.

13. G. Gordon Liddy, *Will: The Autobiography of G. Gordon Liddy* (New York, 1980), 101–102, 120.

14. Leary, *Flashbacks*, 233.

15. Liddy, *Will*, 107ff.

16. James Patterson, *America in the Twentieth Century: A History* (4th ed: Fort Worth, 1994), 441.

17. Alan Talbot, *Power Along the Hudson: Storm King and the Birth of Environmentalism* (New York, 1972), 94.

18. Ibid., 101.

19. Minutes of the Executive Committee meeting, March 18, 1965, in Scenic Hudson archives, Marist College Library.

20. U.S. Court of Appeals for the Second Circuit (no. 106—September Term, 1965, Docket No. 29853), *Scenic Hudson Preservation Conference, Town of Cortlandt, Town of Putnam Valley and Town of Yorktown v. Federal Power Commission and Consolidated Edison Company of New York, Inc.*, 7; also quoted in Talbot, *Power Along the Hudson*, 131.

21. Letter from Pete Seeger, *Harper's* (February 1978), 321.

22. Letter from Frances Reese in ibid., 319.

23. Ross Sandler and David Schoenbrod, eds., *The Hudson River Power Plant Settlement* (New York, 1981), 223: *New York Times*, December 20, 1980, "A Peace Treaty for the Hudson."

24. Scenic Hudson, *Your Valley*, Vol. 1, no. 2, 4, 11.

25. Alec Wilkinson, "The Protest Singer: Pete Seeger and American Folk Music," *The New Yorker*, April 17, 2006, 49.

26. David Dunaway, *How Can I Keep from Singing: Pete Seeger* (New York, 1982), 282.

27. Ibid., 285.

28. Minutes of the Executive Committee meeting, May 10, 1966, in Scenic Hudson Archives, Marist College Library.

29. Paul Fortenoy, *The Sloops of the Hudson River: A Historical and Design Survey* (Mystic, Conn., 1994), 91, 96.

30. Alec Wilkinson, "The Protest Singer: Pete Seeger and American Folk Music," *The New Yorker*, April 17, 2006, 47.

## CHAPTER FIFTEEN. CHANGE IN HIGHER EDUCATION IN THE VALLEY

1. Andrew C. Rieser, "Women's Activism and the Founding of Dutchess Community College, 1955 to 1960," *Dutchess County Historical Society Year Book* 86 (2007–2008), 8.

2. Taped interview with Edna Macmahon in *Dutchess Community College Oral History Project*, Arnold Toback, interviewer and compiler (1976–1977) and phone interview with former President Hall, May 12, 2004.

3. *This is a history of Dutchess Community College, 1957–1997, in the voices and images of the people who made it and in the headlines that announced their achievements* (Poughkeepsie, NY, 1997), 15.

4. Phone interview with James Hall, May 12, 2004.

5. Sarah Bradshaw, "DCC Alumni Found to be Economic Force," *Poughkeepsie Journal*, October 18, 2007.

6. Elizabeth A. Daniels and Clyde Griffen, *Full Steam Ahead in Poughkeepsie: The Story of Coeducation at Vassar, 1966–1974* (Poughkeepsie, NY, 2000), 24.

7. *New Haven Register*, April 4, 1968, and the *Journal Courier*, July 9, 1968. Clippings in CIA Archives, Hyde Park, New York.

8. *Wall Street Journal*, August 7, 1978.

9. George Chevalier, "Growing with High Technology," undated clipping from *Poughkeepsie Journal* in the Fairacre Farms scrapbook, courtesy of Ralph and Doris Adams.

10. Ibid.

## CHAPTER SIXTEEN. IBM DOWNSIZES, BUT THE VALLEY RECOVERS

1. Interview with Frank Bauer, January 16, 2006.

2. *Poughkeepsie Journal*, February 6, 1977, in the first in a series of Schatz Federal Bearing Co. scrapbooks, Adriance Memorial Library.

3. Ibid., January 22, 1981.

4. Ibid., March 5 and March 15, 1981.

5. *Poughkeepsie Journal*, March 2, 2003.

6. "80s Highlights Around the Company," *Fifty Years in Poughkeepsie* (Poughkeepsie, NY, 1991).

7. Ross Bassett, *To the Digital Age: Research Labs, Start-up Companies, and the Rise of MOS Technology* (Baltimore, 2002), 3.

8. Ibid., 300.

9. Ibid, 304.

10. Louis Gerstner, *Who Says Elephants Can't Dance: Inside IBM's Historic Turnaround* (New York, 2002), 79.

11. Ibid., 72.

12. Ibid., 101.

13. Typescript of interview with Fred Nagel, April 2, 2003, 3.

14. Ibid., 2.

15. Ibid., 4.

16. Keith H. Hammonds, "The Town IBM Left Behind," *Business Week* (September 11, 1995), 106.

17. Craig Wolf, "Path Gets Complex after Jobs Recovery," *Poughkeepsie Journal*, February 27, 2005.

18. Craig Wolf, "Slimmer Big Blue, Still a Huge Employer, Chooses Partners," *Poughkeepsie Journal*, February 25, 2002.

19. Ibid.

20. Ibid.

21. Craig Wolf, "IBM Still Has Hefty Share in Tax Rolls," *Poughkeepsie Journal*, September 22, 2001.

22. Craig Wolf, "Industry Changes Redefine IBM's Work Force," *Poughkeepsie Journal*, September 22, 2002.

23. Ibid.

24. Craig Wolf, "IBM Still Has Hefty Share in Tax Rolls."

25. Quoted in Elizabeth Lynch, "Communities Diversify after Layoffs in '90s," *Poughkeepsie Journal*, September 22, 2002, 4-A.

26. Craig Wolf, "Industry Changes Redefine IBM's Workforce."

27. *The New Vassar: Report of the President, 1967–1970* (Poughkeepsie, NY, 1971), 48–49.

28. *Poughkeepsie Journal*, February 27, 2005: "Interview with Carlos Fuentes."

29. Craig Wolf, "Dutchess finds new hurdles to create jobs," *Poughkeepsie Journal*, July 20, 2003.

30. *Poughkeepsie Journal*, March 2, 2003.

## CHAPTER SEVENTEEN. THE NONPROFIT
## SERVICE SECTOR GROWS IN IMPORTANCE

1. *New York Times*, October 28, 2006.

2. *Barron's*, December 4, 2006.

3. Poughkeepsie Journal, *The Hudson Valley: Our Heritage, Our Future* (Poughkeepsie, NY, 2000), 210.

4. Ibid.

5. E-mail from Ron Mullahey to Clyde Griffen, November 29, 2006. The New York Commisssion on Health Care facilities in the twenty-first-century proposal for consolidation of Kingston and Benedictine hospitals is described in the *Poughkeepsie Journal*, November 29, 2006.

6. Shirley Adams quoted in Peter Leonard, "Director Leads Center's Kid-friendly Approach," *Poughkeepsie Journal*, September 28, 2007, F1.

7. *Poughkeepsie Journal*, August 1, 1983.

8. Ibid.

9. Ibid.

10. Interview with Peter Leonard and Sam Busselle, March 29, 2006.

11. *New York Times*, November 6, 2005; *Poughkeepsie Journal*, October 28, 2005, February 25. 2006; and other clippings from the *Journal* provided by Peter Leonard.

12. Typescript of interview with Brian Riddell, February 17, 2005, 3, and "Programs" on Dutchess Outreach Web site.

## CHAPTER EIGHTEEN. MAIN STREET STRUGGLES
## TO RETURN AMID SUBURBAN SPRAWL

1. Bert Burns, "Between You and Me," *Poughkeepsie Journal*, March 7, 1975.

2. *Poughkeepsie Evening News*, September 14, 1977.

3. "Wallace's to Close City Store," *Poughkeepsie Journal*, April 29, 1975, 17.

4. John Nemes, "Merchants to Seek Wallace's Replacement; Confidence Expressed in Future of City Mall," *Poughkeepsie Journal*, May 4, 1975, 5F; also John Zappe, "Wallace Closing Focuses Attention on City's Central Business District," *Poughkeepsie Journal*, May 4, 1975, 1F.

5. George Bernstein, "Luckey Platt to Close City Store," *Poughkeepsie Journal*, June 10, 1981, 5.

6. Robert DePhillipo, "County Employees Request Move to New Offices," *Poughkeepsie Journal*, June 7, 1981, 5.

7. George Bernstein, "Luckey Platt Store Closes Quietly in City," *Poughkeepsie Journal*, July 3, 1981, 5.

8. The Main Mall Commission appointed in 1983 consisted of the business owners Joseph Forman (Up-to-Date) and Paul S. Mancarella (De's Jewelers), building owner Thomas M. Cervone, and citizen members Bruce Avery and Mary Flad. Three years later, the commission hired Felice Entratter as its first executive director.

9. Andrea Simoon, "Memorandum to Tom Aposporos, Chamber of Commerce, Members of the Main Mall Commission and Marketing Committee," April 30, 1986.

10. For an analysis of activities throughout the nation, including the National Trust for Historic Preservation's Main Street Program, see Richard V. Francaviglia, *Main Street Revisited: Time, Space, and Image Building in Small-Town America* (Iowa City, 1996).

11. Letter of submittal to Ms. Felice Entratter, Main Mall Coordinator (February 11, 1987).

12. *City of Poughkeepsie Comprehensive Plan* (Poughkeepsie, NY, 1988), sect. 5, 4.

13. *A Business Enhancement Plan for Downtown Poughkeepsie, New York* (Washington, DC, 1987), 106.

14. Mary Koniz Arnold, "For the Kid in Us," *The Poughkeepsie Beat*, June 25, 1999, 6.

15. Quoted in Arnold, ibid.

16. *Poughkeepsie Journal*, October 26, 2002.

17. "Draft: City of Poughkeepsie Local Waterfront Revitalization Program, Executive Summary," mimeographed, distributed at public hearing June 20, 1988. The original members of the Waterfront Advisory Committee included: Carol Sondheimer, waterfront specialist at Scenic Hudson, chair; John Mylod, executive director of Clearwater; William Linich (a.k.a. "Billy Name" while a resident of Andy Warhol's atelier "The Factory" in New York City); Frank Moore, a city fisherman; and city residents James Schlotzhauer and Harvey Flad. Staff for the committee included Jeff Lipnicky from the city planning department and Anne Conroy, planning consultant with Matthew D. Rudikoff Associates.

18. "Vision Statement for Poughkeepsie Waterfront," *City of Poughkeepsie Local Waterfront Revitalization Program* (Poughkeepsie, NY, 1998), iv.

19. David A. Palieri, *Cognitive Landscapes: Mental Mapping and Urban Perception in Poughkeepsie, New York* (Vassar College, geography BA thesis, 1995), 65–66, and figure 4–8 "Perceived Danger in Poughkeepsie."

20. Joseph Berger, "Poughkeepsie in a Long Tailspin, Now Copes with a Clouded Image," *New York Times*, October 5, 1998, B-1 and B-3.

21. Ibid., B-3.

22. Kimberly P. Harrison, "City's Final Supermarket to Close Doors: Senior Citizens, Low-income Shoppers to be Hit Hardest," *Poughkeepsie Journal*, March 7, 1992, 1A, cited in Beth Munnich, *Access Denied. Supermarket Development and Inner City Food Security: Poughkeepsie, New York* (Vassar College, BA thesis, urban studies, 2003), 17.

23. Mayor Colette Lafuente, interview April 23, 2003, cited in Munnich, 17.

24. Ibid.

25. Frank Clark, interview February 12, 2003, cited in Munnich, 41.

26. City of Poughkeepsie Transit System bus map, 2002, cited in Munnich, 5.

27. Berger, "Poughkeepsie in a Long Tailspin," B-3.

28. Berger, ibid.

29. Thomas J. Lueck, "New Ring of Suburbs Springs Up Around City," *New York Times*, April 29, 1986, A1.

## CHAPTER NINETEEN. CIVIC IDENTITY AND SOCIAL CHANGE IN THE 1990s

1. Nicole Edwards, "Voice for Racial Harmony: Rodney Douglas Continues to Strive to Make a Difference via Plays and Stories," *Poughkeepsie Journal*, April 2, 2004, C-1.

2. Robert D. McFadden, et al., *Outrage: The Story Behind the Tawana Brawley Hoax* (New York, 1990), 29–30.

3. Ibid., 26–29.

4. Ibid., 22–23.

5. John Cronin and Robert F. Kennedy, Jr., *The Riverkeepers* (New York, 1999), 96–97.

6. Ibid.

7. Alison Mountz, *Daily Life in a Transnational Migrant Community: The Fusion of San Agustin Yatareni, Oaxaca and Poughkeepsie,New York* (BA thesis, Department of Geography, Dartmouth College, Hanover, NH, 1995); and Alison Mountz and Richard A. Wright, "Daily Life in the Transnational Migrant Community of San Agustin, Oaxaca, and Poughkeepsie, New York," *Diaspora*, 5, 3 (1996), 403–28.

8. Brian J. Godfrey, "New Urban Ethnic Landscapes," in Christopher Airries and Ines Miyares, eds., *Contemporary Ethnic Geography* (Latham, MD, 2006), 334.

9. Mountz, *Daily Life*, 42.

10. Mountz and Wright, *Daily Life*, 407.

11. Mountz, *Daily Life*, 71.

12. Ibid., 87.

13. Godfrey, "New Urban Ethnic Landscapes," 334.

14. Ibid., 336.

15. Joseph Berger, "Detective's Kindness Helps Awaken a City; After a Death, Poughkeepsie Notices Its 3,000 Mexicans and Their Roots," *New York Times*, January 7, 1999, B-1; see also a photograph of Skip Mannain and comments about his efforts in Joyce C. Ghee and Joan Spence, *Poughkeepsie 1898–1998: A Century of Change* (Charleston, SC, 1999), 126.

16. Larry Hughes, "Mexican's Tragic Death Unites a City," *Poughkeepsie Journal*, April 26, 1998, 5D.

17. Peter Leonard, "Immigrants Add Strength to Community," *Poughkeepsie Journal*, December 27, 1998.

18. Christine Pizzuti, "Housing Group's Dedication Honored," *Poughkeepsie Journal*, September 28, 2007, 1B.

19. Personal comments and interviews in Susan Guerrina, *A Tale of Two Cities, Marketing their Urban Assets: Urban Renewal in the City of Poughkeepsie and Beacon* (Vassar College, BA thesis, geography, 2000), 13.

## CHAPTER TWENTY. CITY AND REGION AT THE END OF THE TWENTIETH CENTURY

1. Craig Wolf, "Planning Group Marks 40 Years of Challenges," *Poughkeepsie Journal*, February 29, 2004.

2. News release of the Regional Plan Association, dated December 13, 1973.

3. *Poughkeepsie Journal*, February 29, 2004.

4. Quoted in Fred Crane, "Lewis Mumford: Regionalism, New York State, and the Mid-Hudson," Richard C. Wiles, ed., *Meeting the Future on Purpose: Papers in Honor of Lewis Mumford* (Annandale-on-Hudson, NY), 1978.

5. Lewis Mumford, *The City in History* (New York, 1961), 554.

6. *The Hudson: The Report of the Hudson River Valley Commission 1966* (Bear Mountain, NY), 85. Governor Rockefeller appointed his brother Laurance, a noted conservationist who would offer funds from the Jackson Hole Preserve foundation to establish the Hudson Highlands State Park in 1970, as chair of the commission. Other members included: William H. Whyte of the American Conservation Association and author of *The Last Landscape* (1968) and *City: Rediscovering the Center* (1988); Thomas Watson, head of IBM; Alan Simpson, president of Vassar College; former Governor Averell Harriman; Henry Heald, president of the Ford Foundation; Lowell Thomas, author and news commentator; Marion Sulzberger Heiskell of the *New York Times*; and banker Frank Wells McCabe.

7. "Memorandum: Preliminary Thoughts Regarding a Legal-Institutional Framework for the Implementation of Hudson River Study Recommendations" (Tarrytown, NY: Raymond, Parish, Pine & Weiner, Inc., October 6, 1978).

8. *Scenic District Management Plan for the Mid-Hudson Historic Scenic Shorelands Area* prepared by Robert M. Toole, Harvey K. Flad, and Robbe Stimson (Albany, NY, 1983). See also Harvey K. Flad, "The Hudson River Shorelands Task Force: Citizen Participation in the Preservation of an Historic Landscape," *Partnership in Conservation: Second Conference of National Trusts* (Edinburgh, Scotland, 1980), 57–61; and Robbe Stimson and Harvey K. Flad, "Preservation of an Historic Rural Landscape: Roles for Public and Private Sectors," *Farmsteads and Market Towns: Preserving the Cultural Landscape* (Albany, NY, 1982).

9. Kenneth Toole, interview, July 24, 2006.

10. *Directions: The Plan for Dutchess County* (Poughkeepsie, NY, 1987), 75.

11. Henry L. Diamond, et al., *Greenways in the Hudson River Valley: A New Strategy for Preserving an American Treasure* (Tarrytown, NY, 1988)

12. Ibid., 6.

13. Klara Sauer, interview, June 20, 2006.

14. Charles E. Little, *Greenways for America* (Baltimore, 1990), 28.

15. American Farmland Trust's 1997 report *Farming on the Edge*, cited in *Agricultural Economic Development for the Hudson Valley* (Saratoga Springs, NY, 2004), 32.

16. American Farmland Trust, *Agricultural Economic Development for the Hudson Valley*, 32, citing Rolf Pendall's 2003 report "Sprawl Without Growth: The Upstate Paradox."

17. Kathleen Norton and Harvey Auster, "City Dwellers Will be Farmers of the Future," *Poughkeepsie Journal*, August 19, 1986, 1. Further stories of Ulster and Dutchess farmers are found in articles published on August 17 and 18, 1986.

18. Matthew Elliot, *Community Gardens* (Vassar College, BA thesis, environmental studies, 2003), 27.

## CHAPTER TWENTY-ONE. MAIN STREET AND THE TWENTY-FIRST-CENTURY CULTURAL LANDSCAPE

1. Hudson River Valley Commission, *Historic Resources of the Hudson* (Tarrytown, NY, 1969), 7.

2. John Russell, cited in R. Simpson and H. K. Flad, "Preservation of an Historic Rural Landscape: Roles for Public and Private Sectors," in *Farmsteads & Market Towns: A Handbook for Preserving the Cultural Landscape* (Albany, NY, 1982).

3. Quoted in Jan Gehorsam, "Crumbling Plaster Is Reality for Daisy Suckley," *Poughkeepsie Journal*, November 13, 1983, 1B. Articles in the same issue refer to other estates and the potential for tourism: "River Estates Struggle to Survive" and "More River Estates May Become Public Preserves."

4. A. L. Huxtable, "Doomsday Notes on a Rotten Game," *New York Times*, September 28, 1969, wherein she declared, "The Downing Landscape . . . is worth the same attention as that given the Sequoias." Local information on the fire was in R. Stearns, "Fire Claims Buildings at Springside," *Poughkeepsie Journal*, August 18, 1969. A history of saving the Springside historic landscape is in Harvey K. Flad, "Matthew Vassar's Springside: '. . . the hand of Art, when guided by Taste,'" in *Prophet with Honor: The Career of Andrew Jackson Downing, 1815–1852*, edited by George B. Tatum and Elisabeth Blair MacDougall (Washington, DC, 1989), 219–57.

5. Quotations from Harvey K. Flad and Craig M. Dalton, "A Tree and Its Neighbors: Creating Community Open Space," *The Hudson River Valley Review*, 21, 2 (Spring 2005), 57–47.

6. Richard Florida, *Cities and the Creative Class* (New York, 2005), 35; data indicating Dutchess County's "creativity index" and "innovation index" is found on 160–63.

7. Ibid., 29.

8. Quoted in *Poughkeepsie: The City That Hopes* (Vassar College, American Culture Program, 2004), 23.

9. Chris Silva, quoted in John W. Barry, "City Lights Up for the Holidays," *Poughkeepsie Journal*, November 30, 2006, D1.

10. Founders of CAP were Poughkeepsie residents Jeep and Carol Johnson, artist Franc Palaia, and photographer Doug Nobiletti. Pioneering and dedicated arts program directors mentioned include: Carole Wolf of Mill Street Loft; Maria Marewski of Children's Media Project; and Diane Pedivillano of the Children's Museum.

11. Randy A. Daniels, Department of State "Objections to Consistency Certification" (Albany, NY, 2005), 11.

12. Quoted in Lexie Averick, *Art-Based Paradigm in Beacon, New York: A Case of Art Revitalization* (Vassar College, BA thesis, urban studies, 2004), 2.

13. Quoted in ibid.

14. Quoted from an article in the *Poughkeepsie Journal*, September 4, 2003 in Averick, ibid., 17.

15. "Arts 'Boom' Fuels Beacon's Rebirth," *Poughkeepsie Journal*, April 7, 1999, quoted in Laurie Pessah, *Beacon's Mill District: Present and Future* (Vassar College, urban studies thesis, 1999). See also "Dia's Entry into the Picture Adds a Centerpiece to Existing Plans for Waterfront Projects" *Poughkeepsie Journal*, March 9, 1999.

16. Lisa W. Foderaro, "Rooms with Views Replace Factories on Hudson's Banks," *New York Times*, October 31, 2005, B-6.

17. Ibid., B-1.

## EPILOGUE. MAIN STREET REVISITED

1. Colette Lafuente, quoted in Elizabeth Lynch, "Parade Marks Street Reopening," *Poughkeepsie Journal*, November 8, 2001, B1.

2. Kevin Cahill, quoted in Vanni Cappelli, "Local Arts Activists Lobby for Increased Funding in Albany," *The Weekly Beat*, March 9, 2007, 3.

3. Ann Davis, et al., *Identifying Growth Trends at the Community Level: A Land-Use Study of Three Dutchess County Communities* (Poughkeepsie, NY, 2007), 5–6.

4. "Riversprawl," editorial, *New York Times*, November 20, 2005, WE-17.

5. Tammy Cilione, "Renaissance Takes Shape in Downtown: Main Street Shops, Eateries Make Comeback," *Poughkeepsie Journal*, November 30, 2003, 20.

6. Ibid., 21.

# Annotated Bibliography

## CHAPTER ONE

On the Hudson River as estuary, see Robert Boyle, *The Hudson River: A Natural and Unnatural History* (New York, 1969) and Stephen Stanne, Roger Panetta, and Brian Forist, *The Hudson: An Illustrated Guide to the Living River* (New Brunswick, NJ, 1996). For perceptions of the valley landscape, turn to Roland Van Zandt, *Chronicles of the Hudson: Three Centuries of Travelers Accounts* (New Brunswick, NJ, 1971); David Schuyler, "The Sanctified Landscape: The Hudson River Valley, 1820 to 1850," in George Thompson, ed., *Landscape in America* (Austin, 1995); and two essays by Harvey Flad, "Following 'The Pleasant Paths of Taste': The Traveler's Eye and New World Landscapes," in *Humanizing Landscapes: Geography, Culture, and the Magoon Collection* (Poughkeepsie, NY, 2000) and "The Hudson River and the Geographic Imagination," *Watershed: The Hudson Valley Art Project*, edited by Miwon Kwon (New York, 2002). For Andrew Jackson Downing's influence, see the reprint edition of his *Treatise* in Jacquetta Haley, *Pleasure Grounds: Andrew Jackson Downing and Montgomery Place* (Tarrytown, NY, 1988).

For surveys and interpretations of major changes over time in or affecting the Hudson valley, see John H. Thompson, ed., *Geography of New York State* (Syracuse, NY, 1966); Carl Carmer, *The Hudson* (New York, 1939); David Ellis, *Landlords and Farmers in the Hudson-Mohawk Region, 1790–1850* (Ithaca, NY, 1946); Louise Zimm, Joseph Emsley, Elwood Corning, and Willitt Jewell, eds., *Southeastern New York: A History of the Counties of Ulster, Dutchess, Orange, Rockland, Putnam* (New York, 1946); Alan Taylor, "The Great Change Begins," *New York History*, 76 (July, 1995); Donald Parkerson, "The Structure of New York Society: Basic Themes in Nineteenth Century Social History," *New York History*, 65 (1984). For early European settlement and the gradual democratization of landholding, see the essays by Henry Cassidy, William McDermott, and John Reilly in Joyce Ghee, et. al, eds., *Transformations of an American County: Dutchess County, New York, 1683–1983* (Poughkeepsie, NY, 1986).

On the career and influence on valley history of its greatest landlord, see Richard Wiles, ed., *The Livingston Legacy: Three Centuries of American History* (Annandale-on-Hudson, NY, 1986) and two articles by Cynthia Kierner: "Landlord and Tenant in Revolutionary New York: The Case of Livingston Manor," *New York History*, 70

(1989) and "Patrician Womanhood in the Early Republic: The Reminiscences of Janet Livingston Montgomery," *New York History*, 73 (1992). On the anti-rent movement, consult Reeve Huston, *Land and Freedom: Rural Society, Popular Protest, and Party Politics in Antebellum New York* (New York, 2000). Thomas Wermuth, *Rip Van Winkle's Neighbors: The Transformation of Rural Society in the Hudson River Valley, 1720–1850* (Albany, NY, 2001) describes the transition in Ulster County from a household to a market economy. For the early exchange economy in Columbia County see Martin Breugel, *Farm, Shop, Landing: The Rise of a Market Society in the Hudson Valley, 1760–1860* (Durham, NC, 2005).

For overviews of the settling of New York, see R. K. McGregor, "Settlement Variation and Cultural Adaptation in the Immigration History of Colonial New York," *New York History*, 73 (1992) and James Darlington, "Peopling the Post-Revolutionary New York Frontier," *New York History*, 74 (1993). On Native Americans in the region, see especially Robert Grumet, "The Ninhams of the Colonial Hudson Valley," *Hudson Valley Regional Review*, 9 (September 1992). On African Americans, see Michael Groth, "The African American Struggle Against Slavery in the Mid-Hudson Valley," *Hudson Valley Regional Review*, 11 (March 1994) and his "Laboring for Freedom in Dutchess County," in Myra B. Armstead, ed., *Mighty Change, Tall Within: Black Identity in the Hudson Valley* (Albany, NY, 2003).

The mid-Hudson valley's four river towns have been well studied for part or all of the nineteenth century. On Hudson, see Ruth Piwonka and Roderic H. Blackburn, *A Visible Heritage: Columbia County, New York, A History in Art and Architecture* (Kinderhook, NY, 1977) and Piwonka, "Hudson," *Hudson Valley Regional Review*, 1 (March, 1985) and Bruce Hall, *Diamond Street: The Story of the Little Town with the Big Red Light District* (Hughsonville, NY, 1994). On Kingston, see Stuart Blumin, *The Urban Threshold: Growth and Change in a Nineteenth-Century American Community* (Chicago, 1976) and Blumin, Glasco, Griffen, Hershberg, and Katz, "Occupation and Ethnicity in Five Nineteenth-Century Cities," *Historical Methods Newsletter*, 7 (1974). On Newburgh, see two essays by Mark Carnes: "The Rise and Fall of a Mercantile Town: Family, Land, and Capital in Newburgh, New York, 1790–1844," *Hudson Valley Regional Review*, 2 (1985) and "From Merchant to Manufacturer: The Economics of Localism in Newburgh, New York, 1845–1900" in ibid., 3 (1986)

## CHAPTER TWO

Edmund Platt, *Eagle's History of Poughkeepsie from the Earliest Settlements, 1683–1905* (Reprint edition, Poughkeepsie, NY, 1987) and Clyde and Sally Griffen, *Natives and Newcomers: The Ordering of Opportunity in Mid-Nineteenth-Century-Poughkeepsie* (Cambridge, Mass., 1978) remain important sources for this chapter as do several essays in *New Perspectives on Poughkeepsie's Past* (Poughkeepsie, NY, 1987): the historical overview of the black community by Lawrence Mamiya and Lorraine Roberts; examination of Poughkeepsie's architectural styles, 1835–1940 by William Rhoads; and studies of the city's Catholic community, 1870–1900 by Louis Zuccarello, and of its changing neighborhoods, 1850–1900 by Clyde Griffen. See also essays in Joyce Ghee, Melodye Kaltz, William McDermott, and Richard Wiles, eds., *Transformations of an American County* (Poughkeepsie, 1986).

Basic primary sources include the U.S. Census since 1850, tax assessment records for the city of Poughkeepsie, and pamphlets of individual businesses and voluntary associations, Local History Room, Adriance Memorial Library; Mercantile Agency (predecessor to Dun and Bradstreet) credit ledgers for Poughkeepsie after 1845 at the Baker Library, Harvard University Business School; *Commemorative Biographical Record of Dutchess County* (Chicago, 1897). The *Poughkeepsie Daily Eagle* and the *Daily Press* were useful for business news and the latter, especially, for reports of strikes by labor. Jonathan Garlock provided information on Knights of Labor organizing in correspondence in 1972 with Clyde Griffen. Patricia Nelson's senior history thesis on the textile industry in Wappingers Falls describes its workforce in 1880.

The history of the Poughkeepsie Railroad Bridge is reported in Carleton Mabee, *Bridging the Hudson: The Poughkeepsie Railroad Bridge and Its Connecting Lines* (Fleischmanns, NY, 2001). For change in transportation, see Gordon L. Moffett, *To Poughkeepsie and Back: The Story of the Poughkeepsie Highland Ferry* (Fleischmanns, NY, 1994) and two 1976 essays by Vassar student Hugh Cosman, "Poughkeepsie and its Railroads" and "The Poughkeepsie and Wappingers Falls Railway," and Lynn Larsen's 1966 essay, "The Extension of the Poughkeepsie City Railroad to Bull's Head and Vassar College." Also useful were a 2004 thesis by William J. Hughes, "History of the Mid-Hudson Bridge Project at Poughkeepsie, N.Y., 1855–1930" and a typescript essay by Megan Floyd that examines "Steamboat Landings and Riverfront Industries in Poughkeepsie, 1871–1873."

The following articles in *Dutchess County Historical Society Yearbooks* were helpful: Jeffrey Arons, "Poughkeepsie Iron Works (Bech's Furnace)," 67 (1982); Peter Edman, "A History of the Curriculum in the Poughkeepsie City School district, 1843–1929," 70 (1985); Jesse Effron, "The Bardavon 1869 Opera House, 1869–1979," 67 (1982); William McDermott, "The Famine Irish Arrive in Poughkeepsie, 1850," 69 (1984); Wilson Poucher, M.D., "Poughkeepsie's Water Supply, 1799–1923," 27 (1942); Susan Puretz, "A History of Garfield Place, Poughkeepsie," 57 (1972); Andrea Zimmermann, "Nineteenth Century Manufacturing Enterprise in Dutchess County," 68 (1983). See also Susan Puretz, *Garfield Place: A Study of a Victorian Street in an Urban Setting* (Poughkeepsie, NY, 1971) and Puretz, *Stages in the Life Cycle of a Street: Evolution of Academy Street, Poughkeepsie, New York* (Poughkeepsie, 1983)

## CHAPTER THREE

The closest counterpart to Matthew Vassar as local civic leader during the Gilded Age was Harvey Eastman, founder and owner of Eastman Business College. See Elizabeth Carter, "Our Almost Forgotten Hero," *Dutchess County Historical Society Yearbook*, 63 (1978); *Eastman Business College Catalogue* (Poughkeepsie, NY, 1886); and the biographical sketch by Clyde Griffen in *The Hudson Valley: Our Heritage, Our Future*. For change in local public education, see Jean Sonkin, "Eight to Four: A Story about the Poughkeepsie Public Schools in 1897 and 1898" (Vassar College essay, 1956).

Histories of individual sports and sport associations provide information on recreation in the late nineteenth century, notably Joseph Poillucci, *Baseball in Dutchess County: When It Was a Game* (Danbury, CT, 2000); Scott Arthur, "Poughkeepsie Yacht Club: Working Men Build a Club," *Dutchess County Historical Society Yearbook*, 74

(1989) and Baltus Van Kleeck, "The Poughkeepsie Tennis Club: Its First 50 Years)," ibid., 44 (1959). See also the Club's *Constitution, Rules, Officers, Members* (1895) and several of its advertisements for fund-raisers, Adriance Library. For a major source of local entertainment, Collingwood's Opera House, see the biography of James Collingwood in *Commemorative Biographical Record* and Jesse Effron, "The Bardavon 1869 Opera House, 1869–1979," *Dutchess County Historical Society Yearbook*, 67 (1982). For the response of one prominent citizen, Edmund H. P. Platt, to events he attended, see the cullings from his diary by Annon Adams, "Mr. Platt Goes to the Collingwood Opera House," *Dutchess County Historical Society Yearbook*, 78 (1993). For a major episode in fund-raising entertainment, see Amy Vernooy, "The Sanitary Fair [1864]," ibid., 32 (1947).

Growing up in the world of the river gentry is described in Geoffrey Ward, *Before the Trumpet: Young Franklin Roosevelt, 1882–1905* (New York, 1986). Two of the estates are described in Charles Snell, *Vanderbilt Mansion Historical Site, New York* (Washington, DC, 1960) and Allen Weinreb, "Staatsburgh: the History of the Lewis-Livingston-Mills Estate" (Draft, 1999). For taste in architecture and landscape among the river gentry of the valley and Poughkeepsie's rich, see David Schuyler, *Apostle of Taste: Andrew Jackson Downing, 1815–1852* (Baltimore, 1996) and Robert M. Toole, "The Prophetic Eye of Taste: Samuel F. B. Morse at Locust Grove," *Hudson Valley Regional Review*, 12 (1995); for Vassar's Springside, see Harvey K. Flad, "Matthew Vassar's Springside: '. . . the Hand of Art, when guided by Taste,'" in George B. Tatum and Elisabeth Blair MacDougall, *Prophet with Honor: The Career of Andrew Jackson Downing, 1815–1852* (Dumbarton Oaks Colloquium on the History of Landscape Architecture XI, Washington, DC, 1989) and John Sears, "Andrew Jackson Downing and Picturesque Tourism at Matthew Vassar's Springside," *Dutchess County Historical Society Yearbook*, 75 (1990); for urban residences see Susan Puretz, "A History of Garfield Place, Poughkeepsie" ibid., 57 (1972); Puretz "Stages in the Life Cycle of a Street: Evolution of Academy Street, Poughkeepsie, New York" (1983); and Barbara Schultz, *Our Irish Roots* (Kingston, NY, 1991).

## CHAPTER FOUR

For description and significance of the urban downtown, or central business district, from the turn of the century through the first half of the twentieth century, see Robert M. Fogelson, *Downtown: Its Rise and Fall, 1880–1950* (New Haven, 2001). For the rise in use of urban parks see Galen Cranz, "The Changing Roles of Urban Parks: From Pleasure Garden to Open Space System," in *Landscape*, 22, 3 (Summer 1978).

Reviews of Poughkeepsie's architecture are found in William B. Rhoads, "Poughkeepsie's Architectural Styles, 1835–1940: Anarchy or Decorum?" in Clyde Griffen, ed., *New Perspectives on Poughkeepsie's Past* (Poughkeepsie, NY, 1988) and Jeanne B. Opdycke, *City of Poughkeepsie Walking & Driving Guide* (Poughkeepsie, NY, 1977). Also see the many volumes of the *National Register Inventory* for Poughkeepsie's buildings shelved in the Dutchess County Planning Department library, and the entries in the American Guide Series, *Dutchess County* (Philadelphia, 1937). Infrastructure improvements at the turn of the twentieth century are noted in Edmund Platt, *Eagle's History*. For a description of Poughkeepsie in the first decade of the twentieth century see M. V. Fuller, "The Rejuvenation of Poughkeepsie," *The American City* 4 (1911).

For an intensive study of retail establishments over a fifty-year period (1890–1940) located between 243 and 397 Main Street in the heart of Poughkeepsie's central business district, see Julie Stephens, "Main Street Poughkeepsie: Market to Hamilton—A Full Three Block Stretch" (typescript, Vassar College History Department, n.d., ca. 1982).

## CHAPTER FIVE

Adriance Library has some reports on immigrants from southern, central, and eastern Europe at the turn of the centuy. Especially useful are Nancy Burger, "Russian Jewish Immigrants in Poughkeepsie" (Vassar College senior thesis, 1972), Eva Goldin, *The Jewish Community of Poughkeepsie*, and the autobiography of Tony di Rosa, *El Piba* (Buenos Aires, 1991). See also John Rinaldi and Lawrence Perretta, *The History of the Italian Center* (Poughkeepsie, 1947). We are indebted to Christine Chiu for her student paper reporting interviews with several Polish-Americans. For Poughkeepsie's African Americans, see Lawrence Mamiya and Lorraine Roberts, "Overview of the Black Community in Poughkeepsie," in Griffen, ed. *New Perspectives on Poughkeepsie's Past*, Mamiya and Patricia Kaurouma, *For Their Courage and For Their Struggles* (The Black Oral History Project of Poughkeepsie, New York, 1978), and Denise Love Johnson, "Black Migration Patterns: A Case Study of the Origin and Development of the Black Population in Poughkeepsie, New York" (Black studies and geography senior thesis, Vassar College, 1973). On the religious activities and aspirations of immigrants, see Louis Zuccarello, "The Catholic Community in Poughkeepsie, 1870–1900: The Period of Testing," in Griffen, ed., *New Perspectives*.

Adriance Library Local History Room's collection of materials for local voluntary associations is invaluable: most useful for this chapter have been histories and materials of the Ferris Heights [neighborhood] Association, the Dutchess County Golf and Country Club, the Poughkeepsie Tennis Club, and especially the annual reports of the Women's City and County Club beginning with 1919. On other sports and recreation, see Joseph V. Poilluci, *Baseball in Dutchess County: When It Was a Game* (Danbury, CT, 2000) and David Montgomery, "The Poughkeepsie Regatta, 1895–1915" (History senior thesis, Vassar College, 1990). A patriotic organization during World War I has been studied by Michael Schroeder, "The Dutchess County Defense Council (April 1917 to November 1920)" (History senior thesis, Vassar College, 1982); see also the well-illustrated *Poughkeepsie's Part in the World War* (1918), Adriance Library. For reports of Ku Klux Klan activities in the valley, see *Poughkeepsie Eagle*, July, 1924.

A number of our interviews on other subjects also touched upon the immigrant experience and assimilation over time. We learned from as well as enjoyed these personal memories in our conversations with Joan and Jonah Sherman, Armine Isbirian, and Doris and Ralph Adams, among others. Assimilation was the subject addressed by Caroline Ware's students in a Vassar class in 1933: see the Ware file, FDR Library. For additional information on recreational activities and social classes in a medium-sized northeastern industrial city (Worcester, Massachusetts), see Roy Rosensweig, *Eight Hours for What We Will: Workers and Leisure in an Industrial City, 1870–1920* (New York, 1983).

## CHAPTER SIX

In the papers of Lucy Maynard Salmon, housed in Special Collections of the Vassar College Library, Folders 57:10, 11, and 13 concern her civic engagement. For a fuller record of her speaking out on public issues, notable in letters to the editors of local newspapers, see her book of clippings, 1902–1908, in the papers, a scrapbook of clippings from the *Poughkeepsie Daily Eagle* for 1898–1904 in Poughkeepsie Document Box, Local History Room, Adriance Memorial Library, and a series of scrapbooks held by the Dutchess County Historical Society. Some of her most important essays have been reprinted in Nicholas Adams and Bonnie Smith, eds., *History and the Texture of Modern Life: Selected Essays, Lucy Maynard Salmon* (Philadelphia, 2001). For her biography, see Louise Fargo Brown, *Apostle of Democracy* (New York, 1941). For the reform work of her Vassar colleague, see Eva Boice, "Woman Suffrage, Vassar College and Laura Johnson Wylie," *The Hudson River Valley Review*, 20 (Spring 2004).

For planning ideas that influenced Lucy Salmon, see John Nolen, *New Towns for Old* (Amherst, MA, 1927). For the actions and reactions of the Poughkeepsie Common Council, see Nancy Mack, "Poughkeepsie: A Case Study of Planning and Zoning in the 1920s" (Senior thesis, Vassar College, 1983). Central to local discussion was *A Plan for the Improvement and Extension of Poughkeepsie, New York: Prepared by Myron Howard West and Staff of the American Park Builders* (Chicago, 1924). On the plight of old cities like Poughkeepsie that did not expand sufficiently through annexation, see David Rusk, *Cities Without Suburbs* (Washington, DC, 1995). The Ferris Heights Association minute books, Volume VIII (1923), show how a residential area concerned with improvements could become eager for annexation. For histories of the city beautification movement and the role of women in civic reform and urban planning in the early decades of the twentieth century, see Alison Isenberg, *Downtown America: A History of the Place and the People Who Made It* (Chicago, 2004).

Fanny R. Sweeny, "A Study of a Few Forms of Public and Private Relief in the City of Poughkeepsie" (MA thesis, Vassar College, 1910) describes the variety of groups in need of assistance and both public and private ventures dedicated to providing it. Helen Thompson of the Tenement House Department of New York City went door to door to document deterioration in housing, especially on the river slope, in her "A Report of a Housing Survey in the City of Poughkeepsie" (1919).

## CHAPTER SEVEN

History of the automobile in America and development of the parkway system is found in: Jon B. Rae, *The American Automobile* (Chicago, 1965); Harvey K. Flad, "Country Clutter: Visual Pollution and the Rural Roadscape," in *The Annals of the American Academy of Political and Social Sciences*, vol. 553 (September 1997); and David Schuyler, *The New Urban Landscape: The Redefinition of Urban Form in Nineteenth Century America* (Baltimore, 1986). For a discussion of the role of the automobile on urban spatial form and residential adaptation see James J. Flink, *The Automobile Age* (Cambridge, MA, 1988) and Peter O. Muller, "Transportation and Urban Form: Stages in the Spatial Evolution of the American Metropolis," in *The Geography of Transportation*, 3rd ed., ed. by Susan Hanson and Genevieve Giuliano (New York, 2004).

The politics of the creation and extension of the Taconic Parkway is found in Robert A. Caro, *The Power Broker: Robert Moses and the Fall of New York* (New York, 1974).

For Franklin Delano Roosevelt's role as historian as well as politician, see Kevin J. Gallagher, "The President as Local Historian: The Letters of F.D.R. to Helen Wilkinson Reynolds," *New York History*, 54, 2 (April 1983); John C. Ferris, "Franklin D. Roosevelt: His Development and Accomplishments as a Local Historian," *Dutchess County Historical Society Yearbook*, 68 (1983); the essays in Nancy Fogel, ed., *FDR at Home* (Poughkeepsie, NY, 2005); and Federal Writers' Project, *American Guide Series: Dutchess County* (Philadelphia, 1937). For his role in designing Dutchess County post offices, see Bernice L. Thomas, *The Stamp of FDR: New Deal Post Offices in the Mid-Hudson Valley* (Fleischmanns, NY, 2002); and William B. Rhoads, "Franklin D. Roosevelt and Dutch Colonial Architecture," *New York History*, 59, 4 (October 1978). For FDR and Eleanor at Val-Kill, see Kenneth S. Davis, *Invincible Summer: An Intimate Portrait of the Roosevelts Based on the Recollections of Marian Dickerman* (New York, 1974), and, for a photographic history, see Richard R. Cain, *Eleanor Roosevelt's Valkill* (Charleston, SC, 2002).

FDR as conservationist is examined in Thomas W. Patton, "The Forest Plantations of Franklin D. Roosevelt at Hyde Park, New York," *Dutchess County Historical Society Yearbook*, 70 (1985); Irving Brant, *Adventures in Conservation with Franklin D. Roosevelt* (Flagstaff, AZ, 1988); and the essays in Henry L. Henderson and David B. Woolner, eds., *FDR and the Environment* (New York, 2005). See also F. Kennon Moody, "F.D.R.: Neighbors and Politics in Dutchess County," *Transformations of an American County: Dutchess County, New York, 1683–1983* (Poughkeepsie, NY, 1986).

## CHAPTER EIGHT

For depictions of local industries and businesses at the beginning of the twentieth Century, see *Illustrated and Descriptive Poughkeepsie, New York* (Poughkeepsie, NY, 1906) and the *Poughkeepsie Eagle* anniversary issue, June 1911. Useful on the city's largest retailer, Luckey, Platt & Co., is *75 Years of Service: The Informal Biography of a Store* (1944). On a seemingly foreign firm, see Michael Sedgwick, "The Pride of Poughkeepsie: A Look at the American FIATs," *Upper Hudson Automobilist*, January 1980. Materials on the history and successful expansion of the Fitchett Dairy were shared by Bernice and Edwin E. Fitchett, Jr. on February 1, 2004. On other individual businesses, see especially the Schatz Federal Bearing Company scrapbook for 1918 to 1945 in the Adriance Memorial Library Local History Room and their collection of materials from other local firms, including De Laval Separator Co. (renamed and so filed under Alfa-Laval), and Smith Brothers Restaurant and Cough Drops. Still invaluable is R. G. and A. R. Hutchinson and Mabel Newcomer, "Study in Business Mortality," *American Economic Review*, 28 (September 1938). Newcomer also contributed "The Little Businessman: A Study of Business Proprietors in Poughkeepsie," in *Business History Review* (Winter 1961). Jonah Sherman kindly shared some annual reports of Chamber of Commerce activities from his extensive collection of materials on the city's history.

On local occupational opportunities, see the U. S. Census Bureau, *Thirteenth Census of the United States* (Washington, DC, 1910), Vol. 4, 263–67 and *Fifteenth Census of the United States* (Washington, DC, 1930), Vol 4, 1107 ff. Also, Florence Brewer, *Choosing an Occupation: The Kinds of Work That Are Open to Women in Poughkeepsie* (Poughkeepsie, 1910). For issues between workers and employers, see the annual reports of the New York State Bureau of Labor Statistics. The mayor's accusation of blacklisting that provoked a judicial inquiry can be tracked in the *Poughkeepsie Eagle*, January to March 1927. On provision for the destitute, see Fanny Sweeney, "A Study of a Few Forms of Public and Private Relief in the City of Poughkeepsie" (MA thesis, Vassar College, 1910).

A history of Woolworth's in the social history of America's downtowns is found in John K. Winkler, *Five and Ten: The Fabulous Life of F.W. Woolworth* (New York, 1940); Robert C. Kirkwood, *The Woolworth Story at Home and Abroad* (New York, 1960); and Jean Maddern Pitrone, *F.W. Woolworth and the American Five and Dime* (Jefferson, NC, 2003).

## CHAPTER NINE

The account of the impact of the Depression in Poughkeepsie comes from Jack Lippmann, "The Depression Comes to Poughkeepsie, 1930–1936," *Dutchess County Historical Society Yearbook* (1981); Ronald Samuelson, "Newspaper Coverage of the Great Depression and the New Deal in Dutchess County, New York: The election of 1932 and the Hundred Days" (Vassar College, history thesis, 1992). For early New Deal intervention in Dutchess, see Civil Works Administration of Dutchess County, "Report of the Executive Director for the Period of Nov. 28, 1933–Feb. 15, 1934," Local History Room, Adriance Library. On WPA projects in Beacon, see Small Collections, WPA Material, FDR Library.

The experience of members of different social groups during the 1930s can be gleaned from personal accounts like Tony diRosa, *El Pibe* (Buenos Aires, 1991) and Bernard Weisberger to Clyde Griffen, a memoir in four extensive e-mails, dated April 15 and 30, May 26 and 27, 2003, and Weisberger's response to questions from Griffen, dated June 12, 2003; also interviews with Maisry MacCracken, February 4, 2004, and Jesse and Leah Effron, December 19, 2003, and January 2004. John Wolf was interviewed by Janet Hays on November 11, 2006. See also Mamiya and Roberts, "Invisible People" and Mamiya and Karouma, *For Their Courage* on the experience of local African Americans.

On the shift toward more vocational education for changing employments on the eve of the Depression, see Peter Edman, "A History of the Curriculum in the Poughkeepsie City School District, 1843–1929," *Dutchess County Historical Society Yearbook* (1985) and also Fox O. Holden, "Occupational Survey, Poughkeepsie, New York" (Poughkeepsie Public Schools, 1939).

On the closing of some of the river estates and their impact on their neighbors, see Martha Bayne, *County at Large* (Poughkeepsie, NY, 1937); Allan Weinreb, "Staatsburgh: the History of the Lewis-Livingston-Mills Estate" (Draft, 1999); Charles W. Snell, *Vanderbilt Mansion* (National Park Service Historical Handbook Series, no. 32, Washington, DC, 1960). For photographs and notes on some of the Livingston houses, see *Landmarks of Dutchess County, 1683–1867* (1969). On the importance of gardens in the great estates, see Henry Noble MacCracken, *Blithe Dutchess* (New York,

1958), and Joel E. Spingarn, "Henry Winthrop Sargent and the Early History of Horticulture and Landscape Gardening in Dutchess County," *Dutchess County Historical Society Yearbook* 22 (1937). Information on local union activities can be found in newspaper clippings from the Depression and war years in the Schatz Federal Bearing Scrapbook, Vol. 1, Adriance Library.

## CHAPTER TEN

Studies of the computer industry and IBM that provide the larger context for IBM in the mid-Hudson valley include Charles Bashe, Johnson Palmer, and Emerson Pugh, *IBM's Early Computers* (Cambridge, MA, 1986); Ross Bassett, *To the Digital Age: Research Labs, Start-up Companies, and the Rise of MOS Technology* (Baltimore, 2002); Alfred Chandler, *Inventing the Electronic Century: The Epic Story of the Computer Electronics and Computer Industries* (New York, 2001); Katherine Fishman, *The Computer Establishment* (New York, 1981); Emerson Pugh, Lyle Johnson, and John Palmer, *IBM's 360 and Early 370 Systems* (Cambridge, MA, 1991); William Rodgers, *Think: A Biography of the Watsons and IBM* (New York, 1969); Robert Sobel, *IBM: Colossus in Transition* (New York, 1981). For the perspectives of top leadership, see two autobiographies: Thomas Watson, Jr., *Father, Son, and Company* (New York, 1990) and Louis Gerstner, *Who Says Elephants Can't Dance: Inside IBM's Historic Turnaround* (New York, 2002). For the viewpoint of Gerstner's successor, Sam Palisano, see his report in *Seven Days at IBM* (Armonk, NY, 2002). See also *IBM, Thirty Years of Management Briefings, 1958 to 1988* (Armonk, NY, 1988). For a broader perspective on corporate paternalism in the twentieth century, see Sanford Jacoby, *Modern Manors: Welfare Capitalism Since the New Deal* (Princeton, 1997).

For IBM in the valley, see the following IBM publications and manuscripts: Daniel Cost, ed., *Fifty Years in Poughkeepsie* (1991); undated typescript, "History of IBM at Poughkeepsie, New York"; *Pages from the Past*, undated and unpaginated IBM Poughkeepsie pamphlet with annual developments there, 1941–1976; IBM, *The Clarence Kenyon Estate* (Poughkeepsie, NY, 1976); *35 Years: Kingston IBM, 1956–1991* (unpaginated publication); undated pamphlet, *IBM Poughkeepsie, New York*, Adriance Library; and Dave Moran, "History Done Oct., 1966 from the Corporation Archives, Harrison" (typescript in External Relations department Files, IBM Poughkeepsie) and also typescript, "Research Laboratory 701 Building" and undated duplicated handout titled "The IBM Country Club, Poughkeepsie, New York"; *IBM: Dedicated to Progress: a historic record of the IBM Dedication Ceremonies and Luncheon held under the auspices of the Poughkeepsie Chamber of Commerce on June 16, 1948* (IBM pamphlet box, Adriance Library). See also Julia Kennedy, "IBM in Dutchess County: A Postwar History of Prosperity" (Vassar College, history senior thesis, 1995). We thank Steven Cole, External Relations, for making available some of this material and for his suggestions and perspective on the local impact of IBM in an interview on April 9, 2002. A photographic record can be found in Mark Lytle, "Images of IBM," *Dutchess County Historical Society Yearbook*, 74 (1989).

## CHAPTER ELEVEN

Retired IBM officers and employers proved to be invaluable sources for this and the preceding chapter: see typescripts of interviews with Ray Boedecker, December 12,

2001; Werner Buchholz, January 15, 2002; Charles Lawson, February 2002; Eric Lindbloom, April 5, 2002; Francis Ritz, April 22, 2002; Bernard Slade, January 28, 2003; and Louis Voerman, Jr., April 22, 2002. Other Poughkeepsie residents we interviewed who helped us understand IBM's relation to city, county, and valley include Anna Buchholz, January 15, 2002; Jack Economou, January 24, 2003; Elizabeth Daniels, January 11, 2001; Julia Dunwell, February 3, 2003; Armine Isberian, January 20, 2003; Lucille Pattison, January 18, 2002; Norma Torney, April 25, 2003; and Jonah and Joan Sherman, April 11, 2002.

The residential concentration of IBMers on individual streets in areas of the town near the South plant and Boardman Road complex appear dramatically in tabulations from Polk's city directories for Poughkeepsie for 1956 and 1964. For comparison of population and economic change between *city* and *town*, see *Dutchess County Data Books* (Poughkeepsie, NY, 1962 and 1974). IBMers' group identity and spatial cohesiveness in residential suburbs located near IBM's plants in the towns of Poughkeepsie and East Fishkill is examined in Klara Sauer, "Is Hopewell Junction a Place?" (typescript for social geography, Vassar College, n.d.). The controversy over the establishment of Spackenkill High School, including interviews with local citizens, is presented in Sandra Markovics, "Maintaining Suburban Community Identity" (Vassar College, American culture senior thesis, 1980); also see Greg Morgan, "The Monolith and the Mini-Metropolis: IBM's Effect on Poughkeepsie" (Vassar College, American culture senior thesis, 1991).

IBM's workforce is described in "Industrial Establishments in Dutchess County" (typescript) and the Industrial Research and Development Commission, "Industrial Opportunities in Dutchess County" (1956), Adriance Library. For change in IBM workforce composition, see the comment in Regional Plan Association, *The Future of Dutchess County* (New York, 1972). For comparison of occupational status and education of heads of household and of family incomes between areas within the town of Poughkeepsie and surrounding townships, see Department of Commerce, *Profile of Business and Industry, Mid-Hudson Area, Business Fact Book, Part 1* (Poughkeepsie, NY, 1976 edition).

## CHAPTER TWELVE

Two major studies of the decades of urban renewal and Model Cities formed the body of this chapter: Harvey K. Flad, "A Time of Readjustment: Urban Renewal in Poughkeepsie, 1955–75," *Dutchess County Historical Society Yearbook*, vol. 72 (1987), reprinted in *New Perspectives on Poughkeepsie's Past*, edited by Clyde Griffen (Poughkeepsie, NY, 1988); and Sandra Opdycke, "With Prosperity All Around: Urban Issues in Poughkeepsie, New York, 1950–1980," *Dutchess County Historical Society Yearbook*, vol. 75 (1990). For a discussion of sprawl in the Poughkeepsie region see *Urban Sprawl: Poughkeepsie and Its Region* (The Poughkeepsie Institute, NY, 2002).

Twentieth-century changes to the downtown cores of America's cities, especially along Main Street, are detailed in Alison Isenberg, *Downtown America: A History of the Place and the People Who Made It* (Chicago, 2004). The impact of the automobile on the postwar urban landscape is found in Jane Holtz Kay, *Asphalt Nation: How the Automobile Took Over America and How We Can Take It Back* (Berkeley, 1997) and James J.

Flink, *The Automobile Age* (Cambridge, MA, 1988). Studies of the politics and social costs of urban renewal in American cities of particular interest to the Poughkeepsie story include: James Q. Wilson, ed., *Urban Renewal: The Record and the Controversy* (Cambridge, MA, 1966), Scott Greer, *Urban Renewal and American Cities* (Indianapolis, 1965), and Jon C. Teaford, *The Rough Road to Renaissance: Urban Revitalization in America, 1940–1985* (Baltimore, 1990). Central city decline, abandoned neighborhoods, and efforts at revitalization in cities across America are detailed in John A. Jakle and David Wilson, *Derelict Landscapes: The Wasting of America's Built Environment* (Avage, MD, 1992).

## CHAPTER THIRTEEN

The urban renewal period in Poughkeepsie has been studied repeatedly by Vassar College students in history, geography, sociology, and urban studies. A selection of works used in this chapter include: Eric B. Marcus, "Main Mall, Portrait of a Failure: The Un-building of Main Street, Poughkeepsie," 1980; Harry Lynch, "Poughkeepsie's Main Mall—Turning the Tide?," 1980; Virginia Maltese, "Gentrification in Poughkeepsie? The Union Street Experience," 1986; Christiana Citron, ed., "A Search for Solutions: Poughkeepsie and the Model Cities Program," 1969; and papers written on Union Street presented in 1971 by Kim Gantz, Ann Silverman, and Nini Brooke. Interviews of Poughkeepsians involved with the major renewal efforts of the period include: Steve and Julie Dunwell, Jack Economou, Jesse Effron, Burt Gold, Jonah Sherman, and Ken Toole.

The nine Model Cities task forces were: crime and delinquency; citizen participation; education; health; housing; manpower and employment; recreation; social services; and transportation. The Model City Agency Board changed membership from 1968 to 1974 as political leadership in the city changed; the number of citizens representing the four impact areas also changed. Friction between administration officials and residents along lines of social class and race with respect to the allocation of federal funds remained a feature of the board's decisions throughout the years of the board's existence.

A short description of PHDC is found in "City of Poughkeepsie, Model Cities Program—A People Program: A Guide to Model Cities Activities in Poughkeepsie" (November 15, 1972). Kenneth Toole, deputy director of county planning, whose home was in the town of Hyde Park, was president of the board during the 1970s and Desti Jackson, an African American home owner in the city, became the first executive director. Adriance Memorial Library has an extensive collection of correspondence, memoranda, and reports of the Model Cities program.

## CHAPTER FOURTEEN

On Poughkeepsie's African Americans before and during the 1960s, see Mamiya and Karouma, *For Their Courage and For Their Struggles* and Mamiya and Roberts, "A Historical Overview of the Black Community in Poughkeepsie," in Griffen, ed., *New Perspectives on Poughkeepsie's Past*. Interview with Jeh and Norma Johnson, March 16, 2003. The following interviews helped us describe aspects of local civic rights activism:

Sandra Opdycke, June 10, 2002; former Mayor Jack Economou, January 24, 2003; Lou Glasse, April 15, 2004; Victor Morris, May 15, 2004. For firsthand accounts of the drug education center in Millbrook and resulting conflict between Leary and Liddy, see Timothy Leary, *Flashbacks: An Autobiography* (Los Angeles, 1982) and G. Gordon Liddy, *Will: The Autobiography of G. Gordon Liddy* (New York, 1980). See also Louis Menand, "Acid Redux: The Life and High Times of Timothy Leary," *The New Yorker*, June 26, 2006.

Alan Talbot, *Power Along the Hudson: Storm King and the Birth of Environmentalism* (New York, 1972) provides a basic narrative of the first decade of the Scenic Hudson Conference's campaign. John Ansley, Special Collections librarian at Marist College, kindly shared recorded interviews by Betsy Pugh with some participants, including Nash Castro. The conclusion of the campaign is documented in Ross Sandler and David Schoenbrod, eds., *The Hudson River Power Plant Settlement* (New York, 1981). Their Appendix C gives a very useful chronology; also helpful are the summary remarks by Russell Train, April 30, 1981. The Marist College library houses the Scenic Hudson collection of records relating to the Storm King Case, 1963–1981, that include minutes of executive committee meetings. Highly critical of Scenic Hudson's delaying tactics was William Tucker, "Environmentalism and the Leisure Class: Protecting Birds, Fishes, and above all Social Privilege" in *Harper's* (December, 1977). For responses from Scenic Hudson members, see especially the letters from Frances Reese and Pete Seeger in the February 1978 issue of *Harper's*. In a phone interview on June 14, 2004, Frances Dunwell told of the post-settlement separation of the new regionally oriented Center for the Hudson Valley from Scenic Hudson.

Pete Seeger shared memories of his interest in the Hudson River, its cleanup, and the campaign for and uses of the Clearwater in a phone conversation on May 17, 2004. He added to the description of that interest in David Dunaway, *How Can I Keep from Singing: Pete Seeger* (New York, 1982). The conversation included Seeger's current view of how small ventures and networking can improve the world. Harvey Flad witnessed the presentation of the certificate of appreciation from the sheriff's office in 2003. For a description of the *Clearwater* sloop and its uses, see the last chapter of Paul Fontenoy, *The Sloops of the Hudson River: A Historical and Design Survey* (Mystic, CT, 1994).

## CHAPTER FIFTEEN

The primary source for the early history of Dutchess Community College is *DCC Oral History Project*, Arnold Toback, interviewer and compiler (1976–1977) that provides taped interviews with principal participants from the administration, staff, and faculty. A less inclusive publication based on that project is *This is a history of Dutchess Community College, 1957–1997 in the voices and images of he people who made it and in the headlines that announced their achievements* (Poughkeepsie, NY, 1997). A phone interview with the first president, James Hall, on May 12, 2004, and conversation with Professor Richard Reitano, then president of the union, on July 10, 2004, complemented those sources. Additional historical information is found in *Dutchess Community College: The 50th Anniversary*, a special issue of the *Dutchess County Historical Society Yearbook*, 8 (2007–2008).

For an overview, see Dennis Murray, "A Lasting Ideal in a Changing World: A History of Marist College," *Dutchess County Historical Society Yearbook*, 74 (1989). Professors Peter O'Keefe and Louis Zuccarello on May 10, 2004, shared their recollections of changes at Marist beginning with the presidency of Brother Linus Foy. A second conversation with Professor O'Keefe followed on July 8, 2004. A recorded interview with Foy is in Marist College library's Special Collections. For a brief description of the brothers' early years in the valley, from the initial training school to a college, see Poughkeepsie Journal, *The Hudson Valley: Our Heritage, Our Future* (Poughkeepsie, NY, 2000). For "The Story of the Move from St. Andrew's on Hudson" and related newspaper clippings see the reference librarian at the Conrad Hilton Library, Culinary Institute of America, Hyde Park, New York.

The account of change at Vassar comes from Elizabeth A. Daniels and Clyde Griffen, *Full Steam Ahead in Poughkeepsie: The Story of Coeducation at Vassar, 1966–1974* (Poughkeepsie, NY, 2000). That story has been brought up to date in Clyde Griffen and Elizabeth Daniels, "Vassar Chooses Coeducation" in Leslie Miller-Bernal and Susan Poulson, eds., *Challenged by Coeducation: Women's Colleges since the 1960s* (Nashville, 2006). The search of the Culinary Institute of America for a less crowded site and its ultimate transfer from New Haven to Hyde Park is documented in rich detail in a collection of newspaper clippings at the CIA's Conrad Hilton Library, kindly shown by CIA Information Services Librarian Christine Crawford-Oppenheimer. Other clippings and *The CIA New Campus Reporter* chronicle events since then at the Hyde Park campus, formerly St. Andrews on Hudson.

Our portrait of change at SUNY New Paltz was shaped by conversations with Professors Sipra Johnson, Richard Varbero, and Gerald Sorin, together with the historical chronology on the college's Web site. Also helpful was George Schnell, "A College and Its Region: Location, Development, and Response," *Journal of Pennsylvania Academy of Science*, 67 (1993). Former president Reamer Kline's *A History of Bard College* provides the foundation. Conversations with Professors Ben LaFarge and Mark Lytle in April 2006 offered their sense of change at Bard with the transition to Leon Botstein's presidency. Agnes Langdon, a previous member of the Bard faculty, shared her reminiscences.

Ralph and Doris Adams described the history of their family's Fairacre Farms business in an interview on February 9, 2005. They kindly shared their company scrapbook that contains clippings from valley newspapers. The fullest account of how their business evolved appeared in *Dutchess Magazine* (Spring 1999). See also *Hudson Valley Magazine*, 25 (November 1996), and the account of Ralph Adams as the person of the year in "Annual Report on Business and Industry," *Poughkeepsie Journal*, February 29, 2004. George Chevalier's "Growing with high technology" (undated clipping in ibid.) shows how far computerization of this retail business has come under Mark Adams in the next generation.

## CHAPTER SIXTEEN

On IBM Poughkeepsie at the peak of its prosperity, see "80s Highlights Around the Company," in Daniel Cost, ed., *Fifty Years in Poughkeepsie* (1991) and *IBM: A Special Company* (September 1989). Ann Davis, Director of the Marist College Bureau of Economic Research, provided data on employment in Dutchess County, 1975–1991, on IBM employees as a percentage of the county's manufacturing workforce, and on average salary in the Hudson valley computer industry. The *Dutchess County Data Book* (1993) provides median household incomes by township.

The history of Schatz Federal Bearing has been derived from newspaper clippings about the company and its employees in the scrapbooks now housed in the Local History Room, Adriance Library. An invaluable retrospective account appears in "Requiem for Schatz: What Killed the Company," *Poughkeepsie Journal*, March 22, 1981. On the fate of another large manufacturer, De Laval, see ibid., September 25, 1986, in the Alfa-Laval folder, Dutchess County Historical Society. An example of its commitment to the ideology of free enterprise can be found in its publication for employees, *The Separator*, VII (April–May 1950) in its editorial, "It Happened Here." On January 16, 2006, Frank Bauer shared his experience working at De Laval under President Neumann and provided a chronology of events, 1954–1975. David Lumb discussed the history of his family's manufacturing firm after World War II in an interview, December 10, 2004. On the efforts of the Sheraton, Wyndham, and Raddison hotel chains to build and run a downtown hotel, see *Poughkeepsie Journal*, September 14, 1977, and September 20 and 28, 1988.

The history of MOS technology and how Silicon Valley competitors employing it ended the profitable heyday of IBM's mainframe business has been ably told in Ross Bassett, *To the Digital Age: Research Labs, Start-up Companies, and the Rise of MOS Technology* (Baltimore, 2002). For statistics on IBM's great downsizing in the early 1990s, see especially the *Fourth Quarter Report* for 1994 of the Marist Bureau of Economic Research and also the *Second Quarter Report* (1992), the *First, Second* and *Third Quarter Reports* (1993) and the *First Quarter Report* (1996). For the perspective of the man hired to chart a new direction for the corporation, see Louis Gerstner, *Who Says Elephants Can't Dance: Inside IBM's Historic Turnaround* (New York, 2002). The cover story of *Business Week*, January 11, 2002 was "IBM's New Boss: Palisano Has a Tough Act to Follow." Palisano's shift in IBM's focus was described by the *New York Times*, January 25, 2004 as "Big Blue's Big Bet: Less Technology, More Touch [services]." In an interview on April 2, 2003, Fred Nagel described how the group of counselors he led, under a New York State grant, tried to help laid-off employees find other employment.

Attempts by valley organizations, in the wake of IBM's contraction to chart ways to improve the regional economy appear in three essays by Craig Wolf: "Planning Group Marks 40 Years of Change," "Group Focuses on Drawing Jobs, Global Marketing," and "The Valley Starts Looking at the Larger Picture," in *Poughkeepsie Journal*, February 29, 1989. See also "Dutchess Empire Zone Still Enlarging," ibid., February 2, 2003, and Wolf, "Path Gets Complex after Jobs Recovery," ibid., February 27, 2005. The experience of the valley's attempts to grow out of the downsizing is presented in Keith H. Hammonds, "The Town IBM Left Behind: Around Poughkeepsie, Big Blue's Fading Seemed Fatal. Here's Why It Wasn't." *Business Week*, September 11, 1995.

## CHAPTER SEVENTEEN

May Mamiya, head social worker at Vassar Brothers Hospital, described current relations between valley hospitals in a conversation on November 12, 2004. See also Poughkeepsie Journal, *The Hudson Valley: Our Heritage, Our Future* (Poughkeepsie, NY, 2000). A very useful analysis of the composition, perspective, and interests of members of the board and the major committees of the Community Chest is Joan Sherman, "Social Planning and Economic Power" (MA thesis, Sarah Lawrence College, 1971). The current diversity in leadership of the Chamber of Commerce as well as the Community Chest can be seen in the Chamber's listing of committee heads and the Chest's Board of Governors on the two organizations' Web sites. Professor Marque Miringoff provided perspective on contemporary social services in the county in an interview on February 19, 2004. Brian Riddell, director of Dutchess Outreach at the Family Partnership Center, described the work of his agency and current problems of funding and restrictive regulations in a February 17, 2005, interview. Lou Glasse provided her summary report of the program of Family Advocacy, January 1972 to March 1973 and the October 1972 series of articles in the *Poughkeepsie Journal* on the problems of the elderly.

## CHAPTER EIGHTEEN

Studies of national efforts at downtown renaissance can be found in Larry R. Ford, *America's New Downtowns: Revitalization or Reinvention?* (Baltimore, 2003), while a case study of a medium-sized former industrial city is reviewed in essays in Joseph L. Scarpaci and Kevi J. Patrick, eds., *Pittsburgh and the Appalachians: Cultural and Natural Resources in a Postindustrial Age* (Pittsburgh, 2006), especially "Downtown Pittsburgh: Renaissance and Renewal," by Edward K. Muller. Specific attention to cities returning their pedestrian malls to urban streets is found in Mary M. Vizard, "Cars Trickle Back to Pedestrian Malls," *New York Times*, December 29, 1991. A review of the political changes in Poughkeepsie during this time is found in Thomas Salvatore Conoscenti, *Shaping the Image of the CBD: A Spatio-Temporal Case Study of the Political Decision-Making Process in Redevelopment in Poughkeepsie's Central Business District, 1854–2002* (BA thesis, Vassar College Geography, 2002).

Planning for Main Mall will be found in *A Business Enhancement Plan for Downtown Poughkeepsie, New York*, prepared for the Common Council and the Main Mall Commission by Hyett-Palma, Inc (Washington, DC, February 1987). Also, see the *City of Poughkeepsie Comprehensive Plan* prepared by the Chazen Companies (Poughkeepsie, NY, November, 1998). Waterfront planning is found in *City of Poughkeepsie Draft Local Waterfront Revitalization Program* prepared by Matthew D. Rudikoff Associates, Inc. (Poughkeepsie, NY, August 1989).

A study of several issues in the overall social health of of the city in the mid-1990s, including quality-of-life issues in several neighborhoods, education, art, music, and media services is found in a fifty-three-page report *Poughkeepsie: The City That Hopes* (Vassar College: American Culture program, 1994).

## CHAPTER NINETEEN

The earliest intensive examination of the Mexican community is found in Alison Mountz, *Daily Life in a Transnational Migrant Community: The Fusion of San Agustin Yatareni, Oaxaca and Poughkeepsie, New York* (BA thesis, Dartmouth College, 1995). Alison, a Poughkeepsie native, spent two years interviewing individuals in Poughkeepsie and lived with families in the village of San Agustin Yatareni. The strong relationship for the migrants and their families of their village with *pokipsi* created a single "transnational locale," according to Mountz, during her years of participant observation in 1993–1994. A decade later, Brian Godfrey, professor of geography at Vassar College, reported on the urban ethnic expression of the Mexican community along Poughkeepsie's Main Street. The local newspaper, the *Poughkeepsie Journal*, has published many articles on the growth of the Mexican community in the city; of particular interest are: a special ten-page report by Mary Beth Pfeiffer, "From Poverty to the Green Valley" (July 16, 1998); Peter Leonard, "Accident Shattered Barrier Between Communities," the newspaper's first article to be published in both English and Spanish (April 26, 1998); Larry Hughes, "Mexican's Tragic Death Unites a City: Residents Open Hearts to Help Send Man Home" (April 26, 1998); Larry Hughes, "Mexican-American Ties Bound Tighter in Valley: Tragic Deaths Foster Greater Understanding" (December 27, 1998); and Elizabeth Lynch, "Hispanic Numbers Rise: Mexicans Are Flocking to the City" (June 27, 2001). Writers for the *Journal*, including Mary Beth Pfeiffer and Peter Leonard, received the 1999 IAPA-Pedro Joaquin Chamorro Inter-American Relations Award from the Inter-American Press Association for their stories "on the life and death of Mexicans in Poughkeepsie."

Along with thousands of pages of newsprint and hours of television, the Tawana Brawley case spawned two hefty books by different journalists who had covered the news over the three-year span: *Outrage: The Story Behind the Tawana Brawley Hoax* by a team of reporters from the *New York Times* headed by Robert D. McFadden (New York, 1990); and *Unholy Alliances: Working the Tawana Brawley Story* by *CBS* television newscasters Mike Taibbi and Anna Sims-Phillips (New York, 1989). Written by reporters based in New York City, both books focus much of their attention on politicians, civil rights activists, and lawyers who were acting on a national stage, such as Governor Mario Cuomo, activist Reverend Al Sharpton, and lawyers Alton H. Maddox and C. Vernon Mason.

Photographs with comments of community activists during the period can be found in Joyce C. Ghee and Joan Spence, *Poughkeepsie 1898–1998: A Century of Change* (Charleston, SC, 1999). Photographs and short histories of selected abandoned buildings in the city can be found in Thomas E. Rinaldi and Robert J. Yasinsac, *Hudson Valley Ruins: Forgotten Landmarks of an American Landscape* (Lebanon, NH, 2006).

## CHAPTER TWENTY

The origins of the Hudson River Valley Commission are detailed in Frances F. Dunwell, *The Hudson River Highlands* (New York, 1991). Discussion of HRVC's position on the Storm King and Danskammer power plants is included in Dunwell as well as in Harvey K. Flad and John F. Sears, "Prepared Testimony in the Matter of Central Hudson Gas & Electric Corp. Danskammer Coal Conversion," NYS Department of Environmental Conservation submitted on behalf of Scenic Hudson, Inc. (Poughkeepsie, NY, 1984). Many other power plants were proposed for the valley. Originally proposed by the U.S. Nuclear Regulatory Commission in 1979, the denial of the Greene County Nuclear Power Plant by the NYS Public Service Commission and the U.S. Atomic Safety and Licensing Board is noted in Harvey Flad. "War Won When Power Plants Lost," *The Hudson Valley: Our Heritage, Our Future* (Poughkeepsie, 2000). Of the many reports by HRVC, see especially *The Hudson* (1966) and *Historic Resources of the Hudson* (1969). Political and planning developments during the period were told through interviews with: Lucille Pattison (January 18, 2002); John Mylod (July 2003); Klara Sauer (May 16, 2006, and June 20, 2006); and Ken Toole (July 24, 2006).

Updates to the 1997 national agricultural census focused on the regional economy are found in the comprehensive technical report *Agricultural Economic Development for the Hudson Valley* published by the American Farmland Trust Northeast Office (Saratoga, Springs, NY, 2004). One family's history on a farm in Columbia County, from pre-Revolutionary farming to twentieth-century U-pick apples can be read in the beautifully written *A Family Place: A Hudson Valley Farm, Three Centuries, Five Wars, One Family* by Leila Philip (New York, 2001). Local farmers tell their stories in "Agriculture at a Crossroads" May/June 2003 edition of *Dutchess* magazine.

The most comprehensive study of land trusts in the Hudson Valley is found in Alice Elizabeth Mulder, *Privately Public: An Exploration of the 'Public' in Private Land Conservation: New York's Hudson Valley* (PhD thesis, Department of Geography, University of Colorado, 2003). Notes on the creation of Minnewaska State Park and Mohonk Preserve can be found in Jack Fagan, *Scenes and Walks in the Northern Shawangunks* (New York, 1999). On the development of Mohonk Mountain House and the Trust, see Larry E. Burgess, *Mohonk: Its People and Spirit* (New Paltz, NY, 1980). The controversy over the future of Minnewaska, including the role of Marriott Hotels, the Phillips family, and representatives of PIPC, including interviews and personal commentaries is told in Jonti Phillips, *Property, Philosophy, Politics, Environmentalism, and the Lake Minnewaska Struggle* (Vassar College, BA thesis, Department of Geography, 1995). The consortium of environmental groups that opposed the Marriot purchase included: Citizens to Save Minnewaska, Friends of Minnewaska (subsequently renamed Friends of the Shawangunks), the Sierrra Club, Sloop Clearwater, Scenic Hudson, National Audubon, and the Appalachian Mountain Cub.

Policies that continued the planning concepts of Henry Heissenbuttel and Kenneth Toole in the 1970s in Dutchess County are found in the 1987 report *Directions: The Plan for Dutchess County* published by the Dutchess County Legislature (Lucille P. Pattison, county executive, and Douglas A. McHoul, chairman), the Dutchess County Planning Board (Robert Hogan, chairman), and the Dutchess County Department of Planning (Roger Akeley, commissioner). Additional background offered by Commissioner Akeley and Senior Planner John Clarke in various informal interviews.

## CHAPTER TWENTY-ONE

Inventories of historic resources of the Hudson River Valley in the late 1960s and early 1970s of particular interest to the Poughkeepsie region include: *Historic Resources of the Hudson*, prepared by the Hudson River Valley Commission (New York, 1969) and *Landmarks of Dutchess County, 1683–1867*, prepared by the Dutchess County Planning Board and published by the New York State Council on the Arts (New York, 1969).

The Hudson Valley Heritage Tourism Agency maintains data on economic impact of tourism in the valley. Figures in our text are from Lisa W. Foderaro, "Tourism Flowing Upriver to the Hudson Valley," *New York Times*, August 21, 2000, and interview with Ann Davis, Bureau of Economic Research, Marist College, in 2002, by Tammy Cilione, "Tourism Gets Italian Lesson, " *Poughkeepsie Journal*, October 10, 2004.

A record of the preservationist battle to save Springside is in Harvey K. Flad, "Matthew Vassar's Springside: '. . . the hand of Art, when guided by Taste,'" in *Prophet with Honor: The Career of Andrew Jackson Downing, 1915–1852*, edited by George B. Tatum and Elisabeth Blair MacDougall, Dumbarton Oaks Colloquium on the History of Landscape Architecture XI (Washington, DC, 1989). Significant documents in the legal proceedings included landscape architect R. M. Toole's 1984 evaluation report and his *Historic Landscape Report for Springside National Historic Landmark, Poughkeepsie, New York* (Saratoga Springs, NY, May 1987).

Community involvement by residents of Hudson and other interveners in the St. Lawrence Cement Plant case is covered in Miriam D. Silverman, *Stopping the Plant: The St. Lawrence Cement Controversy and the Battle for Quality of Life in the Hudson Valley* (Albany, NY, 2006) and Katie Ghilain, *Cultural Landscape Preservation in the Hudson Valley: St. Lawrence Cement's Place in the Evolving Legal Protection of "Place"* (Vassar College, BA thesis in geography, 2006). Historic research by J. Winthrop Aldrich and Ruth Piwonka, and primary documentation from numerous discussions with individuals associated with Scenic Hudson and the Olana Partnership, including Debra DeWan, Warren Reiss, Terry DeWan, and Sara Griffen, and statements by Sam Pratt and other members of Friends of Hudson, and written testimony by Ann Davis, and others.

Descriptions of the bronze horse and the development of Tallix Foundry in Beacon are mentioned in Andrew C. Revkin, "Ages Late, Bronze Horse by Leonardo Comes to Life," *New York Times*, June 26, 1999; Michelle Vellucci, "'Horse' Ready for Journey," *Poughkeepsie Journal*, June 24, 1999; and Nancy Mohr, "A Long Shot Pays Off," *Smithsonian*, 29, 6 (September 1998). The origin and development of Minetta Brook's Hudson Valley Art Project is described in *Watershed Journal*, 1 (October 2002), including essays by the director Diane Shamash, an interview with Lee Balter by editor Miwon Kwon; also information from consultant to the project Mary M. Flad.

Public discourse related to urban revitalization and riverfront developments is presented in many articles and editorials in local and regional newspapers. Examples include "Public Access Is Key to Hudson River's Revival," editorial, *Poughkeepsie Journal*, August 22, 2004. and quotations from local mayors and environmentalists in Lisa W. Foderaro, "Rooms with Views Replace Factories on Hudson's Banks," *New York Times*, October 31, 2005. Comments by Ned Sullivan, executive director of Scenic Hudson, are found in such venues as well as in various issues of the organization's newsletter "Your Valley." Regional economic revitalization through technological "clusters" are projects promoted by the Dutchess County Economic Development Corporation, according to interviews with director Ann Conroy.

## EPILOGUE

Works that describe the stages or eras of Poughkeepsie's development and suggest plans for the future, include: *City of Poughkeepsie Transportation Strategy* by Poughkeepsie-Dutchess County Transportation Council in cooperation with City of Poughkeepsie and Dutchess County Department of Planning (August 1997); *City of Poughkeepsie Draft Comprehensive Plan* (Poughkeepsie, NY, 1998); and Thomas Salvatore

Conoscenti, *Shaping the Image of the CBD: A Spatiotemporal Case Study of the Political Decision-Making Process of Redevelopment in Poughkeepsie's Central Business District, 1854–2002* (Vassar College BA thesis in geography, 2002).

Planning for the valley is found in *Hudson River Valley National Heritage Area, Management and Interpretive Action Plan* (Albany, NY, 2000).

Post-Main Mall studies of perceptions of Poughkeepsie by residents include: Andrew Turgeon, "Pushing Out and Passing Through: Local Perceptions of Poughkeepsie's Urban Development" (Vassar College, 2006). Examples of small city revitalization through limited and creative actions are found in Roberta Brandes Gratz with Norman Mintz, *Cities Back from the Edge: New Life for Downtown* (New York, 1998).

# Illustration Credits

| | |
|---|---|
| ADRIANCE MEMORIAL LIBRARY, local history room | Figures 2.1, 2.3, 3.3, 4.1, 4.2, 4.3, 12.1, 12.3, 12.5, 12.6, 18.1, 18.5 |
| DUTCHESS COUNTY HISTORICAL SOCIETY (10.1–11.1 courtesy IBM) | Figures 3.2, 5.1, 9.2, 9.3, 10.1, 10.2, 10.3, 11.1, 12.2, 12.4, 14.1 |
| VASSAR COLLEGE, special collections | Figures 2.2, 3.1 |
| FRANKLIN D. ROOSEVELT LIBRARY | Figures 7.1, 7.2, 7.3 |
| DUTCHESS COUNTY DEPARTMENT OF PLANNING AND DEVELOPMENT | Figures 19.1, 19.2 |
| SPENCER AINSLEY, *Poughkeepsie Journal* | Figures E.1, E.3, E.5 |
| MEG STEWART, VASSAR COLLEGE | Figures I.1, E.4 |
| TIM ALLRED COLLECTION | Figures 6.1, 16.1, 18.2, 18.3,18.4 |
| FRANC PALAIA | Figure E.2 |

# Index